The Princeton Review

Cracking the GMAT

with Sample Tests on CD-ROM

BY GEOFF MARTZ

2001 EDITION

RANDOM HOUSE, INC.
NEW YORK

www.randomhouse.com/princetonreview

Princeton Review Publishing, L.L.C.
2315 Broadway
New York, NY 10024
E-mail: comments@review.com

ISSN: 1094-0790
ISBN: 0-375-75624-8

GMAT is a registered trademark of the Graduate Management Admission Council, which does not endorse this book.

Macintosh is a registered trademark of Apple Computer, Inc.
System 7 is a registered trademark of Apple Computer, Inc.
Windows™ is a registered trademark of Microsoft® Corporation

Editor: Rachel Warren
Production Editor: Maria Dente
Production Coordinator: Robert McCormack
Illustrations by: The Production Department of The Princeton Review

Manufactured in the United States of America on partially recycled paper.

9 8 7 6 5 4 3 2 1

2001 Edition

ACKNOWLEDGMENTS

Our GMAT course is much more than clever techniques and powerful computer score reports; the reason our results are great is that our teachers care so much about their students. We would like to thank all the teachers who have made the GMAT course so successful, but in particular the core group of teachers and development people who helped get it off the ground: Alicia Ernst, Tom Meltzer, Paul Foglino, John Sheehan, Mark Sawula, Nell Goddin, Teresa Connelly, and Phillip Yee. We would also like to thank Diane Reverand and our agent, Julia Coopersmith; Lesly Atlas for her editing help; and Kristen Azzara and Evelin Sanchez-O'Hara for their production efforts.

Special thanks also go to Jeff Rubenstein and Cathryn Still for lending their expertise to this book.

Finally, we would like to thank the people who truly have taught us everything we know about the GMAT: our students, with a special mention to Bill Lew, our very first GMAT student.

Special thanks to Adam Robinson, who conceived of and perfected the Joe Bloggs approach to standardized tests, and many other techniques in this book.

CONTENTS

Foreword

In 1981, I founded The Princeton Review in order to help prepare high-school students for the SAT. My first course had nineteen students, and it was held in my parents' apartment. Within five years, The Princeton Review had become the largest SAT course in the country.

The Princeton Review's SAT techniques are based in part on what we feel to be essential flaws in the design of the test—flaws that could cause students to score well below their true potential. When we looked at the GMAT (Graduate Management Admission Test), we realized that it contains many of the same flaws as the SAT (both tests are written by the Educational Testing Service). We felt that our techniques for tackling the SAT could be equally useful in tackling the GMAT. So, along with Geoff Martz, one of our veteran teachers and development experts, we designed a course specifically geared for the GMAT. For the past ten years, this course has been taught across the country. It has helped GMAT students attain the same phenomenal score improvements as our SAT students.

How do we do it?

First, unlike many coaches, we don't insist that the student learn dozens of math theorems or memorize all the rules of written grammar. Our extensive examination of the GMAT has shown that the information needed to do well on this test is surprisingly limited. For this reason, we concentrate on a small number of crucial concepts.

Those who have struggled through the GMAT and who've felt that their scores did not reflect their college grades or business acumen probably suspect that there's more to mastering a standardized test than just honing rusty math and verbal skills. So we take our preparation a step further and teach techniques specifically designed to master multiple-choice standardized tests.

Finally, The Princeton Review offers even more than a thorough review and great techniques. Our classes are small (eight to fifteen students) and grouped according to ability. For students who require extra help, we provide smaller group work sessions and even one-on-one tutoring. In addition, we administer several diagnostic GMATs under actual exam conditions.

Unfortunately, many students can't get to our courses. So for you we have written this book. Although the book explains our strongest techniques, it cannot substitute for small classes and great teaching. Still, careful study and practice of the techniques will provide you with the means to boost your score significantly.

To get the maximum effect of our approach, you must practice on actual GMATs. One source of real GMAT questions is a book published by the Educational Testing Service called *The Official Guide for GMAT Review*. Available in bookstores, it contains sample sections of each question type. Other sources of questions are a preparation software put out by ETS, called POWERPREP, and of course the CD-ROM that comes with this book, if you've purchased the CD-ROM version. You can also take one of our GMATs at the following website: tester.review.com. Applying our techniques to questions will prove to you that they work. Make the techniques an integral part of the way you think about tests and you will be comfortable and confident using them when it counts—on the day of your actual GMAT.

If you have any questions about our course, or about academic matters in general, give us a call at 1-800-REVIEW 6.

And finally, in the words of Richard Feynman (Physicist) *"Disregard!"*

Good luck on your GMAT!

John Katzman
President

PART I

Orientation

1
Orientation

WHAT IS THE GRADUATE MANAGEMENT ADMISSION TEST?

The Graduate Management Admission Test (GMAT) is a standardized test used by business schools as one tool to decide whom they are going to let into their M.B.A. programs.

WHAT DOES THE TEST LOOK LIKE?

The GMAT is one of a new generation of tests that are offered only on computer. To take the test, you must go to an approved testing center where you will be seated in front of a secure computer terminal. After a short tutorial in how to use the computer, you will then start the exam, entering your answers on the screen with a mouse. You must compose your essays for the Writing Assessment on the computer as well.

Here's what you'll find on the GMAT:

Important Phone Numbers:

To register for the GMAT: 1-800-GMATNOW

To reach The Princeton Review: 1-800-REVIEW6

1. An interactive tutorial during which you will get a chance to familiarize yourself with the conventions of computerized testing and practice entering answers. You can spend as much time as you like on this tutorial.

2. Two 30-minute essays to be written on the computer using a generic word processing program

3. A 75-minute 37-question math section

4. A 75-minute 41-question verbal section

On average, this gives you two minutes for each math question, and a little less than two minutes for each verbal question.

You must answer a question in order to get to the next question—which means that you can't skip a question and come back to it. And while you are not required to answer every question, your score will be adjusted downward to reflect questions you left undone.

There will be optional 5-minute breaks between each section.

On each of the math and verbal sections, approximately 10 of the questions you encounter will be experimental, and will not count toward your score. These 20 questions, which will be mixed in among the regular questions, are there so the test company can try out new questions for future tests. We'll have much more to say about the experimental questions later.

WHAT INFORMATION IS TESTED ON THE GMAT?

These types of questions are found on the GMAT: regular math Problem Solving; one strange type of math problem called Data Sufficiency; Reading Comprehension; grammar-related questions called Sentence Correction; and logic questions called Critical Reasoning.

WHERE DOES THE GMAT COME FROM?

The GMAT is published by the Educational Testing Service (ETS) under the sponsorship of the Graduate Management Admission Council (GMAC). The council is supposed to oversee ETS. Both ETS and GMAC are private companies. We'll tell you more about them in this chapter.

HOW IS THE GMAT SCORED?

As soon as you've finished taking the GMAT, your computer will calculate and display your unofficial results. Several weeks later, you'll receive a written report from ETS in the mail confirming those results. Most people think of the GMAT score as a single number, but in fact there are four separate numbers:

1. Your total score
    (This is reported on a scale that runs from 200 to 800.)

2. Your verbal score
    (This is reported on a scale that runs from 0 to 60.)

3. Your math score
    (This is also reported on a scale that runs from 0 to 60.)

4. Your Writing Assessment score
    (This is reported on a scale of 1 to 6, in half-point increments; 6 is the highest score.)

Business schools tend to focus on the total score, which means that you may make up for weakness in one area by being strong in another. For example, if your quantitative skills are better than your verbal skills, they'll help pull up your total score. Total scores go up or down in ten-point increments. In other words, you might receive 490 or 500 on the GMAT, but never 494 or 495.

You will also see a percentile ranking next to each score. For example, if you see a percentile of 72 next to your verbal score, it means that 72 percent of the people who took this test scored lower than you did on the verbal section.

ARE GMAT SCORES EQUIVALENT TO SAT SCORES?

No. Even though they both use the same 200 to 800 scale, GMAT scores are not the same as SAT scores. For one thing, the pool of applicants to business schools is much more select than the pool of applicants to colleges. People who take the GMAT have usually already graduated from college. In addition, most have several years of business experience.

The GMAT itself is more complex than the SAT. GMAT questions cover a broader range of topics and have a greater degree of difficulty.

Most people find that their GMAT score is somewhat lower than the score they received on the verbal or math SAT. According to ETS, two-thirds of the people who take the GMAT score between 380 and 590.

ARE NEW GMAT SCORES EQUIVALENT TO OLD GMAT SCORES?

ETS maintains that they are, but many experts disagree. Fairtest, a nonprofit watchdog organization that monitors standardized testing, has been sharply critical of ETS's methodology in calibrating the new scores with the old.

WHAT IS THE PRINCETON REVIEW?

The Princeton Review is a coaching school based in New York City. It has branches in over fifty cities across the country as well as abroad. The Princeton Review's techniques are unique and powerful, and were developed after a study of dozens of real ETS exams. They work because they are based on the same principles that ETS uses in writing the test.

The Princeton Review's techniques for beating the GMAT will help you improve your scores by teaching you to:

1. Think like the test writers at ETS.

2. Take full advantage of the new computer-adaptive logarithms upon which ETS bases the new GMAT.

3. Find the answers to questions you don't understand by using our unique process-of-elimination techniques.

4. Avoid the traps that ETS has set for you (and use those traps to your advantage).

A WARNING

Many of our techniques for beating the GMAT are counterintuitive. Some of them seem to violate common sense. To get the full benefit of our techniques, you must trust them. The only way to develop this trust is to practice the techniques and convince yourself that they work.

But you have to practice them *properly*. If you try our techniques on the practice problems in most popular GMAT coaching books, you will probably decide that they don't work.

Why?

ETS's Auspicious Beginnings

Carl Campbell Brigham, creator of the SAT, developed his earliest standardized tests as mental classification tools for the Army. Brigham, and others like him, used data from test scores to "prove" theories of Nordic white supremacy. Intelligence test scores were quoted in Congressional debates, and shored up support for the passage of the Immigration Restriction Act of 1924.

Because the practice questions in those books are very different from the questions on real GMATs. These books may have Data Sufficiency questions, Sentence Correction questions, and Reading Comprehension questions, but if you compare them with the questions on the real GMAT, you'll find that the resemblance is only superficial. In fact, studying the practice questions and techniques in some of the other books could actually hurt your GMAT score.

One reason these coaching books do not use real GMAT questions is that the Graduate Management Admission Council won't let them. So far, the council has refused to let anyone (including us) license actual questions from old tests. The council has its *own* review book (published jointly with ETS) called *The Official Guide for GMAT Review*. The book boasts that it has 1000 *actual* GMAT test questions.

For this reason, we strongly recommend that you purchase the current edition of *The Official Guide for GMAT Review*. Ignore the suggested methods for answering the questions—they are too time-consuming to be of any use during a real test—and concentrate on the real GMAT questions.

The book can be found in many bookstores, online at www.ets.org, or you can order it by sending a check for $19.95 (within the United States) to:

Graduate Management Admission Test
Educational Testing Service
P.O. Box 6108
Princeton, NJ 08541-6108

By practicing our techniques on real GMATs, you will be able to prove to yourself that the techniques work and increase your confidence when you actually take the test. Of course, another important part of preparing for a computer-adaptive test is taking practice tests on computer. The Princeton Review's GMAT software (available with some editions of this book) gives a very close approximation of the computer-adaptive GMAT, down to the same fonts and approximate scoring algorithms. It includes four complete adaptive tests, and comes in both Macintosh and Windows formats. ETS puts out similar preparation software called *POWERPREP* for $59.95. This includes two computer-adaptive tests, plus additional practice questions. This software has the real advantage of containing actual ETS questions—however many of these questions are taken from *The Official Guide*, which partially diminishes its utility. *POWERPREP* is available only in Windows format.

ETS also offers "The Official GMAT Practice Test." For $59.95, you can take a practice GMAT at the same testing center where you will eventually take the real test—and receive a score that no business schools will ever see. Unfortunately, this practice test is one of the two tests already offered in *POWERPREP*, which, in turn, uses questions taken from *The Official Guide*.

How to Think About the GMAT

What Is ETS?

If you went to ETS to interview for a job, you would be impressed with the working conditions: a beautiful 400-acre estate just outside Princeton, New Jersey. The estate used to be a hunting club, and it boasts a swimming pool, a goose pond, a baseball diamond, lighted tennis courts, jogging trails, an expensive house for the company president, and a chauffeured motor pool.

You would also be impressed with the company's financial structure; ETS is a large private company and it makes a lot of money. (It's also tax–exempt.) It sells the GMAT and the SAT of course, but it also sells about 500 other tests—including those for CIA agents, golf pros, travel agents, firemen, and barbers.

However, what would probably impress you the most, businesswise, is the fact that ETS has pulled off a deal that would in any other field have rendered it liable to antitrust action: ETS has a monopoly.

To Get Into Business School You Can

A) take the GMAT

B) take the GMAT

If you don't like *Time*, you can read *Newsweek*. If you don't like AT&T, there are a host of competitors to choose from. But if you don't like the GMAT ... well, you might as well consider going into social work.

ETS won't mind. They write the entrance test for that, too.

Of course, you can't really blame ETS for trying to hold on to a deal that's as sweet as this one. And in order to do that, ETS must convince both you and the business schools to whom you are applying that the GMAT actually measures something.

There's just one hitch. It doesn't.

What Does the GMAT Measure?

The GMAT is not a test of how smart you are. Nor is it a test of your business acumen. **It's simply a test of how good you are at taking the GMAT.** ETS says that "the GMAT is not a test of knowledge in specific subjects." This is also untrue. In fact, you will learn that by studying the very specific knowledge outlined in this book, you can substantially improve your score.

The GMAT as Job Interview

The first axiom of any how-to book on job interviewing is that you must always tell your interviewer what he or she wants to hear. Whether or not this is good job-hunting advice, it happens to be a very useful strategy on the GMAT. The test writers at ETS think in very predictable ways. You can improve your score by learning to think the way they do and anticipating the kinds of answers that they think are correct.

Not Just GMAT

Here is a partial list of organizations that buy tests from ETS:
The CIA
The Defense Department
The National Security Council
The government of Trinidad and Tobago
National Contact Lens Examiners
The American Society of Heating, Refrigerating, and Air-Conditioning Engineers

Who Writes the GMAT?

Many people believe that GMAT questions are written by university professors or successful executives. This is not true. Virtually all questions are written by ordinary company employees or by college students and other people who are hired part-time from outside ETS.

ETS "examiners" try to write each question so that it can be used in as many as four different tests. Some of the questions from the GMAT have turned up on the SAT.

Is the New Computerized GMAT Better than the Old Paper-and-Pencil Version?

ETS claims that the new test is able to home in on a test taker's level of ability much more precisely than the old test, but many standardized testing experts are dubious.

Among the questionable features of the new GMAT:

- The computer format is likely to discriminate against the computer illiterate.

- Test takers are no longer able to request to see the test they took, in order to determine if it was scored correctly, or if a question had more than one correct answer.

- For the first time ever in standardized testing, experimental questions will be mixed in among the real questions.

- The new format takes away a student's ability to make notes in the margin, or scratch out eliminated choices on the test booklet itself.

Do The Princeton Review Techniques Work on the New GMAT?

The computer-adaptive GMAT contains exactly the same types of questions as the old GMAT—which means that virtually all of the techniques we've been perfecting for the last ten years still work.

The real difference in the computer-adaptive test is its ability to track the test-taker's responses during the exam and offer questions of greater or lesser difficulty based on those responses. This has changed some of our level-of-difficulty strategies, and prompted us to add new ones.

However, we are not asleep. We monitor each new GMAT very closely. Each year, we publish a new edition of this book to reflect the subtle shifts that happen over time, as well as any changes in question type. These changes show up as experimental questions several years before they ever actually make it to the real exam. For the latest information on the computer-adaptive GMAT, please visit our web site at www.review.com.

THE TEST FORMAT HAS CHANGED. ARE THE QUESTIONS THEMSELVES GOING TO CHANGE?

Not anytime soon. While the computerized format may eventually allow ETS to incorporate video and sound into the test, include questions from the individual business schools to which you are applying, and allow short-answer type questions, these innovations are still on the drawing board. ETS has said that for the foreseeable future, the questions will remain in the multiple-choice format—as they have since the test was first administered back in 1954.

Why? Imagine that you're one of ETS's test writers struggling to produce tests that will be taken by over 7 million students each year. Not only must your test question be suitable for the test you are now writing, but it must also be good enough to be included in a file from which future test questions for other tests may be chosen. Under these circumstances, what is needed is a kind of generic question written according to established formulas. Until more of ETS's tests are computer-adaptive, it doesn't make economic sense for them to change the way these questions are constructed.

FORGET ABOUT THE "BEST" ANSWER

The instructions for the GMAT tell you to select the "best" answer to every question. What does "best" answer mean? **It means the answer ETS believes to be the best.**

IS THE GMAT JUST LIKE THE SAT?

The GMAT and the SAT are both prepared by the same organization, so they share the same philosophy. But there are substantial differences between the two tests. The GMAT is a much tougher test, and it contains question types not found on the SAT. Many of the techniques developed by The Princeton Review for the SAT are useful on some sections of the GMAT, but we have also developed new techniques and expanded on some of the old ones.

Is This Book Just Like the Princeton Review Course?

No. You won't have the benefit of taking four computer-adaptive GMATs that are not only scored, but *analyzed* by our computers. You won't get to sit in small classes with ten other highly motivated students who will spur you on. You won't get to work with expert instructors who can assess your strengths and pinpoint your weaknesses. There is no way to put these things in a book.

What you *will* find in this book are some of the techniques and methods that have enabled our students to crack the system—plus a review of the essentials that you cannot afford not to know.

If at all possible, you should take our course. If that is not possible, then use this book.

How to Crack the System

In the following chapters we're going to teach you our method for cracking the GMAT. Read each chapter carefully. Some of our ideas may seem strange at first. For example, when we tell you that it is sometimes easier to answer GMAT questions without actually working out the entire problem, you may think, "This isn't the way I conduct business."

But the GMAT Isn't about Business

We're not going to teach you business skills. We're not going to teach you math and English. We're going to teach you the GMAT.

3

Cracking the System: Basic Principles

How the Computer-Adaptive GMAT Works

To understand how to beat the computer-adaptive GMAT, you have to understand how it works.

Unlike paper-and-pencil standardized tests that begin with an easy question and then get progressively tougher, the computer-adaptive test always begins by giving you a medium question. If you get it right, the computer gives you a slightly harder question. If you get it wrong, the computer gives you a slightly easier question, and so on. The idea is that the computer will zero in on your exact level of ability very quickly, which allows you to answer fewer questions overall, and the computer to make a more finely-honed assessment of your abilities.

What You Will See on Your Screen

During the test itself, what you will see on your screen is the question you're currently working on, with little ovals in front of the five answer choices. To answer the question, you use your mouse to click on the oval of the answer choice you think is correct. Then you press a button at the bottom of the screen to verify that yes, this is the answer you want to pick.

What You Will Never See on Your Screen

What you will *never* see is the score that ETS has assigned you even before you began the exam, and the process by which the computer keeps track of your progress. As you go through the test, the computer will keep revising its assessment of you based on your responses.

Let's watch the process in action. In the left-hand column below, you'll see what a hypothetical test taker—let's call her Jane—sees on her screen as she takes the test. In the right column, we'll show you how ETS keeps track of how she's doing.

(We've simplified this example a bit in the interest of clarity.)

What You'll See:

To regard the overwhelming beauty of the Mojave Desert is <u>understanding the great forces of</u> nature that shape our planet.

- ◯ understanding the great forces of
- ◯ to understand the great forces to
- ◯ to understand the great forces of
- ◯ understanding the greatest forces in
- ◯ understanding the greater forces on

What You *Won't* See:

ETS leads off Jane's verbal section with a medium question, chosen by the computer at random from a bin of medium questions—in this case, a Sentence Correction question. Her score starting out: 500.

current score: *500*

Jane gets the first question right (she chose the third answer down—what we call choice (C)), so her current score goes up to a 540, and the computer selects a harder problem for her second question.

current score: *540*

What You'll See:

Hawks in a certain region depend heavily for their diet on a particular variety of field mouse. The killing of field mice by farmers will seriously endanger the survival of hawks in this region.

Which of the following, if true, casts the most doubt on the conclusion drawn above?

- ◯ The number of mice killed by farmers has increased in recent years.
- ◯ Farmers kill many other types of pests besides field mice without any adverse effect on hawks.
- ◯ Hawks have been found in other areas besides this region.
- ◯ Killing field mice leaves more food for the remaining mice who have larger broods the following season.
- ◯ Hawks are also endangered because of pollution and deforestation.

What You Won't See:

The computer happens to select a Critical Reasoning problem.

Oops. Jane got the second question wrong (the correct answer was the fourth answer down—what we call choice (D)), so her score goes down to a 510, and the computer gives her a slightly easier problem.

current score: 510

What You'll See:

Nuclear weapons being invented, there was wide expectation in the scientific community that all war would end.

- ◯ Nuclear weapons being invented, there was wide expectation in the scientific community that
- ◯ When nuclear weapons were invented, expectation was that
- ◯ As nuclear weapons were invented, there was wide expectation that
- ◯ Insofar as nuclear weapons were invented, it was widely expected
- ◯ With the invention of nuclear weapons, there was wide expectation that

What You Won't See:

Jane has no idea of what the correct answer is on this third question, but she guesses choice (E) and gets it correct. Her score goes up to a 530.

current score: 530

You get the idea. At the very beginning of the test, your score moves up or down in larger increments (perhaps as much as 40 points at a time) than it does at the end, when ETS believes it is merely refining whether you deserve, say, a 610 or a 620.

The questions come from a huge pool of "items" held in the computer in what ETS calls "bins." In theory, there could be as many as 60 different bins available, each with a different level of difficulty. In practice, we believe that ETS has far fewer difficulty bins. This is partly because they are also tracking content. Each of the various kinds of questions on the test must get equal time, and all of the basic subject areas must be covered (for example, the math portion of the test must cover arithmetic, algebra, and geometry). ETS is also tracking what they call "social sensitivity." Several items must appear on every test whose subject matter concerns a minority group. We'll talk more about this later.

THE EXPERIMENTAL QUESTIONS

Unfortunately, almost one-fourth of the questions that you answer won't actually count toward your score. Eleven of the 41 verbal questions and 9 of the 37 math questions are "experimental."

Perhaps the most radical change on the new test is that for the first time ever in standardized testing, the Experimental questions are sprinkled among the real questions.

In the past, ETS would confine the questions that didn't count in an experimental section. This meant that if an Experimental question later turned out to have no correct answer, or if another Experimental question turned out to have *two* correct answers, it was less likely to have a negative impact on a test taker.

However, because the new GMAT mixes real questions with Experimental questions, if you are answering upper-medium problems and you suddenly get one that seems too easy, there are two possibilities: (A) you are about to fall into a trap or (B) it is an Experimental question that actually *is* too easy.

THE PRINCETON REVIEW APPROACH TO THE GMAT

To help you ace the computer-adaptive GMAT, this book is going to provide you with

- The test-taking techniques that have made The Princeton Review famous and which will enable you to turn the inherent weaknesses of the computer-adaptive GMAT to your advantage

- A thorough review of all the major topics covered on the GMAT

- A short diagnostic test to help you predict your current scoring level

- Practice questions to help you raise your scoring level

According to computer-adaptive theory, a test like the GMAT hones in on a test-taker's *general* score level within three or four questions—after which he spends the rest of each section answering questions at about that level and slightly above. Each time he gets one correct, the computer gives him a slightly tougher problem, and more often than not, he gets it wrong—because, after all, this question is beyond his abilities.

Never mind (for the moment) that this is not exactly how it works. People's ability to answer questions depends to a large degree on the subject of those questions. One person might be an algebra ace (and able to answer algebra questions of *any* difficulty level) but rusty in geometry (and thus unable to answer even the simplest geometry problems). Another might be terrific at reading comprehension but lousy at grammar. Sometimes a test taker will really know how to do a problem but will make a careless error; other times she will get a question right by mistake.

KNOW YOUR BIN

According to classic theory, the average test taker spends most of his time answering questions at his level of competency (which he gets right) and questions that are just above his level of competency (which he gets wrong). In other words, most testers will see questions from only a few difficulty "bins."

This means that to raise your score, you must learn to answer questions from the bins immediately *above* your current scoring level. At the back of this book you will find a short diagnostic test to determine your current scoring level, and then bins filled with questions at various scoring levels. When combined with a thorough review of the topics covered on the GMAT, this should put you well on your way to the score you're looking for.

But first, let's begin with some testing strategy.

4

Cracking the System: Intermediate Principles

Imagine for a moment that you are a contestant on *Let's Make a Deal*. It's the final big deal of the day. Monty Hall asks you, "Do you want curtain number one, curtain number two, or curtain number three?"

As you carefully weigh your options, the members of the audience are shouting out *their* suggestions. But you can bet that there is *one* thing no one in the audience is going to shout at you:

"Skip the question!"

It's just not an option. You have to make a choice—and you have to make it *now*. An all-expenses-paid trip around the world, a washer-drier, or a lifetime supply of toilet paper—these are the prizes lurking behind the curtains. One of these choices is much better than the others, but on *Let's Make a Deal*, you have no idea which it is.

LET'S MAKE A GMAT

Normally when you don't know the correct answer on a test, you skip the question and come back to it later. But on the new computer-adaptive GMAT, as in *Let's Make a Deal*, you can never skip the question.

TO GET TO THE NEXT QUESTION, YOU HAVE TO ANSWER THE ONE YOU'RE PRESENTLY ON

Because of the way the GMAT's scoring algorithm works, the question you see on your computer screen at any particular moment depends on your response to the question before. This creates an odd situation for the ETS designers: If they allowed you to skip a question, they wouldn't know which question to give you next.

It's clear from articles ETS test designers have published that they know test takers are at a real disadvantage when they can't skip a problem and come back to it later. Still, the idea of using a computer to administer tests was too tempting to give up. In the end, ETS decided that you should generously be willing to make the sacrifice in the name of progress.

So whether you know the answer to a problem or not, you have to answer it in order to move on.

This means that, like it or not, you are going to have to do some guessing on the GMAT. Ah, but there's guessing, and then there's *guessing*.

IF YOU DON'T KNOW THE RIGHT ANSWER, DON'T YOU DARE JUST PICK AN ANSWER AT RANDOM

This may sound a little loony, but it turns out that you don't always have to know the correct answer to get a question right.

Try answering the following question:

What is the unit of currency in Sweden?

What? You don't know?

Unless you work for an international bank or have traveled in Scandinavia, there is no reason why you should know what the unit of currency in Sweden is. (By the way, the GMAT doesn't ask such factual questions. We're using this one to make a point.) As it stands now, since you don't know the answer, you would have to answer this question at random, right?

Not necessarily. GMAT questions are written in multiple-choice format. One of the five choices has to be the answer. How do you find it?

LOOK FOR WRONG ANSWERS INSTEAD OF RIGHT ONES

Let's put this question into multiple-choice format—the only format you'll find on the GMAT—and see if you still want to answer at random.

What is the unit of currency in Sweden?

○ the dollar
○ the franc
○ the pound sterling
○ the yen
○ the krona

THE PROCESS OF ELIMINATION

Suddenly this question isn't difficult anymore. You may not have known the right answer, but you certainly knew enough to eliminate the wrong answers. Wrong answers are often easier to spot than right answers. Sometimes they just sound weird. At other times they're logically impossible. While it is rare to be able to eliminate all four of the incorrect answer choices on the GMAT, you will almost always be able to eliminate at least one of them—and frequently two or more—by using Process of Elimination. Process of Elimination (POE for short) will enable you to answer questions that you don't have the time or the inclination to figure out exactly. We will refer to POE in every single chapter of this book. It is one of the most important and fundamental tools you will use to increase your score.

Try another example:

Which of the following countries uses the peso as its unit of currency?

○ Russia
○ Canada
○ Venezuela
○ England
○ Chile

This time you can probably only get rid of three of the five answer choices using POE. The answer is clearly *not* Russia, Canada, or England, but most people probably don't know for sure whether the answer is Venezuela or Chile.

You've got the question down to two possibilities. What should you do?

HEADS OR TAILS

A Chilean might flip a peso. You have a fifty-fifty chance of getting this question right, which is much better than if you had guessed at random. And since ETS is forcing you to guess anyway, it makes sense to guess intelligently.

In the chapters that follow, we'll show you specific ways to make use of POE to increase your score. You may feel uncomfortable about using these techniques at first, but the sooner you make them your own, the sooner you'll start to improve your score.

IS IT FAIR TO GET A QUESTION RIGHT WHEN YOU DON'T KNOW THE ANSWER?

If you took any math courses in college you probably remember that the correct answer to a problem, while important, wasn't the only thing you were graded on. Your professor was probably more interested in *how* you got the answer, whether you wrote an elegant equation, or if you used the right formula.

If your equation was correct but you messed up your addition at the end, did you get the entire question wrong? Most college professors give partial credit for an answer like that. After all, what's most important is the mental process that goes into getting the answer, not the answer alone.

On the GMAT, if you don't click the right oval with your mouse, you're wrong. It doesn't matter that you knew *how* to do the problem, or that you clicked the wrong answer *by mistake*. ETS doesn't care: You're just wrong. And a wrong answer means that the running score that ETS is keeping on you will go down by ten or twenty points and you'll be forced to answer several easier questions correctly before you get back to the level where you were.

This really isn't fair. It seems only fitting that you should be able to benefit from the flip side of this situation, which means that if you fill in the *correct* oval, ETS doesn't care how you got that answer either.

SCRATCH PAPER

The Process of Elimination is a powerful tool, but it's only powerful if you keep track of the answer choices you've eliminated. On a computer-adaptive test, you obviously can't cross off choices on the screen—but you *can* cross them off on scratch paper.

The testing center provides each tester with several pieces of blank pink paper. In our course, we encourage our students to spend a couple of minutes during the pre-test tutorial dividing up their scratch paper into boxes, and labeling each box with five answer choices as shown on the next page:

```
┌─────────────────┬─────────────────┐
│ A               │ A               │
│ B               │ B               │
│ C               │ C               │
│ D               │ D               │
│ E               │ E               │
├─────────────────┼─────────────────┤
│ A               │ A               │
│ B               │ B               │
│ C               │ C               │
│ D               │ D               │
│ E               │ E               │
└─────────────────┴─────────────────┘
```

Each letter corresponds to an answer. Of course, the answers on the computer-adaptive GMAT are no longer labeled with letters, but to be able to track the answers you've crossed off, it helps to think of them as if they were. The first answer choice is equivalent to (A), the second to (B), and so on.

Throughout this book, you will see us using scratch paper to keep track of the answer choices that have already been eliminated. By making this part of the ritual of how you take the GMAT, you will be able to prevent careless errors and make your guesses count.

SUMMARY

1. Because of the way that the new GMAT is designed, you will be forced to answer questions whether or not you know the correct answer.

2. However, not knowing the exact answer to a question does not mean that you have to get it wrong.

3. When you don't know the right answer to a question, look for wrong answers instead. This is called POE, or Process of Elimination.

4. The best way to keep track of the answer choices that you've eliminated is to use your scratch paper to cross them off as you go.

5

Cracking the System:
Advanced Principles

The people at ETS think that the new computer-adaptive GMAT is wonderful—and not just because they wrote it, or because it makes them a lot of money. They like it because it ensures that the only problems a test taker gets to see are problems at, and slightly above and below, her level of ability. One of the things they always hated about the paper-and-pencil test was that a student scoring 300 could guess the correct answer to a 700-level question.

BUT ETS HAS THIS LITTLE PROBLEM

The questions on the GMAT are still multiple-choice.

That may not seem like a problem to you, but consider the following situation. Suppose an average student takes the GMAT. He's answered 36 of the 37 problems on the math section. There's one left, and as he looks at this last question, he realizes he has absolutely no idea of how to answer it. However, one of the answer choices just "seems" right. So he picks it.

And gets it right.

ETS gets nightmares just thinking about this situation. That average student was supposed to get 500. He "deserved" 500. But by guessing the correct answer to one last problem, he may have gotten 510.

Ten points more than he "deserved."

ETS'S SOLUTION

ETS's tests wouldn't be worth much if students could routinely guess the correct answer to difficult questions by picking answers that *seemed* right.

So ETS came up with a wonderful solution:

On difficult questions, answer choices that *seem* right to the average student are always wrong.

CHOOSING ANSWERS THAT *SEEM* RIGHT

When we take the GMAT, most of us don't have time to work out every problem completely, or to check and double-check our answers. We just go as far as we can on each problem and then choose the answer that seems correct based on what we've been able to figure out. Sometimes we're completely sure of our answer, and at other times we simply do as much as we can and then follow our hunch. We may pick an answer because it "just looks right," or because something about it seems to go naturally with the question.

WHICH ANSWERS SEEM RIGHT?

That all depends on how high your score is.

Suppose you took the GMAT and scored 800. That means every answer that *seemed* right to you actually *was* right. You picked the answer that seemed right on every question, and every one of those answers was correct.

Now suppose your friend took the GMAT and scored 200. That means every answer that *seemed* right to your friend actually was *wrong*.

Of course, most people who take the GMAT don't score 800 or 200. The average person scores somewhere in-between.

WHAT HAPPENS WHEN THE AVERAGE PERSON TAKES THE GMAT?

The average person picks the answer that *seems* right on every problem. Sometimes these hunches are correct; sometimes they are not.

To be specific:

- ◆ On easy questions, the average person tends to pick the correct answer. The answers that seem right to the average person actually are right on the easy questions.

- ◆ On medium questions, the average person's hunches are right only some of the time. Sometimes the answers that seem right to the average person really are right and sometimes they're wrong.

- ◆ Finally, on difficult problems, the average person's hunches are always wrong. The answers that seem right to the average person on these questions are invariably wrong.

MEET JOE BLOGGS

We're going to talk a lot about "the average person" from now on. For the sake of convenience, let's give him a name: Joe Bloggs. Joe Bloggs is just the average American prospective business-school student. He has average grades from college, and will get an average grade on the GMAT. There's a little bit of him in everyone, and there's a little bit of everyone in him. He isn't brilliant. He isn't dumb. He's just average.

HOW DOES JOE BLOGGS APPROACH THE GMAT?

Joe Bloggs, the average person, spends most of his time answering questions of average difficulty. But whenever he gets several questions right in a row, the computer gives him a more difficult question.

Joe approaches the GMAT just as everybody else does. Whether the question is hard or easy, he always chooses the answer that *seems* to be correct.

Here's an example of what a more difficult problem might look like on a GMAT problem-solving section:

> The output of a factory was increased by 10% to keep up with rising demand. To handle the holiday rush, this new output was increased by 20%. By approximately what percent would the output now have to be decreased in order to restore the original output?
>
> ○ 20%
> ○ 24%
> ○ 30%
> ○ 32%
> ○ 79%

A Little History, Part II

The old ETS scoring machines were susceptible to cheaters, who would blacken more than one square for each question. The women who worked the machines had to visually scan each answer sheet and put cellophane tape over double responses. A University of Chicago student beat this system by marking his second and third choices with tiny dots that the women wouldn't notice but that the machines would. Later in his life, this enterprising young man was convicted of murder.

This question is from an upper medium difficulty bin. Don't bother trying to work the problem out now. You will learn how to do this type of problem (percentage decrease) in the first math chapter.

HOW DID JOE BLOGGS DO ON THIS QUESTION?

He got it wrong.

Why?

Because ETS set a trap for him.

WHICH ANSWER DID JOE BLOGGS PICK ON THIS QUESTION?

Joe didn't think this was a hard problem. The answer *seemed* perfectly obvious. Joe Bloggs picked the middle choice—what we call choice (C). Joe assumed that if you increase production first by 10% and then by 20%, you have to take away 30% to get back to where you started.

ETS led Joe away from the correct answer by giving him an answer that *seemed* right. In fact, the correct answer is choice (B). Here's the same problem with slightly different answer choices. We've changed the choices to make a point:

> The output of a factory was increased by 10% to keep up with rising demand. To handle the holiday rush, this new output was raised by 20%. By approximately what percent would the output now have to be decreased in order to restore the original output?
>
> ○ 21%
> ○ 24%
> ○ 34.2%
> ○ 37%
> ○ 71.5%

If Joe had seen this version, he wouldn't have thought it was an easy question. Now none of the answers would *seem* right to Joe. He would have been forced to guess at random. This would have made the question fairer, but ETS didn't want to take the chance that an *average* person might get this question right by mistake.

Could ETS Have Made This an Easy Question Instead?

Sure, by writing different answer choices.

Here's the same question with choices we've substituted to make the correct answer choice obvious:

> The output of a factory was increased by 10% to keep up with rising demand. To handle the holiday rush, this new output was raised by 20%. By approximately what percent would the output now have to be decreased in order to restore the original output?
>
> ◯ a million %
> ◯ 24%
> ◯ a billion %
> ◯ a trillion %
> ◯ a zillion %

When the problem is written this way, Joe Bloggs can see that the answer has to be choice (B). It seems right to Joe because all the other answers seem obviously wrong.

Profiting from Other People's Bankruptcy

Let's look at a textbook example of how not to run a company.

Suppose you started your own company, with three partners: David Leeson (formerly of Barings Bank), John DeLorean (formerly of General Motors), and Ivan Boesky (formerly of Northview). You have an important business decision to make, and each of your partners gives you his advice. Leeson says, "If you lose a bet on the market, just keep doubling your investment. It always worked for me." DeLorean says, "I have a great investment opportunity for you. Get together $200,000 in cash and call this number in Bolivia." Boesky says, "Listen, what you need is good inside information."

Are you going to make use of the advice of these losers? Sure, you now know three things that you're absolutely not going to do.

The way Joe Bloggs takes a test is a textbook example of how *not* to take a test.

Your Partner on the Test: Joe Bloggs

When you take the GMAT a few weeks or months from now, you'll have to take it on your own, of course. But suppose for a moment that ETS allowed you to take it with Joe Bloggs as your partner. Would Joe be any help to you on the GMAT?

You Probably Don't Think So

After all, Joe is wrong as often as he's right. He knows the answers to the easy questions, but so do you. You'd like to do better than average on the GMAT, and Joe earns only an average score (he's the average person, remember). All things considered, you'd probably prefer to have someone else for your partner.

But Joe might turn out to be a pretty helpful partner, after all. Since his hunches on difficult questions are *always* wrong, couldn't you improve your chances on those questions simply by finding out what Joe wanted to pick, and then picking something else?

If you could use what you know about Joe Bloggs to eliminate one, two, or even three obviously incorrect choices on a hard problem, wouldn't you improve your score by guessing among the remaining choices?

WHATEVER YOUR CURRENT SCORING LEVEL, THE JOE BLOGGS PRINCIPLE CAN HELP YOU

We're going to teach you how to use Joe Bloggs while taking the GMAT.

After you've taken the diagnostic test at the back of this book, the tests in our software products, or the practice tests provided in *The Official Guide to GMAT Review*, you will have some idea, as you take the GMAT, of how you are scoring at any given moment, which means that you'll know approximately the level of difficulty of most of the problems you'll be facing.

If, at the moment, you find yourself facing mostly easy questions, you'll know not to out-think the question by picking hard answers.

If, at the moment, you are facing mostly medium questions, you can concentrate on practicing medium problems and get used to the kinds of traps these types of questions have in store for you.

If, at the moment, you will be facing mostly difficult questions, you can stop and ask yourself, "How would Joe Bloggs answer these questions?" And when you see what *he* would do, you're going to do something else. Why? Because you know that on hard questions, Joe Bloggs is *always* wrong.

SHOULD YOU ALWAYS JUST ELIMINATE ANY ANSWER THAT SEEMS TO BE CORRECT?

No!

Remember what we said about Joe Bloggs:

1. His hunches are often correct on easy questions.

2. His hunches are sometimes correct and sometimes incorrect on medium questions.

3. His hunches are always wrong on difficult questions.

PUTTING JOE BLOGGS TO WORK FOR YOU

In the following chapters, we'll be teaching you many specific problem-solving techniques based on the Joe Bloggs principle. The Joe Bloggs principle will help you:

1. use POE to eliminate incorrect answer choices

2. avoid careless mistakes

A WORD OF CAUTION

If you go through our review of the math and verbal topics covered on the GMAT, do all the drills we provide, and practice our techniques on real GMAT questions, then your scores on practice tests will almost certainly start to go up.

But as your scores improve, the level of difficulty of the questions you will be seeing on the computer-adaptive GMAT will increase as well—which means that you'll have to make adjustments to your use of the Joe Bloggs principle.

SUMMARY

1. Almost everyone approaches the GMAT by choosing the answer that *seems* correct, all things considered.

2. Joe Bloggs is the average person. He earns an average score on the GMAT. On easy GMAT questions, the answers that *seem* correct to him are usually correct. On medium questions, his answers are sometimes correct and sometimes not. On hard questions, the answers that seem correct to him are *always* wrong.

3. By taking a diagnostic test from time to time, you can predict your current scoring level—which, in turn, will tell you what type of questions you will generally be answering: Easy, medium, or difficult.

4. Whatever your current scoring level, the Joe Bloggs principle can help you to eliminate answer choices when you don't know the correct answer.

6

Taking the GMAT

REGISTERING TO TAKE THE GMAT

You can set up an appointment to take the test over the telephone. You will be given a list of various dates and times and testing centers that are located near you. Simply choose the most convenient time and center. You must pay in advance by credit card.

ON THE DAY OF THE REAL TEST

To register for the GMAT Call 1-800-GMATNOW or visit the web site at www.gmat.org

Get up early, have breakfast, and do a couple of GMAT questions you've already seen in order to get your mind working. You don't want to have to warm up on the test itself. Bring a snack to the test center. You'll get two optional 5-minute breaks during the test (one after the essay section, one between the verbal and the quantitative sections). Some people spend the breaks comparing answers in the hallway and getting upset because not only didn't they get the same answers—they didn't even get the same questions. Ignore the people around you. Why assume that they know any more than you do? Use the breaks to eat the food you've brought.

You should also bring a pen or pencil to make notes on the scratch paper ETS provides, as well as a reliable watch. If you like, the computer will give you a constant digital readout of the time remaining in each section, but some students find this distracting and prefer to look at their watches. No calculators are permitted.

AT THE TESTING CENTER

Unlike testing sessions you may have attended in the past, where hundreds of people were lined up to take the same test, you may well be the only person at your testing center taking the GMAT. You'll be asked for two forms of identification. One must be a photo ID. In addition, an employee will take a digital photograph of you before leading you to the computer station where you will take the test. The station consists of a desk with a computer monitor, a keyboard, a mouse, several sheets of scratch paper, and a pencil. Before the test starts, make sure you're comfortable. Is there enough light? Is your desk sturdy? Don't be afraid to speak up; you're going to be spending several hours at that desk.

There will almost certainly be other people in the same room at other computer stations taking other computer-adaptive tests. You might be seated next to someone taking the licensing exam for architects or a test for school nurses, or even a test for golf pros.

None of the people in the room will have necessarily started at the same time. The testing center employee will show you how to start the computer tutorial, but the computer itself will be your proctor from then on. It will tell you how much time you have left in a section, when your time is up, and when to go on to the next section.

The test center employees will be available if you have a question or need additional scratch paper. They will also be monitoring the room for security purposes. Just in case their eagle eyes aren't enough, video and audio systems will record everything that happens in the room.

The process sounds less human than it really is. Our students have generally found the test center employees to be quite nice.

The Tutorial

Before the test begins, ETS will give you an interactive tutorial on all the tools you'll need to use during the exam. If you're used to the latest computer games, you're going to be very disappointed in the graphics of the GMAT. It's mostly black and white, with terrible fonts left over from the era of DOS.

The tutorial teaches you how to use the mouse, select an answer, move on to the next question, see how much time remains in a section, and stop the test if you want to. You'll be able to practice each function until you feel comfortable with it.

Of course, if you aren't already familiar with how to operate a computer, the tutorial they offer right before this very important exam is definitely *not* the time to learn. Anyone who is uncomfortable with computers should spend a number of hours over several weeks getting used to the process.

We encourage our students to become completely familiar with the test experience by practicing with software that mimics the GMAT—either the Princeton Review's GMAT software, or ETS's *POWERPREP*. This way, test takers can use the time allotted for the tutorial to set up their scratch paper for the test to come, including writing down hard-to-remember formulas.

What to Bring to the Test Center

1. your registration ticket
2. a photo ID and one other form of ID
3. a reliable watch
4. a snack

What Your Screen Will Look Like

During most of the test, your screen will look a lot like this:

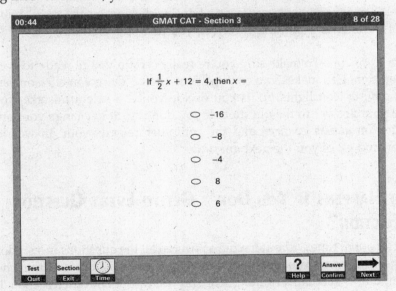

The problem you're working on at any particular moment will be in the middle of the screen (by the way, the answer to this one is the first choice—what we call choice (A)). At the top left will be a readout of the time remaining in the section (if you choose to have it displayed), the name of the section you're taking, the number of the question you're working on, and how many questions remain. At the bottom of the screen are a number of icons:

How Much?

The cost of the GMAT is $150 in the United States, slightly more overseas.

Test Quit—By clicking on this button, you can end the test at any moment. We don't recommend that you do this unless you actually become ill. Even if you decide not to have your test scored (an option they will give you at the end of the exam), you might as well finish—it's great practice, and besides, ETS has no intention of giving you a refund.

Section Exit—By clicking on this button, you will be taken out of the section you're currently working on. The only reason to do this is if you finish a section early and are in a hurry to get to the next section. Most of our students feel that if they are lucky enough to finish early, they'd just as soon have a few moments of rest before the next section begins.

Time—By clicking on this button, you can either make visible or hide the digital countdown at the top left of the screen. Some people like to see how much time is left; others would prefer to look at their watches. When time is almost up, the display will reappear even if you've told it to go away. During the last two minutes, the display will start flashing, and will show you the remaining time in minutes and seconds.

Help—This button gives you a miniature version of the tutorial, explaining what the different icons mean and how to use them.

Next—When you've answered a question by clicking on the small bubble in front of the answer you think is correct, you press this button.

Answer Confirm—To make sure you're really certain you're ready to go to the next question, ETS makes you confirm your choice. Once you click on *next*, the *answer confirm* icon lights up. If you decide you've made a mistake, you can change your answer to the question. If you don't want to change your answer, you click on *answer confirm*, and the computer records your answer to this question and gives you the next question.

WHAT HAPPENS IF YOU DON'T GET TO EVERY QUESTION IN A SECTION?

If you run out of time without having answered all the questions in a section, the computer just moves you on to the next section. As we said in an earlier chapter, the computer is keeping a running score on you throughout each section. If you don't get to answer some questions, the computer deducts points (based on an algorithm that probably wouldn't survive rigorous scientific scrutiny) and gives you a score based on what you *have* answered. It would be theoretically possible to get a GMAT score on the computer-adaptive test by answering only one verbal question and one math question.

It Is Actually in Your Interest to Answer *All* the Questions—Even If you Have to Guess

You might think it would be better to skip any questions you don't have time to answer at the end of a section— but in fact, the reverse is true: if time is running out, you will probably get a slightly higher score by clicking through and answering any remaining questions at random. This is because the penalty for getting a question wrong diminishes sharply toward the end of each section (when the computer has already largely decided your score.) The penalty for each question skipped at the end of a section is actually greater than the penalty for getting one of those last questions wrong.

Zen and the Art of Test-Taking

As you begin a new section, put the last one behind you. Don't get rattled if you think you've done poorly on one part of the test. Most people find that their impression of how they did on a section is often worse than the reality. You should also keep in mind that one-fourth of the questions you'll be taking don't count. Experimental questions are often harder and weirder than real questions. If you feel you've blown a number of problems, there's a good chance at least some of them were Experimental.

At the End of the Test

When you finish, the computer will ask you if you want the test to count. If you say no, you just walk away, the computer will not record your score, and no schools will ever see it. Of course, neither will you. ETS will not let you look at your score and then decide whether or not you want to keep it. If you tell the computer that you want the test to count, then it will give you your unofficial score right then and there on the screen. A few weeks later, you'll receive your verified score in the mail. If you choose to cancel at the test site, you will not be able to change your mind later. By the same token, once you've chosen to *see* your score, you can't cancel it.

One Final Thought before You Begin

No matter how high or low you score on this test, and no matter how much you improve your performance with this book, you should *never* accept the score ETS assigns you as an accurate assessment of your abilities. The temptation to see a high score as evidence that you're a genius, or a low score as evidence that you're an idiot, can be very powerful.

When you've read this book and practiced our techniques on real GMAT questions, you'll be able to judge for yourself whether the GMAT actually measures much besides how well you do on the GMAT.

Think of this as a kind of game—a game you can get good at.

PART II

How to Crack the Math GMAT

GMAT Math:
Basic Principles

What's Covered in the Math Section

The 37 math questions on the GMAT come in two different formats. About half of the questions will be regular Problem Solving questions of the type you're familiar with from countless other standardized tests, such as the SAT. The other half of the questions, mixed in among the regular Problem Solving questions, will be of a type unique to the GMAT; they're called Data Sufficiency questions, and will ask you to determine whether you can answer a math question based on two pieces of information. We've devoted an entire chapter to Data Sufficiency; it follows the math review.

But whether the question falls into the category of Problem Solving or Data Sufficiency, the GMAT questions will test your general knowledge of three subjects:

1. arithmetic

2. basic algebra

3. basic geometry

What Isn't Covered in the Math Section

The good news is that you won't need to know calculus, trigonometry, or any complicated geometry. The bad news is that the specialized, business-type math you're probably good at isn't tested, either. There will be no questions on computing the profit on three ticks of a particular bond sale, no questions about amortizing a loan, no need to calculate the bottom line of a small business.

Ancient History

For the most part what you'll find on the GMAT is a kind of math that you haven't had to think about in years: junior high school and high school math. The GMAT is more difficult than your old nemesis, the SAT, but the Problem Solving on the GMAT tests the same general body of knowledge that's tested by the SAT. Since most people who apply to business school have been out of college for several years, high school math may seem a bit like ancient history to you. In the next few chapters, we'll give you a fast review of the important concepts, and we'll show you some powerful techniques for cracking the system.

Order of Difficulty

The first problem on the computer-adaptive math test will be of medium difficulty. Based on your response to that first question, you will next be presented with an easier or a more difficult problem. ETS says that within 3 or 4 problems, the computer will have honed in on your *approximate* score level. The other 33 questions you'll have to answer will be a mixture of Experimental questions (which don't count toward your score) and questions that will allow ETS to zero in on your exact score.

THE PRINCETON REVIEW APPROACH

Because it's probably been a long time since you've needed to reduce fractions or figure out how many degrees there are in a quadrilateral, the first thing to do is review the information that ETS tests on the GMAT by going through our math review. Along the way, you'll learn some valuable test-taking skills that will allow you to take advantage of some of the inherent weaknesses of standardized testing.

When you've finished the math review, you should read our chapter on Data Sufficiency and then take our diagnostic math test. Based on your approximate score on our diagnostic, you can then practice working through the problems at, or just above, your scoring range. By getting familiar with the general level of difficulty of these problems and the number of steps required to solve them, you can increase your score on the real GMAT.

Always keep in mind that if your purpose is to raise your GMAT score, it's a waste of time to learn math that won't be tested. Don't get us wrong, we think the derivation of π is fascinating, but . . .

EXTRA HELP

Although we can show you which mathematical principles are most important for the GMAT, this book cannot take the place of a basic foundation in math. We find that most people, even if they don't remember much of high school math, pick it up again quickly. Our drills and examples will refresh your memory if you've gotten rusty, but if you have serious difficulties with the following chapters, you should consider a more thorough review. This book will enable you to see where you need the most work. Always keep in mind, though, that if your purpose is to raise your GMAT score, it's a waste of time to learn math that won't be tested.

BASIC INFORMATION

Try the following problem:

> How many even integers are there between 17 and 27?
>
> ○ 9
> ○ 7
> ○ 5
> ○ 4
> ○ 3

This is an easy GMAT question. Even so, if you don't know what an integer is, the question will be impossible to answer. Before moving on to arithmetic, you should make sure you're familiar with some basic terms and concepts. This material isn't difficult, but you must know it cold. (The answer, by the way, is C.)

INTEGERS

Integers are the numbers we think of when we think of numbers. They can be negative or positive. They do not include fractions. The positive integers are:

1, 2, 3, 4, 5, etc.

The negative integers are:

$$-1, -2, -3, -4, -5, \text{ etc.}$$

Zero (0) is also an integer. It is neither positive nor negative.

Ancient History 101

The GMAT will test your (probably rusty) knowledge of high school math.

Positive integers get bigger as they move away from 0; negative integers get smaller. Look at this number line:

2 is bigger than 1, but –2 is smaller than –1.

POSITIVE AND NEGATIVE

Positive numbers are to the right of the zero on the number line above. Negative numbers are to the left of zero on the number line above.

There are three rules regarding the multiplication of positive and negative numbers:

pos. × *pos.* = *pos.*

pos. × *neg.* = *neg.*

neg. × *neg.* = *pos.*

If you add a positive number and a negative number, you're subtracting the number with the negative sign in front of it from the positive number.

$$4 + (-3) = 1$$

If you add two negative numbers, you add them as if they were positive, then put a negative sign in front of the sum.

$$-3 + -5 = -8$$

DIGITS

There are ten digits:

$$0, 1, 2, 3, 4, 5, 6, 7, 8, 9$$

All integers are made up of digits. In the integer 246, there are three digits: 2, 4, and 6. Each of the digits has a different name:

6 is called the units digit

4 is called the tens digit

2 is called the hundreds digit

A number with decimal places is also composed of digits, although it is not an integer. In the decimal 27.63 there are four digits:

7 is the units digit

2 is the tens digit

6 is the tenths digit

3 is the hundredths digit

ODD OR EVEN

Even numbers are integers that can be divided evenly by 2. Here are some examples:

− 4, –2, 0, 2, 4, etc.   (note that 0 is even)

Any integer, no matter how large, is even if its last digit can be divided evenly by 2. Thus 777,772 is even.

Odd numbers are integers that cannot be divided evenly by 2. Here are some examples:

–5, –3, –1, 1, 3, 5, etc.   (note that 0 is not odd)

Any integer, no matter how large, is odd if its last digit cannot be divided evenly by 2. Thus 222,227 is odd.

There are several rules that always hold true with even and odd numbers:

even × *even* = *even*

odd × *odd* = *odd*

even × *odd* = *even*

even + *even* = *even*

odd + *odd* = *even*

even + *odd* = *odd*

It isn't necessary to memorize these, but you must know that the relationships always hold true. The individual rules can be derived in a second. If you need to know "even × even," just try 2 × 2. The answer in this case is even, as "even × even" always will be.

REMAINDERS

If a number cannot be divided evenly by another number, the number that is left over at the end of division is called the remainder.

$$2\overline{)7} \quad \frac{3 \text{ R}1}{}$$

Q: 20,179.01792
In the number above, which of the following two digits are identical?

(A) the tens digit and the hundredths digit

(B) the ones digit and the thousandths digit

(C) the hundreds digit and the tenths digit

(D) the thousands digit and the tenths digit

(E) the thousands digit and the hundredths digit

Consecutive Integers

Consecutive integers are integers listed in order of increasing size without any integers missing in between. For example, –3, –2, –1, 0, 1, 2, 3 are consecutive integers. The formula for consecutive integers is n, $n + 1$, $n + 2$, $n + 3$, etc., where n is an integer.

Some consecutive even integers: –2, 0, 2, 4, 6, 8, etc.

Some consecutive odd integers: –3, –1, 1, 3, 5, etc.

A: D. Both the thousands digit and tenths digit are 0.

Distinct Numbers

If two numbers are distinct, they cannot be equal. For example, if x and y are distinct, then they must have different values.

Prime Numbers

A prime number is a number that can be divided evenly only by two numbers: itself and 1. Thus 2, 3, 5, 7, 11, 13 are all prime numbers. The number 2 is the only even prime number. Neither 0 nor 1 is a prime number. All prime numbers are positive.

Divisibility Rules

If a number can be divided evenly by another number, it is said to be divisible by that number.

Some useful shortcuts:

◆ A number is divisible by 2 if its units digit can be divided evenly by 2. Thus 772 is divisible by 2.

◆ A number is divisible by 3 if the sum of its digits can be divided evenly by 3. We can instantly tell that 216 is divisible by 3, because the sum of the digits (2 + 1 + 6) is divisible by 3.

◆ A number is divisible by 5 if its final digit is either 0 or 5. Thus 60, 85, and 15 are all divisible by 5.

Factors and Multiples

A number is a *factor* of another number if it can be divided evenly into that number. Thus the factors of 15, for example, are 1, 3, 5, and 15.

A number x is considered to be a *multiple* of another number y if y times another integer equals x. For example, 15 is a multiple of 3 (3 × 5); 12 is also a multiple of 3 (3 × 4).

ABSOLUTE VALUE

The *absolute value* of a number is the distance between that number and 0 on the number line. The absolute value of 6 is expressed as $|6|$.

$$|6| = 6$$

$$|-5| = 5$$

STANDARD SYMBOLS

The following standard symbols are frequently used on the GMAT:

Symbol	Meaning
=	is equal to
≠	is not equal to
<	is less than
>	is greater than
≤	is less than or equal to
≥	is greater than or equal to

Don't Ask!

What is 6 divided by 0? The answer is "don't ask." Division by zero is undefined. There is no answer. ETS won't ever put a zero in the denominator. If you're working out a problem and you find yourself with a 0 on the bottom of a fraction, you've done something wrong. By the way, a 0 in the numerator is fine. Any fraction with a 0 on the top is 0.

$$\frac{0}{1} = 0. \ \frac{0}{4} = 0.$$

NOW LET'S LOOK AT THE INSTRUCTIONS

The Problem Solving questions on the GMAT will always have the instructions visible above them, but to avoid wasting time reading these during the test, read our version of the instructions now:

<u>Directions</u>: Solve the following problem, using the scratch paper provided for your computations.

<u>Numbers</u>: This test uses only real numbers; no imaginary numbers are used or implied.

<u>Diagrams</u>: All Problem Solving diagrams are drawn as accurately as possible UNLESS it is specifically noted that a diagram is "not drawn to scale." All diagrams are in a plane unless stated otherwise.

8

The POE and GMAT Math

In chapter 4, we introduced you to the Process of Elimination—a way to find correct answers by eliminating wrong answers. Now we're going to show you how to turn POE into a science.

Here's an example of a typical medium-level problem—the sort of problem that the computer might give you for your very first math question:

> 22% of the cars produced in America are manufac-
> tured in Michigan. If the total number of cars
> produced in America is 40 million, how many cars
> are produced outside of Michigan?
>
> ○
> ○
> ○
> ○
> ○ 31.2 million

ZEN AND THE ART OF TEST WRITING

Let's put ourselves in the place of the ETS test writer who has just written this medium-level math problem. He's finished with his question, and he has his correct answer (31.2 million), but he isn't done yet. He still has four empty slots to fill in. He needs to come up with incorrect numbers for answer choices A, B, C, and D.

He *could* simply choose numbers at random, or numbers that are closely clustered around the correct answer. However, if he did either, test takers who didn't know how to do the problem wouldn't see an obvious answer and might therefore guess at random. The test writer does *not* want test takers to guess at random. If they did, they might actually pick the right answer. So our test writer comes up with incorrect answer choices that whisper seductively, "Pick *me*." If people who don't know how to do the problem are going to guess (and of course they *have* to on the GMAT in order to get to the next question), our test writer wants to make sure they guess wrong.

ETS test writers are very careful in creating incorrect answer choices. They try to figure out all the mistakes a careless test taker might make; then they include those answers among the choices. Here's that same question, now that the ETS test writer has finished it:

> 22% of the cars produced in America are manufac-
> tured in Michigan. If the total number of cars
> produced in America is 40 million, how many cars
> are produced outside of Michigan?
>
> ○   8.8 million
> ○   18 million
> ○   31.2 million
> ○   48.8 million
> ○   62 million

PARTIAL ANSWERS

People often go wrong on GMAT math problems by thinking that they are finished before they really are. The first step in this problem is to find out how many actual cars are produced in Michigan; in other words, we need to know what 22% of 40 million equals. If you aren't sure how to do this, don't worry; we'll show you how to do percent problems in the arithmetic chapter. For the moment, take our word for it that 22% of 40 million equals 8.8 million.

If you were feeling smug about having figured this out, you might just look at the answer choices, notice that the first answer choice (what we call choice (A)) says 8.8 million, and figure that you're done. Unfortunately, the problem didn't ask how many cars were produced in Michigan; it asked how many cars were *not* produced in Michigan.

ETS provided answer choice (A) just in case you got halfway through the problem and decided you'd done enough work. It was a *partial* answer. To find the correct answer you have to subtract 8.8 from 40 million. The correct answer is choice (C), 31.2 million.

HOW DO YOU AVOID PICKING PARTIAL ANSWERS?

You can avoid this mistake by doing two things:

- ◆ When you finish a problem, always take two seconds to reread the last line of the problem to make sure you've actually answered the question.

- ◆ Always think about the level of the problem you're working on to decide whether you've done enough work for ETS to think you "deserve" to get the problem right. For example, if this question were the very first one on the math section of the GMAT, then you would know it is a medium problem—and medium problems always require more than one step. If this question were in the middle of your GMAT math section, you would still have a pretty good idea of its level of difficulty— based on how you are scoring on practice GMATs. If you are normally scoring at around the 50th percentile in math, then you will know that most of the questions you'll be answering will be medium problems that require at least two steps. If you are normally scoring in the 30th percentile, you will know most of the questions you'll be answering will be relatively easy problems that require only one or two simple steps. If you are normally scoring in the 80th percentile, you will know most of the questions you'll be answering will be difficult problems that require at least 3 steps.

CRAZY ANSWERS

The ETS test writers also know that people taking tests do crazy things under pressure. Thus, even though there is no good reason why a person would want to do this, some percentage of the test takers who see this question are going to correctly find 22% of 40, or 8.8, but then *add* it to the original 40. Thus, the ETS test writer will want to include 48.8 among the answer choices. If it weren't there, test takers who'd gotten this answer might realize they had made a mistake and figure out the correct answer, but the ETS test writer would prefer that they just get it wrong.

How else could a test taker go wrong on this problem?

JOE BLOGGS AND GMAT MATH

In chapter 5 we introduced you to Joe Bloggs—the average test taker. Joe just does the first thing that comes into his head. On easy problems, this often gets him the right answer. On difficult questions, his first response is *always* wrong. On medium problems Joe Bloggs's first response is wrong about half the time. On this particular medium problem, what might Joe want to do?

What about just adding the two numbers in the problem together? 22 + 40 equals 62. Or subtracting 22 from 40, which gives you 18. If there's a chance that Joe might pick it, ETS wants it to be there. So the ETS test writers will probably include 62 and 40 among the answer choices. Again, there's no good mathematical reason why a test taker would want to do these things, but ETS knows that you don't always need a good reason to go wrong.

It might strike you that this is pretty unfair. If ETS just picked answers at random, Joe would be much less likely to fall into their traps. However, there is one positive side to ETS's obsession with trap answers:

COMMON SENSE: THE ANTIDOTE TO TRAP ANSWERS

ETS is so caught up in trying to provide answer choices that anticipate all the mistakes a test taker might make on a problem that they often forget to make certain that all of these answer choices make sense. Let's just think about that problem again.

> 22% of the cars produced in America are manufactured in Michigan. If the total number of cars produced in America is 40 million, how many cars are produced outside of Michigan?
>
> ○   8.8 million
> ○   18 million
> ○ 31.2 million
> ○ 48.8 million
> ○   62 million

We want the number of cars produced in places other than Michigan. Forget about math for a moment. Let's just look at the answer choices in the cold light of day. Even if you're rusty on percentages, is there any way that the number of cars produced in the other states could be greater than the total number of cars produced altogether? No way. The answer has to be less than 40 million. Thus, in their zeal to anticipate your potential wrong answers, ETS has given you two answer choices (48.8 and 62) that are just plain crazy.

SCRATCH PAPER

If these two answers are crazy, then cross them off on your scratch paper. It's psychologically very uplifting to see your possible answers narrowed down to only three. Here's what your scratch paper should look like for this question:

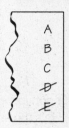

Q: Which of the following numbers is prime?
0, 1, 15, 23, 33

HOW DO YOU PREVENT YOURSELF FROM PICKING CRAZY ANSWERS?

You can prevent yourself from selecting crazy answers by doing two simple things:

- ◆ Before you even start doing any serious math, take a second to use common sense on the problem: Are there any answers that simply don't make sense? If so, cross them off on your scratch paper. This will prevent you from picking them later through carelessness or desperation.

- ◆ If, based on your scores on practice tests, you expect to be seeing mainly medium and difficult problems on the math section of the GMAT, take a second to see if there are any Joe Bloggs answers to cross off.

PSST! HEY, JOE, LOOKING FOR A GOOD TIME?

To come up with answers that will appeal to Joe Bloggs, the ETS test writer has to know how Joe thinks. Fortunately for the test writer, she can draw on over thirty years of statistical information ETS has compiled. From this, she knows that:

1. On difficult math problems, Joe Bloggs is always attracted to easy solutions that he can find in one step.

For example, Joe might just add together the numbers mentioned in the problem.

2. On difficult math problems, Joe Bloggs is attracted to numbers that he has already seen in the problem.

It's pretty silly, but frequently Joe picks a number simply because he remembers it from the problem itself.

Now let's look at the upper-medium problem we showed you in chapter 5, complete with answer choices:

> The output of a factory was increased by 10% to keep up with rising demand. To handle the holiday rush, this new output was increased by 20%. By approximately what percent would the output now have to be decreased in order to restore the original output?
>
> ○　20%
> ○　24%
> ○　30%
> ○　32%
> ○　70%

A: 23. Remember, neither 0 nor 1 is prime.

If the test writer has done her job properly, Joe Bloggs will never even consider the correct answer (24%). He's too smitten by the other answer choices.

Here's how to crack it

As we said in chapter 5, Joe's favorite answer to this question is undoubtedly 30% (what we call choice (C)). Joe notices that the output seems to have increased by 30% and figures that to get rid of that increase, you would have to decrease it by 30%. What Joe has just done is add the two numbers he saw in the problem.

> On medium and difficult math problems, Joe Bloggs is attracted to easy solutions that he can find in one step.

Another answer Joe might be attracted to is choice (A). Twenty (20%) is simply one of the numbers from the problem. There is no logical reason to think this is the correct answer, but Joe isn't always logical.

> On medium and difficult math problems, Joe Bloggs is attracted to answer choices that simply repeat numbers from the problem.

PUTTING EVERYTHING TOGETHER

Here's one last example of an upper medium problem to show how you can use both common sense and the Joe Bloggs principle to help eliminate answers:

> A student took 6 courses last year and received an average grade of 100. The year before, the student took 5 courses and received an average grade of 90. To the nearest tenth of a point, what was the student's average grade for the entire two-year period?
>
> ○　79
> ○　89
> ○　95
> ○　95.5
> ○　97.2

Here's how to crack it

Don't worry if you aren't sure how to solve this problem right now; we'll cover average problems in the next chapter. Let's assume for a moment that you've done our math review, and will be facing mostly medium questions on the math portion of the GMAT.

Even if you knew exactly how to do this problem, it would still make sense for you to eliminate wrong answers before you begin using any serious math. Let's begin by thinking about what Joe Bloggs would like to pick on this question. Joe likes answer choice (C) a lot. He figures that to find the average of the entire two-year period, all he has to do is find that the average of 90 and 100 is 95. If this were an easy problem, he might be right, but we're assuming for the moment that you will be seeing mainly medium problems—so cross it off on your scratch paper.

There are no other obvious Joe Bloggs answers, but it *is* possible to eliminate a couple of other choices by using common sense. The student's average for the first year was 90. The student's average for the second year was 100. Obviously the student's second-year grades are going to bring his average *up*. We may not be sure by exactly how much, but the average for the entire two-year period has to be higher than it was for the first year. Both choices (A) and (B) are less than the first year's average. We can therefore eliminate both of them.

We've eliminated three answer choices. If you know how to solve the problem, go to it. If not, you have a fifty-fifty shot at getting it right anyway. The correct answer is choice (D), 95.5.

SUMMARY

1. The Process of Elimination allows you to eliminate answer choices even when you don't know how to do a problem. There are three types of answers to look for: partial answers, crazy answers, and Joe Bloggs answers.

2. Partial answers: ETS likes to include, among the answer choices, answers that are partial completions of the problem. If you get halfway through a problem and decide that you're done, the number you have arrived at will likely be there, waiting to trip you up. The way to avoid partial answers is to reread the last line of the problem before you pick an answer to make sure you're answering the question they have asked.

3. Crazy answers: ETS also likes to include, among the answer choices, numbers that a test taker may arrive at—even though they don't make much sense. Crazy answer choices can be spotted by taking a step back and looking at the problem and its answers in the cold light of day.

4. Joe Bloggs answers: ETS also likes to include, among the answer choices, numbers that would appeal to Joe Bloggs, the average test taker. Joe is attracted to easy solutions that he can arrive at in one step and answers that repeat numbers from the problem.

9
Arithmetic

Although arithmetic is only one of the three types of math tested on the GMAT, arithmetic problems comprise about half of the total number of math questions. Here are the specific arithmetic topics tested on the GMAT:

1. Axioms and Fundamentals (properties of integers, positive and negative numbers, even and odd). These were covered in chapter 7.

2. Arithmetic Operations

3. Fractions

4. Decimals

5. Ratios

6. Percentages

7. Averages

8. Exponents and Radicals

In this chapter we will first discuss the fundamentals of each topic and then show how ETS constructs questions based on that topic.

ARITHMETIC OPERATIONS

There are six arithmetic operations you will need for the GMAT:

1.	addition $(2 + 2)$	the result of addition is a sum or total
2.	subtraction $(6 - 2)$	the result of subtraction is a difference
3.	multiplication (2×2)	the result of multiplication is a product
4.	division $(8 \div 2)$	the result of division is a quotient
5.	raising to a power (x^2)	in the expression x^2 the little 2 is called an exponent
6.	finding a square root $\left(\sqrt{4}\right)$	$\sqrt{4} = \sqrt{2 \cdot 2} = 2$

WHICH ONE DO I DO FIRST?

In a problem that involves several different operations, the operations must be performed in a particular order, and occasionally ETS likes to see whether you know what that order is. Here's an easy way to remember the order of operations:

Please Excuse My Dear Aunt Sally

The first letters stand for Parentheses, Exponents, Multiplication, Division, Addition, Subtraction. Do operations that are enclosed in parentheses first; then take care of exponents; then multiply, divide, add, and subtract.

DRILL 1

Just to get you started, solve each of the following problems by performing the indicated operation in the proper order. The answers can be found on page 278.

1. $74 + (27 - 24) =$

2. $(8 \times 9) + 7 =$

3. $2[9 - (8 \div 2)] =$

4. $2(7 - 3) + (-4)(5 - 7) =$

It is not uncommon to see a problem like this on the GMAT:

5. $4[-3(3 - 5) + 10 - 17] =$
   - ○ −27
   - ○ −4
   - ○ −1
   - ○ 32
   - ○ 84

There are two operations that can be done in any order, provided they are the only operations involved: **When you are adding or multiplying a series of numbers, you can group or regroup the numbers any way you like.**

$2 + 3 + 4$ is the same as $4 + 2 + 3$

and

$4 \times 5 \times 6$ is the same as $6 \times 5 \times 4$

This is called the *associative law*, but the name will not be tested on the GMAT. The *distributive law* states that $a(b + c) = ab + ac$ and $a(b - c) = ab - ac$.

ETS likes to see whether you remember this. Sometimes the distributive law can provide you with a shortcut to the solution of a problem. If a problem gives you information in "factored form"—$a(b + c)$—you should distribute it immediately. If the information is given in distributed form—$ab + ac$—you should factor it.

DRILL 2

If the following problems are in distributed form, factor them; if they are in factored form, distribute them. Then do the indicated operation. Answers are on page 278.

1. $8(10 + 5)$

2. $(55 \times 12) + (55 \times 88)$

3. $a(b + c - d)$

4. $abc + xyc$

Q: According to the associative law, can you perform the following operations in any order you like?

2 divided by 6 divided by 3 divided by 4.

Hint: The answer is yes *and* no.

A GMAT problem might look like this:

5. If $x = 6$ what is the value of $\dfrac{2xy - xy}{y}$?

○ −30
○ 6
○ 8
○ 30
○ It cannot be determined.

A: There are two ways to approach the problem. You can divide from left to right. Division *must* be performed from left to right. The second way is to convert the several division operations into multiplication:

$2 \times \dfrac{1}{6} \times \dfrac{1}{3} \times \dfrac{1}{4}$.

In this form the operations can be performed in whatever order you find most convenient.

FRACTIONS

Fractions can be thought of in two ways:

◆ A fraction is just another way of expressing division. The expression $\dfrac{1}{2}$ is exactly the same thing as 1 divided by 2. $\dfrac{x}{y}$ is nothing more than x divided by y. In the fraction $\dfrac{x}{y}$, x is known as the numerator and y is known as the denominator.

◆ The other important way to think of a fraction is as $\dfrac{\text{part}}{\text{whole}}$. The fraction $\dfrac{7}{10}$ can be thought of as 7 parts out of a total of 10 parts.

ADDING AND SUBTRACTING FRACTIONS WITH THE SAME DENOMINATOR

To add two or more fractions that have the same denominator, simply add up the numerators and put the sum over the common denominator. For example:

$$\frac{1}{7} + \frac{5}{7} = \frac{(1+5)}{7} = \frac{6}{7}$$

Subtraction works exactly the same way:

$$\frac{6}{7} - \frac{2}{7} = \frac{6-2}{7} = \frac{4}{7}$$

Adding and Subtracting Fractions with Different Denominators

Before you can add or subtract two or more fractions with different denominators, you must give all of them the same denominator. To do this, multiply each fraction by a number that will give it a denominator in common with the others. If you multiplied each fraction by any old number, the fractions wouldn't have their original values, so the number you multiply by has to be equal to 1. For example, if you wanted to change $\frac{1}{2}$ into sixths, you could do the following:

$$\frac{1}{2} \times \frac{3}{3} = \frac{3}{6}$$

We haven't actually changed the value of the fraction, because $\frac{3}{3}$ equals 1. If we wanted to add

$$\frac{1}{2} + \frac{2}{3}$$

$$\frac{1}{2} \times \frac{3}{3} + \frac{2}{3} \times \frac{2}{2}$$

$$\frac{3}{6} + \frac{4}{6} = \frac{7}{6}$$

Multiplying Fractions

To multiply fractions, just multiply the numerators and put the product over the product of the denominators. For example:

$$\frac{2}{3} \times \frac{6}{5} = \frac{12}{15}$$

Reducing Fractions

When you add or multiply fractions, you often end up with a big fraction that is hard to work with. You can usually reduce such a fraction. To reduce a fraction, find a factor of the numerator that is also a factor of the denominator. It saves time to find the biggest factor they have in common, but this isn't critical. You may just have to repeat the process a few times. When you find a common factor, cancel it. For example, let's take the product we just found when we multiplied the fractions above:

$$\frac{12}{15} = \frac{4 \times 3}{5 \times 3} = \frac{4}{5}$$

Get used to reducing all fractions (if they can be reduced) *before* you do any work with them. It saves a lot of time and prevents errors in computation.

DIVIDING FRACTIONS

To divide one fraction by another, just invert the second fraction and multiply:

$$\frac{2}{3} \div \frac{3}{4}$$

is the same thing as

$$\frac{2}{3} \times \frac{4}{3} = \frac{8}{9}$$

You may see this same operation written like this:

$$\frac{\frac{2}{3}}{\frac{3}{4}}$$

Again, just invert and multiply. This next example is handled the same way:

$$\frac{\frac{6}{2}}{3} = \frac{6}{1} \times \frac{3}{2} = \frac{18}{2} = 9$$

CONVERTING TO FRACTIONS

An integer can be expressed as a fraction by making the integer the numerator and 1 the denominator. $16 = \frac{16}{1}$.

The GMAT sometimes gives you numbers that are mixtures of integers and fractions, for example, $3\frac{1}{2}$. It's easier to work with these numbers if you convert them into ordinary fractions. $3\frac{1}{2}$ would be converted like this:

Since the fractional part of this number was expressed in halves, let's convert the integer part of the number into halves as well. $3 = \frac{6}{2}$. Now just add the $\frac{1}{2}$ to the $\frac{6}{2}$. So, $3\frac{1}{2} = \frac{7}{2}$.

COMPARING FRACTIONS

In the course of a problem you may have to compare two or more fractions and determine which is larger. This is easy to do as long as you remember that you can compare fractions directly only if they have the same denominator. Suppose you had to decide which of these three fractions is largest:

$$\frac{1}{2} \quad \frac{5}{9} \quad \frac{7}{15}$$

To compare these fractions directly you need a common denominator, but finding a common denominator that works for all three fractions would be complicated and time consuming. It makes more sense to compare these fractions two at a time. We showed you the classical way to find common denominators when we talked about adding fractions earlier.

Let's start with $\dfrac{1}{2}$ and $\dfrac{5}{9}$. An easy common denominator for these two fractions is 18 (9×2).

$$\dfrac{1}{2} \qquad \dfrac{5}{9}$$

$$\dfrac{1}{2} \times \dfrac{9}{9} \qquad \dfrac{5}{9} \times \dfrac{2}{2}$$

$$= \dfrac{9}{18} \qquad = \dfrac{10}{18}$$

Since $\dfrac{5}{9}$ is bigger, let's compare it with $\dfrac{7}{15}$. Here the easiest common denominator is 45.

Two Shortcuts

One good shortcut to comparing fractions is the bow tie. The idea is that if all you need to know is which fraction is bigger, you just have to compare the new numerators.

$$9 \;\; \dfrac{1}{2} \;\;\diagdown\!\!\!\!\diagup\;\; \dfrac{5}{9} \;\; 10$$

$$10 > 9, \text{ therefore } \dfrac{5}{9} > \dfrac{1}{2}$$

You could also have saved yourself some time on the last problem by a little fast estimation. Again, which is larger? $\dfrac{1}{2}$, $\dfrac{5}{9}$, or $\dfrac{7}{15}$?

Let's think about $\dfrac{5}{9}$ in terms of $\dfrac{1}{2}$. How many ninths equal a half? To put it another way, what is half of 9? 4.5. So $\dfrac{4.5}{9} = \dfrac{1}{2}$. That means $\dfrac{5}{9}$ is *bigger* than $\dfrac{1}{2}$.

Now let's think about $\dfrac{7}{15}$. Half of 15 is 7.5. $\dfrac{7.5}{15} = \dfrac{1}{2}$, which means that $\dfrac{7}{15}$ is *less* than $\dfrac{1}{2}$.

Half Empty or Half Full?

In the GMAT, always think about what's left over. If a pizza is three quarters eaten, there's still one quarter left.

PROPORTIONS

A fraction can be expressed in many ways. $\dfrac{1}{2}$ also equals $\dfrac{2}{4}$ or $\dfrac{4}{8}$, etc. A proportion is just a different way of expressing a fraction. Here's an example:

If 2 boxes hold a total of 14 shirts, how many shirts are contained in 3 boxes?

Here's how to crack it

The number of shirts per box can be expressed as a fraction. What you're being asked to do is express the fraction $\frac{2}{14}$ in a different way.

$$\frac{2(\text{boxes})}{14(\text{shirts})} = \frac{3(\text{boxes})}{x(\text{shirts})}$$

To find the answer, all you need to do is find a value for x such that $\frac{3}{x} = \frac{2}{14}$. The easiest way to do this is to cross-multiply.

$2x = 42$, which means that $x = 21$. There are 21 shirts in 3 boxes.

DRILL 3

The answers to these questions can be found on page 278.

1. $5\frac{2}{3} + \frac{3}{8} =$

2. Reduce $\frac{12}{60}$

3. Convert $9\frac{2}{3}$ to a fraction

4. $\frac{9}{2} = \frac{x}{4}$

Proportions are really ratios. Where a proportion question asks about the number of shirts *per* box, a ratio question might ask about the number of red shirts to blue shirts in a box.

A relatively easy GMAT fraction problem might look like this:

5. $\dfrac{\left(\dfrac{\frac{4}{5}}{\frac{3}{5}}\right)\left(\dfrac{\frac{1}{8}}{\frac{2}{3}}\right)}{\dfrac{3}{4}} =$

- ○ $\frac{3}{100}$
- ○ $\frac{3}{16}$
- ○ $\frac{1}{3}$
- ○ 1
- ○ $\frac{7}{16}$

The Six GMAT Arithmetic Operations

1. addition
2. subtraction
3. multiplication
4. division
5. raising to a power
6. finding a square root

FRACTIONS: ADVANCED PRINCIPLES

Now that you've been reacquainted with the basics of fractions, let's go a little further. More complicated fraction problems usually involve all of the rules we've just mentioned, with the addition of two concepts: part/whole, and the rest. Here's a typical medium fraction problem:

A cement mixture is composed of 3 elements: By weight, $\frac{1}{3}$ of the mixture is sand, $\frac{3}{5}$ of the mixture is water, and the remaining 12 pounds of the mixture is gravel. What is the weight of the entire mixture in pounds?

- ○ 11.2
- ○ 12.8
- ○ 36
- ○ 60
- ○ 180

Q: There are only roses, tulips, and peonies in a certain garden. There are three roses to every four tulips and every five peonies in the garden. Expressed as a fraction, what part of the flowers in the garden are tulips?

EASY ELIMINATIONS

Before we even start doing serious math, let's use some common sense. The weight of the gravel alone is 12 pounds. Since we know that sand and water make up the bulk of the mixture—sand $\frac{1}{3}$, water $\frac{3}{5}$ (which is a bit more than half)—the entire mixture must weigh a great deal more than 12 pounds. Answer choices (A), (B), and (C) are out of the question.

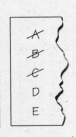

A: To find the answer, find the *whole.* We know the parts are 3 roses, 4 tulips, and 5 peonies. $3+4+5=12=$ the whole. What fractional part of the flowers are tulips? 4 out of a total of 12, otherwise known as $\frac{4}{12}$, or $\frac{1}{3}$.

Here's how to crack it

The difficulty in solving this problem is that sand and water are expressed as fractions, while gravel is expressed in pounds. At first there seems to be no way of knowing what fractional part of the mixture the 12 pounds of gravel represents; nor do we know how many pounds of sand and water there are.

The first step is to add up the fractional parts that we do have:

$$\frac{1}{3} + \frac{3}{5} = \frac{1}{3}\left(\frac{5}{5}\right) + \frac{3}{5}\left(\frac{3}{3}\right) = \frac{14}{15}$$

Sand and water make up 14 parts out of the whole of 15. This means that gravel makes up what is left over—the rest: 1 part out of the whole of 15. Now the problem is simple. Set up a proportion between parts and weights.

$$\frac{1}{15} = \frac{12}{x} \quad \text{pounds (of gravel)} \atop \text{pounds (total pounds)}$$

Cross-multiply: $x = 180$. The answer is choice (E).

DECIMALS ARE REALLY FRACTIONS

A decimal can be expressed as a fraction, and a fraction can be expressed as a decimal.

$$.6 = \frac{6}{10} \text{ ,which can be reduced to } \frac{3}{5}$$

$$\frac{3}{5} \text{ is the same thing as } 3 \div 5$$

$$5\overline{)3.0}^{.6}$$

$$= .6$$

Which would you rather figure out—the square of $\frac{1}{4}$ or the square of 0.25?

There may be a few of you out there who've had so much practice with decimals in your work that you prefer decimals to fractions, but for the rest of us, fractions are infinitely easier to deal with.

Whenever possible, convert decimals to fractions. It will save time and eliminate careless mistakes. Occasionally, however, you will have to work with decimals.

ADDING AND SUBTRACTING DECIMALS

To add or subtract decimals, just line up the decimal points and proceed as usual. Adding 6, 2.5, and 0.3 looks like this:

$$\begin{array}{r} 6.0 \\ 2.5 \\ +\ \ 0.3 \\ \hline 8.8 \end{array}$$

MULTIPLYING DECIMALS

To multiply decimals, simply ignore the decimal points and multiply the two numbers. When you've finished, count all the digits that were to the right of the decimal points in the original numbers you multiplied. Now place the decimal point in your answer so that there are the same number of digits to the right of it. Here are two examples:

.3 times .7 = .21 There were a total of two digits to the right of the decimal point in the original numbers, so we place the decimal so that there are two digits to the right in the answer.

.3 times .232 = .0696 There were a total of four digits to the right of the decimal point in the original numbers, so we place the decimal so that there are four digits to the right in the answer.

DIVIDING DECIMALS

The best way to divide one decimal by another is to convert the number you are dividing by (in mathematical terminology, the divisor) into a whole number. You do this simply by moving the decimal point as many places as necessary. This works as long as you remember to move the decimal point in the number that you are *dividing* (in mathematical terminology, the dividend) the same number of spaces.

For example, to divide 12 by .6, set it up the way you would an ordinary division problem: $.6\overline{)12}$

To make .6 (the divisor) a whole number, you simply move the decimal point over one place to the right. You must also move the decimal one place to the right in the dividend. Now the operation looks like this:

$$6\overline{)120} \quad 6\overline{)120}^{\,20}$$

First Things First

On *all* questions, before you do any serious calculations, take a moment to see whether the answer choices make sense. Eliminate crazy answer choices. Do this first because those "crazy" choices usually reflect the result of a common (but incorrect) approach to the problem. Eliminate first and you won't think (falsely), "Aha, I've got it." Instead, you'll know you took a misstep somewhere.

Whether you prefer decimals or fractions, you must be able to work with both. The ability to work comfortably and confidently with decimals and fractions is vital to GMAT success.

Rounding Off Decimals

9.4 rounded to the nearest whole number is 9.

9.5 rounded to the nearest whole number is 10.

To round off a decimal, look at the digit to the right of the digits place you are rounding to. If that number is 0–4, there is no change. If that number is 5–9, round up.

When ETS asks you to give an approximate answer on an easy question, it is safe to round off numbers. But you should be leery about rounding off numbers on a difficult question. If you're scoring in a high percentile, rounding off numbers will be useful to eliminate answer choices that are out of the ballpark, but not to decide between two close answer choices.

DRILL 4

The answers to these questions can be found on page 278.

1. $\begin{array}{r} 34.26 \\ -.96 \\ \hline \end{array}$

2. $\begin{array}{r} 27.3 \\ \times 9.75 \\ \hline \end{array}$

3. $\dfrac{19.6}{3.22}$

4. $\dfrac{\dfrac{4}{.25}}{\dfrac{1}{.50}}$

On the GMAT, there might be questions that mix decimals and fractions:

5. $\dfrac{\dfrac{3}{10} \times 4 \times .8}{.32}$

   ○ .96
   ○ .333
   ○ 3
   ○ 30
   ○ 96

RATIOS

Ratios are close relatives of fractions. A ratio can be expressed as a fraction and vice versa. The ratio 3 to 4 can be written as $\frac{3}{4}$ as well as in standard ratio format: 3:4.

THERE IS ONLY ONE DIFFERENCE BETWEEN A RATIO AND A FRACTION

One way of defining the *fraction* $\frac{3}{4}$ is to say that there are 3 equal *parts* out of a *whole* of 4.

Let's take the ratio of 3 women to 4 men in a room, which could also be expressed as $\frac{3}{4}$. Is 4 the whole in this ratio? Of course not. There are 3 women and 4 men, giving a total of 7 people in the room. The *whole* in a ratio is the sum of all the parts. If the ratio is expressed as a fraction, the *whole* is the sum of the numerator and the denominator.

Fraction:	Ratio:
part 3	3 women
whole 7	4 men (The *whole* is 7.)

ASIDE FROM THAT, ALL THE RULES OF FRACTIONS APPLY TO RATIOS

A ratio can be converted to a percentage or a decimal. It can be cross-multiplied, reduced, or expanded—just like a fraction. The ratio of 1 to 3 can be expressed as:

$$\frac{1}{3}$$
$$1:3$$
$$0.33\overline{3}$$
$$33\frac{1}{3}\%$$
$$\frac{2}{6}$$
$$\frac{3}{9}$$

AN EASY RATIO PROBLEM

The ratio of men to women in a room is 3 to 4.
What is the number of men in the room if there are
20 women?

Here's how to crack it

No matter how many people are actually in the room, the ratio of men to women will always stay the same: 3 to 4. What you're being asked to do is find the numerator of a fraction whose denominator is 20, and which can be reduced to $\frac{3}{4}$. Just set one fraction equal to another and cross-multiply:

$$\frac{3}{4} = \frac{x}{20} \qquad 60 = 4x, \ x = 15$$

The answer to the question is 15 men. Note that $\frac{15}{20}$ reduces to $\frac{3}{4}$. The two fractions are equal, which is just another way of saying that they're still in the same ratio.

A MORE DIFFICULT RATIO PROBLEM

The ratio of women to men in a room is 3 to 4. If
there are a total of 28 people in the room, how
many women are there?

This problem is more difficult because, while we are given the ratio of women to men, we do not have a specific value for either women or men. If we tried to set this problem up the way we did the previous one, it would look like this: $\frac{3}{4} = \frac{x}{y}$

You can't solve an equation if it has two variables.

Here's how to crack it

The trick here is to remember how a ratio differs from a fraction. If the ratio is 3 parts to 4 parts, then there is a total of 7 parts. This means that the 28 people in that room are made up of groups of 7 people (3 women and 4 men in each group). How many groups of 7 people make up 28 people? 4 groups ($4 \times 7 = 28$).

If there are 4 groups—each made up of 3 women and 4 men—the total number of women would be 4×3, or 12. The number of men would be 4×4, or 16. To check this, make sure that $\frac{12}{16}$ equals $\frac{3}{4}$ (it does) and that 12 + 16 adds up to 28 (it does).

PERCENTAGES

A percentage is just a fraction in which the denominator is always equal to 100. Fifty percent means 50 parts out of a whole of 100. Like any fraction, a percentage can be reduced, expanded, cross-multiplied, converted to a decimal, or converted to another fraction. $50\% = \frac{1}{2} = .5$

AN EASY PERCENT PROBLEM

Q: What is $\frac{1}{4}$% of 40?

The number 5 is what percent of the number 20?

Here's how to crack it

Whenever you see a percent problem, you should be thinking part/whole. In this case, the question is asking you to expand $\frac{5}{20}$ into another fraction in which the denominator is 100. $\frac{\text{part}}{\text{whole}} = \frac{5}{20} = \frac{x}{100}$

$$500 = 20x$$
$$x = 25$$
$$\frac{x}{100} = 25\%$$

PERCENT SHORTCUTS

In the last problem, reducing $\frac{5}{20}$ to $\frac{1}{4}$ would have saved you time if you knew that $\frac{1}{4} = 25\%$. Here are some fractions and decimals whose percent equivalents you should know:

$$\frac{1}{4} = .25 = 25\%$$

$$\frac{1}{2} = .50 = 50\%$$

$$\frac{1}{3} = 0.333 \text{ etc. (a repeating decimal)} = 33\frac{1}{3}\%$$

$$\frac{1}{5} = .20 = 20\%$$

Some percentages simply involve moving a decimal point: To get 10 percent of any number, you simply move the decimal point of that number over one place to the left:

$$10\% \text{ of } 6 = 0.6$$

$$10\% \text{ of } 60 = 6$$

$$10\% \text{ of } 600 = 60$$

◆ To get 1 percent of any number, you just move the decimal point of that number over two places to the left:

$$1\% \text{ of } 600 = 6$$

$$1\% \text{ of } 60 = 0.6$$

$$1\% \text{ of } 6 = .06$$

◆ To find a more complicated percentage, it's easy to break the percentage down into easy-to-find chunks:

20% of 60:   10% of 60 = 6; 20% of 60 is double 10%, so the answer is 2 × 6, or 12.

30% of 60:   10% of 60 = 6; 30% of 60 is three times 10%, so the answer is 3 × 6, or 18.

3% of 200:   1% of 200 = 2; 3% of 200 is just three times 1%, so the answer is 3 × 2, or 6.

23% of 400:   10% of 400 = 40. Therefore 20% equals 2 × 40, or 80.

1% of 400 = 4. Therefore 3% equals 3 × 4, or 12.

Putting it all together, 23% of 400 equals 80 + 12, or 92.

A MEDIUM PERCENT PROBLEM

Like medium and difficult fraction problems, medium and difficult percent problems often involve remembering the principles of part/whole and the rest.

A motor pool has 300 vehicles of which 30% are trucks. 20% of all the vehicles in the motor pool are diesel, including 15 trucks. What percent of the motor pool is composed of vehicles that are neither trucks nor diesel?

○   165%
○   90%
○   65%
○   55%
○   10%

Here's how to crack it

Do this problem one sentence at a time.

1. A motor pool has 300 vehicles, of which 30% are trucks. 30% of 300 = 90 trucks, which means that 210 (the rest) are *not* trucks.

2. 20% of all the vehicles are diesel, including 15 trucks. 20% of 300 = 60 diesel vehicles, 15 of which are trucks, which means there are 45 diesel vehicles that are *not* trucks.

3. What percent of the motor pool is composed of vehicles that are neither truck nor diesel? We know from sentence number 1 that there are 210 nontrucks. We know from sentence number 2 that of these 210 nontrucks, 45 are diesel. Therefore 210 – 45, or 165, are neither diesel nor truck.

The question asks what percent of the entire motor pool these 165 nondiesel nontrucks are.

$$\frac{165}{300} = \frac{x}{100} \qquad 300x = 16{,}500$$

$x = 55$ and the answer is choice (D).

> There's a handy formula for calculating mixed groups. It isn't a priority for you to memorize (you just saw the problem calculated without it), but the formula can be helpful on some questions. Here it is: Group 1 + Group 2 – both + neither = total. Here's what that looks like using the numbers from the vehicle problem. 90 trucks + 60 diesel – 15 diesel trucks + x = 300. 135 + x = 300. x = 165, or 55% of 300.

EASY ELIMINATIONS

1. Since the problem asks us to find a portion of the entire motor pool, it's impossible for that portion to be larger than the motor pool itself. Therefore answer choice (A) 165% is crazy. Also, answer choice (A) was a trap for people who successfully got all the way to the end of the problem and then forgot that the answer was supposed to be expressed as a percent, not as a specific number.

2. If the problem simply asked what percent of the motor pool was not made up of trucks, the answer would be 70%. But since there is a further condition (the vehicles must be both nontruck and nondiesel), the answer must be even less than 70%. This makes answer choice (B) impossible, too.

3. Answer choice (C) is probably a Joe Bloggs answer. You can get it simply by adding 30 + 20 + 15.

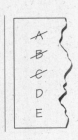

PERCENT INCREASE

Another type of percent problem you may see on the GMAT has to do with *percentage increase* or *percentage decrease*. In these problems the trick is always to put the increase or decrease in terms of the *original* amount. Here's an example:

> The cost of a one-family home was $120,000 in 1980. In 1988, the price had increased to $180,000. What was the percent increase in the cost of the home?
> - ○ 60%
> - ○ 50%
> - ○ 55%
> - ○ 40%
> - ○ 33.3%

Here's how to crack it

The actual increase was $60,000. To find the percent increase, set up the following equation:

$$\frac{\text{amount of increase}}{\text{original amount}} = \frac{x}{100}$$

In this case, $\dfrac{\$60,000}{\$120,000} = \dfrac{x}{100}$ $x = 50$ and the answer is choice (B).

COMPOUND INTEREST

Another type of percentage problem involves *compound interest*. If you kept $1,000 in the bank for a year at 6% simple interest, you would get $60 in interest at the end of the year. Compound interest would pay you slightly more. Let's look at a compound-interest problem:

> Ms. Lopez deposits $100 in an account that pays 20% interest, compounded semiannually. How much money will there be in the account at the end of one year?
> - ○ $118.00
> - ○ $120.00
> - ○ $121.00
> - ○ $122.00
> - ○ $140.00

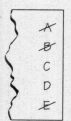

EASY ELIMINATIONS

Joe Bloggs doesn't know how to find compound interest, so he finds simple interest instead. In a compound-interest problem, always calculate simple interest first. $100 at 20% simple interest for one year would turn into $120, which is answer choice (B). Since compound interest is always a *little bit* more than simple interest, we can eliminate answer choices (A) and (B). Answer choice (E) is a great deal more than simple interest, so we can eliminate it, too. Only answer choices (C) and (D) are a *little bit* more than simple interest. We're down to a fifty-fifty guess.

Here's how to crack it

To find compound interest, divide the interest into as many parts as are being compounded. For example, if you're compounding interest semiannually, you divide the interest into two equal parts. If you're compounding quarterly, you divide the interest into four equal parts.

When Ms. Lopez deposited $100 into her account at a rate of 20% compounded semiannually, the bank divided the interest into two equal parts. Halfway through the year, the bank put the first half of the interest into her account. In this case, since the full rate was 20% compounded semiannually, the bank deposited 10% of $100 (10% of $100 = $10). Halfway through the year, Ms. Lopez had $110.

For the second half of the year, the bank paid 10% interest on the $110 (10% of $110 = $11). At the end of the year, Ms. Lopez had $121.00 in her account. She earned $1 more than she would have earned if the account had paid only simple interest. The answer is choice (C).

Reminder!

Averaging problems often have easy eliminations, so be sure to look for them—*before* you solve.

AVERAGES

To find the *average* of a set of n numbers, you simply add the numbers and divide by n. For example:

$$\text{The average of 10, 3, and 5 is } \frac{10+3+5}{3} = 6$$

A good way to handle average problems is to set them up in the same way every time. Whenever you see the word *average*, you should think:

$$\frac{\text{total sum of the items}}{\text{total number of the items}} = \text{average}$$

A ONE-STEP AVERAGE PROBLEM

In a simple problem ETS will give you two parts of this equation, and it will be up to you to figure out the third. For example, ETS might ask:

What is the average of the numbers 3, 4, 5, and 8?

Here's how to crack it

In this case ETS has given us the actual numbers, which means we know the total sum (3 + 4 + 5 + 8 = 20) and the total number of items (there are four numbers). What we're missing is the average.

$$\frac{\text{total sum of the items}}{\text{total number of the items}} = \text{average} \qquad \frac{20}{4} = x \qquad (x = 5)$$

Or ETS might ask:

> If the average of 7 numbers is 5, what is the sum of the numbers?

Here's how to crack it

In this case we know the total number of items and the average, but not the total sum of the numbers.

$$\frac{\text{total sum of the items}}{\text{total number of the items}} = \text{average} \qquad \frac{x}{7} = 5 \qquad (x = 35)$$

A TWO-STEP AVERAGE PROBLEM

This is the same problem you just did, made a little more difficult:

> The average of 7 numbers is 5. If two of the numbers are 11 and 14, what is the average of the remaining numbers?

Here's how to crack it

Always set up an average problem the way we showed you above. With more complicated average problems, take things one sentence at a time. The first sentence yields:

$$\frac{\text{total sum of the average}}{\text{total number of the items}} = \text{average} \qquad \frac{x}{7} = 5 \qquad (x = 35)$$

The sum of *all* the numbers is 35. If two of those numbers are 11 and 14, then the sum of the remaining numbers is 35 − (11 + 14), or 10. The question asks "what is the average of the remaining numbers?" Again, let's set this up properly:

$$\frac{\text{total sum of the remaining numbers}}{\text{total number of the remaining numbers}} = \text{average} \quad \frac{10}{5} = x \quad (x = 2)$$

Why did we divide the total sum of the remaining numbers by 5? There were only 5 remaining numbers!

MEANS

When ETS talks about an average, the words "arithmetic mean" will often follow in parentheses. This is not just to make the problem sound scarier. Arithmetic mean is the precise term for the process of finding an average that we've illustrated in the problems above.

EXPONENTS

An *exponent* is a short way of writing the value of a number multiplied several times by itself. $4 \times 4 \times 4 \times 4 \times 4$ can also be written as 4^5. This is expressed as "4 to the fifth power." The large number (4) is called the base, and the little number (5) is called the exponent.

There are several rules to remember about exponents:

- *Multiplying numbers with the same base:* When you multiply numbers that have the same base, you simply add their exponents.

$$6^2 \times 6^3 = 6^{(2+3)} = 6^5 \qquad (y^4)(y^6) = y^{(4+6)} = y^{10}$$

- *Dividing numbers with the same base:* When you divide numbers that have the same base, you simply subtract the exponents.

$$\frac{3^6}{3^2} = 3^{(6-2)} = 3^4 \qquad \frac{x^7}{x^4} = x^{(7-4)} = x^3$$

- *Raising a power to a power:* When you raise a power to a power, you can simply multiply the exponents.

$$(4^3)^2 = 4^{(3 \times 2)} = 4^6 \qquad (z^2)^4 = z^{(2 \times 4)} = z^8$$

- *Distributing exponents:* When several numbers are inside parentheses, the exponent outside the parentheses must be distributed to all of the numbers within.

$$(4y)^2 = (4)^2(y)^2 = 4^2 \times y^2 = 16 \times y^2$$

There are several operations which *seem* like they ought to work with exponents but don't.

- Does $x^2 + x^3 = x^5$?　　　　NO!

- Does $x^6 - x^2 = x^4$?　　　　NO!

- Does $\dfrac{(x^2 + y^2 + z^2)}{(x^2 + y^2)} = z^2$?　　NO!

Strange Powers Revealed!

Why is any number to the 0 power equal to 1, since any other time we multiply by 0 the result is 0? The answer is that we aren't multiplying by 0 at all. Watch closely now: 3^0 should equal $3^{-1} \times 3^1$, since when you add the exponents you get 3^0. Now, $3^{-1} \times 3^1$ can be rewritten $\dfrac{1}{3} \times 3 = \dfrac{3}{3} = 1$.

In other words, when a base is raised to the 0 power it means multiply the base by its reciprocal, an operation that will always equal 1.

THE STRANGE POWERS OF POWERS

If you raise a positive integer to a power, the number gets larger. For example, $6^2 = 36$. However, raising a number to a power can sometimes have unexpected results:

- If you raise a positive fraction that is less than 1 to a power, the fraction gets *smaller*. $\left(\dfrac{1}{3}\right)^2 = \dfrac{1}{3} \times \dfrac{1}{3} = \dfrac{1}{9}$

- If you raise a negative number to an odd power, the number gets *smaller*.
  $(-3)^3 = (-3)(-3)(-3) = -27$
  (Remember, –27 is smaller than –3.)

- If you raise a negative number to an even power, the number becomes positive.
  $(-3)^2 = (-3)(-3) = 9$
  (Remember, negative times negative = positive.)

- Any number to the first power = itself.

- Any number to the 0 power = 1.

- Any number to the negative power y = the reciprocal of the same number to the positive power y.

  For example, $3^{-2} = \dfrac{1}{3^2} = \dfrac{1}{9}$.

Even More Strange Powers

A radical can be rewritten as a fractional exponent, and vice versa. That is, $\sqrt[3]{5} = 5^{\frac{1}{3}}$. If this all seems a little terrifying, realize that questions that deal with strange powers show up once in a blue moon and only on the very hardest questions.

RADICALS

The square root of a positive number x is the number that, when squared, equals x. For example, the square root of 9 is 3 or –3, because 3 times 3 = 9, and –3 times –3 = 9. However, ETS is interested only in the *positive* square root. So for our purposes the square root of 9 is 3 only. The symbol for a positive square root is $\sqrt{}$.

A number inside the $\sqrt{}$ is called a *radical*. Thus: $\sqrt{4} = 2$

There are several rules to remember about radicals:

1. $\sqrt{x}\sqrt{y} = \sqrt{xy}$. For example, $\sqrt{12}\sqrt{3} = \sqrt{36} = 6$

2. $\sqrt{\dfrac{x}{y}} = \dfrac{\sqrt{x}}{\sqrt{y}}$. For example, $\sqrt{\dfrac{3}{16}} = \dfrac{\sqrt{3}}{\sqrt{16}} = \dfrac{\sqrt{3}}{4}$

3. To simplify a radical, try factoring. For example,
   $\sqrt{32} = \sqrt{16}\sqrt{2} = 4\sqrt{2}$

4. The square root of a positive fraction less than 1 is actually larger than the original fraction. For example, $\sqrt{\dfrac{1}{4}} = \dfrac{1}{2}$

SUMMARY

1. The six arithmetic operations are addition, subtraction, multiplication, division, raising to a power, and finding a square root.

2. These operations must be performed in the proper order (**Please Excuse My Dear Aunt Sally**).

3. If you are adding or multiplying a group of numbers, you can regroup them in any order. This is called the associative law.

4. If you are adding or subtracting numbers with common factors, you can regroup them in the following way:
$$ab + ac = a(b + c)$$
$$ab - ac = a(b - c)$$

   This is called the distributive law.

5. A fraction can be thought of in two ways:

   ◆ Another way of expressing division

   ◆ As a part/whole

6. You must know how to add, subtract, multiply, and divide fractions. You must also know how to raise them to a power and find their roots.

7. Always reduce fractions (when you can) before doing a complicated operation. This will reduce your chances of making a careless error.

8. In tough fraction problems always think *part/whole* and *the rest*.

9. A decimal is just another way of expressing a fraction.

10. You must know how to add, subtract, multiply, and divide decimals.

11. In general it is easier to work with fractions than with decimals, so convert decimals to fractions.

12. A ratio is a fraction in all ways but one:

    A fraction is a $\dfrac{\text{part}}{\text{whole}}$. A ratio is a $\dfrac{\text{part}}{\text{part}}$.

    In a ratio, the whole is the sum of all its parts.

13. A percentage is just a fraction whose denominator is always 100.

14. You must know the percentage shortcuts outlined in this chapter.

15. In tough percent problems, like tough fraction problems, think *part/whole* and *the rest*.

16. In a percentage increase or decrease problem, you must put the amount of the increase or decrease over the *original* amount.

17. In compound interest problems, the answer will always be *a little bit more* than it would be in a similar simple interest problem.

18. To find the average of several values, add the values and divide the total by the number of values.

19. Always set up average problems in the same way:

$$\frac{\text{total sum of the items}}{\text{total number of the items}} = \text{average}$$

20. An exponent is a shorter way of expressing the result of multiplying a number several times by itself.

21. When you multiply numbers with the same base, you simply add the exponents.

22. When you divide numbers with the same base, you simply subtract the exponents.

23. When you raise a power to a power, you multiply the exponents.

24. You *cannot* add or subtract numbers with the same or different bases by adding their exponents.

25. On the GMAT, the square root of a number x is the positive number that when multiplied by itself $= x$.

26. The two radical rules you need to know:

$$\sqrt{x}\sqrt{y} = \sqrt{xy} \qquad \sqrt{\frac{x}{y}} = \frac{\sqrt{x}}{\sqrt{y}}$$

27. There are some unusual features of exponents and radicals:

A. The square root of a positive fraction that's less than 1 is larger than the original fraction.

B. When you raise a positive fraction that's less than 1 to an exponent, the resulting fraction is smaller.

C. When you raise a negative number to an even exponent, the resulting number is positive.

D. When you raise a negative number to an odd exponent, the resulting number is still a negative number.

10

Algebra

About one quarter of the problems on the computer-adaptive GMAT math section will involve traditional algebra.

In this chapter we'll show you some powerful techniques that will enable you to solve these problems without using traditional algebra. The first half of this chapter will discuss these new techniques. The second half will show you how to do the few algebra problems that must be tackled algebraically.

NOT EXACTLY ALGEBRA: BASIC PRINCIPLES

There are certain problems in math that aren't meant to have just one specific number as an answer. Here's an example:

What is two more than 3 times a certain number x?

To find *one* specific number that answers this question, we would need to know the value of that "certain number x." Here's the way ETS would ask the same question:

What is two more than 3 times a certain number x?
○ $3x - 2$
○ $3x$
○ $2x - 3$
○ $2x + 3$
○ $3x + 2$

COSMIC PROBLEMS

In other words, this is kind of a cosmic problem. ETS is asking you to write an equation that will answer this question no matter what the "certain number" is. x could be *any* number, and that equation would still give you the correct answer.

ETS expects you to use algebra to answer this question, but there is a better way. Since the correct answer will work for *every* value of x, why not just pick *one* value for x?

We call this **plugging in**. Plugging in is easy. There are three steps involved:

1. Pick numbers for the letters in the problem.

2. Using your numbers, find an answer to the problem.

3. Plug your numbers into the answer choices to see which choice equals the answer you found in step 2.

Let's look at that same problem again:

What is two more than 3 times a certain number x?

- ○ $3x - 2$
- ○ $3x$
- ○ $2x - 3$
- ○ $2x + 3$
- ○ $3x + 2$

Here's how to crack it

Let's pick a number for x. How about 4? On your scratch paper, write down "$x = 4$" so you will remember what number you've plugged in. By substituting 4 for the x, we now have a specific rather than a cosmic problem. The question now reads,

"What is two more than 3 times 4?"

$3 \times 4 = 12$.

What is 2 more than 12?

14.

Using the number we chose for x, the answer to this question is 14. Write 14 down on your scratch paper and circle it to indicate that it is your answer. All you need to do now is figure out which of the answer choices equals 14 when you substitute 4 for x.

When you're plugging values in, always start with the first answer choice (what we call choice (A)). If that doesn't work, try the last choice (choice (E)), then (B), then (D), then (C). In other words, start from the outside and work toward the center.

Let's start with choice (A), $3x - 2$. Plugging in 4 for x, do we get 14? No, we get 10. Eliminate it.

Go to choice (E), $3x + 2$. Plugging in 4 for x, we get $12 + 2$, or 14. This is the answer we wanted. Choice (E) is the correct answer to this question.

You might be thinking, "Wait a minute. It was just as easy to solve this problem algebraically. Why should I plug in?" There are two answers:

1. This was an easy problem, but plugging in makes even difficult problems easy.

2. ETS has spent hours coming up with all the possible ways you might screw this problem up using algebra. If you make one of these mistakes, your answer will be among the answer choices and you'll pick it and get the question wrong.

USING SCRATCH PAPER

The students in our GMAT course learn to make the use of scratch paper automatic. When plugging in, always write down what number you are plugging in for the variable, and then once you find the answer to the problem in terms of that number, write it down and circle it. Then try each of the answer choices, crossing them off as you eliminate them. Here's what a piece of scratch paper should have looked like for that last problem:

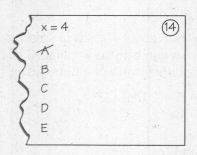

THERE ARE THREE KINDS OF COSMIC PROBLEMS— AND YOU CAN PLUG IN ON ALL OF THEM

A cosmic problem is any problem in which the answer choices are not specific numbers. You can plug in if you see:

1. variables in the answer choices

2. percents in the answer choices (when they are percents of some unspecified amount)

3. fractions or ratios in the answer choices (when they are fractional parts or ratios of unspecified amounts)

VARIABLES IN THE ANSWERS

ETS wants you to use algebra on problems that have variables in the answers, but plugging in is easier, faster, and less likely to produce errors. Here's an example:

> At a photocopy center, the first 10 copies cost x cents each. Each of the next 50 copies costs 5 cents less per copy. From the 61st copy on, the cost is 2 cents per copy. In terms of x, how much does it cost in cents to have 200 copies made?
>
> ○ $60x + 30$
> ○ $50x - 10$
> ○ $50(x - 5)$
> ○ $60x - 110$
> ○ $10x + 490$

Here's how to crack it

Pick a number for x. How about 8?

The first 10 copies = $10 \times 8 = \underline{80 \text{ cents}}$

The next 50 copies each cost 5 cents less than the first 10, so each of these copies cost $8 - 5$ or 3 cents each.

The next 50 copies = $50 \times 3 = \underline{150 \text{ cents}}$

From now on, the cost is 2 cents for any additional copies. We need a total of 200 copies. So far we've done 60 copies. We need an additional 140 copies.

The final 140 copies = $140 \times 2 = \underline{280 \text{ cents}}$

Let's add it all up.

$$\begin{array}{r} 80 \text{ cents} \\ 150 \text{ cents} \\ +280 \text{ cents} \\ \hline 510 \text{ cents} \end{array}$$

This is the answer to the question. All we have to do is find out which answer choice equals 510. Start with choice (A), $60x + 30$, and remember that we plugged in 8 for x. Does $60(8) + 30 = 510$? Yes, it does. The answer to this question is choice (A). (Try the other choices if you're not convinced.)

WHAT NUMBER SHOULD I PLUG IN?

A cosmic problem is designed to work with any number, but you'll find that certain numbers work better than others. Plugging in a number that's simple to use is obviously a good idea. In general you should stick to small numbers. But if the problem concerns hours and days, it might make sense to pick 24. If the problem concerns minutes and hours, a good number would probably be 60.

Avoid 0, 1, and numbers that are already in the problem or the answer choices. Why? If you plug in one of these numbers, you may find that more than one answer choice appears to be correct.

Sometimes the best way to select a number is to use a little common sense. Here's an example:

If Jim can drive the distance k miles in 50 minutes, how many minutes, in terms of k, will it take him to drive 10 miles at the same speed?

- ⬭ $\dfrac{500}{k}$

- ⬭ $\dfrac{k}{50}$

- ⬭ $60k$

- ⬭ $10k$

- ⬭ $\dfrac{50}{k}$

No, *Really*, I Like Algebra

If you're comfortable with algebra, great, it'll come in very handy, but don't think that knowing algebra means you can ignore plugging in. It *will* improve your score. Make it your rule to plug in on every question you can. The technique requires some practice. Plug in on easier questions you might have solved algebraically so that when you're faced with medium and difficult questions plugging in comes naturally.

Q: If 80% of a certain number x is 50% of y and y is 20% of z, then what is x in terms of z?

(A) $5z$

(B) $3z$

(C) $z/4$

(D) $z/5$

(E) $z/8$

Here's how to crack it

ETS wants you to write a complicated equation based on the formula Rate × Time = Distance, or perhaps set up a proportion. But this isn't necessary. Because there are variables in the answer choices, you can simply plug in.

Any number you choose to plug in for k will eventually give you the answer to this problem, but there are some numbers that will make your task even easier.

If it takes Jim 50 minutes to drive k *miles*, how long will it take him to drive *10 miles* at the same rate?

We need a number for k. What if we made k = half of 10? See how the question reads now:

If it takes Jim 50 minutes to drive 5 miles, how long will it take him to drive 10 miles at the same rate?

Suddenly the problem is simple. It will take him twice as long: 100 minutes. Now all we need to know is which of the answer choices equals 100, given that k = 5. Start with answer choice (A). Divide 500 by 5 and you have 100.

The answer to this question is choice (A).

PERCENTS IN THE ANSWERS

ETS wants you to use algebra on certain problems that have percents in the answers, but plugging in is easier and less likely to produce errors. Here's an example:

> A merchant was selling an item at a certain price, then marked it down 20% for a spring sale. During the summer, he marked the item down another 20% from its spring price. If the item sold at the summer price, what percent of the original price did it sell for?
>
> ○ 40%
> ○ 60%
> ○ 64%
> ○ 67%
> ○ 80%

A: The answer is (E). If you plugged in 100 for *x* then you found *y* must equal 160. The question tells us 160 (our *y*) equals 20% of *z*. That means *z* equals 800. Now it should be simple to see that *x* equals *z* divided by 8.

EASY ELIMINATIONS

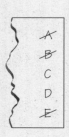

This is a difficult question. The first thing to do here is eliminate any answers that are too good to be true. The number 20 appears twice in this problem. Adding them together gives you answer choice (A). Eliminate choice (A). Joe's favorite answer is probably choice (B). Joe reasons that if an item is discounted 20% and then another 20%, there must be 60% left. Eliminate choice (B). Choice (E) seems too large. The answer is probably choice (C) or (D).

Here's how to crack it

You may have noticed that while this problem gave us lots of information, it never told us the original price of the item. This is another cosmic problem. ETS wants you to write an equation that will work regardless of the original price of the item. But since this problem is supposed to work for *any* original amount, we may as well pick *one* amount.

Let's plug in 100. *When you are dealing with a percent problem, 100 is usually a convenient number.* The merchant was selling the item for $100. He discounted it by 20% for the spring sale. 20% of $100 is $20, so the spring price was $80. For the summer, he discounted it again, by 20% of the spring price. 20% of $80 is $16. Therefore he took $20 and then $16 off the original price. The summer price is $64.

The question asks what percent of the original price the item sold for. It sold for $64. What percent of 100 is 64? 64%. The answer is choice (C).

FRACTIONS OR RATIOS IN THE ANSWERS

ETS wants you to use traditional math on certain problems with fractions or ratios in the answer choices, but plugging in is easier, faster, and less likely to produce errors. Here's an example:

> Half the graduating class of a college was accepted by a business school. One-third of the class was accepted by a law school. If one-fifth of the class was accepted to both types of school, what fraction of the class was accepted only by a law school?
>
> ○ $\frac{1}{60}$
>
> ○ $\frac{2}{15}$
>
> ○ $\frac{1}{3}$
>
> ○ $\frac{1}{2}$
>
> ○ $\frac{4}{5}$

Here's how to crack it

You may have noticed that while this problem gave us lots of fractions to work with, it never told us how many people were in the graduating class. This is yet another cosmic problem. ETS wants you to find a fractional *part* without knowing what the specific *whole* is. Since this problem is supposed to work with *any* number of people in the graduating class, we may as well pick *one* number.

Checking Your Work

Because you're plugging in and using real numbers it's much easier to catch a mistake should you make one. If the numbers you plug in are realistic, the answer should be realistic. If, in solving the copy shop problem, you came up with an answer that indicated making 200 copies cost $500, you'd know you'd taken a misstep. But when working with variables alone it's almost impossible to see what a realistic answer might or might not be. In a sense, by plugging in you're checking your work as you go.

This problem will work with any number, but some numbers are easier to work with than others. For example, if we chose 47 for the number of people in the graduating class, that would mean that $23\frac{1}{2}$ people were accepted by a business school; while this might make a good plot for a Stephen King novel, wouldn't it be easier to pick a number that can be divided evenly by all the fractions in the problem? One number that is evenly divisible by 2, 3, and 5 is 30. So let's plug in 30 for the number of people in the graduating class.

One half of the class got into business school. $\left(\frac{1}{2} \text{ of } 30 = 15\right)$

One third of the class got into law school. $\left(\frac{1}{3} \text{ of } 30 = 10\right)$

One fifth of the class got into both. $\left(\frac{1}{5} \text{ of } 30 = 6\right)$

ETS wants to know what fraction of the class was accepted only by a law school. Ten people were accepted by a law school, but 6 of those 10 were also accepted by a business school. Therefore 4 people out of 30 were accepted only by a law school. Reduced, $\frac{4}{30}$ is $\frac{2}{15}$, so the answer is choice (B).

WORKING BACKWARD

Any cosmic algebra problem can be solved, as we have seen, by plugging in numbers. But not all algebra problems are cosmic. What about a problem that asks for a specific numeric answer?

> A company's profits have doubled for each of the 4 years it has been in existence. If the total profits for those 4 years were $30 million, what were the profits in the first year of operation?

There is only one number in the whole world that will answer this question. If you tried plugging in amounts for the first year of operation in hopes of happening upon the correct answer, you would be busy for a very, very long time.

ETS expects you to use algebra to answer this question. They want you to assign a variable for the first year's profits, say x, in which case the second year's profits would be $2x$, the third year's profits would be $4x$, and the fourth year's profits would be $8x$. Altogether, we get $15x = 30$, and $x = 2$.

Unfortunately, it is extremely easy to make a mistake when you set up an equation. You could add up the number of xs incorrectly, or think that the profits of the third year were equal to $3x$. While this is not a difficult problem, it does represent the potential difficulties of using algebra.

ETS expects you to use algebra to answer this question, but *there is a better way*. Each time ETS asks you to find a specific numeric answer, they are forced to give you five clues. Here is how ETS would ask this question:

A company's profits have doubled for each of the 4 years it has been in existence. If the total profits for the last 4 years were $30 million, what were the profits in the first year of operation?

- ◯ $1 million
- ◯ $2 million
- ◯ $4 million
- ◯ $4.5 million
- ◯ $6 million

Here's how to crack it

Without answer choices this problem is complicated, and the only way to solve it is to use algebra. Now, however, there are only five possible answers. One of them has to be correct. Why not **work backward** from the answer choices?

Working backward is easy. There are three steps involved:

1. Always start with the middle answer choice (what we call choice (C)). Plug that number into the problem and see whether it makes the problem work.

2. If choice (C) is too small, choose the next larger number.

3. If choice (C) is too big, choose the next smaller number.

Numeric answers on the GMAT are always given in order of size (with one or two rare exceptions). Therefore, when you're working backward, always start with answer choice (C). Plug that number into the problem and see whether it works. If it does, you've already found the answer. If it's too big, you can try a lower number. If it's too small, try a larger number.

Let's try answer choice (C).

If the first year's profits were	$4 million
the second year's profits would be	$8 million
the third year's profits would be	$16 million
and the fourth year's profits would be	$32 million
the total profits =	$60 million

This is too big. The total profits were only $30 million. We don't even have to look at choice (D) or (E), which are even bigger. We can eliminate choices (C), (D), and (E).

Let's try answer choice (B).

If the first year's profits were	$2 million
the second year's profits would be	$4 million
the third year's profits would be	$8 million
and the fourth year's profits would be	$16 million
the total profits =	$30 million

Bingo! The correct answer is choice (B). Note that if choice (B) had been too big, the only possible answer would have been choice (A).

When to Work Backward

You can work backward as long as:

A. The answer choices are numbers.

B. The question is relatively straightforward. For example, it's easy to work backward on a question that asks, "What is x?" It's difficult and not worth the bother to work backward on a problem that asks, "What is $(x + y)$?"

> If x is a positive number such that $x^2 + 5x - 14 = 0$, what is the value of x?
>
> ○   −7
> ○   −5
> ○   0
> ○   2
> ○   5

A: The answer is C. Be sure to follow these questions carefully. It's Patrick who reads $\frac{1}{2}$ as much as Amy, not Bob.

Here's how to crack it

There is only one number in the world that will make this problem work, and fortunately it has to be one of the five answer choices. Let's work backward. Start with the middle choice, (C). (Zero squared) plus (zero times 5) minus 14 does *not* equal 0. Eliminate it. We don't have to try choice (A) or (B) because the problem asks for a positive number. Let's try choice (D). (Two squared) plus (5 times 2)—we're up to 14 so far—minus 14 *does* equal 0. The answer is choice (D).

Easy Eliminations

Obviously, if x is a positive number, choices (A), (B), and (C) are out of the question.

Working Backward: Advanced Principles

Sometimes when you're working backward you'll be able to eliminate choice (C), but you may not be sure whether you need a larger number or a smaller one. Rather than waste time trying to decide, just try all the answer choices until you hit the right one. You'll never have to try more than four of them.

> Today Jim is twice as old as Fred, and Sam is 2 years younger than Fred. Four years ago Jim was 4 times as old as Sam. How old is Jim now?
>
> ○   8
> ○   12
> ○   16
> ○   20
> ○   24

Here's how to crack it

One of these five answer choices is the right answer.

Let's work backward.

Start with choice (C). Jim is 16 years old today. He is twice as old as Fred, so Fred is 8. Sam is 2 years younger than Fred, so Sam is 6. Therefore, 4 years ago

Jim was 12 and Sam was 2. If these numbers agree with the rest of the problem, then choice (C) is the answer to this question. The problem says that four years ago Jim was 4 times as old as Sam. Does 2 times 4 equal 12? No. Choice (C) is the wrong answer. Does anybody want to guess which direction to go in now? Rather than hem and haw, just try the other answers until you get the right one.

Let's try choice (D). Jim is 20 years old today. He is twice as old as Fred, so Fred is 10. Sam is 2 years younger than Fred, so Sam is 8. Therefore, four years ago Jim was 16 and Sam was 4. If these numbers agree with the rest of the problem, choice (D) is the right answer. The problem says that four years ago Jim was 4 times as old as Sam. Does 4 times 4 equal 16? Yes. The answer is choice (D).

Must Be/Could Be

From time to time ETS will write a question that contains the words "must be," "could be," or "cannot be." This type of problem can almost always be solved by plugging in, *but you may need to plug in more than one number*. Here's an example:

> If x and y are consecutive integers, which of the following must be an even integer?
>
> ○ x
>
> ○ y
>
> ○ $\dfrac{xy}{2}$
>
> ○ $\dfrac{x}{y}$
>
> ○ xy

Here's how to crack it

Plug in numbers for x and y. How about 2 for x and 3 for y? Now go through each of the answer choices. Using these numbers, choice (A) is even, but because of the words "must be," we cannot assume that it will *always* be even, or that this is necessarily the right answer. Keep going. Using the numbers we plugged in, choices (B) and (C) turn out to be odd, and (D) is not an integer. Since the question asks us for an answer that is *always* even, we can eliminate all of these. However, choice (E) is also even. We're down to either choice (A) or (E). Which is correct?

Try plugging in a different set of numbers. The problem concerns even and odd numbers, so this time let's try an odd number first. How about 3 and 4? This time choice (A) is odd. Eliminate. Choice (E) is still even; this must be our answer.

BASIC ALGEBRA

Plugging in and working backward will take care of most of your algebraic needs, but there are a few other types of problems that require some knowledge of basic algebra. After reading the rest of this chapter and working out the problems contained in it, if you still feel rusty, you might want to dig out your old high-school algebra book.

SOLVING EQUALITIES

Even the simplest equalities can be solved by working backward, but it's probably easier to solve a *simple* equation algebraically. If there is one variable in an equation, isolate the variable on one side of the equation and solve it. Here's an example:

If $x - 5 = 3x + 2$, then $x =$

- ⬭ -8
- ⬭ $-\dfrac{7}{2}$
- ⬭ -7
- ⬭ $\dfrac{10}{3}$
- ⬭ $\dfrac{7}{5}$

Here's how to crack it

Get all of the *x*s on one side of the equation. If we subtract *x* from both sides we have:

$$
\begin{array}{rcl}
x - 5 &=& 3x + 2 \\
\underline{-x} & & \underline{-x} \\
-5 &=& 2x + 2
\end{array}
$$

Now subtract 2 from both sides:

$$
\begin{array}{rcl}
-5 &=& 2x + 2 \\
\underline{-2} & & \underline{-2} \\
-7 &=& 2x
\end{array}
$$

Finally, divide both sides by 2:

$$
\frac{-7}{2} = \frac{2x}{2}
$$

$x = -\dfrac{7}{2}$. The answer is choice (B).

The Solvability Rule

You must have at least as many distinct equations as you have variables for the equations to be solvable. That is, if you are trying to figure out what x, y and z are, you need at least three distinct equations.

SOLVING INEQUALITIES

To solve inequalities, you must be able to recognize the following symbols:

> is greater than

< is less than

≥ is greater than or equal to

≤ is less than or equal to

Q: Are the following equations distinct?

(1) $3x + 21y = 12$

(2) $x + 7y = 4$

As with an equation, you can add a number to or subtract a number from both sides of an inequality without changing it; you can collect similar terms and simplify them.

In fact, an inequality behaves just like a regular equation except in one way: *If you multiply or divide both sides of an inequality by a negative number, the direction of the inequality symbol changes.* For example,

$$-2x > 5$$

To solve for x, you would divide both sides by –2, just as you would in an equality. But when you do, the sign flips:

$$\frac{-2x}{-2} < \frac{5}{-2}$$

$$x < -\frac{5}{2}$$

SOLVING SIMULTANEOUS EQUATIONS

It's impossible to solve one equation with two variables. But if there are two equations, both of which have the same two variables, then it is possible to solve for both variables. An easy problem might look like this:

If $3x + 2y = 6$ and $5x - 2y = 10$ then $x = ?$

To solve simultaneous equations, add or subtract the equations so that one of the variables disappears.

$$\begin{array}{rl} 3x + 2y = & 6 \\ 5x - 2y = & 10 \\ \hline 8x \quad\;\; = & 16 \qquad x = 2 \end{array}$$

In more difficult simultaneous equations, you'll find that neither of the variables will disappear when you try to add or subtract the two equations. In such cases you must multiply both sides of one of the equations by some number in order to get the coefficient in front of the variable that you want to disappear to be the same in both equations. This sounds more complicated than it is. A difficult problem might look like this:

If $3x + 2y = 6$ and $5x - y = 10$, then $x = ?$

Let's set it up the same way:

$$3x + 2y = 6$$
$$5x - y = 10$$

Unfortunately, in this example neither adding nor subtracting the two equations gets rid of either variable. But look what happens when we multiply the bottom equation by 2:

$$3x + 2y = 6$$
$$(2)5x - (2)y = (2)10$$

or

$$3x + 2y = 6$$
$$\underline{+\ 10x - 2y = 20}$$
$$13x \quad = 26 \qquad x = 2$$

Quadratic Equations

On the GMAT, quadratic equations always come in one of two forms: factored or unfactored. Here's an example:

$$\overset{factored}{(x + 2)(x + 5)} = \overset{unfactored}{x^2 + 7x + 10}$$

The first thing to do when solving a problem that involves a quadratic equation is to see which form the equation is in. If the quadratic equation is in an unfactored form, factor it immediately. If the quadratic equation is in a factored form, unfactor it. ETS likes to see whether you know how to do these things.

To unfactor a factored expression, just multiply it out:

$$(x + 2)(x + 5) = (\ x + 2)(x + 5)$$
$$= (x \text{ times } x) + (x \text{ times } 5) + (2 \text{ times } x) + (2 \text{ times } 5)$$
$$= x^2 + 5x + 2x + 10$$
$$= x^2 + 7x + 10$$

To factor an unfactored expression, put it into the following format and start by looking for the factors of the first and last terms.

$$x^2 + 2x - 15$$
$$= (\quad)(\quad)$$
$$= (x\quad)(x\quad)$$
$$= (x\quad 5)(x\quad 3)$$
$$= (x + 5)(x - 3)$$

Quadratic equations are usually set equal to 0. Here's an example:

> What are all the values of x that satisfy the equation $x^2 + 4x + 3 = 0$?
>
> ◯   −3
> ◯   −1
> ◯   −3 and −1
> ◯   3 and 4
> ◯   4

A: No. Look at what equation #2 looks like multiplied by 3.
$$3(x + 7y) = 3(4)$$
or $3x + 21y = 12$.
Multiply both sides by 3 and equation #1 and #2 are identical.
When one equation can be multiplied to produce the other, the equations are identical, not distinct.

Here's how to crack it

This problem contains an unfactored equation, so let's factor it.

$$x^2 + 4x + 3 = 0$$
$$(x)(\quad x) = 0$$
$$(x3)(\quad x1) = 0$$
$$(x + 3)(x + 1) = 0$$

In order for this equation to be correct, x must be either -3 or -1. The correct answer is choice (C).

Note: This problem would also have been easy to solve by working backward. It asked a specific question, and there were five specific answer choices. One of them was correct. All you had to do was try the choices until you found the right one. Bear in mind, however, that in a quadratic equation there are usually two values that will make the equation work.

FETISHES OF GMAT TEST WRITERS

There are two types of quadratic equations the test writers at ETS find endlessly fascinating. These equations appear on the GMAT with great regularity in both the Problem Solving format and the Data Sufficiency format:

$$(x + y)^2 = x^2 + 2xy + y^2$$

$$(x + y)(x - y) = x^2 - y^2$$

Memorize both of these. As with all quadratic equations, if ETS presents the equation in factored form, you should immediately unfactor it; if it's unfactored, factor it immediately.

If $\dfrac{x^2-4}{x+2} = 5$, then $x =$

- ⃝ 3
- ⃝ 5
- ⃝ 6
- ⃝ 7
- ⃝ 9

Here's how to crack it

This problem contains one of ETS's fetishes. It is unfactored, so let's factor it:

$$\frac{(x+2)(x-2)}{(x+2)} = 5$$

The $(x + 2)$s cancel out, leaving us with $(x - 2) = 5$. $x = 7$ and the answer is choice (D).

RATE × TIME = DISTANCE

Any problem that mentions planes, trains, cars, bicycles, distance, miles per hour, or any other travel-related terminology is asking you to write an equation based on the formula *rate × time = distance*. This formula is easy to reconstruct if you forget it; just think of a real-life situation. If you drove at 50 miles per hour for 2 hours, how far did you go? That's right, 100 miles. We just derived the formula. The rate is 50 miles per hour. The time is 2 hours. The distance is 100 miles.

> Pam and Sue drove to a business meeting 120 miles away in the same car. Pam drove to the meeting and Sue drove back along the same route. If Pam drove at 60 miles per hour and Sue drove at 50 miles per hour, how much longer, in minutes, did it take Sue to travel the distance than it did Pam?
>
> ○ 4
> ○ 10
> ○ 20
> ○ 24
> ○ 30

Here's how to crack it

As soon as you see the words "drove" and "travel," make a little chart for yourself:

$$R \times T = D$$

Pam _____

Sue _____

The problem says the meeting was 120 miles away from wherever they started. This tells us not only how far Pam drove but how far Sue drove as well, since she returned along the same route. We are also given the rates of both women.

Let's fill in the chart with the information we have:

$$R \times T = D$$

Pam $60 \times ? = 120$

Sue $50 \times ? = 120$

60 times what equals 120? It took Pam 2 hours to drive to the meeting. 50 times what equals 120? It took Sue 2.4 hours to drive back from the meeting. Sue took .4 hours longer, but the problem asks for the answer in minutes. .4 equals $\frac{4}{10}$ or $\frac{2}{5}$. There are 60 minutes in an hour, so just find $\frac{2}{5}$ of 60. The answer is choice (D), 24 minutes.

WORK PROBLEMS

Another type of GMAT problem that requires an equation is the work problem. These are easy to spot because they always involve two people (or factories or machines) working at different rates. In these problems the trick is not to think about how long it takes to do an entire job, but rather how much of the job can be done in *one hour*.

> If Sam can finish a job in 3 hours and Mark can finish a job in 12 hours, in how many hours could they finish the job if they worked on it together at their respective rates?
>
> ○ 1
>
> ○ $2\frac{2}{5}$
>
> ○ $2\frac{5}{8}$
>
> ○ $3\frac{1}{4}$
>
> ○ 4

Here's how to crack it

If Sam can finish a job in 3 hours, then in one hour he can finish $\frac{1}{3}$ of the job. If Mark can finish a job in 12 hours, then in one hour he can finish $\frac{1}{12}$ of the job. Working together, how much of the job can they do in one hour?

$$\frac{1}{3} + \frac{1}{12} = \frac{1}{x}$$

Now we only need to solve for x. First find a common denominator for $\frac{1}{3}$ and $\frac{1}{12}$.

$$\frac{1}{3} + \frac{1}{12} = \frac{1}{x}$$

$$\frac{4}{12} + \frac{1}{12} = \frac{1}{x}$$

$$\frac{5}{12} = \frac{1}{x}$$

Cross-multiply and divide. $x = 2\frac{2}{5}$. The answer is choice (B).

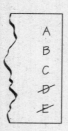

EASY ELIMINATIONS

It stands to reason that two men working together would take less time to finish a job than they would if each of them worked alone. Since Sam, working alone, could finish the job in 3 hours, it must be true that the two of them, working together, could do it in less time. The answer to this question has to be less than 3. Therefore we can eliminate answer choices (D) and (E).

FUNCTIONS

You know you've hit a function problem by the sensation of panic and fear you get when you see some strange symbol ($ or # or * or Δ) and say, "I studied for two months for this test and somehow managed to miss the part where they told me about $ or # or * or Δ." Relax. Any strange-looking symbol on the GMAT is just a function, and on this test, functions are easy.

A function is basically a set of directions. Let's look at an example:

If $x * y = 3x - y$, then what is 4 * 2?

What the first half of this problem says is that for any two numbers with a * between them, you must multiply the number on the left by 3 and then subtract the number on the right. These are the directions. The second half of the problem asks you to use these directions with two specific numbers: 4 * 2.

To solve this problem, all we need to do is plug the specific numbers into the set of directions:

$$x * y = 3x - y$$
$$4 * 2 = 3(4) - (2)$$
$$= 12 - 2$$
$$= 10$$

Functions don't always involve two variables. Sometimes they look like this:

If $\Delta x = x$ if x is positive, or $2x$ if x is negative, what is $\dfrac{\Delta 30}{\Delta - 5}$?

- ○ −12
- ○ −6
- ○ −3
- ○ 6
- ○ 30

Let's take this one step at a time. In this case the directions say that the function of any number x is simply that same number x, if x is positive. However, if the number x is negative, then the function of that number is $2x$. Thus:

$$\frac{\Delta 30}{\Delta - 5} = \frac{30}{2(-5)} = \frac{30}{-10}$$ or −3. The answer is choice (C).

Easy Eliminations

Joe has no idea what to do with Δ, so he just ignores it. Because $\frac{30}{-5} = -6$, Joe picks answer choice (B). On the other hand, Joe might also think he can reduce functions. In other words, he might think he could do this:

$$\frac{\Delta 30}{\Delta - 5} = \Delta - 6$$

The function of −6 = −12, so Joe might also select answer choice (A).

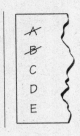

PROBABILITY

Just the word is enough to cause math phobes to run for the exits— but, at least as it appears on the GMAT, probability really isn't all that bad. Here's an easy example:

> If you rolled a six-sided die (with faces numbered one through six) one time, what is the probability that it would land with the "2" side facing upward?

Well, of course, there's only one possibility of this happening, and there are six possible outcomes, so there's a one-in-six chance. In essence, this is all that probability is about. On the GMAT, probability is usually expressed as a fraction: The total number of possibilities is always the denominator. The number of possibilities that match what you want is the numerator. In the example above, that translates to $\frac{1}{6}$.

Let's make this example a little harder:

> If you rolled a six-sided die (with faces numbered one through six) one time, what is the probability that it would land with either the "2" side facing upward or the "3" side facing upward?

The total number of possible outcomes (the denominator) is still the same: 6. But the numerator is different now. There are two possibilities that would match what we want, so the numerator becomes 2. The probability is $\frac{2}{6}$ or $\frac{1}{3}$.

Let's make the example a little harder still.

> If you rolled a six-sided die (with faces numbered one through six) two times, what is the probability that it would land with the "2" side facing up <u>both</u> times?

Obviously, the odds of this happening are much smaller. How do you figure out the probability of something happening over a series of events? It's actually pretty easy. To find the probability of a series of events, you multiply the probabilities of each of the individual events. Let's start with the first roll of the die. We already figured out that the probability of the die landing with its "2" side facing up on a *single* toss is $\frac{1}{6}$. Now, let's think about the *second* toss. Well, actually, the probability of this happening on the second toss is exactly the same: $\frac{1}{6}$.

However, to figure out the probability of the "2" side facing upward on *both* tosses, you multiply the first probability by the second probability: $\frac{1}{6} \times \frac{1}{6} = \frac{1}{36}$.

Here's an example of a moderately difficult GMAT problem.

> There are 8 job applicants sitting in a waiting room— 4 women and 4 men. If two of the applicants are selected at random, what is the probability that both will be women?
>
> ○ $\frac{1}{2}$
>
> ○ $\frac{3}{7}$
>
> ○ $\frac{1}{4}$
>
> ○ $\frac{3}{14}$
>
> ○ $\frac{1}{10}$

Here's how to crack it

Let's take the first event in the series. The total number of possibilities for the first selection is 8, because there are 8 applicants in the room. Of those 8 people, 4 are women, so the probability that the first person chosen will be a woman is $\frac{4}{8}$ or $\frac{1}{2}$. You might think that the probability would be exactly the same for the second choice (in which case you would multiply $\frac{1}{2} \times \frac{1}{2}$ and choose answer choice (C)), but in fact, that's not true. Let's consider: the first woman has just left the room, and they are about to choose another applicant at random. How many total people are now in the room? Aha! Only 7. And how many of those 7 are women? Only 3. So the probability that the second choice will be a woman is actually only $\frac{3}{7}$, which is choice (B). But we aren't done yet. We have to figure out the probability that BOTH choices in this series of two choices will be women. The probability that the first will be a woman is $\frac{1}{2}$. The probability that the second will be a woman is $\frac{3}{7}$. The probability that they both will be women is $\frac{1}{2} \times \frac{3}{7}$, or $\frac{3}{14}$. The answer is choice (D).

SUMMARY

1. Most of the algebra problems on the GMAT are simpler to solve *without* algebra, using two Princeton Review techniques: *plugging in* and *working backward*.

2. Plugging in will work on any cosmic problem—that is, any problem that does not include specific numbers in the answer choices. You can always plug in if you see:

   - variables in the answer choices
   - fractional parts in the answer choices
   - ratios in the answer choices

   You can usually plug in when you see:

   - percentages in the answer choices

3. Plugging in is easy. There are three steps:

   A. Pick numbers for the variables in the problem.

   B. Using your numbers, find an answer to the problem.

   C. Plug your numbers into the answer choices to see which choice equals the answer you found in Step B.

4. When you plug in, try to choose convenient numbers—those that are simple to work with and make the problem easier to manipulate.

5. When you plug in, avoid choosing 0, 1, or a number that already appears in the problem or in the answer choices.

6. On problems with variables in the answers that contain the words "must be" or "could be," you may have to plug in more than once to find the correct answer.

7. Working backward will solve algebra problems that are *not* cosmic—in other words, problems that are highly specific. You can always work backward on an algebra problem if the answer choices contain specific numbers and if the question being asked is relatively straightforward.

8. Working backward is easy. There are three steps:

   A. Always start with answer choice (C). Plug that number into the problem and see whether it makes the problem work.

   B. If choice (C) is too small, choose the next larger number.

   C. If choice (C) is too big, choose the next smaller number.

9. If you see a problem with a quadratic equation in factored form, the easiest way to get the answer is to unfactor the equation immediately. If the equation is unfactored, factor it immediately.

10. Memorize the factored and unfactored forms of the two most common quadratic equations on the GMAT:

$$(x + y)^2 = x^2 + 2xy + y^2$$
$$(x + y)(x - y) = x^2 - y^2$$

11. On problems containing inequalities, remember that when you multiply or divide both sides of an inequality by a negative number, the sign flips.

12. In solving simultaneous equations, add or subtract one equation to or from another so that one of the two variables disappears.

13. Any travel-related problem is probably concerned with the formula **Rate × Time = Distance**.

14. The key to work problems is to think about how much of the job can be done in one hour.

15. A function problem has strange symbols like $, Δ, or *, but it is really just a set of directions.

16. Probability problems can be solved by putting the total number of possibilities in the denominator, and the number of possibilities that match what you are looking for in the numerator.

11
Geometry

Fewer than a quarter of the problems on the computer-adaptive GMAT will involve geometry. And while this tends to be the math subject most people remember least from high school, the good news is that the GMAT tests only a small portion of the geometry you used to know. It will be relatively easy to refresh your memory.

The Brain Dump

Since the GMAT doesn't provide formulas, some students use the time set aside for the tutorial at the beginning of the exam to write down formulas they tend to forget on their scratch paper.

The bad news is that unlike the SAT, the GMAT does not provide you with the formulas and terms you'll need to solve the problems. You'll have to memorize them.

The first half of this chapter will show you how to eliminate answer choices on certain geometry problems without using traditional geometry. The second half will review all the geometry you need to know in order to answer the problems that must be solved using more traditional methods.

CRAZY ANSWERS

Eliminating choices that don't make sense has already proven to be a valuable technique on arithmetic and algebra questions. On geometry questions you can develop this technique to the point where it becomes an art form. The reason for this is that many geometry problems come complete with a diagram *drawn to scale*.

Most people get so caught up in solving a geometry problem geometrically that they forget to look at the diagram to see whether their answer is reasonable.

CRAZY ANSWERS ON EASY QUESTIONS

How big is angle *x*?

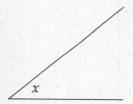

Obviously you don't know exactly how big this angle is, but it would be easy to compare it with an angle whose measure you *do* know exactly. Let's compare it with a 90-degree angle:

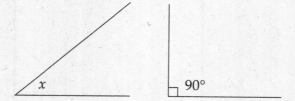

Angle *x* is less than 90 degrees. How much less? It looks as though it's about half of a 90-degree angle, or 45 degrees. Now look at the following problem, which asks about the same angle, *x*:

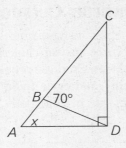

In the figure above, if *BC* = *CD*, and angle *ADC* = 90 degrees, then what is the value of *x*?

- ⭕ 45
- ⭕ 50
- ⭕ 70
- ⭕ 75
- ⭕ 100

Here's how to crack it

This is a relatively easy problem, but before you launch into solving it, it's still a good idea to take a moment to decide whether any of the answer choices are clearly unreasonable. We've already decided that angle *x* is less than 90 degrees, which means that the last answer choice (what we call choice (E)) can be eliminated. How much less is it? Well, we estimated before that it was about half, which rules out answer choices (C) and (D) as well.

There is another way to eliminate choices (C) and (D). We can compare angle *x* with the other marked angle in the problem—angle *DBC*. If the answer to this problem is choice (C), then angle *x* should look like angle *DBC*. Does it? No. Angle *x* looks a little bit smaller than angle *DBC*, which means that both choices (C) and (D) can be eliminated.

Eliminating crazy answers will prevent you from making careless mistakes on easy problems. (By the way, we'll show you how to solve this problem using geometry later in the chapter.)

CRAZY ANSWERS ON DIFFICULT QUESTIONS

If it's important to cross off crazy answer choices on easy questions, it's even more important to eliminate crazy answer choices when you're tackling a *medium* or *difficult* geometry problem. On these problems, you may not know how to find the answer geometrically, and even if you do, you could still fall victim to one of the traps ETS has placed in your path. Take a look at the following difficult geometry problem:

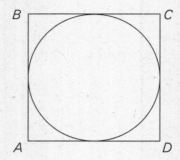

In the figure above, circle *C* is inscribed inside square *ABCD* as shown. What is the ratio of the area of circle *C* to the area of square *ABCD*?

○ $\dfrac{\pi}{2}$

○ $\dfrac{4}{\pi}$

○ $\dfrac{\pi}{3}$

○ $\dfrac{\pi}{4}$

○ $\dfrac{2}{\pi}$

Here's how to crack it

This is a difficult problem, but before you start guessing at random, let's see whether you can eliminate any of the answer choices just by looking at the diagram and using some common sense.

The problem asks you for the ratio of the area of the circle to the area of the square. Just by looking at the diagram, you can tell that the circle is smaller than the square. The correct answer to this question has to be the ratio of a smaller number to a bigger number. Let's look at the answer choices.

In choice (A), the ratio is π over 2. An approximate value of π is 3, so this really reads $\dfrac{3}{2}$.

Is this the ratio of a smaller number to a bigger number? Just the opposite. Therefore choice (A) is a crazy answer. Eliminate it.

In choice (B), the ratio is 4 over π. This really reads $\frac{4}{3}$.

Is this the ratio of a smaller number to a bigger number? No. Choice (B) is a crazy answer. Eliminate it.

In choice (C), the ratio is π over 3. This really reads $\frac{3}{3}$.

Is this the ratio of a smaller number to a bigger number? No. Choice (C) is a crazy answer. Eliminate it.

Answer choices (D) and (E) both contain ratios of smaller numbers to bigger numbers, so they're both still possibilities. However, we've eliminated three of the answer choices without doing any math. If you know how to solve the problem geometrically, then proceed. If not, guess and move on. (By the way, we will show you how to solve this problem using geometry later in the chapter.)

THE BASIC TOOLS

In eliminating crazy answers, it helps to have the following approximations memorized.

$$\pi \approx 3$$
$$\sqrt{1} = 1$$
$$\sqrt{2} \approx 1.4$$
$$\sqrt{3} \approx 1.7$$
$$\sqrt{4} = 2$$

It's also useful to have a feel for the way certain common angles look:

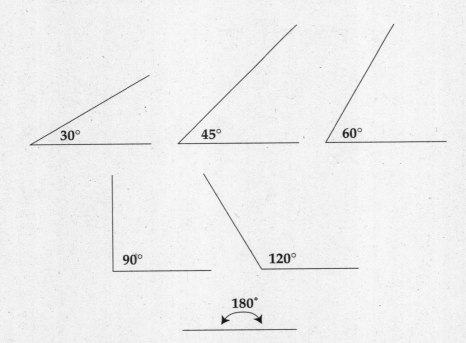

GETTING MORE PRECISE

When a geometry problem contains a diagram that's drawn to scale, you can get even more precise in eliminating wrong answer choices.

How?

By measuring the diagram.

The instructions to the GMAT CAT say that unless a diagram is marked "not drawn to scale," it is drawn "as accurately as possible." ETS finds it possible to draw diagrams very accurately indeed. All you need now is something with which to measure the diagram. Fortunately the folks at ETS provide you with a ruler—your scratch paper. You can use one of the straight edges of your scratch paper to construct a ruler, and by holding it up to the computer screen, you can measure the diagram.

Look at the problem below:

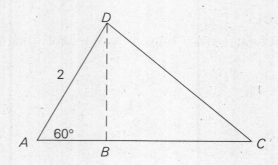

In the figure above, if a line segment connecting points B and D is perpendicular to AC and the area of triangle ADC is $\dfrac{3\sqrt{3}}{2}$, then $BC = ?$

○ $\sqrt{2}$

○ $\sqrt{3}$

○ 2

○ $3\sqrt{3}$

○ 6

Here's how to crack it

Find any straight-edged piece of paper and make a dot somewhere along the top edge. Put this dot on point *A* in the diagram. Now turn the edge of your piece of paper so that it lines up along *AD* and mark another dot along the edge of the paper next to point *D*. Here's how it should look:

Q: Is making a ruler cheating?

You now have a ruler. The distance between the dots at the top of your scrap paper is exactly the same as the distance between points *A* and *D* on the diagram. Use the ruler to measure the distance between point *B* and *C*.

If you measure carefully, you'll notice that the distance between *A* and *D* is the same as the distance between *B* and *C*—exactly 2. Let's look at the answer choices. Because you memorized the values we told you to memorize earlier, you know that answer choice (A) is equal to 1.4. Eliminate it. Answer choice (B) is equal to 1.7. This is close enough for us to hold on to it while we look at the other choices. Choice (C) is exactly what we're looking for—2. Choice (D) is 3 times 1.7, which equals 5.1. This is much too large. Choice (E) is even larger. Eliminate (D) and (E). We're down to choices (B) and (C). The correct answer is choice (C).

Three important notes

1. Diagrams in questions using the problem-solving format may be drawn to scale (unless otherwise indicated), but they are not *all* drawn to the *same* scale. A ruler that measures 2 on one diagram won't measure 2 on another. For every new problem with a diagram, you will have to make a new ruler.

2. Diagrams marked "not drawn to scale" cannot be measured. In fact, the drawings in these problems are often purposely misleading to the eye.

3. Drawings in questions using the Data Sufficiency format of the GMAT are *not* drawn to scale. They *cannot* be estimated with your eye or with a ruler.

WHAT SHOULD I DO IF THERE IS NO DIAGRAM?

Draw one. It's always difficult to imagine a geometry problem in your head. The first thing you should do with any geometry problem that doesn't have a diagram is sketch it out on your scratch paper. And when you draw the diagram, try to draw it to scale. That way, you'll be in a position to estimate.

A: NO.

WHAT SHOULD I DO IF THE DIAGRAM IS NOT DRAWN TO SCALE?

The same thing you would do if there were no diagram at all—draw it yourself. Draw it as accurately as possible so you'll be able to see what a realistic answer should be.

BASIC PRINCIPLES: FUNDAMENTALS OF GMAT GEOMETRY

The techniques outlined above will enable you to eliminate many incorrect choices on geometry problems. In some cases, you'll be able to eliminate every choice but one. However, there will be some geometry problems on which you will need geometry. Fortunately, ETS chooses to test only a small number of concepts.

For the sake of simplicity, we've divided GMAT geometry into five basic topics:

1. degrees and angles

2. triangles

3. circles

4. rectangles, squares, and other four-sided objects

5. solids and volume

DEGREES AND ANGLES

There are 360 degrees in a circle. It doesn't matter how large or small a circle is, it still has precisely 360 degrees. If you drew a circle on the ground and then walked a quarter of the distance around it, you would have traveled 90 degrees of that circle. If you walked halfway around the circle, you would have traveled 180 degrees of it.

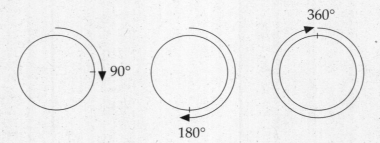

An angle is formed when two line segments extend from a common point. If you think of that point as the center of a circle, the measure of the angle is the number of degrees enclosed by the lines when they pass through the edge of the circle.

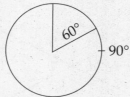

A line is just a 180-degree angle.

l is the symbol for a line. A line can be referred to as *l* or by naming two points on that line. For example, in the diagram below both points *A* and *B* are on the line *l*. This line could also be called line *AB*. Also, the part of the line that is between points *A* and *B* is called a line segment. *A* and *B* are the end points of the line segment.

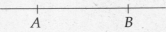

If a line is cut by another line, as in the diagram below, angle *x* and angle *y* add up to one straight line, or 180 degrees. If you knew that angle *x* equaled 120 degrees, you could find the measure of angle *y* by subtracting 120 degrees from 180 degrees. Thus angle *y* would equal 60 degrees.

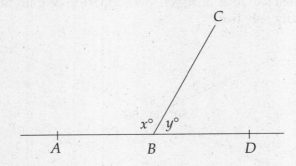

Note that in the diagram above, angle *x* could also be called angle *ABC*, with *B* being the point in the middle.

When two lines intersect—as in the diagram below—four angles are formed. The four angles are indicated by letters.

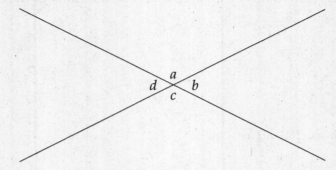

The four angles add up to 360 degrees (remember the circle).

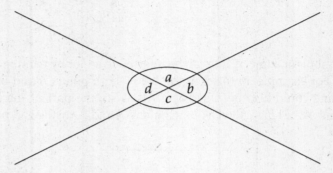

$a + b + c + d = 360$. Angle a + angle b, since they add up to a straight line, are equal to 180 degrees. Angle b + angle c also add up to a straight line, as do $c + d$ and $d + a$. Angles that are opposite each other are called *vertical angles* and have the same number of degrees. For example, in the diagram above, angle a is equal to angle c. Angle d is also equal to angle b.

Therefore when two lines intersect, there appear to be four different angles, but there are really only two:

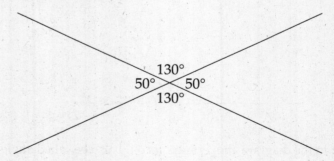

Two lines in the same plane are said to be parallel if they extend infinitely in both directions without touching. The symbol for parallel is | |.

Look at the diagram below:

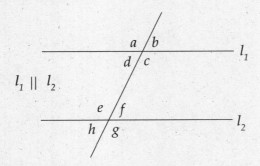

l_1 || l_2

The Number of Billionaires in America

1987	49
1988	51
1989	67
1990	66
1991	71

Source: *Forbes*, 1991

When two parallel lines are cut by a third line, there appear to be eight separate angles, but there are really only two. There is a big one (greater than 90°) and a little one (less than 90°). Angle a (a big one) is also equal to angles c, e, and g. Angle b (a little one) is also equal to angles d, f, and h.

If two lines intersect in such a way that one line is perpendicular to the other, all the angles formed will be 90-degree angles. These are also known as right angles:

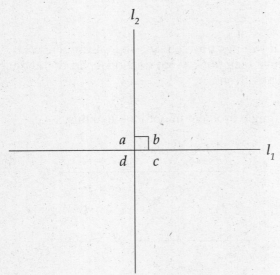

Angles a, b, c, and d each equal 90 degrees. The little box at the intersection of the two lines is the symbol for a right angle.

DRILL 5 (Angles and Lengths)

In the following figures, find numbers for all the variables. The answers to these problems can be found on page 278.

The answers to these problems can be found on page 278.

In a Problem Solving question, if it doesn't say *not drawn to scale* then it *is* drawn to scale. When they give you a scale drawing, use it to eliminate answers that are out of proportion.

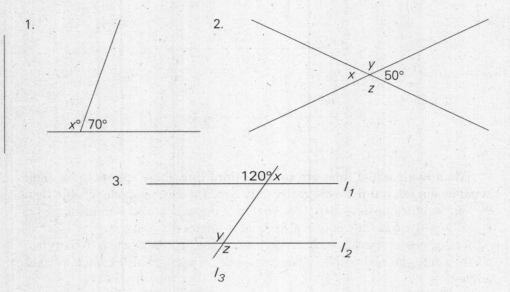

1.

2.

3.

4. If a driver has traveled 270 degrees around a circular race track, what fractional part of the track has he driven?

A real GMAT angle problem might look like this:

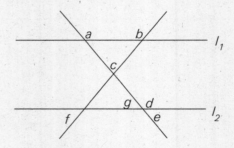

Note: Figure not drawn to scale.

5. In the figure above, if $l_1 \parallel l_2$, then which of the following angles must be equivalent?

   ○ *a* and *b*
   ○ *g* and *f*
   ○ *d* and *e*
   ○ *a* and *d*
   ○ *f* and *d*

TRIANGLES

A triangle is a three-sided figure that contains three interior angles. The interior angles of a triangle always add up to 180 degrees. Several kinds of triangles appear on the GMAT:

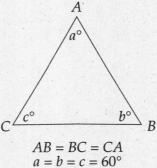

$$AB = BC = CA$$
$$a = b = c = 60°$$

The 180° Rule, Part II

When a question involving angles has a triangle or several triangles in it, remember the rule of 180 degrees. Apply that rule in every possible way you can. It is one of ETS's favorite items. They seem to have a neverending bag of tricks when it comes to questions in which they can use the simple rule of 180 degrees.

An *equilateral* triangle has three sides that are equal in length. Because the angles opposite equal sides are also equal, all three angles in an equilateral triangle are also equal.

An *isosceles* triangle has two sides that are equal in length. The angles opposite those equal sides are also equal.

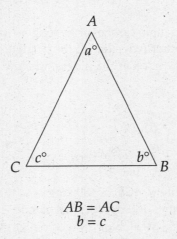

$$AB = AC$$
$$b = c$$

A *right* triangle has one interior angle that is equal to 90 degrees. The longest side of a right triangle (the one opposite the 90-degree angle) is called the *hypotenuse*.

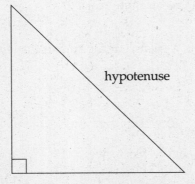

EVERYTHING ELSE YOU NEED TO KNOW ABOUT TRIANGLES

1. The sides of a triangle are in the same proportion as its angles. For example, in the triangle below, which is the longest side?

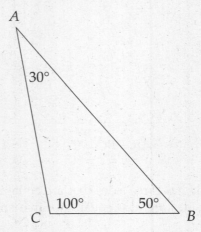

Remembering how to order the 1, 2, √3 sides of a 30-60-90 triangle is easy if you remind yourself that the largest side goes opposite the largest angle and the smallest side opposite the smallest angle, *and* if you remind yourself that √3 is roughly 1.7, okay?

The longest side is opposite the largest angle. The longest side in the triangle above is *AB*. The next longest side would be *AC*.

2. One side of a triangle can never be longer than the sum of the lengths of the other two sides of the triangle, or less than their difference. Why? Look at the diagram below:

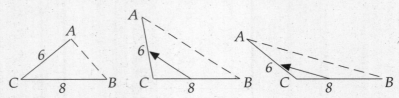

At the point where angle *ACB* = 180 degrees, this figure ceases to be a triangle. Angle *ACB* becomes 180 degrees when side *AB* equals the sum of the other two sides, in this case 6 + 8. Side *AB* can never quite reach 14.

By the same token, if we make angle *ACB* smaller and smaller, at some point, when angle *ACB* = 0 degrees, the figure also ceases to be a triangle. Angle *ACB* becomes 0 degrees when side *AB* equals the difference of the other two sides, in this case 8 – 6. So *AB* can never quite reach 2.

3. The *perimeter* of a triangle is the sum of the lengths of the three sides.

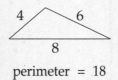

perimeter = 18

4. The *area* of a triangle is equal to $\dfrac{\text{height} \times \text{base}}{2}$

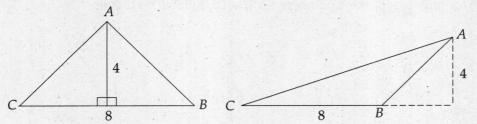

In both of the above triangles, the area = $\dfrac{4 \times 8}{2}$ = 16.

In a right triangle, the height also happens to be one of the sides of the triangle:

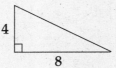

5. Don't expect triangles to be right side up:

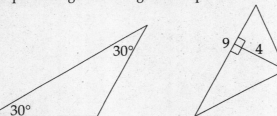

This is an *isosceles* triangle.   The area of this triangle is $\dfrac{9 \times 4}{2}$, or 18.

6. In a right triangle, the square of the hypotenuse equals the sum of the squares of the other two sides. In the triangle below:

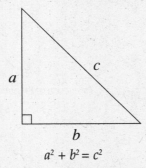

$$a^2 + b^2 = c^2$$

This is called the *Pythagorean Theorem*. ETS loves to test this theorem, but usually you won't actually have to make use of it if you've memorized a few of the most common right-triangle proportions. The Pythagorean triangle that comes up most frequently on the GMAT is one that has sides of lengths 3, 4, and 5, or multiples of those numbers. Look at the following examples:

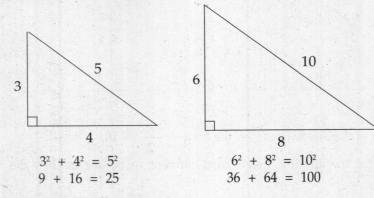

$$3^2 + 4^2 = 5^2 \qquad 6^2 + 8^2 = 10^2$$
$$9 + 16 = 25 \qquad 36 + 64 = 100$$

Some other Pythagorean triangles:

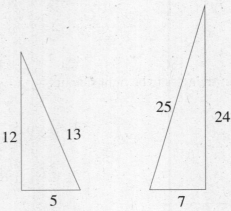

There are two other kinds of right triangles that ETS loves to test. These are a little complicated to remember, but they come up so often that they're worth memorizing.

7. A *right isosceles* triangle is one that always has the following proportions:

For example:

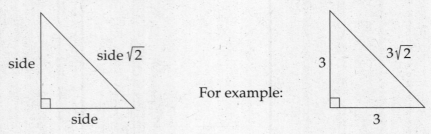

8. A *30-60-90* triangle is one that always has the following proportions:

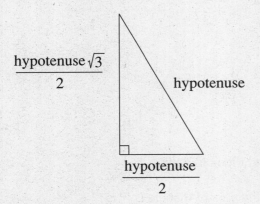

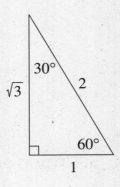

DRILL 6 (Triangles)

Find the value of the variables in the following problems. The answers can be found on page 278.

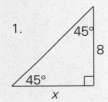

4. What value must x be less than in the triangle below? What value must x be greater than?

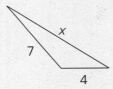

5. In the square *ABCD* below, what is the value of line segment *AC*?

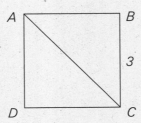

6. In the triangle below, what is the value of the line segment *BC*?

A real GMAT triangle problem might look like this:

7. In the diagram below, if the area of triangle *LNP* is 32, then what is the area of triangle *LMN*?

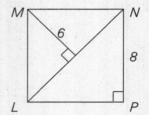

Note: Figure not drawn to scale.

○ 24

○ $24\sqrt{2}$

○ $24\sqrt{3}$

○ 32

○ 48

CIRCLES

A line connecting any two points on a circle is called a *chord*. The distance from the center of the circle to any point on the circle is called the *radius*. The distance from one point on the circle through the center of the circle to another point on the circle is called the *diameter*. The diameter is equal to twice the radius.

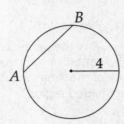

radius = 4
diameter = 8
AB is a chord

The rounded portion of the circle between points *A* and *B* is called an *arc*. The *area* of a circle is equal to πr^2.

The *circumference* (the length of the entire outer edge of the circle) is equal to $2\pi r$ or πd.

DRILL 7 (Circles)

Answer the following questions. The answers can be found on page 278.

1. In the circle below with center O, what is the area of the circle? What is the circumference?

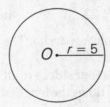

2. If the area of a circle is 36π, what is the circumference?

3. In the circle below with center O, if the arc *RT* is equal to $\dfrac{1}{6}$ of the circumference, what is the value of angle *x*?

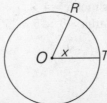

A real GMAT circle problem might look like this:

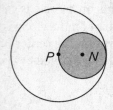

4. In the figure above, *P* is the center of the larger circle, and *N* is the center of the smaller, shaded circle. If the radius of the smaller circle is 5, what is the area of the unshaded region?

○ 100π
○ 75π
○ 25π
○ 20π
○ 10π

RECTANGLES, SQUARES, AND OTHER FOUR-SIDED OBJECTS

A four-sided figure is called a *quadrilateral*. The perimeter of any four-sided object is the sum of the lengths of its sides. A *rectangle* is a quadrilateral whose four interior angles are each equal to 90 degrees.

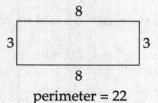

perimeter = 22

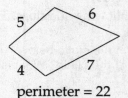

perimeter = 22

The area of a rectangle is *length × width*. The area of the rectangle above is therefore 3 × 8, or 24.

A *square* is a rectangle whose four sides are all equal in length. The perimeter of a square is therefore just four times the length of one side. The area of a square is the length of one of its sides squared. For example,

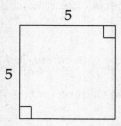

perimeter = 4 × 5 = 20
area = 5 × 5 = 25

A *parallelogram* is a quadrilateral in which the two pairs of opposite sides are parallel to each other and equal to each other, and in which opposite angles are equal to each other. A rectangle is obviously a parallelogram, but so is a figure like this:

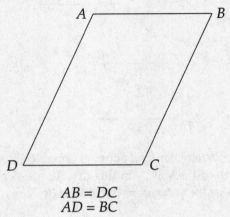

$$AB = DC$$
$$AD = BC$$

Angle ADC = angle ABC, and angle DAB = angle DCB.
The area of a parallelogram equals *base × height*.

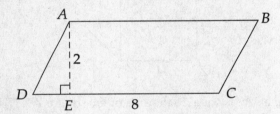

The area of parallelogram $ABCD$ = 8×2 = 16. (If you are having trouble picturing this, imagine cutting off triangular region ADE and sticking it onto the other end of the figure. What you get is a rectangle with dimensions 8 by 2.)

SOLIDS, VOLUME, AND SURFACE AREA

The GMAT will occasionally ask you to find the volume or surface area of a three-dimensional object.

Advanced Principle #1: Advance!

With GMAT geometry, just get going. Wade in there and do something. With each piece you add to the puzzle the next piece to look for becomes evident.

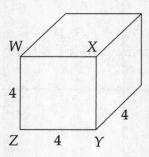

The volume of the *rectangular solid* above is equal to the area of the rectangle *ABCD* times the depth of the solid—in this case 12 × 6, or 72. Another way to think of it is *length × width × depth* = 3 × 4 × 6, or 72.

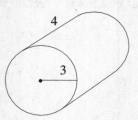

The volume of a *cube* is equal to the area of the square *WXYZ* times the depth of the cube, or again, *length × width × depth*. In the case of a cube, the length, width, and depth are all the same, so the volume of a cube is always the length of any side, cubed. The volume of this cube is 4 × 4 × 4, or 64.

The volume of a *cylinder* is equal to the area of the circular base times the depth. The area of this circle is 9π. Thus the volume of the cylinder is 36π.

You may need to find the surface area of a solid. Surface area is just the sum of the areas of all the two-dimensional outer surfaces of the object. The surface area of a rectangular solid is just the sum of the two-dimensional areas of each of the six faces of the solid. For example, in the rectangular solid below, the surface area would be

Face 1:	3	×	4	= 12
Face 2:	3	×	4	= 12
Face 3:	3	×	2	= 6
Face 4:	3	×	2	= 6
Face 5:	4	×	2	= 8
Face 6:	4	×	2	= $\frac{8}{52}$

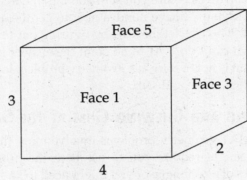

GMAT GEOMETRY: ADVANCED PRINCIPLES

All geometry problems (even easy ones) involve more than one step. Remember the first problem we looked at in this chapter?

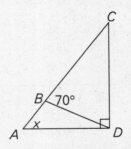

In the figure above, if *BC* = *CD* and angle *ADC* = 90 degrees, then what is the value of *x*?

- ○ 45
- ○ 50
- ○ 70
- ○ 75
- ○ 100

Here's how to crack it

Just by looking at the figure, we were able to eliminate answer choices (C), (D), and (E). Now let's solve the problem using geometry. The figure includes two—actually three—different triangles: *ABD, BCD,* and *ACD*. ETS wants even this easy problem to be a little challenging; there must be more than one step involved. To find angle *x*, which is part of triangles *ABD* and *ACD*, we must first work on triangle *BCD*.

What do we know about triangle BCD? The problem itself tells us that BC = CD. This is an isosceles triangle. Since angle DBC equals 70, so does angle BDC. Angle BCD must therefore equal 180 minus the other two angles. Angle BCD = 40. In the diagram, write in the measure of angle BCD.

Now look at the larger triangle, ACD. We know that angle ACD = 40, and that angle ADC = 90. What does angle x equal? Angle x equals 180 minus the other two angles, or 50 degrees. The answer is choice (B).

With GMAT geometry you shouldn't expect to be able to see every step a problem involves before you start solving it. Often, arriving at the right answer involves saying, "I have no idea how to get the answer, but since the problem says that BC = CD, let me *start* by figuring out the other angle of that triangle. Now what can I do?" At some point the answer usually becomes obvious. The main point is not to stare at a geometry problem looking for a complete solution. Just wade in there and *start*.

WALKING AND CHEWING GUM AT THE SAME TIME

Most GMAT geometry problems involve more than one geometric concept. A problem might require you to use both the properties of a triangle and the properties of a rectangle; or you might need to know the formula for the volume of a cube in order to find the dimensions of a cube's surface area. The difficult geometry problems do not test more complicated concepts—they just pile up easier concepts.

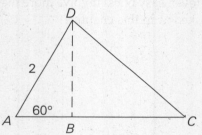

In the figure above, if a line segment connecting points B and D is perpendicular to AC, and the area of triangle ADC is $\dfrac{3\sqrt{3}}{2}$, then BC =

○ $\sqrt{2}$

○ $\sqrt{3}$

○ 2

○ $3\sqrt{3}$

○ 6

Here's how to crack it

We already got the correct answer to this question by measuring; now let's solve it using geometry. If we draw in the line DB (which is perpendicular to AC), we form a 30-60-90 triangle on the left side of the diagram (triangle ADB). The hypotenuse of this triangle is 2. Using the rules we've learned, the measurements of triangle ADB are as follows:

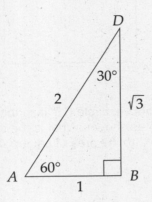

Thus $DB = \sqrt{3}$. At first you might think we're no closer to the solution, but don't despair. Just look for somewhere else to start. The problem tells us that the area of triangle ADC is $\dfrac{3\sqrt{3}}{2}$. The area of a triangle is $\dfrac{\text{base} \times \text{height}}{2}$. DB is the height. Let's find out what the base is. In other words, $\dfrac{\text{base} \times \sqrt{3}}{2} = \dfrac{3\sqrt{3}}{2}$, so the base equals 3. We know from the 30-60-90 triangle that $AB = 1$. What is BC? 2. The answer is choice (C).

PLUGGING IN ON GEOMETRY?

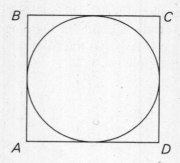

In the figure above, circle C is inscribed inside square *ABCD* as shown. What is the ratio of the area of circle C to the area of square *ABCD*?

○ $\dfrac{\pi}{2}$

○ $\dfrac{4}{\pi}$

○ $\dfrac{\pi}{3}$

○ $\dfrac{\pi}{4}$

○ $\dfrac{2}{\pi}$

Here's how to crack it

We already saw this problem in the first half of the chapter when we discussed eliminating crazy answers. As you recall, we were able to eliminate answer choices (A), (B), and (C) because we determined that the correct answer had to be the ratio of a smaller number to a bigger number.

Now let's solve this problem completely. You may have noticed that the answer choices do not contain *specific numbers* for the areas of the two figures—all we have here are *ratios* in the answer choices. Sound familiar? That's right! This is just another cosmic problem, and the best way to solve it is to plug in.

To find the area of the circle, we need a radius. Let's just pick one—3. If the radius is 3, the area of the circle is 9π. Now let's tackle the square. The circle is inscribed inside the square, which means that the diameter of the circle is also the length of the side of the square. Since the radius of the circle is 3, the diameter is 6. Therefore the side of the square is 6, and the area is 36.

The problem asks for the ratio of the area of the circle to the area of the square:

$$\frac{9\pi}{36} = \frac{\pi}{4} \qquad \text{The answer is choice (D).}$$

SUMMARY

1. While the geometry found on the GMAT is rudimentary, you will have to memorize all of the formulas that you'll need because they are not provided on the test.

2. Always study any problem drawn to scale very closely in order to eliminate crazy answer choices.

3. You must know the following approximate values: $\pi \approx 3$ $\sqrt{2} \approx 1.4$ $\sqrt{3} \approx 1.7$

4. You must be familiar with the size of certain common angles:

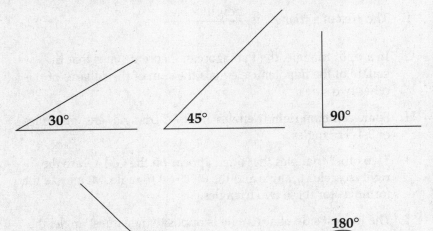

5. You can estimate problem-solving diagrams very precisely by using the edge of your scratch paper as a ruler.

6. You can *never* estimate from drawings on Data Sufficiency problems.

7. When no diagram is provided, draw your own, and make it to scale.

8. When the diagram is not drawn to scale, redraw it.

9. Degrees and angles:

   A. A circle contains 360 degrees.

   B. When you think about angles, remember circles.

   C. A line is a 180-degree angle.

   D. When two lines intersect, four angles are formed, but in reality there are only two pairs of identical angles.

   E. When two parallel lines are cut by a third line, eight angles are formed, but in reality there are only two sets of identical angles: a set of big ones and a set of little ones.

10. Triangles:

  A. Every triangle contains 180 degrees.

  B. An equilateral triangle has three equal sides and three equal angles, each of which measures 60 degrees.

  C. An isosceles triangle has two equal sides, and the angles opposite those sides are also equal.

  D. A right triangle contains one 90-degree angle.

  E. The perimeter of a triangle is the sum of the lengths of its sides.

  F. The area of a triangle is $\dfrac{\text{height} \times \text{base}}{2}$.

  G. In a right triangle, the Pythagorean theorem states that the square of the hypotenuse equals the sum of the squares of the other two sides.

  H. Some common right triangles are 3-4-5 triangles and multiples of 3-4-5 triangles.

  I. Two other triangles that often appear on the GMAT are the right isosceles triangle and the 30-60-90 triangle. Memorize the formulas for these two triangles.

  J. The longest side of a triangle is opposite the largest angle; the shortest side is opposite the smallest angle.

  K. One side of a triangle can never be as large as the sum of the two remaining sides, nor can it ever be as small as the difference of the two remaining sides.

11. Circles:

   A. The circumference of a circle is $2\pi r$ or πd, where r is the radius of the circle and d is the diameter.

   B. The area of a circle is πr^2, where r is the radius of the circle.

12. Rectangles, squares, and other four-sided objects:

   A. Any four-sided object is called a quadrilateral.

   B. The perimeter of a quadrilateral is the sum of the lengths of the four sides.

   C. The area of a rectangle, or of a square, is equal to length times width.

   D. The area of a parallelogram is equal to altitude times base.

13. Solids and volume:

   A. The volume of most objects is equal to their two-dimensional area times their depth.

   B. The volume of a rectangular solid is equal to length times width times depth.

   C. The volume of a cylinder is equal to the area of the circular base times depth.

14. GMAT geometry problems always involve more than one step, and difficult GMAT geometry problems may layer several concepts. Don't be intimidated if you don't see the entire process that's necessary to solve the problem. Start somewhere. You'll be amazed at how often you arrive at the answer.

12
Data Sufficiency

About half of the 37 math questions on the GMAT will be Data Sufficiency questions. Such questions exist on no other test in the world.

WHAT IS DATA SUFFICIENCY?

Data Sufficiency *is* weird. For the vast majority of students it is also the easiest question type to improve on. At the moment you may hate Data Sufficiency; you might have looked at it once and said, "This is too bizarre, I can't deal." Mostly, Data Sufficiency is just new. Follow this chapter closely, and your score should soar.

This type of question requires some getting used to. When you take the exam, you may notice that some of the people sitting at computers nearby will spend at least the first ten minutes of the math section just reading the directions for Data Sufficiency. To avoid being one of those unfortunate people, look at our version of the directions:

Directions: Each of the data sufficiency problems below consists of a question and two statements, labeled (1) and (2), in which certain data are given. You have to decide whether the data given in the statements are <u>sufficient</u> for answering the question. Using the data given in the statements <u>plus</u> your knowledge of mathematics and everyday facts (such as the number of days in July or the meaning of *counterclockwise*), you are to fill in oval

○ if statement (1) ALONE is sufficient, but statement (2) alone is not sufficient to answer the question asked;

○ if statement (2) ALONE is sufficient, but statement (1) alone is not sufficient to answer the question asked;

○ if BOTH statements (1) and (2) TOGETHER are sufficient to answer the question asked, but NEITHER statement ALONE is sufficient;

○ if EACH statement ALONE is sufficient to answer the question asked;

○ if statements (1) and (2) TOGETHER are NOT sufficient to answer the question asked, and additional data specific to the problem are needed.

Numbers: All numbers used are real numbers.

Figures: A figure in a data sufficiency problem will conform to the information given in the question, but will not necessarily conform to the additional information given in statements (1) and (2).

You may assume that lines shown as straight are straight and that angle measures are greater than zero.

You may assume that the position of points, angles, regions, etc., exist in the order shown.

All figures lie in a plane unless otherwise indicated.

Note: In questions that ask for the value of a quantity, the data given in the statements are sufficient only when it is possible to determine exactly one numerical value for the quantity.

Example:

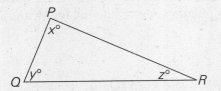

In $\triangle PQR$, what is the value of x?

(1) $PQ = PR$

(2) $y = 40$

Explanation: According to statement (1), $PQ = PR$; therefore, $\triangle PQR$ is isosceles and $y = z$. Since $x + y + z = 180$, $x + 2y = 180$. Since statement (1) does not give a value for y, you cannot answer the question using statement (1) by itself. According to statement (2), $y = 40$; therefore, $x + z = 140$. Since statement (2) does not give a value for z, you cannot answer the question using statement (2) by itself. Using both statements together, you can find y and z; therefore, you can find x, and the answer to the problem is C.

Basic Principles

You can see why it is absolutely necessary to learn these directions NOW. You shouldn't even have to glance at them when you take the test. Let's start with a simple example:

Example 1

What is x?
(1) $2x + 4 = 14$
(2) $x + y = 7$

○   if statement (1) ALONE is sufficient, but statement (2) alone is not sufficient to answer the question asked;

○   if statement (2) ALONE is sufficient, but statement (1) alone is not sufficient to answer the question asked;

○   if BOTH statements (1) and (2) TOGETHER are sufficient to answer the question asked, but NEITHER statement ALONE is sufficient;

○   if EACH statement ALONE is sufficient to answer the question asked;

○   if statements (1) and (2) TOGETHER are NOT sufficient to answer the question asked, and additional data specific to the problem are needed.

Here's how to crack it

Cover up statement (2). Based on statement (1) *alone,* can we answer the question "What is x?" Yes. Using algebraic manipulation, we can do the following:

$$2x + 4 = 14$$
$$\underline{-\;\;\;\;4\;\;\;\;-4}$$
$$2x = 10 \qquad \text{So } x = 5$$

Note that the question isn't asking us what x equals. The question asks only whether the information provided is sufficient to *find out* what x equals.

In this case it is. Statement (1) gives us enough information to answer the question "What is x?"

If statement (1) is sufficient, you have narrowed your answer choice down to two possibilities:

○   if statement (1) ALONE is sufficient, but
    statement (2) alone is not sufficient to
    answer the question asked;

           or

○   if EACH statement ALONE is sufficient to
    answer the question asked;

Now forget you ever saw statement (1). Cover it up with your finger and look only at statement (2). Based on statement (2) *alone,* can we find a single value for x?

No. The statement tells us that $x + y = 7$, in which case there are many possible values of x: If y equaled 2, then x could equal 5. On the other hand, if y equaled 3, then x could equal 4. Statement (2) is *not* sufficient to give us a single value for x.

Since (1) is sufficient and (2) is not, the answer to this question is

○   if statement (1) ALONE is sufficient, but
    statement (2) alone is not sufficient to
    answer the question asked;

Because this answer choice is always the *first* one listed, we like to refer to it as choice (A).

Let's look at the same problem with the two statements reversed:

The Equation Rule I

You must have as many equations as you have variables for the data to be sufficient. For example: $x = y + 1$ cannot be solved without another *distinct* equation. For more on this see page 95 in the section on solving simultaneous equations.

Example 2

What is x?

(1) $x + y = 7$
(2) $2x + 4 = 14$

○   if statement (1) ALONE is sufficient, but statement (2) alone is not sufficient to answer the question asked;

○   if statement (2) ALONE is sufficient, but statement (1) alone is not sufficient to answer the question asked;

○   if BOTH statements (1) and (2) TOGETHER are sufficient to answer the question asked, but NEITHER statement ALONE is sufficient;

○   if EACH statement ALONE is sufficient to answer the question asked;

○   if statements (1) and (2) TOGETHER are NOT sufficient to answer the question asked, and additional data specific to the problem are needed.

The Equation Rule II (part i)

Just because there is only one variable doesn't mean an equation has *just one solution*. When an equation has one variable and that variable is to an *odd* power the equation has only one solution.

Here's how to crack it

Cover up statement (2) and look at statement (1). Well, we know from the previous example that $x + y = 7$ does not give us a single value for x. So this time statement (1) is *not* sufficient.

In the first example, by deciding that statement (1) was sufficient, we narrowed our answer down to choice (A) or (D).

In this example, however, because (1) is *not* sufficient, we can eliminate answer choices (A) and (D).

Now cover up statement (1) and look at statement (2). Well, we already know from the first example that $2x + 4 = 14$ gives us a single value for x.

Since we know that (2) is sufficient, but (1) is not, the answer is

○   if statement (2) ALONE is sufficient, but statement (1) alone is not sufficient to answer the question asked;

Because this answer choice is always the *second* one listed, we like to refer to it as choice (B).

SCRATCH PAPER AND DATA SUFFICIENCY

Because Data Sufficiency is potentially so confusing, it is extremely important that test takers take advantage of their scratch paper to make notes. The first step in doing this is getting used to thinking of the five answer choices as A,B,C,D, and E.

Again, here are the answer choices that you'll see on the test, and the letters we strongly suggest that you think of them as:

○ if statement (1) ALONE is sufficient, but statement (2) alone is not sufficient to answer the question asked; = A

○ if statement (2) ALONE is sufficient, but statement (1) alone is not sufficient to answer the question asked; = B

○ if BOTH statements (1) and (2) TOGETHER are sufficient to answer the question asked, but NEITHER statement ALONE is sufficient; = C

○ if EACH statement ALONE is sufficient to answer the question asked; = D

○ if statements (1) and (2) TOGETHER are NOT sufficient to answer the question asked, and additional data specific to the problem are needed. = E

Example 3

What is x?

(1) $x + y = 7$
(2) $y = 2$

○ if statement (1) ALONE is sufficient, but statement (2) alone is not sufficient to answer the question asked;

○ if statement (2) ALONE is sufficient, but statement (1) alone is not sufficient to answer the question asked;

○ if BOTH statements (1) and (2) TOGETHER are sufficient to answer the question asked, but NEITHER statement ALONE is sufficient;

○ if EACH statement ALONE is sufficient to answer the question asked;

○ if statements (1) and (2) TOGETHER are NOT sufficient to answer the question asked, and additional data specific to the problem are needed.

Here's how to crack it

Cover up statement (2) and look only at statement (1). By itself, (1) is not sufficient to answer the question. Eliminate answer choices (A) and (D).

Cover up statement (1) and look at statement (2). By itself, this statement tells us what y equals, but we need a value for x. Eliminate answer choice (B).

We're down to answer choice (C) or (E).

Now let's look at the two statements at the same time. Since we know from the second statement that $y = 2$, we can substitute for y in the first statement. Now it reads $x + 2 = 7$.

Do we have a single value for x? You bet!

Since neither statement by itself is sufficient, but both statements together are sufficient, the answer is choice (C).

Example 4

What is x?

(1) $2x + 4 = 14$
(2) $3x = 15$

○ if statement (1) ALONE is sufficient, but statement (2) alone is not sufficient to answer the question asked;

○ if statement (2) ALONE is sufficient, but statement (1) alone is not sufficient to answer the question asked;

○ if BOTH statements (1) and (2) TOGETHER are sufficient to answer the question asked, but NEITHER statement ALONE is sufficient;

○ if EACH statement ALONE is sufficient to answer the question asked;

○ if statements (1) and (2) TOGETHER are NOT sufficient to answer the question asked, and additional data specific to the problem are needed.

Here's how to crack it

Cover up statement (2). Based on statement (1) *alone*, can we get a single value for x? Yes. Using algebraic manipulation, we can determine that $x = 5$.

Since statement (1) is sufficient, we are already down to two possible answer choices: (A) or (D).

Now cover up statement (1). Based on statement (2) *alone*, can we get a single value for x? Yes. Using algebraic manipulation, we again find that $x = 5$.

Since each statement alone is sufficient, the answer is choice (D).

Example 5

What is x?

(1) $x + y = 7$
(2) $y + z = 3$

○ if statement (1) ALONE is sufficient, but statement (2) alone is not sufficient to answer the question asked;

○ if statement (2) ALONE is sufficient, but statement (1) alone is not sufficient to answer the question asked;

○ if BOTH statements (1) and (2) TOGETHER are sufficient to answer the question asked, but NEITHER statement ALONE is sufficient;

○ if EACH statement ALONE is sufficient to answer the question asked;

○ if statements (1) and (2) TOGETHER are NOT sufficient to answer the question asked, and additional data specific to the problem are needed.

Equation Tricks and Traps

$x + 3y - 7 = x^2(x^{-1}) + y$
This looks like two variables in one equation, which would mean we need at least one more equation to solve, but look again. Since $x^2(x^{-1}) = x^{(2-1)} = x$, each side of the equation has only one x. The xs can be subtracted, leaving you with just one variable, y. The equation can be solved.

Here's how to crack it

Cover up statement (2). Based on statement (1) alone, can we get a single value for x? No. Eliminate answer choices (A) and (D).

Cover up statement (1). Based on statement (2) alone, we still can't arrive at a single value for x. Eliminate answer choice (B).

We're down to answer choice (C) or (E).

Looking at both statements together, can we find a single value for x?

No. Because there are three different variables in the two equations, x could have many different values.

Since statements (1) and (2) are not sufficient by themselves *or* together, the answer is choice (E).

Drill 8 (Data Sufficiency Basics)

The answers can be found on page 279.

1. What is the value of x?
   - (1) $x^2 = 4$
   - (2) $x < 0$

   - ○ statement (1) BY ITSELF is sufficient to answer the question but statement (2) is not sufficient by itself;
   - ○ statement (2) BY ITSELF is sufficient to answer the question but statement (1) is not sufficient by itself;
   - ○ neither statement is sufficient by itself, but the two statements IN COMBINATION are sufficient to answer the question;
   - ○ EACH statement by itself is sufficient to answer the question;
   - ○ NEITHER statement (1) nor statement (2) is sufficient to answer the question separately or in combination.

2. What is the value of xy?
   - (1) $x^2 = 4$
   - (2) $y = 0$

   - ○ statement (1) BY ITSELF is sufficient to answer the question but statement (2) is not sufficient by itself;
   - ○ statement (2) BY ITSELF is sufficient to answer the question but statement (1) is not sufficient by itself;
   - ○ neither statement is sufficient by itself, but the two statements IN COMBINATION are sufficient to answer the question;
   - ○ EACH statement by itself is sufficient to answer the question;
   - ○ NEITHER statement (1) nor statement (2) is sufficient to answer the question separately or in combination.

3. What is the value of xy?

   (1) $x^2 = 4$
   (2) $y^2 = 9$

   ○ statement (1) BY ITSELF is sufficient to answer the question but statement (2) is not sufficient by itself;

   ○ statement (2) BY ITSELF is sufficient to answer the question but statement (1) is not sufficient by itself;

   ○ neither statement is sufficient by itself, but the two statements IN COMBINATION are sufficient to answer the question;

   ○ EACH statement by itself is sufficient to answer the question;

   ○ NEITHER statement (1) nor statement (2) is sufficient to answer the question separately or in combination.

DANISH DATA SUFFICIENCY

In the examples above you may have noticed that we were already using the Process of Elimination. In Data Sufficiency a little knowledge goes a long way. Suppose you saw the following Data Sufficiency problem:

How tall is Frank?

(1) Frank is 6′2″.
(2) Frank er en stor mand.

○ if statement (1) ALONE is sufficient, but statement (2) alone is not sufficient to answer the question asked;

○ if statement (2) ALONE is sufficient, but statement (1) alone is not sufficient to answer the question asked;

○ if BOTH statements (1) and (2) TOGETHER are sufficient to answer the question asked, but NEITHER statement ALONE is sufficient;

○ if EACH statement ALONE is sufficient to answer the question asked;

○ if statements (1) and (2) TOGETHER are NOT sufficient to answer the question asked, and additional data specific to the problem are needed.

Equation Tricks and Traps

Some equations are not distinct. When one equation can be multiplied to equal the other equation, the equations are not distinct. For example:
$$x + y = 4$$
$$4x + 4y = 16$$
These are not distinct equations. There is not enough data yet to solve for x or y.

When we don't know something about a problem, our first impulse is just to skip the whole thing. On the computer-adaptive GMAT, of course, you can't do that; to get to the next question, you have to answer the one you're on. So should you guess at random?

Since you probably don't speak Danish, you have no idea whether the second statement is sufficient to answer the question.

However, it would be a mistake to guess at random.

Heads You Win; Tails You Lose

Let's focus on what you DO know. Cover up statement (2). Based on statement (1) *alone*, do you know how tall Frank is? Of course. He is 6'2". Since statement (1) is sufficient, the answer to this question is either

    A. Statement (1) alone is sufficient

       or

    D. EACH statement ALONE is sufficient

By using POE, you've narrowed your choice down to two possibilities. You now have a fifty-fifty chance of getting this question correct, even though you have no idea what statement (2) means.

On Scratch Paper, It Comes Down to AD or BCE

Just by figuring out whether or not the first statement answers the question, you've done some great eliminating. If the first statement works, you are down to A or D. If it doesn't, you're down to the remaining choices: B, C, or E.

AD or BCE. Memorize it; these are *always* your options. And it makes sense to write it down this way on your scratch paper. If the first statement answers the question by itself, write down AD on your scratch paper. Then cover up statement (1) and look at statement (2). If (2) also answers the question, circle D on your scratch paper and mark it on your computer screen. If it doesn't, circle A on your scratch paper and mark it on your screen.

If the first statement does NOT answer the question, then write down BCE on your scratch paper. Then cover up statement (1) and look at statement (2). If (2) answers the question by itself, you're done: Circle B on your scratch paper and pick it on your screen. If (2) does not answer the question by itself, cross off B. You're down to C or E.

Equation Tricks and Traps

Sometimes ETS will ask you for the value of two variables put together, for example, what is the value of $(x + y)$? Don't think of this as solving for two variables. It is the same as solving for the expression as a whole.
For example:
$4x + 4y = 16$
has a solution. Divide both sides by 4: $x + y = 4$.

MORE DANISH DATA SUFFICIENCY

As long as you know *something* about a Data Sufficiency problem, you can do some shrewd guessing. Look at the following problem:

How tall is Frank?

(1) Frank is pretty tall.

(2) Frank es en stor mand.

○ if statement (1) ALONE is sufficient, but statement (2) alone is not sufficient to answer the question asked;

○ if statement (2) ALONE is sufficient, but statement (1) alone is not sufficient to answer the question asked;

○ if BOTH statements (1) and (2) TOGETHER are sufficient to answer the question asked, but NEITHER statement ALONE is sufficient;

○ if EACH statement ALONE is sufficient to answer the question asked;

○ if statements (1) and (2) TOGETHER are NOT sufficient to answer the question asked, and additional data specific to the problem are needed.

Since statement (1) does not give you a specific height, it is not sufficient to answer the question. So what are you down to? BCE. Write it down on your scratch paper. Now, let's cover it up and look at statement (2). Based on statement (2) *alone*, can you tell exactly how tall Frank is? Well, again, not unless you speak Danish.

By using POE in this case, you've narrowed your choice down to three possibilities—a one-in-three shot—even though the only thing you knew for certain about this problem was that one of the statements *did not* work.

Can't Make Heads or Tails of the First Statement?

If you're having trouble understanding the first statement, skip it for a minute and look at the second statement. If it is sufficient, you can eliminate answer choices (A), (C), and (E) and be down to a fifty-fifty guess—choice (B) or (D). If it is not sufficient, you can eliminate answer choices (B) and (D), and have a one-in-three shot at getting the problem right.

Look at the following problem:

How tall is Frank?

(1)   Frank er en stor mand.
(2)   Frank is pretty tall.

○   if statement (1) ALONE is sufficient, but statement (2) alone is not sufficient to answer the question asked;

○   if statement (2) ALONE is sufficient, but statement (1) alone is not sufficient to answer the question asked;

○   if BOTH statements (1) and (2) TOGETHER are sufficient to answer the question asked, but NEITHER statement ALONE is sufficient;

○   if EACH statement ALONE is sufficient to answer the question asked;

○   if statements (1) and (2) TOGETHER are NOT sufficient to answer the question asked, and additional data specific to the problem are needed.

Since we have no idea what statement (1) says, let's cover it up and look at statement (2). Based on statement (2) *alone*, can you tell exactly how tall Frank is? Of course not. Since (2) is not sufficient, you can rule out choices (B) and (D).

By using POE in this case, you've narrowed your choice down to three possibilities—a one-in-three shot—even though the only thing you knew for certain about this problem was that one of the statements *did not* work.

Data Sufficiency Math versus Problem Solving Math

In terms of mathematical content, Data Sufficiency problems test the same kinds of topics tested by the regular math problems. You'll find problems involving integers, percents, averages, ratios, algebra, and geometry. Only the format is different.

Let's do a "regular" math problem and then turn it into a Data Sufficiency problem.

A certain factory has filled 92 orders. If the total number of orders on file is 230, what percent of the orders have been filled?

○ 20%
○ 30%
○ 40%
○ 50%
○ 60%

If you've already done the math review in the preceding chapters, this problem should be pretty easy. It's a percent problem, and as soon as you see the word "percent," you should be thinking:

$$\frac{\text{part}}{\text{whole}} = \frac{92}{230} = \frac{x}{100}$$

(The answer, by the way, is (C), 40%.)

Now let's turn this same problem into a Data Sufficiency problem.

If a certain factory has filled 92 orders, what percent of the total number of orders has been filled?

(1)   The total number of orders on file is 230.
(2)   The number of orders the factory has already filled represents two-fifths of the total number of orders.

○ if statement (1) ALONE is sufficient, but statement (2) alone is not sufficient to answer the question asked;

○ if statement (2) ALONE is sufficient, but statement (1) alone is not sufficient to answer the question asked;

○ if BOTH statements (1) and (2) TOGETHER are sufficient to answer the question asked, but NEITHER statement ALONE is sufficient;

○ if EACH statement ALONE is sufficient to answer the question asked;

○ if statements (1) and (2) TOGETHER are NOT sufficient to answer the question asked, and additional data specific to the problem are needed.

Here's how to crack it

Although the problem is now in a different format, the math involved is exactly the same. Again, as soon as you see the word "percent," you should think

$$\frac{\text{part}}{\text{whole}}$$

Without looking at the two statements, let's look at the information contained in the question itself and set that up as a part-over-whole equation:

$$\frac{\text{part}}{\text{whole}} = \frac{92}{?} = \frac{x}{100}$$

As this equation stands, there is no way to find a value for x. We have the *part* (the number of orders that have already been filled), but we do not have the *whole* (total number of orders).

Cover up statement (2). Does statement (1) alone give us the missing whole? Yes, it does. Therefore, the answer to this question is either choice (A) or (D).

Now cover up statement (1). Statement (2) expresses the number of orders already filled as a fraction of the total number of orders. Remember, a fraction is *also* a part over whole. Let's see what we have:

$$\frac{\text{part}}{\text{whole}} \; \frac{2}{5} = \frac{x}{100}$$

Can we find a value for x in this equation? Of course. Therefore statement (2) is also sufficient, and the answer to this question is choice (D).

Drill 9

The answers can be found on pages 279–80.

1. How many people attended the Rose Seminar this year?

   (1)   70 people sent in deposits to attend the Rose Seminar this year.

   (2)   60% of the people who sent deposits to attend the Rose Seminar this year actually attended.

   ○   statement (1) BY ITSELF is sufficient to answer the question but statement (2) is not sufficient by itself;

   ○   statement (2) BY ITSELF is sufficient to answer the question but statement (1) is not sufficient by itself;

   ○   neither statement is sufficient by itself, but the two statements IN COMBINATION are sufficient to answer the question;

   ○   EACH statement by itself is sufficient to answer the question;

   ○   NEITHER statement (1) nor statement (2) is sufficient to answer the question separately or in combination.

2. Luxo paint contains only alcohol and pigment. What is the ratio of alcohol to pigment in Luxo paint?

(1) Exactly 7 ounces of pigment are contained in a 12-ounce can of Luxo paint.

(2) Exactly 5 ounces of alcohol are contained in a 12-ounce can of Luxo paint.

○ statement (1) BY ITSELF is sufficient to answer the question but statement (2) is not sufficient by itself;

○ statement (2) BY ITSELF is sufficient to answer the question but statement (1) is not sufficient by itself;

○ neither statement is sufficient by itself, but the two statements IN COMBINATION are sufficient to answer the question;

○ EACH statement by itself is sufficient to answer the question;

○ NEITHER statement (1) nor statement (2) is sufficient to answer the question separately or in combination.

3. A car drives along a straight road from Smithville to Laredo, going through Ferristown along the way. What is the total distance by car from Smithville to Laredo?

(1) The distance from Smithville to Ferristown is $\frac{3}{5}$ of the entire distance.

(2) The distance from Ferristown to Laredo is 12 miles.

○ statement (1) BY ITSELF is sufficient to answer the question but statement (2) is not sufficient by itself;

○ statement (2) BY ITSELF is sufficient to answer the question but statement (1) is not sufficient by itself;

○ neither statement is sufficient by itself, but the two statements IN COMBINATION are sufficient to answer the question;

○ EACH statement by itself is sufficient to answer the question;

○ NEITHER statement (1) nor statement (2) is sufficient to answer the question separately or in combination.

Math Is Math Is Math

All Data Sufficiency problems are just standard math problems in a new format. Look for the clue that tells you what to do, then see whether the two statements provide you with enough information to answer the question.

. . . Except on "Yes or No" Questions

Leave it to ETS to come up with a way to give you five different answer choices on a "yes or no" question. Let's look at an example:

> Did candidate x receive more than 40% of the 30,000 votes cast in the general election?
>
> (1) Candidate y received 45% of the votes.
> (2) Candidate x received exactly 11,000 votes.
>
> ○ if statement (1) ALONE is sufficient, but statement (2) alone is not sufficient to answer the question asked;
>
> ○ if statement (2) ALONE is sufficient, but statement (1) alone is not sufficient to answer the question asked;
>
> ○ if BOTH statements (1) and (2) TOGETHER are sufficient to answer the question asked, but NEITHER statement ALONE is sufficient;
>
> ○ if EACH statement ALONE is sufficient to answer the question asked;
>
> ○ if statements (1) and (2) TOGETHER are NOT sufficient to answer the question asked, and additional data specific to the problem are needed.

Here's how to crack it

When all is said and done, the answer to this question is either yes or no.

Cover up statement (2). Does statement (1) alone answer the question? If you were in a hurry, you might think so. Many people just assume that statement (1) is talking about candidate x—in which case, they get the problem wrong. Other people notice that statement (1) is talking about candidate y but assume that these are the only two candidates running in the election (in which case, since candidate y received 45%, candidate x must have received 55%). Since the problem doesn't *say* that there were only two candidates, statement (1) doesn't answer the question.

Now cover up statement (1) and let's look at statement (2). This seems more promising. Like the problem we saw earlier involving factory orders, this problem is also about percents, so again we think:

$$\frac{\text{part}}{\text{whole}} \quad \frac{11,000}{30,000} = \frac{x}{100}$$

Using algebraic manipulation, we learn that $x = 36.6\%$. At which point many people say, "The guy got less than 40%—this statement doesn't answer the question, either."

But they're wrong.

JUST SAY NO

Broken down to its basics, the question we were asked was, "Did he get more than 40% of the vote—yes or no?"

Statement (2) *does* answer the question. The answer is, "No, he didn't."

On a yes or no Data Sufficiency problem, if a statement answers the question in the "affirmative" *or* in the negative, it is sufficient. The answer to the question above is choice (B).

HOW TO KEEP IT ALL STRAIGHT

Since there will be several "yes or no" Data Sufficiency problems on your GMAT, it's a good idea to have a strategy. When yes or no questions involve variables, there's a good way to keep everything straight. Here's an example:

> Is x an integer?
>
> (1) $5x$ is a positive integer
> (2) $5x = 1$
>
> ⬭ if statement (1) ALONE is sufficient, but statement (2) alone is not sufficient to answer the question asked;
>
> ⬭ if statement (2) ALONE is sufficient, but statement (1) alone is not sufficient to answer the question asked;
>
> ⬭ if BOTH statements (1) and (2) TOGETHER are sufficient to answer the question asked, but NEITHER statement ALONE is sufficient;
>
> ⬭ if EACH statement ALONE is sufficient to answer the question asked;
>
> ⬭ if statements (1) and (2) TOGETHER are NOT sufficient to answer the question asked, and additional data specific to the problem are needed.

Here's how to crack it

As always, cover up statement (2). Look only at statement (1). Let's plug in a value for x, a number that anyone, even Joe Bloggs, might pick. How about 2? We know that $5 \times 2 = 10$, which is a positive integer. Is 2 an integer? Yes.

What we've just found is *one case* in which the answer to this question is yes. If x is *always* an integer, then the answer is always yes, and statement (1) is sufficient. If x is *never* an integer, the answer would always be no, and statement (1) would *still* be sufficient (remember, a sufficient answer to a "yes or no" question can be *no*).

But if statement (1) gives us an answer that is sometimes yes and sometimes no, then the statement is not sufficient.

By plugging in, we found *one case* in which the answer to the question is yes. Now all we need to do is see whether we can find *one case* in which the answer to the question is no. The statement says,

> (1) $5x$ is a positive integer

Most numbers we could plug in for x to make the statement true are integers. Is there ANY value of x that makes the statement true, but isn't an integer, itself? What if x were $\dfrac{1}{5}$?

We know that $5 \times \dfrac{1}{5} = 1$, which *is* a positive integer; but now x is *not* an integer. By plugging in $\dfrac{1}{5}$, we have found one case in which the answer is no. Since statement (1) gives us an answer that is sometimes yes and sometimes no, the statement is not sufficient. Now we're down to (B), (C), or (E).

Cover up statement (1) and look at statement (2):

    (2) $5x = 1$

To make this statement true, x *must* equal $\dfrac{1}{5}$. Is x an integer? No. We have now found *one case* in which the answer is no. Is there any other number we could plug in for x that would make the statement true? No.

Since statement (2) gives us an answer that is *always* no, the statement is sufficient, and the answer to this question is choice (B).

Dr. Livingstone, I Presume?

The test makers at ETS like to see whether they can get you to make careless assumptions. Here's an example:

> Two people went into an executive trainee program at the same time. How much more money per week does trainee A now earn than trainee B?
>
> (1)   Trainee A earns $300 per week more than she did when she began the program.
> (2)   Trainee B earns $100 more per week than she did when she began the program.
>
>   ◯ if statement (1) ALONE is sufficient, but statement (2) alone is not sufficient to answer the question asked;
>
>   ◯ if statement (2) ALONE is sufficient, but statement (1) alone is not sufficient to answer the question asked;
>
>   ◯ if BOTH statements (1) and (2) TOGETHER are sufficient to answer the question asked, but NEITHER statement ALONE is sufficient;
>
>   ◯ if EACH statement ALONE is sufficient to answer the question asked;
>
>   ◯ if statements (1) and (2) TOGETHER are NOT sufficient to answer the question asked, and additional data specific to the problem are needed.

Here's how to crack it

In this problem everyone's first impression is that the answer is choice (C) (both statements together are sufficient). Most people make the perfectly natural assumption that both trainees started at the same salary. But do we *know* this?

NEVER ASSUME

If you are answering questions from medium or difficult bins, you can never assume *anything*. The answer to this question is choice (E) because the two trainees may have had different starting salaries.

At a business dinner, people were offered coffee or tea. If all the diners had either coffee or tea, how many of the diners had tea?

(1) Of 60 people at the dinner, 10% had tea.
(2) Fifty-four people had coffee.

○ if statement (1) ALONE is sufficient, but statement (2) alone is not sufficient to answer the question asked;

○ if statement (2) ALONE is sufficient, but statement (1) alone is not sufficient to answer the question asked;

○ if BOTH statements (1) and (2) TOGETHER are sufficient to answer the question asked, but NEITHER statement ALONE is sufficient;

○ if EACH statement ALONE is sufficient to answer the question asked;

○ if statements (1) and (2) TOGETHER are NOT sufficient to answer the question asked, and additional data specific to the problem are needed.

Here's how to crack it

Statement (1) is sufficient because 10% of 60 = 6. Now look at statement (2). At first glance this seems sufficient as well. We just found out from statement (1) that there were a total of 60 people at the dinner. If 54 of them had coffee, then the other 6 had tea, which agrees with the number we got in statement (1). There is only one hitch: Statement (2) by itself does not tell us the total number of people at the dinner. We are subconsciously relying on information in statement (1).

Just Because One Statement Seems to Agree with the Other Doesn't Mean That it is Necessarily Saying the Same Thing

If statement (2) had said "two people had coffee," you might have eliminated it right away. But because it seemed to agree with statement (1), it became much more tempting. Just remember: When you look at statement (2), *always cover up statement (1) and forget you ever saw it.* The answer to this question is choice (A).

CRACKING DATA SUFFICIENCY: ADVANCED PRINCIPLES

It is particularly important to know your approximate GMAT scoring level when you're doing Data Sufficiency questions. If you will mainly be answering easy questions, then by concentrating on the principles we've shown you so far, you will get most of these questions right.

But if you will be answering mainly medium and difficult questions, then you have to learn to anticipate the level of complexity of medium and difficult Data Sufficiency problems. Some of the medium problems will contain traps that ETS hopes will trip you up. We'll show you some of ETS's favorite traps in just a minute.

On the difficult problems, virtually every question contains a trap. By learning to recognize the traps ETS has set for you, you can eliminate them. Sometimes all that remains is the correct answer.

JOE'S FAVORITE ANSWERS

Joe Bloggs's initial reaction to a difficult Data Sufficiency question is, "I don't know how to do this." This statement doesn't seem to help Joe in answering the question. Therefore on questions he perceives to be difficult, Joe's favorite answer is usually choice (E) (statements (1) and (2) TOGETHER are not sufficient).

His second favorite answer is choice (C) (BOTH statements TOGETHER are sufficient, but neither statement alone is sufficient). Joe likes choice (C) because he assumes that a difficult question like this one will need a lot of information.

Joe's favorite answers on tough Data Sufficiency questions are choices (E) and (C), but that doesn't mean that these will never be the answer to difficult questions. We should eliminate choice (E) and/or (C) *only* when they are Joe Bloggs's first or second impulse.

If $yz \neq 0$, what is the value of $\dfrac{x^4 y^3 z^2}{y^2 y^1 z^2}$?

(1) $x = 3$
(2) $y = 5$

○ if statement (1) ALONE is sufficient, but statement (2) alone is not sufficient to answer the question asked;

○ if statement (2) ALONE is sufficient, but statement (1) alone is not sufficient to answer the question asked;

○ if BOTH statements (1) and (2) TOGETHER are sufficient to answer the question asked, but NEITHER statement ALONE is sufficient;

○ if EACH statement ALONE is sufficient to answer the question asked;

○ if statements (1) and (2) TOGETHER are NOT sufficient to answer the question asked, and additional data specific to the problem are needed.

Here's how to crack it

If you know from practice tests that you will be seeing mainly medium and difficult math problems on the GMAT, you will know that this is a tough problem. Joe's *first* impulse here might be to pick answer choice (E). He sees an expression with xs, ys, and zs, but the two statements underneath give values only for x and y.

If Joe thinks for a minute, he might realize that there is a z^2 in the numerator and a z^2 in the denominator. These cancel out, eliminating all the zs in the expression. Joe's *second* impulse might be to pick answer choice (C). He now sees an equation with xs and ys, and assumes he will need values for both in order to answer the question.

Having eliminated Joe's answers, we're down to choices (A), (B), or (D). If that's as far as you have time to get on this problem, guess and move on. You have a one-in-three shot of getting it right—good odds.

The correct answer is answer choice (A). The $y^2 y^1$ in the denominator can be consolidated as y^3. The ys cancel out.

When Joe Thinks a Tough Question Is Easy

The only time the correct answer to a tough Data Sufficiency question will actually turn out to be (E) or (C) is when Joe is convinced that the question is easy.

What was the combined average attendance at games at Memorial Stadium for the months of June and July?

(1) The average attendance per game for the month of June was 23,100, and the average attendance per game for the month of July was 25,200.

(2) There were 20 games played in June at the stadium and 22 games played in July.

○ if statement (1) ALONE is sufficient, but statement (2) alone is not sufficient to answer the question asked;

○ if statement (2) ALONE is sufficient, but statement (1) alone is not sufficient to answer the question asked;

○ if BOTH statements (1) and (2) TOGETHER are sufficient to answer the question asked, but NEITHER statement ALONE is sufficient;

○ if EACH statement ALONE is sufficient to answer the question asked;

○ if statements (1) and (2) TOGETHER are NOT sufficient to answer the question asked, and additional data specific to the problem are needed.

Here's how to crack it

Joe thinks this is an easy one. Statement (1) gives us the average attendance for June and the average attendance for July. Joe probably decides this is sufficient by itself. He thinks you can get the total average of the two months by averaging the two averages. (You—having completed our chapter on arithmetic—know better.) Joe looks at statement (2) and doesn't see any attendance figures at all. He picks answer choice (A).

Because he is convinced that this is an easy question and that the answer is choice (A), Joe Bloggs never even considers his two favorite answers—choices (E) and (C). *This* time he *knows* he's right!

But, of course, he is wrong. The answer to this question is choice (C). An average is the *total* sum of values divided by the total number of values. We need to know the number of games in each month in order to find out the *total* number of people attending.

PUTTING IT ALL TOGETHER

Eliminating Joe Bloggs answers gives you an enormous advantage on Data Sufficiency problems. But by coupling this technique with POE, you can do even better. Remember our Danish question?

How tall is Frank?

(1)   Frank is 6'2".
(2)   Frank er en stor mand.

○   if statement (1) ALONE is sufficient, but statement (2) alone is not sufficient to answer the question asked;

○   if statement (2) ALONE is sufficient, but statement (1) alone is not sufficient to answer the question asked;

○   if BOTH statements (1) and (2) TOGETHER are sufficient to answer the question asked, but NEITHER statement ALONE is sufficient;

○   if EACH statement ALONE is sufficient to answer the question asked;

○   if statements (1) and (2) TOGETHER are NOT sufficient to answer the question asked, and additional data specific to the problem are needed.

Using POE and completely ignoring statement (2), we were able to get down to a fifty-fifty choice. Since statement (1) unequivocally answers the question, we knew the answer had to be choice (A) or (D). Now suppose you also knew that this was a tough question. How would you know? Because your scores on practice tests indicate that the ETS computer will mainly be throwing medium and difficult questions at you. We were already down to a fifty-fifty choice. The answer is choice (A) or (D).

Now, consider for a moment: Which of the two remaining choices does Joe like?

Since Joe doesn't know anything about statement (2), he'll probably choose (A). If this is a tough question, there's no way Joe's answer could be correct. In that case we'd better pick answer choice (D).

Here's one last example:

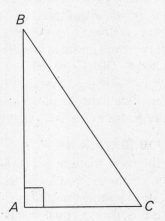

19. If the perimeter of right triangle *ABC* above is $3+3\sqrt{3}$, what is the area of the triangle?

(1) $AC \neq AB$.
(2)   Angle *ABC* = 30 degrees.

- ○ if statement (1) ALONE is sufficient, but statement (2) alone is not sufficient to answer the question asked;

- ○ if statement (2) ALONE is sufficient, but statement (1) alone is not sufficient to answer the question asked;

- ○ if BOTH statements (1) and (2) TOGETHER are sufficient to answer the question asked, but NEITHER statement ALONE is sufficient;

- ○ if EACH statement ALONE is sufficient to answer the question asked;

- ○ if statements (1) and (2) TOGETHER are NOT sufficient to answer the question asked, and additional data specific to the problem are needed.

Here's how to crack it

The area of a triangle is $\frac{1}{2}$ *base* × *height*. Joe looks at statements (1) and (2) and sees neither the length of the base nor the length of the height. Joe likes choice (E) a lot on this problem. He doesn't see how he can get the area of the triangle from this information. Joe might also be tempted by choice (C) just because it seems like he is being given an awful lot of information; maybe, he reasons, there's some formula he doesn't know about.

Let's look at the problem seriously now. Cover up statement (2). Statement (1) tells us only that two of the sides of the triangle are not equal. Is there any conceivable way that this information could help us find the base and the height of the triangle? No, statement (1) doesn't answer the question. Since statement (1) is not sufficient by itself, we can eliminate answer choices (A) and (D).

We are left with three choices: (B), (C), or (E).

Are any of these choices Joe Bloggs answers? Well, yes. We decided a moment ago that choice (E) was definitely Joe Bloggs and that, in fact, choice (C) might be as well. It therefore seems quite likely that the answer is choice (B).

Here's how ETS wants you to crack it

Statement (2) tells us that the right triangle is a 30-60-90 triangle. If you have already read our chapter on geometry, you know that the dimensions of a 30-60-90 triangle are always in the same proportion: The short side (the side opposite the 30-degree angle) is always equal to half the hypotenuse, and the middle side is always equal to the short side times $\sqrt{3}$. If we call the short side x, then the hypotenuse is $2x$ and the middle side is $x\sqrt{3}$. Thus the formula for the perimeter of a 30-60-90 triangle is $3x + x\sqrt{3}$, where x is the side opposite the 30-degree angle. If we set this equal to the actual perimeter of the triangle, we can solve for x.

$$3x + x\sqrt{3} = 3 + 3\sqrt{3}$$

After a lot of work solving for x, it turns out that $x = \sqrt{3}$. This is equal to the base of our triangle. We can now figure out the height, which would be the short side ($\sqrt{3}$) times $\sqrt{3}$, or 3. If we know the base and the height, we can figure out the area, which means that statement (2) is sufficient, and the answer is choice (B).

Wait a minute! If the base is $\sqrt{3}$ and the height is 3, doesn't this agree with statement (1) that $AC \neq AB$? Sure, but so what? Just because statement (1) seems to *agree* with statement (2) doesn't mean that it says the same thing.

THAT WAS A LOT OF WORK

This problem was very difficult and took a long time if you actually tried to solve it mathematically, the way ETS wanted you to. You will notice that we got the same answer within only a few seconds by using a combination of POE and the Joe Bloggs technique.

Using our method isn't infallible, but if you *know* you will mostly be answering tough questions, this technique will help you on problems you have neither the time nor the inclination to figure out mathematically.

SUMMARY

1. The instructions for Data Sufficiency questions are very complicated. Memorize them now. Here is a pared-down checklist:

    ○ if statement (1) ALONE is sufficient, but statement (2) alone is not sufficient to answer the question asked;

    ○ if statement (2) ALONE is sufficient, but statement (1) alone is not sufficient to answer the question asked;

    ○ if BOTH statements (1) and (2) TOGETHER are sufficient to answer the question asked, but NEITHER statement ALONE is sufficient;

    ○ if EACH statement ALONE is sufficient to answer the question asked;

    ○ if statements (1) and (2) TOGETHER are NOT sufficient to answer the question asked, and additional data specific to the problem are needed.

2. To aid in scratch-paper eliminations, think of these answer choices as A, B, C, D, and E.

3. Use the Process of Elimination to narrow down the field. If you *know* that one statement is sufficient, you are already down to a fifty-fifty guess: A or D. If you *know* that one statement is *not* sufficient, you are already down to a one-in-three guess: B, C, or E.

4. If you are stuck on statement (1), skip it and look at statement (2). POE will be just as helpful.

5. The math content of the Data Sufficiency questions is exactly the same as it is on the regular math questions.

6. As you would in the regular math problems, look for the clues that tell you how to solve Data Sufficiency problems.

7. On "yes or no" questions, a statement is sufficient if it always gives us the *same* answer: always yes or always no. If the answer is sometimes yes and sometimes no, the statement is insufficient.

8. On medium and difficult Data Sufficiency problems, you must be on guard against careless assumptions.

9. On *difficult* Data Sufficiency problems:

   ◆ If Joe Bloggs *thinks* the problem is difficult, his favorite answers are choices (E) ("there isn't enough information") and (C) ("this problem needs all the information it can get").

   ◆ If Joe Bloggs thinks the problem is easy, he will be drawn to choices (A), (B), or (D).

10. On difficult Data Sufficiency problems, Joe's answer is always wrong.

PART III

How to Crack the Verbal GMAT

13

Sentence Correction

Sentence Corrections make up roughly a third of the 41 questions on the verbal section of the GMAT—approximately 14 questions that will be interspersed throughout the verbal section. A Sentence Correction question consists of one long sentence that is partly underlined. You have to decide whether the sentence is grammatically correct as it's written, or if it is not, which of the answer choices best replaces the underlined portion.

Before we begin, take a moment to read the following instructions. They are a close approximation of the instructions you'll see on the real GMAT. Be sure you know and understand these instructions before you take the GMAT. If you learn them ahead of time, you won't have to waste valuable seconds reading them on the day of the test.

> <u>Directions</u>: Part or all of each sentence that follows has been underlined. If you think the sentence is correct as written, pick the first answer choice, which simply repeats the underlined portion exactly. If you think there is something wrong with the sentence as written, choose the answer choice that best <u>replaces</u> the underlined portion of the sentence.
>
> Sentence correction questions are designed to measure your correct use of grammar, your ability to form clear and effective sentences and your capacity to choose the most appropriate words. Pick the answer that best states what was meant in the original sentence, avoiding constructions which are awkward, unclear, or which unnecessarily repeat themselves.

THE BAD NEWS

It's important to understand the fine print of the instructions you've just read. The test writers at ETS ask you to choose the "best" answer, by which they mean the answer that they think is right. The bad news is that some of the "correct" answer choices for the GMAT's sentence correction questions will probably not sound correct to you. The rules of English as interpreted by ETS are very different from the rules of English that govern what we read in newspapers or hear on television or speak in our everyday lives.

How many times have you heard your boss, or a television anchorperson, or a president of the United States, make the following statement?

"Hopefully, we will know the answer to that question tomorrow."

While you probably don't want to make a habit of correcting people's grammar, you should know that this sentence is not technically correct. According to ETS, the president was supposed to say, "It is hoped that we will know the answer to that question tomorrow." It may be of some comfort to you that your boss, the television anchorperson, and the president of the United States would all get a question like this wrong if they took the GMAT.

GMAT ENGLISH

GMAT English should be studied the same way you would approach any other foreign language. It has its own rules and its own internal logic. GMAT English has much in common with American English, but if you rely solely on your ear, you may get into trouble.

Confronted with a poorly constructed sentence, most of us could find *a* way to fix it. Most of the time we would probably break the sentence into two separate sentences (GMAT sentences are often too long and unwieldy). Unfortunately, on this test we are forced to find *the* way to fix the sentence; that is to say, ETS's way to fix it.

To do well on sentence correction, you will have to learn GMAT English.

THE GOOD NEWS

ETS test writers try to stick to the basics. If they tested a controversial point of grammar, they might be proven wrong. They don't want to have to change their minds after a test is given and mail 20,000 letters explaining why they're changing the answer key (something that has happened from time to time in the past). The easiest way to avoid trouble is to test a handful of the rules of standard written English.

There are huge books devoted exclusively to the correct use of English. You could spend the next six weeks just studying grammar and never even scratch the surface of the subject. The good news is that this won't be necessary. Although there are hundreds of rules of standard written English that could be tested, the GMAT concentrates on only a few.

In other words, GMAT English is fairly easy to learn.

SENTENCE CORRECTION: CRACKING THE SYSTEM

In this chapter we'll show you the most common types of errors that are tested in GMAT sentences, and how to spot them. We'll show you how ETS chooses the four incorrect choices for each question, and we'll show you how to use Process of Elimination to make your life a lot easier.

To forestall the objections of the expert grammarians out there, let us say at the outset that this discussion is not designed to be an all-inclusive discussion of English grammar. You are reading this chapter to do well on Sentence Correction *as it appears on the GMAT*. Thus, if we seem to oversimplify a point or ignore an arcane exception to a rule, it is because we do not feel that any more detail is warranted. Remember, this isn't English; it's GMAT English.

ORDER OF DIFFICULTY

The computer-adaptive GMAT will be choosing questions for you from a large pool based on your responses to previous questions. Theoretically, the computer knows which questions in its pool are easy and which are difficult. However, when it comes to sentence correction, most of our students find that they can't tell the difference; "easy" questions often seem as poorly worded as "difficult" questions. You will discover that The Princeton Review techniques make the relative difficulty of Sentence Correction questions pretty meaningless.

PROCESS OF ELIMINATION

Most people approach Sentence Correction questions the same way. They read the original sentence and then read the entire sentence again, substituting the first answer choice for the underlined part. Then they go back and do the same thing for the second, third, and fourth answer choices. This approach is both laborious and confusing. It's hard to keep five different versions of the same sentence straight, especially when all five of them are awkward.

The Princeton Review approach uses Process of Elimination to narrow down the choices before you have to start reading the answers carefully. Since there are relatively few types of errors that appear in Sentence Correction questions, we will focus on teaching you how to spot these errors. Once you've spotted the error in a sentence you'll be able to go through the answer choices and eliminate any that also contain that error. Then you can decide among the remaining choices.

SCRATCH PAPER

Effective use of POE on the computer-adaptive GMAT always involves scratch paper, and *always* involves thinking of the answer choices as A, B, C, D, and E, even though they are not labeled that way onscreen. As you eliminate answer choices, you should cross them off on the scratch paper.

BASIC PRINCIPLES

Let's look at a Sentence Correction question that's written in a way that you will unfortunately never see on the real GMAT—with only the correct answer listed:

> Registered brokerage firms have been required to record details of all computerized program trades made in the past year so that government agencies <u>will be able to decide whether they should be banned</u>.
>
> ○
> ○
> ○
> ○
> ○ will be able to decide whether program trades should be banned

Piece of cake, right? It gets a little harder when they throw in the other four answer choices. Don't worry if you aren't sure why the last answer choice—what we call answer choice (E)—is better than the original sentence. We will cover how to spot this type of error (pronoun reference) a little later in the chapter. For now, it's enough to know that the "they" in the underlined portion of the sentence was ambiguous. It wasn't clear whether "they" referred to "registered brokerage firms," "details," or the "computerized program trades."

Don't bother saying it was perfectly obvious that "they" referred to the program trades. This is GMAT English, remember? It doesn't matter if *you* knew what the sentence meant. The sentence had to be clear to the ETS test writer who wrote it.

ZEN AND THE ART OF TEST WRITING

Let's put ourselves in the place of the GMAT test writer who wrote this question. He has just finished his sentence and he has his correct answer, but he isn't finished yet. He still has to write four other answer choices. It's actually kind of difficult to come up with four answer choices that seem plausible but are wrong. If the test writer makes the incorrect choices too obviously wrong, Joe Bloggs might be able to pick the correct answer without having really understood the rule of English involved. If the test writer makes the incorrect answer choices too subtle, Joe won't find one that seems right to him, and therefore might guess at random. The test writer does *not* want Joe to guess at random. If Joe guesses at random, he might actually pick the right answer.

ONE DOWN, FOUR TO GO

Selecting the correct answer was easy for our test writer—after all, *he* wrote the question. He will probably spend much more time on the incorrect answer choices.

Answer choice (A)

Coming up with the first wrong answer choice is also easy for our test writer; the first of the answer choices (what we call answer choice (A)) is always a repeat of the underlined part of the original sentence. Obviously, this is the choice to select if you think that the sentence is correct as it's written. Two down, three to go.

IF YOU CAN'T SELL A LEMON, REPACKAGE IT

To see whether Joe has spotted the error in the sentence, the ETS test writer will include the *same error* in at least one, and usually two, of the other answer choices. If Joe didn't like the error in the original sentence, maybe he'll like it better surrounded by different words. Look at the same sentence again, this time with two incorrect answer choices that include the error found in the original sentence:

> Registered brokerage firms have been required to record details of all computerized program trades made in the past year so that government agencies <u>will be able to decide whether they should be banned</u>.
>
> ○ will be able to decide whether they should be banned
> ○ **should be able to decide whether they should be banned**
> ○ **should be able to decide whether they can be banned**
> ○ will be able to decide whether program trades should be banned

The GMAT on the GMAT:

"The GMAT has two primary limitations: (1) it cannot and does not measure all the qualities important for graduate study in management and other pursuits; (2) there are psychometric limitations to the test—for example, only score differences of certain magnitudes are reliable indicators of real differences in performance. Such limits should be taken into consideration as GMAT scores are used."
Source: The Official Guide for GMAT Review

Joe Bloggs has no idea what point of grammar is being tested in this question. He picks answers because they sound good. Our test writer is hoping that one of these answer choices will sound better to Joe than the correct answer. Both choices change the sentence, but both also still contain the ambiguous word "they," and both are still wrong.

ALMOST RIGHT

Our test writer has one more kind of trap to insert into question. This time the trap isn't for Joe Bloggs; it's for the person who has spotted the error in the sentence but is in too big a hurry to make fine distinctions.

Usually one of the incorrect answer choices will actually fix the original error—*but will create some new error in the process.*

Spotting the original error is all well and good, but our test writer wants to make sure you really "deserve" to get this one right. So include an answer choice that's almost right. It will be a close variation of the "best" answer; it will correct the mistake in the original sentence, but it will be *wrong.*

Here's the same sentence with an answer choice that fixes the original mistake but creates a new one:

> Registered brokerage firms have been required to record details of all computerized program trades made in the past year so that government agencies <u>will be able to decide whether they should be banned</u>.
>
> ○ will be able to decide whether they should be banned
> ○ should be able to decide whether they should be banned
> ○ should be able to decide whether they can be banned
> ○ **will be able to decide whether program trades should be able to be banned**
> ○ will be able to decide whether program trades should be banned

Answer choice (D) fixes the original problem; there is no longer an ambiguous "they" in the sentence. Our test writer is hoping that anyone who has spotted the original error will read just far enough to see that answer choice (D) fixes it, but not far enough to see that there is something else wrong. What's wrong? On the GMAT, only animate objects are "able" to do anything.

THREE DOWN, TWO TO GO

Let's look at the entire problem, now that our test writer has finished it, and count our blessings.

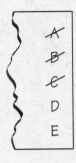

Registered brokerage firms have been required to record details of all computerized program trades made in the past year so that government agencies <u>will be able to decide whether they should be banned</u>.

- ○ will be able to decide whether they should be banned
- ○ should be able to decide whether they should be banned
- ○ should be able to decide whether they can be banned
- ○ will be able to decide whether program trades should be able to be banned
- ○ will be able to decide whether program trades should be banned

Here's how to crack it

By spotting what was wrong in the original sentence, we could have eliminated three of the five answer choices. Choice (A) merely repeated the original sentence word for word. Choices (B) and (C) contained the same error that was found in the original sentence.

We're down to choice (D) or (E). Both fix the original error. What's the difference between them? Three words. If you don't see why one is correct and the other isn't, don't soul-search. Just click on one answer and move on. The correct answer is choice (E).

OUR BASIC APPROACH

To use POE, you must be able to spot the errors in the original sentences. Fortunately, as we said before, ETS leans heavily on only a few major types of errors. Just recognizing these errors should enable you to answer many of the roughly 15 Sentence Correction problems. There are two ways to do this:

Plan A

The first step in your sentence correction strategy should be to read the original sentence, looking for the very specific errors that ETS likes to test. As soon as you spot an error, you can eliminate any answer choices that repeat this error. Then, having gotten rid of several choices, you can actually read the remaining choices carefully to see which is best.

But what happens if you finish the sentence without spotting one of these errors? Unfortunately, you can't skip the question and come back to it later. So what do you do?

Plan B

If you don't spot the error as you read the original sentence, then the second step in your sentence correction strategy is to go straight to the answer choices to look for clues. Here are the answer choices to a real GMAT problem:

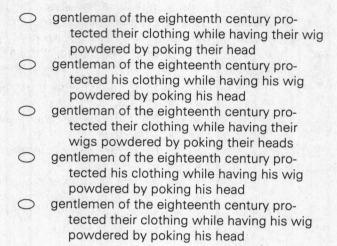

- ○ gentleman of the eighteenth century pro-
  tected their clothing while having their wig
  powdered by poking their head
- ○ gentleman of the eighteenth century pro-
  tected his clothing while having his wig
  powdered by poking his head
- ○ gentleman of the eighteenth century pro-
  tected their clothing while having their
  wigs powdered by poking their heads
- ○ gentlemen of the eighteenth century pro-
  tected his clothing while having his wig
  powdered by poking his head
- ○ gentlemen of the eighteenth century pro-
  tected their clothing while having his wig
  powdered by poking his head

Forget about the original sentence entirely for a moment (pretty easy, since we didn't give it to you). Just look at the first word of each of the choices. Does anything strike you?

By examining the answer choices, you will often find an excellent hint as to what kind of error you might be looking for in the original sentence. For example, in the answers above, ETS is offering you a choice of the singular noun "gentleman" and the plural noun "gentlemen." A further fast scan of the answer choices would reveal a choice of pronouns referring back to the nouns. What type of error might be involved if we're seeing singular nouns with plural pronouns? Aha. Pronoun reference.

Even if the answer choices do not provide a clue, all is not lost. Remember how our ETS test writer constructs wrong answer choices: The test writer likes to throw in one or more answer choices that fix the original error but create new errors in the process. You may not have been able to spot the original error, but you'll probably see the *new* errors in the bogus answer choices.

As you read the remaining answer choices, look for differences. Sometimes the realization that one answer choice is exactly the same as another with the exception of a couple of words will enable you to choose between them.

When you've eliminated everything you can, guess and move on.

The combination of Plan A and Plan B should allow you to get most of the Sentence Completion questions correct—once you've learned one other important concept:

THE MOST COMMON ERROR IS *NO* ERROR

About one-fifth of the Sentence Correction sentences are fine just the way they are. If a sentence is correct as is, the "best" answer is the first answer choice (what we call choice (A)), which repeats the original sentence. According to the law of averages, two or three of the Sentence Correction questions you will see on the GMAT will contain no error.

How do you tell when there is nothing wrong with a sentence?

You can tell that a sentence is correct by the *absence* of any of the other types of errors that we're going to show you how to spot. Try not to use your ear —at least not at first. As you read each sentence, you'll be marking off a mental checklist of likely ETS errors. If you come to the end of the list without having found a specific error, go to plan B and look for differences in the answer choices. If you still haven't found an error in the original sentence, chances are very good that there was none.

We'll come back to (A)s later in the chapter, after you've learned how to spot the major errors.

BEFORE WE START, SOME BASIC TERMINOLOGY

You won't be asked to name the parts of speech on the GMAT. However, an acquaintance with some of these terms is necessary to understand the techniques we're about to show you.

- ◆ A *noun* is a word that's used to name a person, place, thing, or idea.

- ◆ A *verb* is a word that expresses action.

Here is a very basic sentence:

> *Sue opened the box.*

In this sentence, *Sue* and *box* are both nouns, and *opened* is a verb. *Sue* is considered the subject of this sentence because it is the person, place, or thing about which something is being said. *Box* is considered the object of the sentence because it receives the action of the verb.

- ◆ An *adjective* is a word that modifies a noun.

- ◆ An *adverb* is a word that modifies a verb, adjective, or adverb.

- ◆ A *preposition* is a word that notes the relation of a noun to an action or a thing.

- ◆ A *phrase* is a group of words acting as a single part of speech. A phrase is missing either a subject or a verb or both.

- ◆ A *prepositional phrase* is a group of words beginning with a preposition. Like any *phrase*, a prepositional phrase does not contain both a subject and a verb.

Here's a more complicated version of the same sentence.

> *Sue quickly opened the big box of chocolates.*

In this sentence, *quickly* is an adverb modifying the verb *opened*. *Big* is an adjective modifying the noun *box*. *Of* is a preposition because it shows a relation between *box* and *chocolates*. *Of chocolates* is a prepositional phrase that acts like an adjective by modifying *box*.

B-School Lingo

Net Net: End result

◆ A *pronoun* is a word that takes the place of a noun.

◆ A *clause* is a group of words that contains a subject and a verb.

Here's an even more complicated version of the same sentence:

> *Because she was famished, Sue quickly opened the big box of chocolates.*

There are two clauses in this sentence. *Sue quickly opened the big box of chocolates* is considered an independent clause because it contains the main idea of the sentence, and could stand by itself. *Because she was famished* is also a clause (it contains a subject and a verb) but it cannot stand by itself. This is known as a dependent clause. The word *she* is a pronoun referring to the noun *Sue*.

THE MAJOR ERRORS OF GMAT ENGLISH

1. PRONOUN ERRORS

There are two main types of pronoun errors. The first is called *pronoun reference*. You saw an example of this in the sentence about program trading above. Take a look at a simple example:

> *Samantha and Jane went shopping, but she couldn't find anything she liked.*

This type of mistake used to drive Harold Ross, the founding editor of *The New Yorker*, crazy. He was famous for scrawling "Who he?" in the margins of writers' manuscripts. It is supposed to be absolutely clear who is being referred to by a pronoun. In the example above, the pronoun "she" could refer to either Samantha or Jane. The pronoun is ambiguous and must be fixed. You can fix it in three different ways:

> *Samantha and Jane went shopping, but Samantha couldn't find anything she liked.*

> *Samantha and Jane went shopping, but Jane couldn't find anything she liked.*

> *Samantha and Jane went shopping, but they couldn't find anything they liked.*

The second type of pronoun error is called *pronoun number* (singular or plural). Here is a simple example:

> *The average male moviegoer expects to see at least one scene*
> *of violence per film, and they are seldom disappointed.*

In this case, the pronoun "they" clearly refers to the average male moviegoer, so there is no ambiguity of reference. However, "the average male moviegoer" is *singular*. "They" cannot be used to take the place of a singular noun. There is really only one way to fix this sentence.

> *The average male moviegoer expects to see at least one scene*
> *of violence per film, and he is seldom disappointed.*

ETS is very fond of both of these types of errors, and routinely makes use of them. By the way, as we mentioned earlier, you don't have to memorize any of the terminology we use. You simply have to recognize a GMAT English error when you see it.

Q: What is the easiest way to spot a pronoun error?

How Do You Spot a Pronoun Error?

That's easy. Look for pronouns.

A pronoun is a word that replaces a noun. Here's a list of common pronouns. (You don't need to memorize these—just be able to recognize them.)

Singular

I, me
he, him
she, her
you
it
each
another
one
other
such
mine
yours
his, hers
ours
this

Plural

we, us
they, them
both
these
those

Can Be Singular or Plural

some
any
you
who
which
what
that

Every single time you spot a pronoun, you should immediately ask yourself the following two questions:

- ◆ Is it completely clear, not just to me but to a pedantic ETS test writer, who or what the pronoun is referring to?

- ◆ Does the pronoun agree in number with the noun it is referring to?

Let's look at an example:

> While Brussels has smashed all Western European tourism revenue records <u>this year, they still lag well behind in exports</u>.
>
> ○ this year, they still lag well behind in exports
> ○ in the past year, they still lag well behind in exports
> ○ in the past year, it lags still well behind in exports
> ○ this year, they lag still well behind in exports
> ○ this year, it still lags well behind in exports

A: Look for pronouns!

Here's how to crack it

<u>Plan A</u>: As you read the sentence for the first time, look to see if there is a pronoun. There is: "they." Let's make sure the pronoun is being used correctly. Who is the "they" supposed to refer to? Brussels. Is Brussels plural? No, it's the name of a city.

Now that you've spotted the problem, go through the answer choices. Any answer choice with the pronoun "they" in it has to be wrong. You can cross off answer choices (A), (B), and (D). You're down to answer choices (C) and (E).

Both of the remaining answer choices solve the original problem. Read them carefully. If you aren't sure, take a guess. If you said answer choice (E), you were right. The adverb "still" in answer choice (C) must go in front of the verb.

<u>Plan B</u>: Now, what if Plan A lets you down, and you don't spot the error as you read the sentence in the first place? There is always Plan B. Go straight to the answer choices and ask yourself how they are different. Obviously, they differ in several ways—but one huge difference is that some answer choices use the pronoun "they" while others use the pronoun "it." This is a clue that will remind you to check pronoun reference and number.

2. MISPLACED MODIFIERS

Misplaced modifiers come in several forms, but ETS's favorite looks like this:

> *Coming out of the department store, John's wallet was stolen.*

When a sentence begins with a participial phrase (just a fancy term for a phrase that starts with a verb ending in -*ing*), that phrase is supposed to modify the noun or pronoun immediately following it.

Was the "wallet" coming out of the department store? No.

There are two ways to fix this sentence.

First, we could change the second half of the sentence so that the noun or pronoun that comes after the participial phrase is actually what the phrase is supposed to refer to:

> *Coming out of the department store, John was robbed of his wallet.*

Or, we could change the first half of the sentence into an adverbial clause (which contains its own subject) so that it is no longer necessary for the first half of the sentence to modify the noun that follows it:

> *As John was* coming out of the department store, his wallet was stolen.

Other forms of misplaced modifiers:

A. Participial phrases preceded by a preposition:

> *On leaving the department store, John's wallet was stolen.*

(Corrected version: On leaving the department store, John was robbed of his wallet.)

B. Adjectives:

> *Frail and weak, the heavy wagon could not be budged by the old horse.*

(Corrected version: Frail and weak, the old horse could not budge the heavy wagon.)

C. Adjectival phrases:

> *An organization long devoted to the cause of justice, the mayor awarded a medal to the American Civil Liberties Union.*

(Corrected version: An organization long devoted to the cause of justice, the American Civil Liberties Union was awarded a medal by the mayor.)

In each of these examples, the modifying phrase modified the wrong noun or pronoun.

HOW DO YOU SPOT A MISPLACED MODIFIER?

That's easy. *Whenever a sentence begins with a modifying phrase that's followed by a comma, the noun or pronoun right after the comma should be what the phrase is referring to.* Every single time you see a sentence that begins with a modifying phrase, check to make sure that it modifies the right noun or pronoun. If it doesn't, you've spotted the error in the sentence.

The correct answer choice will either change the noun that follows the modifying phrase (the preferred method) or change the phrase itself into an adverbial clause so that it no longer needs to modify the noun.

Let's look at two examples:

> <u>Written in 1961, Joseph Heller scored a literary hit with his comedic first novel, *Catch-22*.</u>

- ○ Written in 1961, Joseph Heller scored a literary hit with his comedic first novel, *Catch-22*.
- ○ Written in 1961, Joseph Heller scored a literary hit with *Catch-22*, his comedic first novel.
- ○ Written in 1961, *Catch-22*, the comedic first novel by Joseph Heller, was a literary hit.
- ○ *Catch-22*, which was written in 1961 by Joseph Heller, scored a literary hit with his comedic first novel.
- ○ *Catch-22*, the comedic first novel, scored a literary hit for Joseph Heller by its being written in 1961.

Here's how to crack it

Plan A: As you read the sentence for the first time, go through your checklist. Is there a pronoun error in the sentence? No. Does the sentence begin with a modifying phrase? Yes. Now we're getting somewhere. Let's check to see if the modifying phrase actually modifies what it is *supposed to*. Does it? No. "Joseph Heller" is not what was written in 1961. This is a misplaced modifier.

Now that you've spotted the error, look through the other answer choices and eliminate any that contain the same error. Choice (B) contains the same error. Get rid of it. You're down to choices (C), (D), and (E).

Now, there are really only two ways to fix this kind of error, as you know. Do any of the answer choices change the noun that follows the modifying phrase? Yes, answer choice (C). This is probably the right answer. Read through the other two choices just to make sure there's nothing better. Choices (D) and (E) contain awkward constructions. Choice (C) is the "best" answer.

Plan B: If you don't spot the error as you read the sentence for the first time, you have a second chance to spot it by looking for differences in the answer choices. Several contain a participial phrase followed by the noun the phrase is supposed to modify. But in one of those choices, the noun following the phrase is different. Hmmm. Could this be a misplaced modifier?

Although not quite as liquid an investment as a money-market account, financial experts recommend a certificate of deposit for its high yield.

- ◯ Although not quite as liquid an investment as
- ◯ Although it is not quite as liquid an investment as
- ◯ While not being quite as liquid an investment as
- ◯ While it is not quite as liquid as an investment
- ◯ Although not quite liquid an investment as

Here's how to crack it

Plan A: Go through your checklist. Is there a pronoun in this sentence? Yes, the third to last word of the sentence is a pronoun, but it clearly refers back to the certificate of deposit. False alarm. Does the sentence begin with a modifying phrase? Yes. Now we're getting warmer. Check to see whether the modifying phrase modifies what it's supposed to modify. Does "although not quite as liquid an investment . . ." refer to financial experts? No. This is a misplaced modifier.

The clearest way to fix this sentence would be to change the noun that follows the modifying phrase:

> *Although not quite as liquid an investment as a money-market account, a certificate of deposit is recommended by financial experts for its high yield.*

However, you can't fix *this* sentence that way for the very good reason that only the first phrase of the sentence was underlined. This time, you'll have to find a way to fix the modifying phrase itself. Look for an answer choice that changes the modifying phrase into an adverbial clause with its own subject and verb.

Choices (A), (C), and (E) do not have subjects and can therefore be eliminated immediately. Choices (B) and (D) each have a subject—in both cases, the word "it"—turning the modifying phrases into adverbial clauses. However choice (D) contains a new error: The word "as" has been moved, leaving "money-market" stranded in the middle of the sentence with no function. While it sounds atrocious, choice (B) is the "best" answer.

Plan B: Again, if you didn't spot the error as you read the original sentence, the answer choices were there to provide you with a clue. Of the five answer choices, two turned the beginning phrase into a clause by means of the pronoun "it." By noticing this, you might be reminded to check for a misplaced modifier.

A close relative of a misplaced modifier is a *dangling modifier*. You can spot the two errors in the same way. Here's a simple example:

Q: What is a tip-off to a misplaced modifier error?

Before designing a park, the public must be considered.

Again, this sentence starts with a modifying phrase followed by a comma. The noun following the comma is what the modifying phrase is supposed to modify. Does it? No! "The public" didn't design the park. A dangling modifier differs from a misplaced modifier in that a dangling modifier doesn't just modify the wrong word; it doesn't modify any word.

To fix this sentence, we would have to insert whoever is designing the park into the sentence:

Before designing a park, the architect must consider the public.

3. PARALLEL CONSTRUCTION

There are two kinds of ETS sentences that test parallel construction. The first is a sentence that contains a list, or has a series of actions set off from one another by commas. Here's an example:

> *Among the reasons cited for the city councilwoman's decision not to run for reelection were the high cost of a campaign, the lack of support from her party, and desiring to spend more time with her family.*

When a main verb controls several phrases that follow it, each of those phrases has to be set up in the same way. In the sentence above, three reasons were listed. The three reasons *were* (main verb):

> the high cost of a campaign
> the lack of support from her party
> and
> desiring to spend more time with her family

A: A modifying phrase followed by a comma. To correct it, make sure that what comes after the comma is modified by what comes before it.

The construction of each of the three reasons is supposed to be parallel. The first two items on the list are phrases that are essentially functioning as nouns: The high *cost* (of a campaign); the *lack* (of support from her party). However, the third item on the list seems more like a verb than a noun. How could we change the word "desiring" to a noun? If you said, "the desire," you were absolutely correct. It should read:

> the high cost of a campaign
> the lack of support from her party
> and
> *the desire* to spend more time with her family.

The second kind of ETS sentence that tests parallel construction is a sentence that's divided into two parts. Here's an example:

> *To say that the song patterns of the common robin are less complex than those of the indigo bunting is doing a great disservice to both birds.*

If the first half of a sentence is constructed in a particular way, the second half must be constructed in the same way. The first half of this sentence begins, "To . . . "; therefore, the second half has to begin the same way:

> *To say that the song patterns of the common robin are less complex than those of the indigo bunting is to do a great disservice to both birds.*

How Do You Spot Parallel Construction?

That's easy. Every time you read a Sentence Correction problem, look to see if you can find a series of actions, a list of three things, or a sentence that is divided into two parts.

Here's an example:

> In a recent survey, the Gallup poll discovered that the average American speaks 1.3 languages, buys a new car every 5.2 years, <u>drinks 14 gallons of alcoholic beverages every year, and forgot to pay at least one bill per quarter</u>.
>
> ○ drinks 14 gallons of alcoholic beverages every year, and forgot to pay at least one bill per quarter
> ○ drinks 14 gallons of alcoholic beverages every year, and forgets to pay at least one bill per quarter
> ○ can drink 14 gallons of alcoholic beverages every quarter and forgot to pay at least one bill per quarter
> ○ drinks 14 gallons of alcoholic beverages every year, and forgets at least to pay one bill per quarter
> ○ drank 14 gallons of alcoholic beverages every year, and forgets to pay at least one bill per quarter

Here's how to crack it

Plan A: As you read the sentence for the first time, run through your checklist. Is there a pronoun? No. Does the sentence begin with a modifying phrase? Yes, but the word after the phrase is what is supposed to be modified, so this is not a misplaced modifier. Is there a series or list of three things or a series of actions? Yes. Let's see if all the actions are parallel. The average American . . .

> speaks (1.3 languages)
> buys (a new car . . .)
> drinks (14 gallons . . .)
> and
> forgot (to pay . . .)

The first three verbs are all in the present tense, but the fourth one is in the past tense. The problem in this sentence is a lack of parallel construction.

Now that you know what the error is, go through the answer choices. Any choice that contains the word "forgot" is wrong. We can eliminate choices (A) and (C). Choice (E), even though it fixes the parallel construction of the fourth verb, changes the construction of the third verb. Eliminate it.

Choices (B) and (D) have perfect parallel construction. If you aren't sure which one is correct, guess and move on. If you picked choice (B), you were right. In choice (D), the adjectival phrase "at least" had to be in front of "one bill."

Plan B: The error on which this question hinges is easy to spot if you use Plan B. Clearly, what is at issue is the verb that begins the underlined portion of the sentence. Why would the ETS test writers be changing around the form of this verb? Aha! They do it in order to create a parallel construction problem.

4. Tense

On the GMAT, tense problems are often just a matter of parallel construction. In general, if a sentence starts out in one tense, it should probably stay there. Let's look at an example:

> When he was younger he walked three miles every day and
> has lifted weights too.

The clause "when he was younger" puts the entire sentence firmly in the past. Thus the two verbs that follow should be in the past tense as well. You may not have known the technical term for "has lifted" (the present perfect tense) but you probably noticed that it was inconsistent with "walked" (the simple past tense). The sentence should read:

> When he was younger he walked three miles every day and
> lifted weights too.

Here are the tenses that come up on the GMAT:

Tense	Example
present	He *walks* three miles a day.
simple past	When he was younger, he *walked* three miles a day.
present perfect	He *has walked* three miles a day for the last several years.
past perfect	He *had walked* three miles a day until he bought his motorcycle.
future	He *will walk* three miles a day, starting tomorrow.

It isn't important that you know the names of these tenses as long as you understand how they're used. As we said before, a sentence that begins in one tense should generally stay in that tense. For example, a sentence that begins in the present perfect (which describes an action that has happened in the past, but is potentially going on in the present as well) should stay in the present perfect.

B-School Lingo

OOC: out of cash
Opportunity Costs: the cost of pursuing an opportunity, e.g., B-school tuition and the forfeiture of two years' income

> *He has walked three miles a day for the last several years, and has never complained.*

One exception to this rule is a sentence that contains the past perfect (in which one action in the past happened before another action in the past). By definition, any action set in the past perfect must have another action that comes after it, set in the simple past.

> *He had ridden his motorcycle for two hours when it ran out of gas.*

The only other exceptions to this rule come up when one action in a sentence clearly precedes another:

> *The dinosaurs are extinct now, but they were once present on the earth in large numbers.*

In this case, the sentence clearly refers to two different time periods: "now," which requires the present tense, and a period long ago, which requires the past tense.

How Do You Spot Tense Errors?

That's easy. Using Plan A, look for changes in verb tense in the sentence. Using Plan B, look for changes in verb tense *in the answer choices*. If the answer choices give you several versions of a particular verb themselves, then you should be looking to see which one is correct. Here's an example:

A doctor at the Amsterdam Clinic maintains that if children eat a diet high in vitamins and <u>took vitamin supplements, they will be less likely to catch</u> the common cold.

- ○ took vitamin supplements, they will be less likely to catch
- ○ took vitamin supplements, they are less likely to catch
- ○ take vitamin supplements, they were less likely of catching
- ○ take vitamin supplements, they will be less likely of catching
- ○ take vitamin supplements, they are less likely to catch

Here's how to crack it

Plan A: As you read the sentence, go through your checklist. There is one pronoun ("they") in the sentence, but in this case it clearly refers only to the children. Is there a modifying phrase? No. Is there a list of things or a series of actions? Not really. Are the verb tenses inconsistent? Hmm. Now we're getting somewhere. The first verb "maintains" is in the present tense. So is the verb "eat." But the third verb, "took," which is supposed to be a parallel action with "eat," is in the past tense.

Look at the dependent clause that is partially underlined.

> . . . *that if children* eat *a diet high in vitamins and* <u>took</u>
> <u>vitamin supplements</u> . . .

Obviously, the two verbs are inconsistent with each other, and since only one of them is underlined, that's the one that must be wrong. The correct sentence must have a "take" in it, so we can eliminate choices (A) and (B). Choice (C) puts the rest of the sentence in the past tense, so scratch (C). Choice (D) puts the rest of the sentence in the future tense. This *might* be acceptable, but the choice also uses the incorrect idiomatic expression "likely of catching." The correct answer to this question is Choice (E), which keeps the entire sentence in the present tense.

Plan B: If you don't spot the error as you read the original sentence, look at the answer choices. Aha! (A) and (B) offer us "took" while (C), (D), and (E) offer us "take." One of these two alternatives must be right. Why would the ETS test writers be offering us this choice of present and past tense verbs? Clearly, this is a tense question.

5. SUBJECT–VERB AGREEMENT ERRORS

Nouns that Sound Plural, but Aren't

The Netherlands (the name of any city, state, or country)
Tom or John (any two singular nouns connected by an "or")
the family
the audience
politics
measles
the number
the amount

A verb is supposed to agree with its subject. Let's look at an example:

> *The number of arrests of drunken drivers are increasing every year.*

ETS likes to separate the subject of a sentence from its verb with several prepositional phrases, so that by the time you get to the verb you've forgotten whether the subject was singular or plural.

The subject of the sentence above is "number," which is singular. The phrase "of arrests of drunken drivers" modifies the subject. The verb of this sentence is "are," which is plural. If we set off the prepositional phrase with parentheses, this is what the sentence looks like:

> *The number (of arrests of drunken drivers) are . . .*

To fix this sentence we need to make the verb agree with the subject:

> *The number (of arrests of drunken drivers) is increasing every year.*

How to Spot Subject–Verb Agreement Errors

Cover up the prepositional phrases between the subject and the verb of each clause of the sentence so you can see whether there is an agreement problem. You should also be on the lookout for nouns that sound plural but are in fact singular:

Some nouns that are generally singular

> The Netherlands (the name of any city, state, or country)
> Tom or John (any two singular nouns connected by an "or")
> the family
> the audience
> politics
> measles
> the number
> the amount

Q: A parallel construction error can be recognized by what giveaways?

You are already on the lookout for pronouns since they're first on your checklist. Sometimes pronouns can be the subject of a sentence, in which case the verb has to agree with the pronoun. There are some pronouns that people tend to think are plural when they are in fact singular:

Singular pronouns
> each
> everyone
> everybody
> nobody

Let's look at an example of a subject-verb error as it might appear on the GMAT:

> Many political insiders now believe that the dissension in Congress over health issues <u>decrease the likelihood for significant action being</u> taken this year to combat the rising costs of healthcare.

- ○ decrease the likelihood for significant action being
- ○ decrease the likelihood that significant action will be
- ○ decrease the likelihood of significant action to be
- ○ decreases the likelihood for significant action being
- ○ decreases the likelihood that significant action will be

Here's how to crack it

<u>Plan A</u>: As you read the sentence for the first time, run through your mental checklist. Is there a pronoun, a modifying phrase, a list of several things, a series of parallel actions, or a change in tense? Not this time. Let's check for subject-verb agreement. The subject of the independent clause is "insiders" and the correct verb, "believe," follows almost immediately, so there's no problem in the main clause.

However, let's look at the dependent clause that follows "That the dissension over health issues decrease the likelihood…"

In this clause, the subject is "dissension," not "health issues." Remember to put parentheses around any prepositional phrases. It should look like this:

> …the dissension (over health issues) decrease…

Is this correct? No, the singular "dissension" needs the singular verb "decreases." Looking at the answers, we can immediately eliminate choices (A), (B), and (C). Now let's examine choices (D) and (E). Both fix the subject-verb error, but choice (D) uses the unidiomatic expression "likelihood for," and it also uses "being" instead of "will be." The correct answer is choice (E).

<u>Plan B</u>: If you don't spot the error as you read the sentence the first time, it takes only a second to look at the answer choices and see that one big difference in the answer choices is the form of the verb "decrease," which means this is a subject-verb issue.

> A: A list or a series of actions set off by commas. Every item in the list or series should take the same form.

6. Apples-and-Oranges

Another error that ETS likes to include is what we call apples and oranges. Here's a simple example:

> *The people in my office are smarter than other offices.*

Taken literally, this sentence compares "the people in my office" with "other offices." This is what we call an apples-and-oranges sentence. It compares two dissimilar things (in this case, "people" and "offices.") To fix this sentence, we need to make the comparison clear. There are two ways to do this:

> *The people in my office are smarter than the people in other offices.*
>
> *or*
>
> *The people in my office are smarter than those in other offices.*

We hope that you recognized "those" as a pronoun that takes the place of "the people." The correct answer to an apples-and-oranges question on the GMAT almost invariably involves the use of a pronoun ("that" or "those") rather than a repetition of the noun.

Apples-and-oranges problems also come up when you compare two actions:

> *Synthetic oils burn less efficiently than natural oils.*

In this case, what is being compared is not the two types of oil, but how well each type of oil *burns*. You could fix this by changing the sentence to read,

> *Synthetic oils burn less efficiently than natural oils burn.*

However, ETS would rather that you fix it by replacing the second verb (in this case, "burn") with a replacement verb ("do" or "does.") Here is how ETS would like to see this sentence rewritten:

> *Synthetic oils burn less efficiently than do natural oils.*

How Do You Spot Apples-and-Oranges?

Q: What is an indication of an apples-and-oranges error?

Look for sentences that make comparisons. These sentences often include words such as "than," "as," "similar to," and "like." When you find one of these comparison words, check to see whether the two things being compared are really comparable.

Let's look at an example.

> Doctors sometimes have difficulty diagnosing viral pneumonia because the early symptoms of this potentially deadly illness <u>are often quite similar to the common cold</u>.
>
> ○ are often quite similar to the common cold
> ○ often resemble that of the common cold
> ○ are often quite similar to those of the common cold
> ○ are often quite similar to the common cold's symptom
> ○ quite often are, like the common cold, similar

Here's how to crack it

<u>Plan A</u>: Go through your checklist; do you see any suspicious pronouns, misplaced modifiers, unparallel constructions, needless shifts in tense, or subject-verb problems? Good. There aren't any. Do you see any comparison words? Yes, the sentence uses "are similar to." Let's see exactly what is being compared. The symptoms of one illness are being compared directly to . . . another illness. Aha! This is an apples-and-oranges error. To make this sentence correct, we need to compare the *symptoms* of one illness to the *symptoms* of the other, and the way ETS would prefer that we do it is by using a replacement pronoun.

If we look at the answer choices, we can eliminate choices (A) and (E) because neither makes any attempt to compare symptoms to symptoms. Choice (B) looks promising because it uses the replacement pronoun "that"; however, "symptoms" is plural, and therefore can't be replaced by the singular "that." Choice (D) seems promising because it looks like it's trying to compare symptoms to symptoms—but if you look more closely, you'll notice that the last word of choice (D) is "symptom," which is singular. The correct answer is choice (C).

<u>Plan B</u>: There are often clues to apples-and-oranges questions in the answer choices as well. Just as you should be on the lookout for words like "similar to" in the sentences themselves, you can also often spot apples-and-oranges problems by looking for replacement nouns such as "that of" and "those of," or replacement verbs such as "than do" and "than does" in the answer choices.

7. Quantity Words

ETS likes to see if you know how to indicate quantity. Here's an example.

> *On the flight to Los Angeles, Nancy had to choose among two*
> *dinner entrees.*

If there were more than two items being compared, then "among" would be correct. However, if there are only two choices available, the correct quantity word should be "between."

> *On the flight to Los Angeles, Nancy had to choose between*
> *two dinner entrees.*

Here are the comparison quantity words that come up on the GMAT most frequently:

if two items	if more than two items
between	among
more	most
better	best
less	least

Another type of quantity word that shows up on the GMAT from time to time involves things that can be counted as opposed to things that can't. For example, if you were standing in line at a buffet, and you didn't want as big a serving of soup as the person in front of you received, which of the following would be correct?

Singular Pronouns

either
neither
each
everyone
everybody
nobody
no one

A: A comparison could indicate an A & O error. Check that the two things being compared are comparable.

Could I have fewer soup, please?

or

Could I have less soup, please?

If an item can't be counted, the correct adjective would be "less." However, if we were talking about french fries (which can be counted) the correct adjective would be "fewer."

countable items	non-countable items
fewer	less
number	amount, quantity
many	much

HOW DO YOU SPOT QUANTITY WORD ERRORS?

That's easy. Look for quantity words. Whenever you see a "between," check to see if there are only two items being discussed in the sentence. (If there are more, you'll need an "among.") Whenever you see an "amount," make sure that whatever is being discussed cannot be counted. (If the sentence is talking about the "amount" of people, then you'll need to change it to "number.")

Here's what a "between–among" quantity word error might look like on the GMAT:

Of the many decisions facing the energy commission as it meets to decide on new directions for the next century, the question of the future of nuclear energy <u>is for certain the more perplexing</u>.

- ○ is for certain the more perplexing
- ○ is certainly the most perplexing
- ○ it seems certain, is the most perplexed
- ○ is certainly the more perplexing
- ○ it seems certain, is perplexing the most

Here's how to crack it

<u>Plan A</u>: If your checklist includes quantity words, the word "more" will set off red flags as you read the sentence. If there were two decisions facing the energy commission, then "the more perplexing" would be correct. However, the sentence says there are "many" decisions. Therefore the sentence must read, "the most perplexing."

This allows us to eliminate choices (A) and (D) immediately. Choice (C) gives the impression that it is the *question* that is perplexed. Eliminate it. Choice (E) incorrectly positions "the most" after the word it is supposed to modify. The correct answer is choice (B).

<u>Plan B</u>: If you don't notice the quantity word in the question itself, you'll probably notice the series of different quantity words ("more" and "most") in the answer choices.

8. IDIOM

ETS likes to test certain idiomatic expressions. Here's an easy example:

> *There is little doubt that large corporations are indebted for
> the small companies that broke new ground in laser optics.*

It is incorrect to say you are indebted *for* someone.

> *There is little doubt that large corporations are indebted to
> the small companies that broke new ground in laser optics.*

Idiomatic errors are difficult to spot because there is no one problem to look for. In fact, there are really no rules. Each idiom has its own particular usage. There is no real reason why an idiomatic expression is correct. It is simply a matter of custom.

However, you haven't been speaking English for the past twenty years for nothing. The main similarity between GMAT English and American English is that they both use the same idiomatic expressions.

You already know them.

HOW DO YOU SPOT IDIOMATIC ERRORS?

If you've gone through the first seven items on your checklist—pronouns, misplaced modifiers, parallel construction, tense, subject-verb agreement, apples-and-oranges, and quantity words—and still haven't found an error, try pulling any idiomatic expressions out of the sentence so that you can see whether they're correct.

Then make up your own sentence using the suspect idiom:

> *I am indebted for my parents for offering to help pay for
> graduate school.*

Does that sound right? Of course not. I am indebted *to* my parents. Usually if you take the expression out of the long and awkward sentence and use it in an everyday sentence, the error (if there is one) will be obvious. Here's what an idiom question might look like on the GMAT:

> The administration of a small daily dose of aspirin
> has not only been shown to lower the risk of heart
> attack, <u>and it has also been shown to help</u> relieve
> the suffering of arthritis.
>
> ○   and it has also been shown to help
> ○   and it has also been shown helpful to
> ○   but it has also been shown to help
> ○   but it has been shown helpful in addition for
> ○   in addition it has also been shown helping

Here's how to crack it

Plan A: As always, run through your checklist. Is there a pronoun in the sentence? Yes, but if you check the answer choices, you'll discover that the same pronoun appears in each one. Obviously, pronoun error is *not* what is being tested this time. Is there a modifying phrase? No. So much for misplaced modifiers. Is there a list of things or a series of actions? No. To be sure that there really is no parallel construction problem we should look at the two halves of the sentence as well. The first half, " . . . has been shown," matches the second half, " . . . has also been shown," and both are in the same tense, so there is no problem with either parallel construction or tense. There are no comparison words either, so we don't have to worry about apples-and-oranges. Could there be something wrong with an idiomatic expression in the original sentence? Let's try a sentence of our own.

Not only is he nasty . . .

How would you finish this sentence? If you said something like " . . . but he is also disgusting," you would be absolutely correct. In GMAT English, "not only. . ." is always followed somewhere in the same sentence by "but . . . also." Let's look at the answer choices to see which can be eliminated. (A), (B), and (E) all use some other conjunction instead of "but," which means that the only possible answers are (C) and (D). Choice (D) uses "in addition" instead of "also." This *might* not be fatal, but then keep reading after the underlining: "<u>helpful in addition for</u> relieve the suffering of arthritis." If the word "for" seems to stick out, it is because we need to form the infinitive case of "relieve" by using "to." Thus, the correct answer is (C).

Plan B: If you didn't spot the idiomatic error in the sentence itself, the first word of each of the answer choices gives you a clue. Does the sentence need an "and," a "but," or an "in addition?"

Q: What is the rule when looking for tense errors?

THE IDIOMS MOST COMMONLY TESTED ON THE GMAT

There are, of course, thousands of idiomatic expressions that ETS could test on the GMAT. But here are a handful that seem to come up all the time.

A: Keep the same tense throughout the sentence.

not only . . . but also . . .
not so much ... as ...
defined as
regard as
neither ... nor ...
modeled after
based on
a result of
to result in
a debate over
a responsibility to
responsible for
different from
a consequence of
so ... as to be ...
so (adjective) that
depicted as
as great as
as good as, or better than
distinguish from
attribute to
credited with

ONE LAST EXAMPLE:

The foresight <u>that was evident in the court's selection of an independent trustee</u> to oversee the provisions of the agreement will probably go unremarked by the press.

- ◯ that was evident in the court's selection of an independent trustee
- ◯ that was evident by the court's selection of an independent trustee
- ◯ evidenced with the court's selection of an independent trustee
- ◯ evidenced of the court's selection of an independent trustee
- ◯ that was evident of the court's selection of an independent trustee

Here's how to crack it

Plan A: As you read the sentence, go through your checklist. Is there a pronoun? No. Does the sentence begin with a modifying phrase? No. Is there a list of three things or a series of actions? No. Is there a tense error? No. Is there a subject-verb problem? No. Is there a comparison word such as "similar" or "than?" No. Are there any quantity words to check? No. Do any expressions in the sentence seem suspicious? No.

We have checked off all of the items on our list. Maybe nothing is wrong with this sentence. The "best" answer to this question is choice (A).

Plan B: In cases like this where there is nothing wrong, you want to be careful not to go off on a wild goose chase. The idea behind Plan B is to look for clues that will lead you to spot one of the major errors that ETS likes to test. If all you're doing is trying out each of the answers in turn to see which one sounds better, you aren't really using Plan B. If you can't spot one of the major errors in the sentence or in the answer choices, you have to start considering that the sentence might be correct as written.

IF YOU'RE REALLY GUNG HO

You can expand your checklist to include as many types of errors as you like. Obviously the more types of errors you can identify, the better prepared you'll be to take the test. But you should bear in mind that while there are other types of errors that we haven't discussed, these errors don't come up very often on the GMAT. Some of the errors to consider: redundant words, misuse of the subjunctive mood, and the use of the passive voice when the active voice is possible. If you're seriously gunning to get every Sentence Correction question correct, you should dig out your old grammar book from high school and study it carefully. You should also take as many of the real ETS Sentence Correction sections in the *Official Guide for GMAT Review* as you can; pay special attention to the idiomatic expressions that come up in these sections, since these are sometimes repeated.

SUMMARY

1. GMAT English is different from American English. You have to learn the rules.

2. Fortunately, Sentence Correction questions test only a handful of rules. Once you learn them, you will be able to score quite well on this question-type.

3. There are two Princeton Review techniques that together will help you to ace Sentence Correction: Plan A, in which you look for specific errors as you read the sentence, and Plan B, in which you treat differences among the answer choices as clues that will help you spot the error.

4. Make a checklist of errors to look for when you read a Sentence Correction question. The most common are:

    A. *Pronouns*: If a sentence contains a pronoun, check to see whether it clearly refers to the noun it is replacing; also check to see whether the pronoun agrees in number with the noun to which it refers.

    B. *Misplaced modifiers:* If the sentence begins with a modifying phrase, check to make sure that the noun it modifies comes directly after the modifying phrase.

    C. *Parallel construction:* If a sentence contains a list of things, or actions, or is broken up into two halves, check to make sure the parts of the sentence are parallel.

    D. *Tense:* If the answer choices contain different verb tenses, make sure that the tense of the verb or verbs in the original sentence is correct. For the most part, verb tense should be consistent throughout a sentence.

    E. *Subject-verb agreement:* ETS sometimes puts extraneous prepositional phrases between the subject and the verb. Cover up these phrases so that you can see whether the subject and the verb of each clause in the sentence agree with each other.

F. *Apples-and-oranges:* When a sentence makes a comparison, check to see whether the two things being compared are comparable.

G. *Quantity words:* Whenever you see a quantity word (countable vs. uncountable; two vs. three or more) check to see if it is being used correctly.

H. *Idiom:* If a sentence contains an idiomatic expression that seems wrong to you, try taking the expression out of the sentence and creating a sentence of your own with the suspect expression.

5. If you've spotted the error, go through the answer choices and eliminate any that contain the same error. Then look at the remaining answer choices and find the one that fixes the sentence.

6. If you can't find the error, first look to the answer choices for clues. Then consider the possibility that there might not be an error.

7. About one-fifth of the sentences are correct as they are. When a sentence is correct, the answer is choice (A), which simply repeats the sentence word for word.

8. Once you've gained confidence in your ability to spot the major errors, you should expand your checklist to include other types of errors.

14

Reading Comprehension

Reading Comprehension questions make up roughly a third of the 41 questions on the verbal section of the GMAT—approximately 14 questions. Unlike the other questions on the test, Reading Comprehension questions come in clumps of three or four, and are based on reading passages that range from 200 to 350 words in length.

Before we begin, take a moment to read the following instructions, which are a close approximation of the instructions you will find on the real GMAT.

> Directions: Read the passage below, then answer questions based on your knowledge of what has been directly said in the passage or what can be inferred from it. You may have to use the scroll bar to see the entire passage. Answer each question by clicking the oval in front of the best response.

Be sure you know and understand these instructions before you take the GMAT. If you learn them ahead of time, you won't have to waste valuable seconds reading them on the day you take the test.

GMAT READING COMPREHENSION: CRACKING THE SYSTEM

It's important to know the instructions at the top of each group of Reading Comprehension questions on the GMAT, but it's much more important to understand what these instructions mean. ETS's instructions don't tell you everything you need to know about GMAT Reading Comprehension questions. The rest of this chapter will teach you what you do need to know.

Our techniques will enable you to:

1. read quickly in a way that will allow you to understand the main idea of the passage,

2. eliminate answer choices that could not possibly be correct,

3. take advantage of outside knowledge,

4. take advantage of inside information (about the way ETS's test writers think), and

5. find answers in some cases *without reading the passage.*

BASIC PASSAGE TYPES

There are only three types of passages on the GMAT:

1. *The social science passage*: This usually concerns a social or historical issue. For example, you might see a passage about world food shortages or the history of a civil rights movement.

2. *The science passage*: This might describe a scientific phenomenon, such as gravitation or plate tectonics.

3. *The business passage*: This usually discusses a business-related topic. For example, you might see a passage about the privatization of state-owned industries, or the causes of inflation.

The subject matter for one of the passages on each test may concern a minority group. There are certain useful techniques that can be used on this passage. We'll tell you more about that later in the chapter.

ORDER OF DIFFICULTY

The level of difficulty of the passages you see will depend on how you are doing on the exam—but unlike all the other questions on the GMAT, the three to four Reading Comprehension questions based on each passage are *not* arranged in order of difficulty. You will see the same questions based on this passage, regardless of how you answer them. ETS found it too hard to write lots of different questions based on such brief passages.

WHAT YOU WILL SEE ON YOUR SCREEN

The reading passage appears on the left side of the screen. The questions appear one at a time on the right side of the screen, so you can always refer back to the passage. You can't see the next question until you answer the one before, and as always, you can't go back to a previous question once you've moved on.

Here's an example of what the screen will look like:

Sentence Correction Review

Q: How do you find quantity word mistakes?

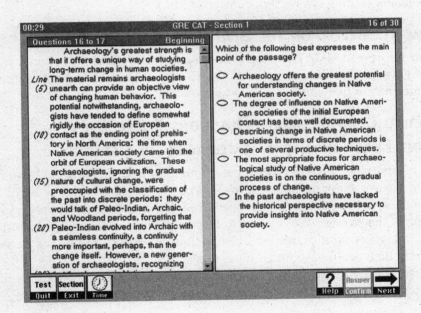

THE LONG AND THE SHORT OF IT

The reading passages come in two lengths—the shorter passages fit completely on the computer screen, but the longer passages will require you to use a scroll bar to read them entirely. For those of you who are unfamiliar with a scroll bar, it is the long vertical gray bar just to the right of the passage in the diagram on the preceding page. If you place your mouse at the arrow at the bottom of the bar and hold down the mouse button, the passage will "scroll" down, enabling you to see the second half of the passage. To get back up, do the same thing to the arrow at the top of the scroll bar.

IS THIS LIKE NORMAL READING?

GMAT reading has nothing to do with normal reading. For one thing, no one in his right mind would ever read one of these passages of his own free will. They are almost always boring. For another, if you've spent any time on the Internet, you know that reading off a computer screen is much more tiring than reading from a printed page.

IS THIS LIKE BUSINESS READING?

GMAT reading has even less to do with business reading. If your boss asked you to analyze a quarterly report and make a presentation of all the points it raised, you would go home and spend hours going over it. You would look for important information, anticipate questions, and memorize statistics.

Business reading is a careful, painstaking process.

HOW TO SUCCEED ON THE GMAT

If you try to read GMAT passages the way you read quarterly reports, you'll never have time for the questions. Worse, you'll have spent a lot of time absorbing information that you don't need to know.

READING COMPREHENSION QUESTIONS COVER ONLY A TINY FRACTION OF THE MATERIAL IN THE PASSAGE

Each reading passage comes with three or four questions. You probably assumed that to answer these questions correctly you would need to know all of the information in the passage, but this isn't true. The questions cover only a small portion of the passage. We're going to teach you how to identify the important parts and ignore most of the rest. The less time you spend reading the passage, the more time you'll have for earning points.

There are two types of questions in Reading Comprehension and neither requires you to memorize specific information:

1. *General questions*: To answer these, you need to have an understanding of the main idea and, perhaps, the *structure* of the passage.

Sentence Correction Review

A: Look for quantity words and know whether the noun they modify is countable or not countable. (See the lists on pages 189–190).

2. *Specific questions*: Since you'll be asked about only a few specific pieces of information, it's silly to try to remember all of the specific information contained in a passage. It makes much more sense to have a vague idea of where specific information is located in the passage. That way you'll know where to look for it if you need it.

GMAT READING: THE PRINCETON REVIEW METHOD

Think of a GMAT reading passage as a house. The main idea of the passage is like the overall plan of the house; the main idea of each paragraph is like the plan of each room. Reading the passage is like walking quickly through the house. You don't want to waste time memorizing every detail of every room; you want to develop a general sense of the layout of the house.

Later, when ETS asks you what was sitting on the table beside the chair in the master bedroom, you won't know the answer off the top of your head, but you will know exactly where to look for it. And you'll be able to answer more questions in less time than someone who has tried to memorize every detail.

TAKING NOTES

As you make your fast read, you'll probably want to write a one- or two-word summary of each paragraph on your scratch paper. This is partly to make yourself articulate what the main idea of each paragraph is—but it is also in order to remember them. Have you ever had the experience of reading an entire passage, getting to the end, and then saying, "I have no idea what I just read?"

Most GMAT passages inspire exactly that thought.

STEP ONE: READ FOR THE MAIN IDEA

Take a look at the first paragraph of a sample GMAT passage:

> Biologists have long known that some types of electromagnetic radiation such as X rays and gamma rays can be dangerous to human beings. Operating at a frequency of 10^{18} through 10^{22} mhz, these rays, which are well above the visible light spectrum, were first detected in the early years of the 20th century.

Here's how to crack it

The first sentence of a paragraph should always be read carefully since it is so often the key to understanding the entire paragraph. This first sentence was no exception: It tells you that the paragraph is about two types of radiation and their danger to humans. On your scratch paper, jot down a couple of key words to encapsulate the main idea.

However, once you've got the main idea, it isn't necessary to pay a lot of attention to the other sentences in the paragraph. For example, you probably noticed that while the second sentence included some specific facts, it added nothing to our understanding of the main point of the paragraph. Later, if ETS asks you a specific question about this radiation, you can go back and find the answer; it will still be there.

Sentence Correction Review

Q: How do you spot an error in idiom?

THINK OF THIS AS *VARIABLE* SPEED READING

Until you know what the main idea of a paragraph is, you want to read very carefully. However, as soon as you've got a handle on what's going on, you can speed up. Let your eyes glaze over when you get to the small details. Until ETS asks you about them, who cares?

Sentence Correction Review

A: Become familiar with the check list on pages 195–196.

The goal is to spend no more than a minute or two "reading" the entire passage. Impossible? Sure, if you're going to insist on reading the way you normally do. Just remember that you don't get any points for reading the passages; when you take the real GMAT the proctor will *not* be walking around the test room awarding extra points for great reading technique. You get points for *answering questions*.

Try reading the second paragraph in the way we've suggested above:

> However, until now, no one has ever suggested that microwave radiation might also be harmful. In preliminary laboratory results, Cleary and Milham have found elevated growth rates in cancer cells exposed to low doses of microwaves. Cleary exposed cancer cells to levels of radiation that are commonly found in microwave ovens and found that the abnormal cells grew 30 percent faster than did unexposed cells. Milham's study focused on ham radio operators who are commonly exposed to levels of radiation slightly higher than those emitted by cellular telephones. He discovered elevated levels of myeloid leukemia.

Here's how to crack it

Reading the first sentence carefully, we realize that this paragraph is going off on a tangent thought. In fact, the passage is *not* going to be about the dangers of X rays or gamma rays; it is going to be about the possible dangers of microwaves. Now that we have the main idea, we can afford to skim or skip over the rest of the paragraph. If ETS asks us later about Cleary or Milham, we'll know where to find them, but until then, we can let this part of the passage pass in a blur.

Now try reading the last paragraph of the passage:

> The methodology of Cleary and Milham has been questioned by other scientists in the field. However, no one seriously disputes that their preliminary findings must be taken seriously or that new studies should be set up to try to duplicate their results. Although federal guidelines for how much electromagnetic energy can be allowed to enter the work and home environment have been made more stringent since they were first implemented in 1982, the recent studies pose troubling questions about the safety of microwaves.

Here's how to crack it

The first word of the second sentence ("however") let us know that the author was going to come back to the original point: Microwaves may be dangerous. Was this a conclusion? You bet.

In retrospect, the organization of the passage is pretty clear.

- The *first* paragraph states the dangers of other types of waves.

- The *second* paragraph talks about the dangers of microwaves as shown by two studies.

- The *third* questions the two studies, but decides that, on balance, microwaves may indeed be dangerous.

STEP TWO: AS YOU READ, LOOK FOR STRUCTURAL SIGNPOSTS

Certain words instantly tell you a lot about the structure of a passage. For example, if you were reading a paragraph that began, "There are three reasons why the Grand Canyon should be strip-mined," at some point in the paragraph you would expect to find three reasons listed. If a sentence begins, "on the one hand," you would expect to find an "on the other hand" later in the sentence. These structural signposts show an alert reader what's going to happen later in a passage. Here are some structural signposts to look out for on the GMAT.

TRIGGER WORDS

The second paragraph you just read began with a word which probably automatically clued you in to the fact that a change was on its way: The word was "however."

Trigger words (such as "however" and "but") always signal a change in the direction of a passage. Here's a simple example:

First paragraph: Most economists believe that the budget deficit will take years to remedy . . .

Second paragraph: HOWEVER (trigger word), some economists believe there may a fast solution to the problem.

In this example the trigger word signals that the second paragraph will modify or qualify what has gone before. A trigger word at the beginning of any paragraph is a sure sign that this paragraph will disagree with what was stated in the preceding one.

Trigger words are important even if they do not appear at the beginning of a paragraph; they always signal a change of meaning, even if it is only within a sentence. Here are the trigger words that often appear on the GMAT:

but
although (even though)
however
yet
despite (in spite of)
nevertheless
nonetheless
notwithstanding
except
while
unless
on the other hand

CONTINUING-THE-SAME-TRAIN-OF-THOUGHT WORDS

Some structural signposts let you know that there will be no contradiction, no change in path. If you see a "first of all" it stands to reason that there will be a "second of all" and perhaps a "third." Other signs of continuation:

in addition
by the same token
likewise
similarly
this (implies a reference to preceding sentence)
thus (implies a conclusion)

One other continuing structural element that appears on the GMAT is not a word. Sentences or fragments that appear inside *parentheses* often contain information you'll need to answer a question. You should make a mental note of any sentence or fragment that is enclosed in parentheses.

YIN-YANG WORDS

One of ETS's all-time favorite types of passage contrasts two opposing viewpoints, and certain words immediately give this away. See if you can supply the second half of the following sentences:

> The traditional view *of the causes of global warming focuses on the burning of fossil fuel* . . .

(Second half: However, the *new* view is that there is some other cause.)

> Until recently, *it was thought that the Mayan civilization was destroyed as a result of drought* . . .

(Second half: However, *now* we believe that they were destroyed by space invaders.)

> The classical *model of laissez-faire capitalism does not even admit the possibility of government intervention* . . .

(Second half: But the *rock and roll* version of laissez-faire capitalism says, "Let me just get my checkbook.")

Before 1960, it was commonly assumed that the atom was the smallest particle in the universe . . .

(Second half: However, *after 1960* scientists began to suspect that there was something even smaller.)

Whenever you spot a "yin" word, you should realize that there is a "yang" on the way. Some other yin-yang words:

Yin	Yang
generally	(however, this time . . .)
the old view	(however, the new view . . .)
the widespread belief	(but the in-crowd believes . . .)
most scientists think	(but Doctor Spleegle thinks . . .)
on the one hand	(on the other hand . . .)

GETTING THROUGH THE PASSAGE FASTER

Structural elements like these can help you understand a passage faster, with less "reading" and less wear and tear on your brain. When you spot one of these signposts, make a mental note. If it actually starts a paragraph, you might begin your three-word synopsis of the paragraph with a big "but." A structural signpost is usually more important to your understanding of a passage than any individual fact within that passage.

STEP THREE: ATTACK THE QUESTIONS

Once you've grasped the main ideas of the paragraphs, you can attack the questions aggressively. As we noted earlier, each passage is followed by up to four questions of varying levels of difficulty. These questions *generally* follow the organization of the passage. In other words, a question about the first paragraph will probably come before a question about the second paragraph.

GENERAL QUESTIONS

- ◆ "What is the primary purpose of this passage?"

- ◆ "What is the author's tone?"

- ◆ "Which of the following best describes the structure of the passage?"

Each of the questions above is a general question. A two-minute "read" using the techniques we've shown you over the last few pages should be all that you need to answer the general questions—without going back to the passage. Always try to answer a general question in your own words *before* you look at the answer choices.

Sentence Correction Review: Quantity Comparison Words

comparing two items
between
more
better
less

comparing more than two items
among
most
best
least

USING POE TO ELIMINATE WRONG ANSWERS ON GENERAL QUESTIONS

Once you have your *own* idea of what the answer should be, it's time to use POE to zero in on *ETS*'s answer. In the chapter on Sentence Correction, you learned that it's often easier to eliminate incorrect answers than to select the correct answers. The Process of Elimination is just as useful on Reading Comprehension questions. How can you use POE to eliminate wrong answers to general questions?

General questions have general answers. Thus, we can eliminate any answer to a general question that focuses on only one part of the passage or is too specific in some other way. We can also eliminate answers which cite information that's not in the passage at all. For example, here's a question based on the passage you have already read:

> The main topic of the passage is
> ○ the health hazards of X rays and gamma rays on humans
> ○ the overly severe federal guidelines on radiation
> ○ the potential dangers of microwaves
> ○ to compare and contrast the work of Cleary and Milham
> ○ the limits of study methodology in science

Here's how to crack it

In spite of the fact that X rays and gamma rays were mentioned in the first sentence, we know that this was just an introductory thought to get to the real idea of the passage—the danger of microwaves. So eliminate choice (A). The federal guidelines in choice (B) were mentioned in the passage, but only at the very end. Could this be the main idea of the entire passage? No way. Choice (C) is the correct answer, and exactly what we should be expecting from our fast "read." While Cleary and Milham are discussed several times, they are never compared, so we can eliminate choice (D). And while the passage mentions that the methodologies of the two scientists have been questioned, this is not the main idea, so we can eliminate choice (E) as well.

SPECIFIC QUESTIONS

> ◆ "The passage suggests which of the following about the laboratory results on microwaves mentioned in line 12?"

> ◆ "According to the passage, a study of ham radio operators might be expected to find which of the following?"

Each of the questions above is a specific question. Specific questions have specific answers which you'll now need to find. Naturally, your two-minute "read" has not equipped you with the answers to these questions, but every specific question gives you a clue about where to look for the answer.

LINE NUMBERS

How do you find the answer to the following question?

> "The passage suggests which of the following about the federal guidelines on microwaves mentioned in line 12?"

That's easy: It has a line number. All you have to do is go back to the cited line or lines and read starting a little above them until you come to the answer to the question.

LEAD WORDS

How do you find the answer to *this* question?

> "According to the passage, a study of ham radio operators might be expected to find which of the following?"

When a question seems to be specific but gives no line number, look for a catchy word or phrase in the question. For example, in this question, there's a very clear specific reference: "ham radio operators." We call this a **lead** phrase. Now that you know what you're looking for, run your finger down the passage on the screen as you scroll until you see your lead word or phrase. When you find it, you will have almost certainly found your answer.

Try this technique out right now by running your finger down the passage below until you find "ham radio operators." Don't read; just look:

> Biologists have long known that some types of electromagnetic radiation such as X rays and gamma rays can be dangerous to human beings. Operating at a frequency of 10^{18} through 10^{22} mhz, these rays, which are well above the visible light spectrum, were first detected in the early years of the 20th century.
>
> However, until now, no one has ever suggested that microwave radiation might also be harmful. In preliminary laboratory results, Cleary and Milham have found elevated growth rates in cancer cells exposed to low doses of microwaves. Cleary exposed cancer cells to levels of radiation that are commonly found in microwave ovens and found that the abnormal cells grew 30 percent faster than did unexposed cells. Milham's study focused on ham radio operators who are commonly exposed to levels of radiation slightly higher than those emitted by cellular telephones. He discovered elevated levels of myeloid leukemia.

The methodology of Cleary and Milham has been questioned by other scientists in the field. However, no one seriously disputes that their preliminary findings must be taken seriously or that new studies should be set up to try to duplicate their results. Although federal guidelines for how much electromagnetic energy can be allowed to enter the work and home environment have been made more stringent since they were first implemented in 1982, the recent studies pose troubling questions about the safety of microwaves.

USING POE TO ELIMINATE WRONG ANSWERS ON SPECIFIC QUESTIONS

Specific questions have very specific answers. Before you even go to the answer choices, you should usually be able to point to the exact spot in the passage where the answer to the question is to be found.

Once you go to the answer choices, you'll probably be able to eliminate several right away. However, if you are down to two possibilities, don't try to prove one of the answers right. Look for something in the passage that will make one of the answers *wrong*. It's often easier to find the flaw in an incorrect answer. For example, here's a question (complete with answer choices) based on the passage you have already read:

> According to the passage, a study of ham radio operators might be expected to find which of the following?
>
> ○ The presence of X rays and gamma rays
> ○ Unusual cells growing 30% faster than normal
> ○ A level of radiation exposure similar to that found in users of microwave ovens
> ○ Higher levels of a particular type of leukemia
> ○ Levels of radiation identical to those emitted by cellular phones

Here's how to crack it

The lead words, "ham radio operators" led us to the second half of the second paragraph. If you haven't already, read the relevant sentences and get an idea of what you might expect the answer to be.

Now, go to the answer choices. Would a study of ham radio operators find the presence of X rays and gamma rays? Well, neither are mentioned in *this* paragraph. The *first* paragraph did mention these rays—but only to introduce the dangers of microwaves. So much for choice (A).

Both choices (B) and (C) were mentioned in this paragraph, but only in connection with *Cleary's* work—which had nothing to do with ham radio operators.

You might have been torn between choices (D) and (E) since both come from the right place in the passage. Don't try to decide which is correct. Look for a reason why one of them is *wrong*. Let's attack choice (E). It says that ham operators were exposed to levels of radiation identical to those emitted by cellular phones. Is that *exactly* what the passage said? Well, no. According to the passage, ham radio operators were exposed to slightly *higher* levels. Choice (E) is history. The correct answer must be choice (D).

INFERENCE QUESTIONS

"Which of the following can be inferred from the passage about the level of radiation from cellular telephones?"

Although this question asks you to draw an inference, you'll find that ETS's idea of an inference will be much more timid than yours. GMAT inferences go at most a *tiny* bit further than the passage itself. If your thoughts about this type of question becomes too subtle, you'll get it wrong. Here's an example:

Which of the following can be inferred from the passage about the studies conducted by Cleary and Milham?

- ⬭ Cleary's results were better documented than Milham's.
- ⬭ Neither study is scientifically valid.
- ⬭ Both studies indicated that microwaves were more harmful than X rays.
- ⬭ The final results were not in at the time the article was written.
- ⬭ The results of both studies were based on the same scientific data.

Here's how to crack it

The passage never said that one study was better than the other, so eliminate answer choice (A). While both studies were questioned in the third paragraph, it would be inferring far too much to say that neither was scientifically valid. Eliminate choice (B). The passage never said that microwaves were more harmful than X rays. It seems likely that they are less harmful. Eliminate choice (C). The results of both studies were called "preliminary" in paragraph two. Thus, choice (D) seems so obvious that you might almost hesitate to call it an inference. This is exactly the kind of inference that ETS feels comfortable making. Choice (E) was not just *not* stated. It is likely to be false. Cleary concentrated on cancerous cells exposed to levels of radiation equivalent to microwave ovens. Milham studied ham radio operators. The correct answer was (D).

Q: What is the purpose of skimming the passage?

ADVANCED POE: ATTACKING DISPUTABLE ANSWER CHOICES

Say you've eliminated two answer choices on a Reading Comprehension question, but you can't decide which of the remaining three choices is best. All three seem to be saying the same thing. How do you choose between them? The test writers at ETS want their correct answers to be indisputable so that no one will ever be able to complain.

Here are three statements. Which of them is indisputable?

○ Shaw was the greatest dramatist of his time.
○ Shaw's genius was never understood.
○ Shaw was a great dramatist, although some critics disagree.

Shaw's status as a playwright will always be a matter of opinion. If ETS made the first statement the correct answer to a Reading Comprehension question, people who got the question wrong might argue that not everyone considers Shaw the greatest dramatist of his time.

If ETS made the second statement the correct answer to a Reading Comprehension question, people who got the question wrong could argue that someone, somewhere in the world, must have understood poor old Shaw.

The third statement, by contrast, is indisputable. Most critics would agree that Shaw was *a* great dramatist. If there are any critics who do not, ETS covers itself with a little disclaimer; "although some critics disagree." The third statement is so vague that no one could possibly argue with it.

In general, an answer choice that is highly specific and unequivocal is *disputable* and is therefore usually not the correct answer.

An answer choice that is general and vague is *indisputable* and is therefore often the correct answer.

HOW TO PICK AN INDISPUTABLE ANSWER CHOICE

Certain words make a statement so vague that it is almost impossible to dispute. Here are some of these words:

usually
sometimes
may
can
some
most

If a statement says that Shaw is *sometimes* considered to be the greatest dramatist ever, who can dispute that?

How to Avoid a Disputable Answer Choice

Certain words make a statement so specific that it's easy to dispute. Here are some of these words:

> always
> must
> everybody
> all
> complete
> never

If a statement says that Shaw is *always* considered to be the greatest dramatist ever, who couldn't dispute that?

What Does Wally Want to Pick?

The GMAT was created in 1954. Although it is now administered on computer, the *philosophical* outlook of the test has remained pretty much the same. Every year the same information is tested in pretty much the same way. The GMAT is frozen in time. It harkens back to a more innocent era—a time when there were answers to every question, and America was always right, and all of our problems were on the way to being solved. ETS reading passages are still largely written from that perspective.

It is a perspective you may not understand, since you probably weren't around in the 1950s. But we've all experienced that era indirectly, in the form of 1950s television sitcoms. Think of the GMAT as the test Wally Cleaver would have had to take if he'd decided to go to business school.

Whenever you're in doubt about an answer, it always helps to ask yourself whether Wally would have felt comfortable selecting that answer.

Respect for Professionals

ETS has tremendous respect for all professionals—doctors, scientists, economists, writers, and artists. After all, Dr. Kildare never got sued for malpractice, and Wally would feel very uncomfortable selecting an answer choice that implied that any professional was a terrible person.

By the same token, it would be unusual to find a correct answer choice that took any but the lightest digs at America. Our country is pretty much beyond ETS's reproach.

Moderate Emotion

ETS avoids strong emotions on the GMAT. If Wally took the GMAT, he would never pick an answer choice that took too strong a position about anything. The author's tone might be "slightly critical," but it will not be "scornful and envious." The author's tone might be "admiring," but it will never be "wildly enthusiastic."

> **Reading Comprehension trigger words that signal a change in meaning:**
> - but
> - although (even though)
> - however
> - yet
> - despite (in spite of)
> - nevertheless
> - nonetheless
> - notwithstanding
> - except
> - while
> - unless
> - on the other hand

THE MINORITY PASSAGE

For many years minority groups have complained—justifiably—that ETS tests discriminate against them. ETS responded to this criticism by adding a minority passage to many of its tests. One of the reading passages on the GMAT you take will almost certainly be about some oppressed group—African-Americans, Mexican-Americans, women.

Designed to answer charges that ETS tests are biased, the minority passage is invariably positive in tone. This doesn't make the test any fairer to minorities, but it does sometimes make the test easier to beat. Any answer choice that expresses negative views of the minority in question is almost certainly wrong. Try the following example:

> The author considers women's literature to be
>
> ○ derivative
> ○ lacking in imagination
> ○ full of promise and hope
> ○ much better than the literature being written
>   by men today
> ○ uninteresting

Here's how to crack it

You don't need to see the passage to answer this question. The whole purpose of the minority passage is to illustrate to everyone how broad-minded and unbiased the GMAT really is. *Derivative*, *lacking in imagination*, and *uninteresting* all express negative opinions of literature written by (what ETS considers to be) a minority group. Wally would never have picked choices (A), (B), or (E).

Answer choice (D) goes too far in the other direction. As far as Wally and ETS are concerned, women's literature is just as good as, but no better than, anyone else's. The answer must be choice (C).

PUTTING ALL THIS TO WORK

Now that you know something about how to tackle GMAT passages and what to look for in them, try the sample passage below. Find the main idea of each paragraph (and if you like, jot down a few key words about each on scratch paper); look for structural signposts along the way.

Try to spend no more than two minutes "reading." Remember, you only get points for answering questions. (At the end of this chapter you will find the scratch paper notes that one of our teachers made when she "read" the passage.)

Remember, ETS will give you no more than four questions per passage. We've included a few extra questions just for practice.

Until recently, corporate ideology in the United States has held that bigger is better. This traditional view of the primacy of big, centralized companies is now being challenged as some of the giants of American business are being outperformed by a new generation of smaller, streamlined businesses. If it was the industrial revolution that spawned the era of massive industrialized companies, then perhaps it is the information revolution of the 1990s that is spawning the era of the small company.

For most of this century, big companies dominated an American business scene that seemed to thrive on its own grandness of scale. The expansion westward, the growth of the railroad and steel industries, an almost limitless supply of cheap raw materials, plus a population boom that provided an ever-increasing demand for new products (if not a cheap source of labor) all coincided to encourage the growth of large companies.

But rapid developments in the marketplace have begun to change the accepted rules of business, and have underscored the need for fast reaction times. Small companies, without huge overhead and inventory, can respond quickly to a technologically advanced age in which new products and technologies can become outmoded within a year of their being brought to market.

Of course, successful emerging small companies face a potential dilemma in that their very success will tend to turn them into copies of the large corporate dinosaurs they are now supplanting. To avoid this trap, small companies may look to the example of several CEOs of large corporations who have broken down their sprawling organizations into small, semi-independent divisions capable of making the leap into the next century.

ATTACKING THE QUESTIONS

While you skim a passage, be aware of its structure. Is one theory presented and then discounted? Are there lists of items? Does it provide two schools of thought? Trigger words, which act as structural signposts, can help you uncover a passage's structure.

1. The primary purpose of the passage is to

   ⬭ present evidence that resolves a contradiction in business theory

   ⬭ discuss reasons why an accepted business pattern is changing

   ⬭ describe a theoretical model and a method whereby that model can be tested

   ⬭ argue that a traditional ideology deserves new attention

   ⬭ resolve two conflicting explanations for a phenomenon

Here's how to crack it

This is a general question, and general questions always reflect the structure of the passage. The first words of the passage were "until recently." We hope you recognized right away that this was "yin-yang" terminology, as was "this traditional view." Obviously this passage was about to present a *new* view.

The old view, according to the passage, was that in America large companies were always better off than small companies. Of course, the new view is that smaller companies are now doing better than big companies. This was probably enough for you to answer all the general questions in this section, but let's look quickly at the rest of the passage: Paragraph two gave historical reasons why bigger used to be better; paragraph three explained why this was no longer true today; and paragraph four concludes by talking about how small companies can stay successful as they inevitably get bigger. Let's look at the answer choices.

(A) In yin-yang passages, new is virtually always better than old. There is really no contradiction here, and besides, how could a 250-word passage "resolve" anything definitively? Eliminate it.

(B) This is the correct answer. It mirrors the yin-yang structure of the passage—the accepted pattern of almost a century is now changing.

(C) If you picked this one, you were thinking too hard. Perhaps you thought the primacy of the small company was the new theoretical model, about to be tested. However, the passage seems to imply that the decline of large companies and the ascendancy of small companies started before anyone even realized what was happening, let alone came up with some smart theory about it.

(D) Was the author arguing that in fact the traditional view that "bigger is better" is actually correct after all? Nope. Eliminate it.

(E) GMAT passages virtually never "resolve" anything. How could you hope to resolve a complex issue in 250 words? While there are two conflicting elements in this passage, they are not conflicting explanations for a single phenomenon.

2. According to the passage, all of the following are examples of developments that helped promote the growth of large companies earlier in this century EXCEPT

- ⟳ the growth of the railroad industry
- ⟳ America's westward expansion
- ⟳ an almost inexhaustible source of raw materials
- ⟳ the existence of an inexpensive source of labor
- ⟳ the development of an industry to produce steel

Here's how to crack it

This is a specific question without a line number, but you probably knew just where to look. Which paragraph gave historical background on the growth of large companies? If you said paragraph two, you are absolutely correct.

The first time you "read" this passage, you may have skipped over the specifics in this paragraph since they weren't necessary to understand the purpose of the paragraph. Now, of course, you are interested. But even if you had spent twenty minutes you didn't really have memorizing the entire passage, wouldn't you still have wanted to peek back at this paragraph just to make sure you remembered it correctly? Since you were going to have to look back anyway, it made sense to skip over the details the first time around. Remember, there was no guarantee that there would even be a question about this information. It is not unusual to find GMAT passages whose questions completely ignore whole paragraphs at a time.

This is an "except" question, which means that every answer choice is correct but one. The answer to this question was buried inside the parentheses in lines 19–20: "(if not a cheap source of labor.)" The answer to this question is choice (D).

3. The author's attitude toward the traditional view expressed in lines 1–7 can best be described as

- ⟳ scornful and denunciatory
- ⟳ dispirited and morose
- ⟳ critical but respectful
- ⟳ admiring and deferential
- ⟳ uncertain but interested

Here's how to crack it

You could eliminate two of these answer choices without even reading the passage. Wally would never have chosen an answer that described an attitude toward the ideology of companies like General Motors in terms like "scornful and denunciatory" or "dispirited and morose." As far as the passage is concerned, the traditional ideology no longer works, so we can pretty much rule out choice (D), admiring and deferential. Choice (E) is a little too vague. Both choices

(A) and (B) are so strong and out in left field that we can safely eliminate them. The only possible answer is choice (C).

4. It can be inferred from the passage that which of the following actions would be most consistent with the traditional ideology described in the passage?
   ○ Splitting a manufacturing company into several smaller divisions
   ○ Bringing a new product to market within a year
   ○ Creating a department to utilize new emerging technologies
   ○ Expanding an existing company in anticipation of growing demand
   ○ Cutting inventory and decreasing overhead

Here's how to crack it

The trick in inference questions is to infer as little as possible. The traditional ideology is that bigger is better. Which of the answer choices shows a situation getting bigger? The correct answer is choice (D). Choices (A) and (E) both illustrate the process of downsizing as described in the passage. Choices (B) and (C) illustrate the lean-and-mean tactics attributed in the passage to small companies.

5. According to the passage, to avoid the trap posed by "the potential dilemma" mentioned in line 32, emerging successful small companies will have to do which of the following?
   ○ Turn for advice to the industry analysts who earlier predicted the problems of large companies
   ○ Avoid taking paths that will make them too successful
   ○ Learn to embrace the traditional ideology of large corporations
   ○ Create small interconnected divisions rather than expanding in traditional ways
   ○ Hire successful CEOs from other firms

Here's how to crack it

Whenever you see a specific question with line numbers, always remember to read a little above and a little below the cited line. In this case, we are not interested so much in the "dilemma" as we are in avoiding the trap posed by the dilemma. The answer to this question is in the last three lines of the passage. Let's look at the answer choices:

(A) is an interesting idea, but it is not said in the passage, so we can eliminate it.

(B) has the right idea, but takes it too far. It is practically un-American to think that a company would try not to become too successful.

(C) The traditional ideology is what got the big companies into trouble. Eliminate.

(D) This is the correct answer, and a nice paraphrase of what was said in the last three lines of the passage.

(E) The passage suggests that small companies could learn from these CEOs, but does not suggest that the small companies *hire* the CEOs.

6. Which of the following best describes the organization of the first paragraph of the passage?

○ A conventional model is dismissed and an alternative is introduced.
○ An assertion is made and a general supporting example is given.
○ Two contradictory points of view are presented and evaluated.
○ A historical overview is given to explain a phenomenon.
○ A new theory is described and then qualified.

Here's how to crack it

This is a structure question, pure and simple. Let's look at the answers:

(A) correctly describes this yin-yang paragraph.

(B) ignores the structure of the passage.

(C) is close, but fails to show that one point of view is considered superior to the other.

(D) describes paragraph two instead of paragraph one.

(E) The word "qualified" means "limited." The author seems to like the idea of the small company, and certainly doesn't qualify it in the first paragraph.

7. It can be inferred from the passage that small companies are better able to adapt to the new business climate due to which of the following factors?

    I. low overhead and inventory
    II. the ability to predict when new products will become outmoded
    III. the capacity to change quickly to meet new challenges

  ◯ I only
  ◯ II only
  ◯ III only
  ◯ I and III only
  ◯ I, II, and III

B-School Lingo

Run the Numbers: analyze quantitatively

Here's how to crack it

I, II, III questions are nasty because you have to answer three questions in order to get one right. Where in the passage were small companies actually described? If you said paragraph three, you were absolutely correct. Since this is an inference question, we need to make sure we don't infer too far. Let's look at statement I. Can we infer that small companies are better able to adapt because of low inventory? Sure. In lines 25–26 the passage reads, "Small companies, without huge overhead and inventory. . ."

Since we know that statement I works, we can cross off choices (B) and (C); why? Because neither includes statement I. Let's look at statement II. While it seems likely that the ability to predict ahead of time which products are going to become outmoded would help small companies adapt faster, there is no indication in the passage that anyone has the ability to predict ahead. If you aren't sure about statement II, you can skip it and go on to statement III. This statement is definitely true. It is a paraphrase of line 25. The correct answer is choice (D).

HERE'S WHAT YOUR SCRATCH PAPER SHOULD LOOK LIKE AFTER YOU'VE FINISHED READING THIS PASSAGE

1) Traditional view: bigger is better
New view: small is better

2) Hist. reasons for big companies' success

3) reasons for small companies' success

4) danger for small companies: getting too big

SUMMARY

1. Reading Comprehension questions make up roughly a third of the 41 questions on the verbal section of the GMAT—approximately 14 questions. The three types of passages that may appear on the test are social science, science, and business.

2. Reading Comprehension questions are not presented in any order of difficulty.

3. GMAT reading has little to do with regular reading, and even less to do with business reading. GMAT passages contain many more pieces of information than you'll be tested on. Trying to remember all this useless information is silly.

4. Read a passage for its main idea. This will enable you to answer the general questions, and give you a good idea of where to look for the answers to specific questions. Specific facts are unimportant at this stage. Skim them. Write notes on your scratch paper.

5. Structural signposts can help you see how a passage is organized. Look for trigger words, continuing-the-same-train-of-thought words, and yin-yang constructions.

6. Answers to specific questions can be found either through **line numbers** or **lead words**. When line references are given, read a little above and a little below them.

7. Attack answer choices that are disputable. Specific, strong statements are often wrong. Vague, wimpy statements are often correct.

8. The tone of a minority passage is invariably positive. This can sometimes help you to answer questions even if you haven't had time to read the entire passage.

9. If the Beaver's older brother, Wally, wouldn't have liked a particular answer, there's a good chance it's wrong. Wally wouldn't have liked answers that

    A. are disrespectful to professionals
    B. are too strong
    C. condone prejudicial attitudes

10. I, II, III questions are best tackled by POE.

15

Critical Reasoning

Critical Reasoning questions make up roughly a third of the 41 questions on the verbal section of the GMAT— approximately 14 questions. They consist of very short reading passages (typically twenty to 100 words). Each of these passages is followed by one or two questions. These questions are supposed to test your ability to think clearly. ETS says that "no knowledge of the terminology and of the conventions of formal logic is presupposed." Nevertheless, you'll find that while it may not be presupposed, some knowledge of the rudiments of formal logic—as applied by The Princeton Review—can substantially increase your score.

THE HISTORY OF CRITICAL REASONING

Over the years ETS has tried several different formats in an attempt to test reasoning ability.

The original GMAT contained a section called Best Arguments. In 1961, ETS replaced this section ("in part because research indicated that [doing so] would increase the predictive effectiveness of the test") with something called Organization of Ideas. In 1966, this section was also phased out, and for six years reasoning ability went unmeasured by ETS. In 1972, ETS tried again, with a section called Analysis of Situations. Finally, on the October 1988 version of the GMAT, ETS unveiled Critical Reasoning for the first time.

WELL, NOT EXACTLY THE *FIRST* TIME

In fact, Critical Reasoning looks a lot like Best Arguments. ETS has used this type of question for years on the LSAT and the GRE—respectively, the Law School Admission Test and the Graduate Record Exam.

Before we begin, take a moment to read a close approximation of the instructions at the beginning of each Critical Reasoning question:

> Directions: After reading the question, pick the
> best answer among the choices that follow.

Obviously you won't need to read these instructions again.

HOW TO ATTACK THE CRITICAL REASONING QUESTIONS

The terseness of ETS's instructions implies that all you need on these questions is common sense. Common sense will certainly help, but you should also understand a bit about the formal logic on which Critical Reasoning is based.

Like the other types of questions found on the GMAT, Critical Reasoning questions tend to be predictable. There are only a few question types, and as you learn how the test writers use their smattering of formal logic to write Critical Reasoning questions, you'll be able to anticipate the answers to certain of those questions.

In this chapter we'll teach you how to:

1. use clues in the questions to anticipate the kind of answer you're looking for in a passage

2. analyze and attack the passages in an organized fashion

3. understand the basic structure of the passages

4. use Process of Elimination to eliminate wrong choices

A Word about GMAT Logic

GMAT logic is different from the formal logic you may have studied in college. Our review of GMAT logic is not intended to be representative of logic as a whole. We don't intend to teach you logic; we're going to teach you *GMAT* logic.

The Passage

Most Critical Reasoning passages are in the form of *arguments* in which the writer tries to convince the reader of something. Here's an example:

> In the past 10 years, advertising revenues for the magazine *True Investor* have fallen by 30%. The magazine has failed to attract new subscribers, and newsstand sales are down to an all-time low. Thus, sweeping editorial changes will be necessary if the magazine is to survive.

There are three main parts to an argument.

The Conclusion: This is what the author is trying to convince us of.

The Premises: These are the pieces of evidence the author gives to support the conclusion.

The Assumptions: These are unstated ideas or evidence without which the entire conclusion might be invalid.

In the passage above, the author's *conclusion* is found in the last line:

> *Thus, sweeping editorial changes will be necessary if the magazine is to survive.*

To support this, the author gives three pieces of evidence, or *premises*: Advertising revenue is down; there are no new subscribers; and very few people are buying the newspaper at the newsstand.

Are there any *assumptions* here? Well, not in the passage itself. Assumptions are never stated by the author. They are parts of the argument that have been left out. Even the best thought-out argument has assumptions. In this case one important assumption the author seems to be making is that it was the old editorial policy that caused the problems the magazine is now encountering.

A Critical Reasoning passage is not necessarily made up of only these three parts. The passage might contain other information as well—extraneous ideas, perhaps, or statements of an opposing point of view. It's also possible that some important part of an argument will be missing—its conclusion, for example. Sometimes ETS will ask *you* to supply the conclusion.

THIS IS NOT LIKE READING COMPREHENSION

Reading Comprehension passages are long and filled with useless facts. By now you've gotten used to reading these passages for their structure, letting your eyes skip over factual data you probably won't be tested on anyway.

By contrast, Critical Reasoning passages are quite short, and every single word should be considered carefully; shades of meaning are very important. Because the passages are relatively short, you will probably never have to use the scroll bar to see them in their entirety.

THE QUESTION

Reading Comprehension Review

A: Do not infer! Stick as closely as possible to the passage.

Immediately after the passage, there will be a question. There is usually only one question per passage—which means it is essential that you *always read the question first*.

The question contains important clues that will tell you what to look for as you read the passage.

THERE ARE EIGHT QUESTION TYPES

Here are examples of the eight major question types you'll see (we'll go into much greater detail later in the chapter):

1. What is the conclusion in the passage above?

As you read the passage, you'll be looking to identify and separate the premises from the conclusion.

2. What conclusion is best supported by the passage above?

The passage connected to this type of question will simply be a list of premises. You will have to supply your own conclusion.

3. The passage above assumes that . . .

As you read the passage in question, you will be looking for an unstated premise on which the argument depends.

4. Which of the following, if true, would most strengthen the conclusion drawn above?

This type of question is like an assumption question in that it is asking you to find an unstated premise on which the argument depends, and then bolster it.

5. Which of the following, if true, would most seriously weaken the conclusion of the passage above?

This type of question, like an assumption question, is asking you to find an unstated premise of the argument and attack it.

6. Which of the following can best be inferred from the passage above?

This question, like inference Reading Comprehension questions, is at most asking you to go a tiny, tiny bit further than the passage does.

7. Which of the following most resembles the method used by the author to make the point above?

This type of question asks you to find an argument in the answer choices that mimics the original argument.

8 Which of the following best resolves the apparent contradiction in the passage above?

This type of question asks you to pick an answer choice that explains an inconsistency between two incompatible facts.

While the wording of the questions may vary, these are the question types you'll see. Each type of question has its own strategy.

THE ANSWER CHOICES

As you read through this chapter you will notice that certain sentences keep coming up again and again in our discussions of how to eliminate wrong answers.

"This answer choice goes too far."

"That choice is out of the scope of the argument."

SCOPE

Scope is the single most valuable tool to eliminate answer choices in Critical Reasoning questions. It takes a little practice to figure out how scope works. We'll give you an introduction to the concept here, but you'll need to work through the entire chapter (and practice on the questions in our software or in *Official Guide for GMAT Review*) to understand it completely.

Here's an example:

> In an effort to save money, a country's government is considering reducing its military spending. However, without military contracts, crucial industries in that country face bankruptcy, which could disrupt the economy. Thus, the same government that is reducing its military spending will eventually

Reading Comprehension Review

Trigger words that signal a conclusion:
therefore
thus
so
hence
implies
indicates

have to provide these industries with money for peacetime research and development.

Which of the following states the conclusion of the passage above?

- ◯ The necessity of providing money to keep crucial industries from going bankrupt will discourage the government from reducing its military budget.
- ◯ If the government decreases its military budget, it will eventually be forced to increase its military budget to its former level.
- ◯ The industries that receive research and development money will be successful in their efforts to convert to peacetime manufacturing.
- ◯ In the event of war, this country would be unprepared for military conflict.
- ◯ Reducing military spending to save money will result in some increases in other types of spending.

We will be discussing how to do this type of question (find-the-conclusion) very shortly, but for now we're going to summarize the argument and skip right to the answer choices in order to illustrate how to use scope as an elimination technique. The argument states that a country wants to save money by decreasing its military budget; however, in order to keep the industries that depend on military contracts from collapsing, the country will have to *spend* some additional money as well.

ETS REWARDS NARROW MINDS

In the Critical Reasoning section it is easy to think too much. The first answer choice (what we call answer choice (A)) might look very tempting at first, because it seems to take the argument to its logical conclusion: "Hey, if cutting military spending is going to end up *costing* the country money, they may as well not do it." But the ETS test writers consider answer choice (A) to be outside the scope of this argument. In fact, if you think about it, we have no idea whether the government will be discouraged or not, or even whether the costs of supplying research and development money will be greater than the savings in military spending. This answer goes much further than the argument itself.

Choice (B) goes too far as well. Perhaps cutting military spending will turn out to be a bad idea, but even if that is true, how do we know that the country will then eventually decide to increase military spending? What might happen in the future is well outside the scope of this argument.

We can eliminate choice (C) for the same reason, since it merely goes off on a tangent to speculate as to the ultimate fate of the industries mentioned in the passage. Whether these industries succeed in making the transition to peacetime manufacturing is not crucial to this argument.

If you are tempted by choice (D), you're still thinking too much. When a country reduces its military spending, you could argue that it might be less prepared for war—but that is way outside the scope of this passage. Be careful not to impose your own value judgments or thought processes on these questions.

Choice (E) may have seemed simplistic when you first read it. You might even have thought that it wasn't really a conclusion at all, that it was more like a summary. However, this is the answer the ETS test writer would choose. And remember, *she's* the one who makes up the answer key. Choice (E) stayed within the scope of the argument.

Q: What is the very first thing you should do when starting a Critical Reasoning passage?

USING SCRATCH PAPER

As you eliminate answer choices, it's vital that you physically cross them off on your scratch paper. This will prevent you from wasting time rereading answer choices you've already eliminated.

FIND-THE-CONCLUSION QUESTIONS

Here's a typical find-the-conclusion question. Remember, always read the question first so you will know what to look for in the passage.

> When young students first look at modernist abstract painting, their eyes are assailed by a seemingly meaningless mass of squiggles. It is only after a study of the history of art and the forces which led up to abstraction that it is possible to appreciate the intellectual sophistication of modern art. Thus, a high-school study of modern art should always begin with a study of the history of art.
>
> Which of the following is the main point of the passage above?
>
> ○ To understand the history of art, it is necessary to study modern art.
> ○ Young students are unable to appreciate fully the complexities of modern art.
> ○ An understanding of the history of art is essential to an understanding of modern art.
> ○ To understand abstract art, students must first study the history of art.
> ○ A high-school study of modern art will have little relevance to students who lack a historical perspective.

Since you read the question first, you knew as you began reading the passage that you would need to separate the conclusion of the argument from its premises. Before you start analyzing the passage, here are a few pointers:

How to Find the Conclusion If it is Stated in the Passage

A: Read the question! This will allow you to focus on what the question is asking when reading the passage.

◆ Look for conclusions at the beginning and end of a passage. Most arguments follow one of two common structures:

Premise, premise, premise, conclusion
or
conclusion, premise, premise, premise.

Therefore the conclusion can often be found in the first or last sentence of the passage.

◆ Look for the same kinds of structural signposts we showed you in the Reading Comprehension chapter. Words like

therefore	hence
thus	implies
so	indicates that

often signal that a conclusion is about to be made.

◆ Look for a statement that cannot stand alone; in other words, a statement that needs to be supported by premises.

◆ If you can't find the conclusion, look for the premises instead. These are the parts of the argument that support the conclusion.

Premises are often preceded by another kind of signpost. Words like

because	in view of
since	given that

signal that evidence is about to be given to support a conclusion.

Now Let's Analyze the Passage

When young students first look at modernist abstract painting, their eyes are assailed by a seemingly meaningless mass of squiggles. It is only after a study of the history of art and the forces that led up to abstraction that it is possible to appreciate the intellectual sophistication of modern art. Thus, a high-school study of modern art should always begin with a study of the history of art.

Which of the following is the main point of the passage above?

- ⬭ To understand the history of art, it is necessary to study modern art.
- ⬭ Young students are unable to appreciate fully the complexities of modern art.
- ⬭ An understanding of the history of art is essential to an understanding of modern art.
- ⬭ To understand abstract art, high school students must first study the history of art.
- ⬭ A high-school study of modern art will have little relevance to students who lack a historical perspective.

Here's how to crack it

Look at the first sentence of the passage. If this is the conclusion, it must be supported by other statements in the passage. Does the second sentence, for example, support the first? No, it goes on to make another point. The first sentence is probably not the conclusion. Look at the last sentence. This seems more like a conclusion. It follows the word "thus"—conclusion signpost—and makes a statement that cannot stand alone. Furthermore, the rest of the passage seems to be leading up to this sentence. We've found our conclusion. The passage can be broken down as follows:

1. Students don't understand modern art. (premise)

2. To understand modern art, it is necessary to study art history. (premise)

3. Therefore, students who study modern art should first study art history. (conclusion)

Let's look at the answer choices:

- ⬭ To understand the history of art, it is necessary to study modern art.

This statement actually reverses the second premise. Not only is it not the conclusion, it's not even a premise. Eliminate.

- ⬭ Young students are unable to appreciate fully the complexities of modern art.

This statement is the first premise, not the conclusion. Eliminate.

- ⬭ An understanding of the history of art is essential to an understanding of modern art.

This is a correct statement of the second premise, but, again, it is not the conclusion.

- ⬭ To understand abstract art, high school students must first study the history of art.

This looks pretty good. It's a restatement of the last sentence of the passage.

○ A high-school study of modern art will have little relevance to students who lack a historical perspective.

This choice may seem a little tempting at first. To be sure, it is *a* conclusion—and it begins with the same words found in the last sentence of the passage. The question you must ask yourself is whether this statement encapsulates the conclusion found in the passage. The conclusion in the passage states that a high-school study of art should begin with art history. This answer choice does not restate the conclusion—it goes further to explain why students need art history. In other words, it is outside the scope of the argument.

SUPPLY-YOUR-OWN-CONCLUSION QUESTIONS

Supply-your-own-conclusion questions are much more common than find-the-conclusion questions. The passage gives you a list of premises. You then have to decide which of the answer choices is the best conclusion to the passage. Here's an example:

> Fewer elected officials are supporting environmental legislation this year than at any time in the last decade. In a study of thirty elected officials, only five were actively campaigning for new environmental legislation. This comes at a time when the public's concern for the environment is growing by leaps and bounds.
>
> Which of the following conclusions is best supported by the passage above?
>
> ○ More elected officials are needed to support environmental legislation.
> ○ Elected officials have lost touch with the concerns of the public.
> ○ The five elected officials who actively campaigned for new environmental legislation should be congratulated.
> ○ If the environment is to be saved, elected officials must support environmental legislation.
> ○ If elected officials are truly to represent their constituents, many of them must increase their support of environmental legislation.

B-School Lingo

Sharks: aggressive students who smell blood and move in for the kill

Shark Comment: comment designed to gore a fellow student in class discussion

Soft Courses: touchy-feely courses such as human resources and organizational behavior

Soft Skills: conflict resolution, teamwork, negotiation, and oral and written communication

Slice and Dice: run all kinds of quantitative analysis on a set of numbers

Here's how to crack it

Having read the question first, you know that this passage will have several premises but no conclusion. Your job is to find a conclusion among the answer choices. Here are some guidelines:

- Conclusions are supported by *all* the evidence in the passage. As you look at each answer choice, check to see whether the potential conclusion is supported not by some of the premises but by all of them. A statement that follows from only one of the premises will not be the conclusion.

- Because the conclusion in this type of question is not in the passage, the answer cannot be just a restatement of a sentence from the passage.

- Several answer choices will be obviously wrong. Eliminate these first, then decide which of the remaining answers follows most clearly from the premises.

- Be wary of answer choices that go further than the scope of the original argument. For example, if the passage has given you several noncontroversial facts about advertising, do not select an answer choice that says advertising is a waste of time.

Q: Most arguments can be divided into what three parts?

Let's attack the answer choices:

○ More elected officials are needed to support environmental legislation.

This statement ignores the last premise of the passage—that the *public* is becoming more and more concerned about the environment. A conclusion must be supported by all its premises. Eliminate.

○ Elected officials have lost touch with the concerns of the public.

This is *a* conclusion, but it goes beyond the scope of the argument and ignores parts of the first two premises that relate to the environment.

○ The five elected officials who actively campaigned for new environmental legislation should be congratulated.

This statement, while consistent with the sentiments of the author, again does not deal with the last premise, relating to the concerns of the public.

○ If the environment is to be saved, elected officials must support environmental legislation.

This answer choice again ignores the last premise in the passage. The correct conclusion to this passage must support all of its premises. Eliminate.

○   If elected officials are truly to represent their constituents, many of them must increase their support of environmental legislation.

Bingo. This conclusion is supported by all the premises, and it does not go beyond the scope of the argument.

ASSUMPTION QUESTIONS

An assumption question asks you to identify an unstated premise of the passage from among the answer choices. As you read the passage, what you will be looking for is a gap in the underlying logic of the argument—a gap that can only be closed by stating out loud what is now only being assumed. There are many different kinds of assumptions the ETS test writers can use, but let's get you started by identifying three: causal assumptions, statistical assumptions, and analogy assumptions.

CAUSAL ASSUMPTIONS

ETS is extremely fond of these, and makes use of them several times on every GMAT. Causal arguments take an effect and suggest a cause for it. Here's a simplified example:

Every time I wear my green suit, people like me. Therefore, it is my green suit that makes people like me.

The author's conclusion (it is the green suit that makes people like him) is based on the premise that every time he wears it, he has observed that people like him. But this argument relies on the assumption that there is no other possible cause for people liking him. Perhaps he always wears a red tie with his green suit, and it's really the tie that people like.

Whenever you spot a cause being suggested for an effect, ask yourself whether there might be an alternate cause.

ANALOGY ASSUMPTIONS

An argument by analogy compares one situation to another, ignoring the question of whether the two situations are comparable.

Studies indicate that use of this product causes cancer in laboratory animals. Therefore, you should stop using this product.

The author's conclusion (you should stop using the product) is based on the premise that the product causes cancer in laboratory animals. This argument is not really complete. It relies on the assumption that since this product causes cancer in laboratory animals, it will also cause cancer in humans.

Whenever you see a comparison in a Critical Reasoning passage, you should ask yourself: Are these two situations really comparable?

STATISTICAL ASSUMPTIONS

A statistical argument uses statistics to "prove" its point. Remember what Mark Twain said: "There are lies, damned lies, and statistics."

> *Four out of five doctors agree: The pain reliever in Sinutol is the most effective analgesic on the market today. You should try Sinutol.*

The conclusion (you should try Sinutol) is based on the premise that four out of five doctors found the pain reliever in Sinutol to be the most effective. However, a literal reading of the passage tells us that the statistic that the author uses in support of his conclusion is only based on the opinions of five doctors (all of whom may be on the board of directors of Sinutol). The author's conclusion is based on the *assumption* that four out of *every* five doctors will find Sinutol to be wonderful. This may be correct, but we do not know for sure. Therefore, the most we can say about the conclusion is that it may be true.

Whenever you see statistics in an argument, always be sure to ask yourself the following question: Are the statistics representative?

Neither analogy nor statistical arguments are as prevalent on the GMAT as causal arguments.

HOW TO ATTACK THE ANSWER CHOICES ON AN ASSUMPTION QUESTION

Assumptions plug holes in the argument and help make a conclusion true. Here are some guidelines for spotting assumptions among the answer choices:

- Assumptions are never stated in the passage. If you see an answer choice that comes straight from the passage, it is not correct.

- Assumptions support the conclusion of the passage. Find the conclusion in the passage, then try out each answer choice to see whether it makes the conclusion stronger.

- Assumptions frequently turn on the gaps of logic we've just been discussing. If the argument proposes a cause for an effect, you should ask yourself whether there might be some other cause. If the argument uses statistics, you should probably ask yourself whether the statistics involved are representative. If the argument offers an analogy, you should ask yourself whether the two situations are analogous.

A: Causal assumptions. If an argument states that one event caused another, always ask yourself whether an alternative causal explanation exists.

Now Let's Try the Passage

Q: What are some helpful approaches to finding the conclusion?

Many people believe that gold and platinum are the most valuable commodities. To the true entrepreneur, however, gold and platinum are less valuable than opportunities that can enable him to further enrich himself. Therefore, in the world of high finance, information is the most valuable commodity.

The author of the passage above makes which of the following assumptions?

○ Gold and platinum are not the most valuable commodities.
○ Entrepreneurs are not like most people.
○ The value of information is incalculably high.
○ Information about business opportunities is accurate and will lead to increased wealth.
○ Only entrepreneurs feel that information is the most valuable commodity.

Here's how to crack it

The question tells you that you are looking for an assumption, which means that as you read, you'll be looking for a hole in the argument.

Since an assumption supports the conclusion, it's a good idea to know what the conclusion is. Can you identify it? It was in the last sentence, preceded by "therefore": "In the world of high finance, information is the most valuable commodity."

As you read the passage, keep your eyes open for potential holes in the argument. For example, as you read it might occur to you that the author is assuming that there is no such thing as bad information. Anyone who has ever taken a stock tip knows the error in that assumption.

Don't be upset if you can't find a hole in the argument as you read. The answer choices will give you a clue.

Let's attack the answer choices:

○ Gold and platinum are not the most valuable commodities.

Does this support the conclusion? In a way, it does. If information is supposed to be the most valuable commodity, it might help to know that gold and platinum are not the most valuable commodities.

However, saying that gold and platinum are *not* the most valuable commodities does not necessarily mean that information *is* the most valuable commodity.

○ Entrepreneurs are not like most people.

If most people find gold and platinum to be the most valuable commodities, while entrepreneurs prefer information, then it *could* be inferred that entrepreneurs are not like most people. Does this support the conclusion, though? Not really. Remember, ETS rewards narrow thinking.

○ The value of information is incalculably high.

This answer merely restates the conclusion. Remember, we're looking for an assumption, which is an *unstated* premise. In addition, this answer goes beyond the scope of the argument. To say that information is valuable does not mean that its value is "incalculable."

○ Information about business opportunities is
accurate and will lead to increased wealth.

This is the correct answer. If the business information is not accurate, it could not possibly be valuable. Therefore this statement supports the conclusion by plugging a dangerous hole in the argument.

○ Only entrepreneurs feel that information is
the most valuable commodity.

Does this statement strengthen the conclusion? Actually, it might weaken it. The conclusion states that "in the world of high finance, information is the most valuable commodity." Presumably the world of high finance is not composed exclusively of entrepreneurs. If only entrepreneurs believe information to be the most valuable commodity, then not everyone in the world of high finance would feel the same way.

> A: Look at the beginning or
> end of the passage and be
> familiar with conclusion
> flag words (see list on
> page 228).

STRENGTHEN-THE-ARGUMENT QUESTIONS

If a question asks you to strengthen an argument, it is saying that the argument can be strengthened; in other words, again, you're going to be dealing with an argument that has a gap in its logic.

Like assumption questions, strengthen-the-argument questions are really asking you to find this gap and then fix it with additional information. Here are some guidelines for spotting strengthen-the-argument statements among the answer choices:

◆ The correct answer will strengthen the argument with *new* information. If you see an answer choice that comes straight from the passage, it's wrong.

◆ The new information you're looking for will support the conclusion of the passage. Find the conclusion in the passage, then try out each answer choice to see whether it makes the conclusion stronger.

◆ Strengthen-the-argument questions frequently turn on the gaps of logic we've already discussed. If the argument proposes a cause for an effect, you should ask yourself whether there might be some other cause. If the argument uses statistics, you should probably ask yourself whether the statistics involved are representative. If the argument offers an analogy, you should ask yourself whether the two situations are analogous.

Now Let's Try the Passage

It has recently been proposed that we adopt an all-volunteer army. This policy was tried on a limited basis several years ago, and was a miserable failure. The level of education of the volunteers was unacceptably low, while levels of drug use and crime soared among army personnel. Can we trust our national defense to a volunteer army? The answer is clearly "No."

Which of the following statements, if true, most strengthens the author's claim that an all-volunteer army should not be implemented?

○ The general level of education has risen since the first time an all-volunteer army was tried.

○ The proposal was made by an organization called Citizens for Peace.

○ The first attempt to create a volunteer army was carried out according to the same plan now under proposal and under the same conditions as those that exist today.

○ A volunteer army would be less expensive than an army that relies on the draft.

○ The size of the army needed today is smaller than that needed when a volunteer army was first tried.

Here's how to crack it

You know from reading the question first that you're expected to fix a flaw in the argument. Even better, the question itself tells you the conclusion of the passage: "An all-volunteer army should not be implemented."

Since the reasoning in a strengthen-the-argument question is going to contain gaps, it pays to see whether the argument is statistical, causal, or analogous. You may have noticed that the argument *does*, in fact, use an analogy. The author is basing his conclusion on the results of one previous experience. In effect he is saying, "The idea didn't work then, so it won't work now." This is the potential flaw in the argument.

If you didn't spot the argument by analogy, don't worry. You would probably have seen it when you started attacking the answer choices:

○ The general level of education has risen since the first time an all-volunteer army was tried.

Does this support the author's conclusion? Actually, it may weaken the conclusion. If the general level of education has risen, it could be argued that the level of education of army volunteers is also higher. This would remove one of the author's objections to a volunteer army. Eliminate.

◯ The proposal was made by an organization
called Citizens for Peace.

This is irrelevant to the author's conclusion. You might have wondered whether a group called Citizens for Peace was the right organization to make suggestions about the army. Attacking the reputation of a person in order to cast doubt on that person's ideas is a very old pastime. There's even a name for it: an ad hominem fallacy. An ad hominem statement does not strengthen an argument. Eliminate.

◯ The first attempt to create a volunteer army
was carried out according to the same
plan now under proposal and under the
same conditions as those that exist today.

This is the correct answer. The passage as it stands is potentially flawed because we cannot know that a new attempt to institute an all-volunteer army would turn out the same way it did before. This answer choice provides new information that suggests that the two situations *are* analogous.

◯ A volunteer army would be less expensive
than an army that relies on the draft.

Does this support the conclusion? No. In fact, it makes a case *for* a volunteer army. Eliminate.

◯ The size of the army needed today is smaller
than that needed when a volunteer army
was first tried.

Like answer choice (D), this answer contradicts the conclusion of the passage. If we need a smaller army today, maybe we would be able to find enough smart and honest volunteers to make a volunteer army work. Eliminate.

WEAKEN-THE-ARGUMENT QUESTIONS

If a question asks you to weaken an argument, it implies that the argument can be weakened; in other words, once again you're going to be dealing with unstated premises and a logical gap.

Like assumption questions and strengthen-the-argument questions, weaken-the-argument questions are really asking you to find a hole in the argument. This time, however, you don't need to fix the hole. All you have to do is expose it. Here are some guidelines for finding weaken-the-argument statements among the answer choices:

◆ The statement you'll be looking for should weaken the *conclusion* of the passage. Find the conclusion in the passage, then try out each answer choice to see whether it makes the conclusion less tenable.

◆ Weaken-the-argument questions frequently turn on the gaps of logic that we've already discussed. If the argument proposes a cause for an effect, ask yourself whether there might be some other cause. If the argument uses statistics, ask yourself whether

Always stick to the passage. The easiest way to strengthen an argument is to strengthen the conclusion. You can do this by presenting new evidence. Any answer choice that comes from the passage will probably be wrong. New evidence or assumptions, whether statistical, analogy, or causal, must support the conclusion.

the statistics involved are representative. If the argument offers an analogy, ask yourself whether the two situations are analogous.

Now Let's Try the Passage

Assumption Guidelines

(1) Assumptions are never stated in the passage.

(2) An assumption must support the conclusion; eliminate answer choices that do not strengthen the conclusion.

(3) Assumptions frequently work to fill in gaps in the reasoning of the argument.

Look to see if the assumption, whether it is statistical, analogy, or casual, links the evidence to the conclusion.

The recent turnaround of the LEX Corporation is a splendid example of how an astute chief executive officer can rechannel a company's assets toward profitability. With the new CEO at the helm, LEX has gone, in only three business quarters, from a 10 million dollar operating loss to a 22 million dollar operating gain.

A major flaw in the reasoning of the passage above is that

○ the passage assumes that the new CEO was the only factor that affected the corporation's recent success

○ the recent success of the corporation may be only temporary

○ the chief executive officer may be drawing a salary and bonus that will set a damaging precedent for this and other corporations

○ the author does not define "profitability"

○ rechanneling assets is only a short-term solution

Here's how to crack it

You know from reading the question that you'll need to find a flaw in the reasoning of the argument. As you read the passage, look for the conclusion. The correct answer choice will weaken this conclusion. In this passage the conclusion is in the first sentence: "The recent turnaround of the LEX Corporation is a splendid example of how an astute chief executive officer can rechannel a company's assets toward profitability."

Because this is a weaken-the-argument question that will almost certainly contain a gap in its reasoning, you should look to see whether the argument is causal, statistical, or analogical. In this case the argument is causal. The passage implies that the sole cause of the LEX Corporation's turnaround is the new CEO. While this *may* be true, it is also possible that there are other causes. If you didn't spot the causal argument, don't worry. You would probably have seen it when you attacked the answer choices. Let's do that now:

○ the passage assumes that the new CEO was the only factor that affected the corporation's recent success

This is the correct answer. The new chief executive officer may not have been the cause of the turnaround—there may have been some other cause we don't know about.

○ the recent success of the corporation may be
   only temporary

It may be hasty to crown LEX with laurels after only three economic quarters, but this statement doesn't point out a flaw in the *reasoning* of the passage. Eliminate.

○ the chief executive officer may be drawing a
   salary and bonus that will set a damaging
   precedent for this and other corporations

This answer choice may seem tempting because it's not in favor of the new CEO. But this alone doesn't represent a major flaw in the reasoning of the passage. Eliminate.

○ the author does not define "profitability"

An author can't define every word he uses. Profitability seems a common enough word, and a change in the balance sheet from minus 10 million to plus 22 million seems to qualify. Eliminate.

○ rechanneling assets is only a short-term
   solution

Like the second answer choice (what we call choice (B)), this statement implies that all the votes aren't in yet. This does not affect the reasoning of the argument, however. Eliminate.

INFERENCE QUESTIONS

Like inference questions in Reading Comprehension, Critical Reasoning inference questions do not really ask you to make an inference. In fact, you will often find that the answer to a Critical Reasoning inference question is so basic that you won't believe it could be correct the first time you read it. Inference questions often have little to do with the conclusion of the passage; instead they might ask you to make inferences about one or more of the premises.

In film and videotape, it is possible to induce viewers to project their feelings onto characters on the screen. In one study, when a camera shot of a woman's face was preceded by a shot of a baby in a crib, the audience thought the woman's face was registering happiness. When the same shot of the woman's face was preceded by a shot of a lion running toward the camera, the audience thought the woman's face was registering fear. Television news teams must be careful to avoid such manipulation of their viewers.

Which of the following can be inferred from the passage?

○ Television news teams have abused their
   position of trust in the past.

○ The expression on the woman's face was, in
   actuality, blank.
○ A camera shot of a baby in a crib provoked
   feelings of happiness in the audience.
○ Audiences should strive to be less gullible.
○ The technique for manipulating audiences
   described in the passage would work with
   film or videotape.

Here's how to crack it

This is an inference question. ETS is probably not interested in the conclusion of the passage. You'll be looking for a statement that seems so obvious that it almost doesn't need saying. Let's attack the answer choices:

○ Television news teams have abused their
   position of trust in the past.

If you chose this answer, you inferred too much. The passage doesn't say that news teams have ever abused their position of trust. Eliminate.

○ The expression on the woman's face was, in
   actuality, blank.

The audience had no idea what the expression on the woman's face was, and neither do we. It would make sense for the woman's face to be blank, but we don't know whether this is so. This answer goes too far.

○ A camera shot of a baby in a crib provoked
   feelings of happiness in the audience.

This is the correct answer. The passage says that the audience projects its own feelings onto characters on the screen. If the audience believes the woman's face reflects happiness, then that must have been their own reaction.

○ Audiences should strive to be less gullible.

This statement goes way beyond the intent of the passage. Eliminate.

○ The technique for manipulating audiences
   described in the passage would work with
   film or videotape.

Again, this statement goes too far to be the correct answer to an inference question. Eliminate.

MIMIC-THE-REASONING QUESTIONS

Mimic-the-reasoning questions ask you to recognize the reasoning in a passage and follow the same line of reasoning in one of the answer choices. The best way to understand the passage associated with a reasoning question is to simplify the terms. Here's an example: "If it rains, I will stay home today." We could simplify this by saying, "If A, then B."

Q: What is the most effective way to eliminate answer choices in Critical Reasoning questions?

World-class marathon runners do not run more than six miles a day when they are training. Therefore, if you run more than six miles a day, you are not world-class.

Which of the following statements supports its conclusion in the same manner as the argument above?

○ Sprinters always run in the morning. If it is morning, and you see someone running, it will not be a sprinter.

○ Paint never dries in less than three hours. If it dries in less than three hours, it is not paint.

○ Little League games are more fun for the parents than for the children who actually play. Therefore, the parents should be made to play.

○ If a car starts in the morning, chances are it will start again that evening. Our car always starts in the morning, and it always starts in the evening as well.

○ If you sleep less than four hours a night, you may be doing yourself a disservice. Studies have shown that the most valuable sleep occurs in the fifth hour.

A: Scope! If something is out of scope—if it does not refer back to the passage—then you should eliminate it.

Here's how to crack it

First, simplify the argument in the passage. World-class marathon runners do not run more than six miles a day when they are training. (If A, then B.) Therefore, if you run more than six miles a day, you are not world-class. (If not B, then not A.)

Now let's attack the answer choices:

○ Sprinters always run in the morning. If it is morning, and you see someone running, it will not be a sprinter.

Just because this answer choice is also about running doesn't mean the reasoning will be the same. In fact, it is unlikely that ETS would use the same subject matter for the correct answer. If we simplify this argument, we get: If A, then B. If B, then not A. Is this the same reasoning used in the passage? No. Eliminate.

○ Paint never dries in less than three hours. If it dries in less than three hours, it is not paint.

If we simplify this argument, we get: If A, then B. If not B, then not A. This is the correct answer.

○ Little League games are more fun for the parents than for the children who actually play. Therefore, the parents should be made to play.

Simplifying this argument, we get . . . not much. The reasoning here is totally different. Also, note that the subject matter here is still about sports. Eliminate.

Q: How do you tackle an assumption question?

○ If a car starts in the morning, chances are it will start again that evening. Our car always starts in the morning, and it always starts in the evening as well.

If we simplify this argument, we get: If A, then B. If always A, then always B. That doesn't sound right. Eliminate.

○ If you sleep less than four hours a night, you may be doing yourself a disservice. Studies have shown that the most valuable sleep occurs in the fifth hour.

Simplifying this argument, we get . . . again, not much. The reasoning in this answer choice is very different from the reasoning in the passage. Eliminate.

RESOLVE-THE-PARADOX QUESTIONS

Some GMAT questions ask you to resolve an apparent paradox or explain a possible discrepancy. In these questions, the passage will present you with two seemingly contradictory facts. Your job is to find the answer choice that allows both of the facts from the passage to be true.

Here's an example:

In 1994, the TipTop airline reported an increase in the total number of passengers it carried from the year before, but a *decrease* in total revenues—even though prices for its tickets on all routes remained unchanged during the two-year period.

Which of the following, if true, best reconciles the apparent paradox described above?

○ TipTop Airlines was a victim of a mild recession in 1994.
○ Total passenger miles were up in 1994.
○ Fuel costs remained constant during the two-year period.
○ Passengers traveled shorter (and thus less expensive) distances in 1994.
○ TipTop did not buy any new airplanes or equipment in 1994.

Here's how to crack it

First, restate the contradiction in your own words.

"TipTop's profits went down even though they flew more passengers."

Now, let's see which of the answer choices makes both of the facts in the argument true.

○ TipTop Airlines was a victim of a mild recession in 1994.

If TipTop was affected by a recession, that might explain a loss of revenues. But since ticket prices remained the same, it would not explain how the number of passengers could have increased at the same time. Eliminate.

○ Total passenger miles were up in 1994.

If total passenger miles were up, and prices remained the same, there is no way that there could have been a loss of revenues. We can eliminate this choice as well.

○ Fuel costs remained constant during the two year period.

If fuel costs had *not* remained constant, the company's profits might have fallen. An increase in fuel prices could have increased their costs and cut into profits. But it would not have cut into total *revenues*, which is what we are concerned with in this passage. Of course, since choice (C) told us that the costs remained constant, this choice has no bearing on the argument at all. Eliminate.

○ Passengers traveled shorter (and thus less expensive) distances in 1994.

Bingo! If passengers traveled on short, inexpensive flights, then they paid less money. In spite of the increase in number of passengers, the money they paid could have added up to less than that of the year before. This is the best answer, but always remember to read all the choices anyway.

○ TipTop did not buy any new airplanes or equipment in 1994.

This answer is much like the third choice (what we call choice (C)). If TipTop *had* bought new planes, it might have cut into its profits, but it would not have had any bearing on revenues. Of course, since this choice told us that TipTop did not buy any planes, there is no relevance at all. Eliminate.

A: Because assumptions are unstated, eliminate any answer choices that are stated in the passage. Also, look for the three types of reasoning— statistical, analogical, and causal— each of which may be used as an assumption.

SUMMARY

1. Critical Reasoning is made up of short passages. Each of these passages is followed by one or two questions, for a total of roughly 14 questions.

2. ETS says that no formal logic is required to answer these questions, but in fact some knowledge of the rudiments of GMAT logic *will* increase your score.

3. There are three parts to an argument:

   A. the conclusion

   B. the premises

   C. assumptions

4. Critical Reasoning is not like Reading Comprehension:

   A. You should never skim; each word is important

   B. You should always read the question first

   C. Most of the Reading Comprehension techniques we have shown you are inappropriate for Critical Reasoning.

5. Always read the question first because it will contain clues that will help you to find the answer as you read the passage. As you eliminate answer choices, cross them off on your scratch paper.

6. In Critical Reasoning, the most important POE technique is eliminating answers that are outside the scope of the argument.

7. There are eight question types. Each type has its own strategy.

   A. *Find-the-Conclusion Questions*
   Break the argument down into its parts and look for signposts. A conclusion must be supported by its premises.

   B. *Supply-the-Conclusion Questions*

   C. *Assumption Questions*

   Assumptions are unstated premises that support the conclusion. Look for a flaw in the argument that is fixed by the assumption.

Q: How would you approach a strengthening- or weakening-the-argument question?

D. *Strengthen-the-Argument Questions*

Look for an answer choice with information that supports the conclusion.

E. *Weaken-the-Argument Questions*

These questions ask you to find the answer choice that points out flaws in the reasoning of passages.

F. *Inference Questions*

Like Reading Comprehension inference questions, these questions do not actually want you to infer. Unlike most Critical Reasoning questions, these questions will concern the *premises*, not the conclusion.

G. *Mimic-the-Reasoning Questions*

This type of question asks you to find an argument in one of the answer choices that mimics the method of reasoning used in the original argument. Most of these questions can be answered by simplifying (if A, then B).

H. *Resolve-the-Paradox Questions*

This type of question asks you to pick an answer choice that explains an apparent contradiction between two incompatible facts.

8. In assumption questions, weaken-the-argument questions, and strengthen-the-argument questions, there are three types of assumptions that students should be on the look out for. These are, in order of the frequency:

A. causal assumptions—Ask yourself whether there might be an alternate cause.

B. assumptions of analogy—Ask yourself whether the two situations are analogous.

C. statistical assumptions—Ask yourself whether the statistics are representative.

A: Expose the assumption and build it up to strengthen the argument or tear it down to weaken the argument.

PART IV

How to Crack the Writing Assessment

16

Writing Assessment

After you finish the computer-adaptive tutorial, the first thing you will be asked to do on the GMAT is write two essays using a word processor program and the computer keyboard. You will have 30 minutes for each essay. You will not be given the essay topics in advance, nor will you be given a choice of topics. The writing assessment is scored separately from the rest of the GMAT.

WHY ADD ESSAYS TO THE GMAT?

The business schools themselves asked ETS to make the addition. Recent studies have indicated that verbal skills are more important to success in business (and in business school) than had been previously thought.

The business schools have also had to contend with a huge increase in the number of applicants from overseas. Admissions officers at the business schools were finding that the application essays they received from outside the United States did not always accurately reflect the abilities of the students who were supposed to have written them. To put it more bluntly, some of these applicants were paying native English speakers to write their essays for them.

The GMAT writing assessment is thus at least partly a check on the writing ability of foreign applicants who now make up more than one-third of all applicants to American business schools.

At the business schools' request, all schools to which you apply now receive, in addition to your writing assessment score, a photocopy of the actual essays you wrote.

HOW DO THE SCHOOLS USE THE WRITING ASSESSMENT?

If you are a citizen of a non-English-speaking country, you can expect the schools to look quite closely at both the score you receive on the essays you write and the essays themselves. If you are a native English speaker with reasonable verbal scores and English grades in college then the writing assessment is not likely to be a crucial part of your package.

On the other hand, if your verbal skills are *not* adequately reflected by your grades in college, or in the other sections of the GMAT, then a strong performance on the writing assessment could be extremely helpful.

HOW WILL THE ESSAYS BE SCORED?

When you get your GMAT score back from ETS, you will also receive a separate score for the writing assessment. Each essay is read by two readers, each of whom will assign your writing a grade from 1-6, in half-point increments (6 being the highest score possible). If the two scores are within a point of each other, they will be averaged. If there is a more than one-point spread, the essays will be read by a third reader, and scores will be adjusted to reflect the third scorer's evaluation.

ETS uses the "holistic" scoring method to grade essays; your writing will be judged not on small details but rather on its overall impact. The ETS essay readers are supposed to ignore small errors of grammar and spelling. Considering that these poor readers are going to have to plow through over 600,000 essays each year, this is probably just as well.

WHO ARE THESE READERS ANYWAY?

Well, let's talk about the first reader first. We'll put this in the form of a multiple-choice question:

Your essays will initially be read by

 (A) captains of industry

 (B) leading business school professors

 (C) college TAs working part time

If you guessed (C) you're doing just fine. Each essay will be read first by part-time employees of ETS, mostly culled from graduate school programs. However, you might have a hard time guessing who (or should we say, what) will read your essays second.

WHAT ARE THESE READERS ANYWAY?

As of February 1999, the second reader of your essays will be a computer. Yes, you heard right. That well-known arbiter of creative writing and syntax, a software program called the "E-rater," will read and grade your essay. If the computer and the human reader disagree, the essay in question will be read by a third, human, reader, who will make the final decision. ETS says this is a cost-cutting measure.

HOW MUCH TIME DO THEY DEVOTE TO EACH ESSAY?

The human graders get two minutes, tops. They work in eight-hour marathon sessions (nine to five, with an hour off for lunch). The humans are each required to read thirty essays per hour. Obviously, these poor graders do not have time for an in-depth reading of your essay. They probably aren't going to notice how carefully you thought out your ideas, or how clever your analysis was. Under pressure to meet their quota, they are simply going to be giving it a fast skim. By the time your reader gets to your essay, she will probably have already seen over a hundred—and no matter how ingenious you were in coming up with original ideas, she's already seen them.

The computer grader, of course, takes even less time. It scores your essay by comparing it to other essays on the same topic. In other words, if you actually did come up with an original point, the computer not only wouldn't recognize it—it would probably penalize you for not coming up with one of the more obvious points it was programmed to find.

SO HOW DO YOU SCORE HIGH ON THE GMAT ESSAYS?

On the face of it, you might think it would be pretty difficult to impress these jaded human readers and rote computer readers, but it turns out that there are some very specific ways to persuade them of your superior writing skills.

WHAT ETS DOESN'T WANT YOU TO KNOW

In a 1982 internal study, two ETS researchers analyzed a group of essays written by actual test takers and the grades that those essays received. The most successful essays had one thing in common. Which of the following characteristics do you think it was?

◆ Good organization

◆ Proper diction

◆ Noteworthy ideas

◆ Good vocabulary

◆ Sentence variety

◆ Length

◆ Number of paragraphs

WHAT YOUR ESSAY NEEDS IN ORDER TO *LOOK* LIKE A SUCCESSFUL ESSAY

The ETS researchers discovered that the essays that received the highest grades from ETS essay graders had one single factor in common.

Length.

To ace the Writing Assessment, you need to take one simple step: *Write as much as you possibly can.* Each essay should include at least four indented paragraphs.

HOW DOES THE WORD PROCESSING PROGRAM WORK?

ETS has created a very simple program to allow students to compose their essays on the screen. Compared to any of the commercial word processing programs, this one is extremely limited, but it does allow the basic functions: You can move the cursor with the arrow keys, and you can delete, copy, and paste.

If you're a computer novice, don't worry. You don't *have* to use any of these functions. With just the backspace key and the mouse to change your point of insertion, you will be able to use the computer like a regular typewriter.

However, if you can't type you really do have a problem. There is not enough time to write an effective essay using the hunt-and-peck method of typing. Nor is there enough time to write your essay long-hand and then type it into the computer. If you aren't used to typing or using a computer word processor, you should definitely make it a point to practice on a friend's computer for a couple of weeks before the test.

The ETS booklet describes an "outstanding" Analysis of an Issue essay as one that: "explores ideas and develops a position on the issue with insightful reasons and/or persuasive examples, is clearly well organized, demonstrates superior control of language, including diction and syntactic variety, demonstrates superior facility with the conventions of standard written English . . ."

Here's what your screen will look like during the AWA section of the test:

A new medical test that allows the early detection of a particular disease will prevent the deaths of people all over the world who would otherwise die from that disease. The test has been extremely effective in allowing doctors to diagnose the disease 6 months to a year before it would have been spotted by conventional means.

Discuss how logically convincing you find this argument. In explaining your point of view, be sure to analyze the line of reasoning and the use of evidence in the argument. Also discuss what, if anything, would make the argument more sound and persuasive, or would help you to better evaluate its conclusion.

The argument that this new medical test|

[Cut]

[Paste]

[Undo]

The question always appears at the top of your screen. Below it, in a box, will be your writing area (where you can see a partially completed sentence). When you click inside the box with your mouse, a winking cursor will appear, indicating that you can begin typing. The program supports the use of many of the normal computer keys:

The *backspace* key removes text to the left of the cursor.

The *delete* key removes text to the right of the cursor.

The *arrow* keys move the cursor up, down, left, or right.

The *home* key moves the cursor to the beginning of a line.

The *end* key moves the cursor to the end of a line.

The *enter* key moves the cursor to the beginning of the next line.

Page up moves the cursor up one page.

Page down moves the cursor down one page.

You can also use the icons on the right of the screen to copy and paste words, sentences, or paragraphs. To do this, first you have to highlight the desired text by clicking on the starting point with your mouse and then holding down the mouse button while you drag it to the ending point. Then (while this may seem counterintuitive) click on the *cut* button. This deletes the text you've selected from the screen, but also stores it in the computer's memory. Now, just move the cursor to wherever you would like the selected text to reappear, and click on the *paste* button. The selected text will appear in that spot.

If you make a mistake, you simply click on the *undo* button, which will undo whatever operation you have just done. You can undo a cut, a paste, or even the last set of words you've typed in. Unfortunately, unlike many word processing programs, ETS's program does not have a *redo* button, so be careful what you decide to undo.

Sentence Correction Review

When confronted with a Sentence Correction question, remember your hit-list of Sentence Correction errors:

- pronouns
- misplaced modifiers
- parallel construction
- tense
- subject-verb agreement
- apples and oranges
- quantity words
- idiom

Obviously, this small box is not big enough to contain your entire essay. However, by hitting the *page up* and *page down* buttons on your keyboard, or by using the arrows on your keyboard, you will be able to go forward and backward to reread what you have written and make corrections.

DOES SPELLING COUNT?

Officially, no. ETS essay readers are supposed to ignore minor errors of spelling and grammar. However, the readers wouldn't be human (so to speak) if they weren't influenced favorably by an essay that had no obvious misspelled words or unwieldy constructions. Unfortunately, there is no spell-check function in the word processing program.

WHAT WILL THE ESSAY TOPICS LOOK LIKE?

There are two types of essay topics: Analysis of an Issue and Analysis of an Argument. Here's an example of each:

Analysis of an Issue

Reacting to statistics of increased crime and violence, some advocates have argued that it is necessary for the entertainment industry to police itself by censoring television programs and popular music lyrics. However, civil liberties advocates argue that it has not been demonstrated that watching television violence or listening to violent lyrics in songs leads to real violence.

Which do you find more compelling, the call for censorship of entertainment media or civil libertarians' response to it? Explain your position, using relevant reasons and/or examples drawn from your own experience, observations, or reading.

Analysis of an Argument

A new medical test that allows the early detection of a particular disease will prevent the deaths of people all over the world who would otherwise die from the disease. The test has been extremely effective in allowing doctors to diagnose the disease 6 months to a year before it would have been spotted by conventional means.

Discuss how logically convincing you find this argument. In explaining your point of view, be sure to analyze the line of reasoning and the use of evidence in the argument. Also discuss what, if anything, would make the argument more sound and persuasive, or would help you to better evaluate its conclusion.

You will have to write one essay on each topic.

THE WRITING ASSESSMENT: BASIC PRINCIPLES

You might think that there is really no way to prepare for the writing assessment (other than by practicing writing over a long period of time, and by practicing your typing skills). After all, you won't find out the topic of the essay they'll ask you to write until you get there, and there is no way to plan your essays in advance.

OH YES, YOU CAN *TOO* PLAN YOUR ESSAYS IN ADVANCE

In fact, there are some very specific ways to prepare for the GMAT essays that go beyond length and good typing skills. Of course, if all you had to worry about were the ETS graders, these techniques might not be necessary. However, your GMAT essays are being sent to the schools to which you're applying. Just in case the admissions officers decide to read them, you want them to be good.

So how can you prepare ahead of time?

CREATING A TEMPLATE

When a builder builds a house, the first thing he does is construct a frame. The frame supports the entire house. After the frame is completed, he can nail the walls and windows to the frame. We're going to show you how to build the frame for the perfect GMAT essay. Of course, you won't know the exact topic of the essay until you get there (just as the builder may not know what color his client is going to paint the living room), but you will have an all-purpose frame on which to construct a great essay no matter what the topic is.

We call this frame the *template*.

PRECONSTRUCTION

Just as a builder can construct the windows of a house in his workshop weeks before he arrives to install them, so can you pre-build certain elements of your essay.

We call this *preconstruction*.

In the rest of this chapter we'll show you how to prepare *ahead of time* to write essays on two topics you won't see until they appear on your screen. Let's begin with the Analysis of an Issue essay.

ANALYSIS OF AN ISSUE

Writing the Analysis of an Issue essay requires a series of steps.

Step 1: Read the topic.

Step 2: Decide the general position you are going to take—you need to take a stand on the issue.

Step 3: Brainstorm. Come up with a bunch of supporting ideas or examples. It helps to write these down on a piece of scratch paper. These supporting statements are supposed to help convince the reader that your main thesis is correct.

Step 4: Look over your supporting ideas and throw out the weakest ones. There should be three to five left over.

Step 5: Write the essay on screen, using all the preconstruction and template tools you're going to be learning in this chapter.

Step 6: Read over the essay and do some editing. The GMAT readers will not take away points for spelling or grammatical mistakes, but you want your organization to be as well-reasoned as possible.

WHAT THE READERS ARE LOOKING FOR

The essay topic for the Analysis of an Issue will ask you to choose a side on an issue and develop coherent reasons or examples in defense of your position. You aren't required to know any more about the subject than would any normal person. As far as ETS is concerned, it doesn't even matter which side of the argument you take—as long as your essay is well written. So what constitutes a well-written essay?

The essay readers will be looking for four characteristics as they skim at the speed of light through your Analysis of an Issue essay. According to a booklet prepared by ETS, "an outstanding essay . . .

- explores ideas and develops a position on the issue with insightful reasons and/or persuasive examples,

- is clearly well organized,

- demonstrates superior control of language, including diction and syntactic variety,

- demonstrates superior facility with the conventions of standard written English, but may have minor flaws."

To put it more simply, they're looking for good organization, good supporting examples for whatever position you've taken, and reasonable use of the English language. Let's start with good organization and the easiest way to accomplish it—the template.

A SAMPLE TEMPLATE

You will want to come up with your own template, but here is an elementary example of one, just to get you started:

Paragraph 1:

The issue of _____

is a controversial one. On the one hand, _____

_____.

On the other hand, _____

_____.

However, in the final analysis, I believe that _____

_____ .

Paragraph 2:

One reason for my belief is that _____

_____

_____

_____ .

Paragraph 3:

Another reason for my belief is _____

_____

_____

_____ .

Paragraph 4:

Perhaps the best reason is _____

_____

_____

_____ .

Paragraph 5:

For all these reasons, I therefore believe that _____

_____

_____

_____ .

B-SCHOOLS REVIEWED

According to 15,000 students surveyed, "students don't develop strong marketing skills" at:

Brigham Young University
Boston University
Northeastern University
University of Washington
Rensselaer Polytechnic
 Institute
University of Kansas
University of Texas/Arlington
University of Denver
University of Pennsylvania
University of Chicago

Let's try fitting the Analysis of an Issue topic we've already seen into this organizational structure.

Essay topic 1:

> *Reacting to statistics of increased crime and violence, some advocates have argued that it is necessary for the entertainment industry to police itself by censoring television programs and popular music lyrics. However, civil liberties advocates argue that it has not been demonstrated that watching television violence or listening to violent lyrics in songs leads to real violence.*
>
> Which do you find more compelling, the call for censorship of entertainment media or civil libertarians' response to it? Explain your position, using relevant reasons and/or examples drawn from your own experience, observations, or reading.

How would this topic fit into the first paragraph of our template? Take a look.

The issue of censorship of popular TV programs and music lyrics is a controversial one. On the one hand, increased crime and violence are causing a disintegration of the framework of our society. On the other hand, free speech is one of our most important freedoms, guaranteed by the constitution. However, in the final analysis, I believe that the dangers of subjecting impressionable young minds to questionable values makes self-censorship by the entertainment industry a viable alternative.

> The key to an Analysis of an Issue essay is to be clear about which side you are on.

If we were writing the rest of this essay, we would start giving supporting examples and reasons for our position, but for now, let's concentrate on the first paragraph. Could we have used this template to take the other side of the argument? Sure. Here's how that would look:

The issue of censorship of popular TV programs and music lyrics is a controversial one. On the one hand, free speech is one of our most important freedoms, guaranteed by the constitution. On the other hand, increased crime and violence are causing a disintegration of the framework of our society. However, in the final analysis, I believe that the principle of free speech is too precious to allow censorship in any form.

OKAY, IT WORKS WITH THAT TOPIC, BUT WILL IT WORK WITH ANOTHER?

Of course. Let's try the same template with another topic.

Essay topic 2:

> *Everyone agrees that countries need governing, and yet the cost of government seems to increase every year. Government bureaucracy is often blamed for these increases and while some people feel that these increasing costs are only to be expected, others have argued that our federal bureaucracy needs to be overhauled.*
>
> Which do you find more compelling, the acceptance of the increasing cost of government, or the call for an overhaul of federal bureaucracy? Explain your position, using relevant reasons and/or examples drawn from your own experience, observations, or reading.

The issue of the overhaul of our federal bureaucracy is a controversial one. On the one hand, federal jobs employ a huge number of Americans, making any attempt to prune the federal payroll both difficult and painful. On the other hand, the percentage of our tax-dollars spent simply on the upkeep of this huge bureaucratic juggernaut is rising at an alarming rate. However, in the final analysis, I believe that the political and financial price of bureaucratic reform would be too high.

As you can see, this template will fit practically any situation. To prove it, let's try it out on one of the great philosophical arguments of our time.

TASTES GREAT/LESS FILLING

Essay topic X:

> *Some people say that they drink light beer because it tastes great. Others say they drink it because it's less filling.*
>
> Which reason for drinking light beer do you find more compelling? Explain your position, using relevant reasons and/or examples drawn from your own experience, observations, or reading.

The issue of whether light beer is so popular because of its taste or because you can drink more of it without it filling you up is a controversial one. On the one hand, light beer does have a pleasingly mild taste. On the other hand, light beer also offers a sharply reduced number of calories . However, in the final analysis, I believe that light beer is so popular because of its great taste.

NOW YOU TRY IT

Read the following topic carefully. Decide which side of the argument you want to be on, and then fill in the blanks of the first paragraph of this template.

You may have noticed in the previous examples that to make this particular template work most effectively, the first "on the one hand" should introduce the argument that you are ultimately going to support. The "on the other hand" should be the argument you are going to disprove. The sentence beginning "however, in the final analysis" will return to the point of view that you believe in.

Essay topic 3:

> One of the primary reasons cited by doctors as justification for increases in the fees they charge patients is the increasing cost to the doctors themselves of malpractice insurance. These doctors say that a cap on monetary awards in malpractice cases would result in lower costs for health care. Patient groups contend, however, that some malpractice is so heinous that there should be no limit set on the financial award.
>
> Which do you find more compelling, the call for a cap on medical malpractice awards or the response to it? Explain your position, using relevant reasons and/or examples drawn from your own experience, observations, or reading.

The issue of _____

_____ is a controversial one. On the one hand,

_____

_____.

On the other hand, _____

_____.

However, in the final analysis, I believe that _____

_____.

B-School Lingo

Valuation: adds up projected future cash flow into current dollars

Value-Based Decision Making: applying values and ethics to the process of business

If you were completing the entire essay, now you would write paragraphs giving support to your belief, but for right now let's concentrate on that first paragraph. Here's one way Topic 3 could have gone:

The issue of <u>capping malpractice awards</u> is a controversial one. On the one hand, <u>health care costs are rising so quickly that drastic measures are needed to contain them</u>. On the other hand, <u>when an individual's life is ruined as a result of a doctor's negligence, that individual deserves fair recompense</u>. However, in the final analysis, I believe that <u>by capping the awards at a reasonable amount we can both lower the cost of health care and protect the rights of victims of malpractice</u>.

ARE THERE OTHER TEMPLATES?

There are many ways to organize an Analysis of an Issue essay, and we'll be showing you a few variations, but the important thing is that you bring with you to the exam a template you have practiced using and are comfortable with. Whatever the topic of the essay and whatever your personal mood that day, you don't want to have to think for a second about how your essay will be organized. By deciding on a template in advance you will already have your organizational structure down before you get there.

That said, it's important that you develop your *own* template, based on your own preferences and your own personality. Of course, yours may have some similarities to one of ours, but it should not mimic ours exactly—for one thing, because it's pretty likely that when this edition of our book comes out, the folks who write the GMAT will read it, and they might take a dim view of anyone who blatantly copies one of our templates word-for-word.

CUSTOMIZING YOUR TEMPLATE

Your organizational structure may vary in some ways, but it will always include the following elements: *The first paragraph* should illustrate to the reader that you have understood the topic, and that you have chosen a position. To do this, first restate the topic, then say how you feel about it. The first paragraph does not have to be more than a couple of sentences.

In the *second, third, and fourth paragraphs* you will develop examples and ideas to support your thesis. *The last paragraph* should sum up your position on the topic, using slightly different wording from the first paragraph.

Here are some alternate ways of organizing your essay.

The Analysis of an Issue Essay in Six Steps

Step 1: Read the topic.

Step 2: Decide your position, for or against.

Step 3: Brainstorm for about five minutes.

Step 4: Select the strongest three to four supporting ideas.

Step 5: Write the essay, using preconstruction and template tools.

Step 6: About two minutes before time is up, read over your essay and correct for spelling or grammar mistakes.

Variation 1:

1st paragraph: State both sides of the argument briefly before announcing what side you are on

2nd paragraph: Support your argument

3rd paragraph: Further support

4th paragraph: Further support

5th paragraph: Conclusion

Variation 2:

1st paragraph: State your position

2nd paragraph: Acknowledge the arguments in favor of the *other* side

3rd paragraph: Rebut each of those arguments

4th paragraph: Conclusion

Variation 3:

1st paragraph: State the position you will eventually contradict, i.e. "Many people believe that . . . ."

2nd paragraph: Contradict that first position, i.e. "However, I believe that . . ."

3rd paragraph: Support your position

4th paragraph: Further support

5th paragraph: Conclusion

SO MUCH FOR ORGANIZATION. NOW, WHAT ABOUT SUPPORT?

We've shown you how templates and structure words can be used to help the organization of your essay. However, organization is not the only important item on the essay reader's checklist. You will also be graded on how you support your main idea.

THE KEY TO GOOD SUPPORT: BRAINSTORMING

Learning to use the structural words we've just been discussing is in fact a way to bring pre-built elements into the GMAT examination room with you. Along with a template, they will enable you to concentrate on your ideas without worrying about making up a structure from scratch. But what about the ideas themselves?

After reading the essay topic, you should take a couple of minutes to plan out your essay. First, decide which side of the issue you're going to take. Then, begin brainstorming. On a piece of scratch paper, write down all the reasons and persuasive examples you can think of in support of your essay. Don't stop to edit yourself; just let them flow out.

The Three Types of GMAT Logic

(1) Statistical
(2) Analogical
(3) Causal

If you think better on the computer, you can write out your outline and supporting ideas directly on the screen. Just remember to erase them before the time for that essay is over.

Then go through what you've written to decide on the order in which you want to make your points. You may decide, on reflection, to skip several of your brainstorms—or you may have one or two new ones as you organize.

Here's an example of what some brainstorming might produce in the way of support for Analysis of an Issue topic #1:

Main Idea: Censorship of television programs and popular music lyrics would be a mistake.

Support:

1. Freedom of speech was one of the founding principles of this country. It has been too hard won for us to give it up.

2. Who would perform this censorship, and how would we ensure that there was no political agenda attached to it?

3. Once started, censorship of violent content is hard to stop or to curb. Where would we draw the line? *Hamlet*? *Bambi*?

4. So far, the evidence of different studies is contradictory. The causal link between violence on television and real violence has not yet been convincingly proven.

5. While upsetting to many, the lyrics of such entertainers as Snoop Doggy Dogg continue a long tradition of protest of social conditions that has stretched over the centuries and has included such artists as Bob Dylan and Woody Guthrie.

After you've finished brainstorming, look over your supporting ideas and throw out the weakest ones. In general, examples from your personal life are less compelling to readers than examples from history or current events. There should be three to five ideas left over. Plan the order in which you want to present these ideas. You should start with one of your strongest ideas.

GETTING SPECIFIC

The GMAT readers are looking for supporting ideas or examples that are, in their words, "insightful" and "persuasive." What do they mean? Suppose you asked your friend about a movie she saw yesterday, and she said, "It was really cool."

Well, you'd know that she liked it, and that's good—but you wouldn't know much about the movie. Was it a comedy? An action adventure? Were the characters sexy? Did it make you cry?

The GMAT readers don't want to know that the movie was cool. They want to know that you liked it because:

Fastest growing professions

% increase by year 2005	
Paralegal	85%
System analyst	79%
Physical therapist	76%
Psychologist	64%
Travel agent	62%
Corrections officer	61%
Flight attendant	60%
Computer programmer	56%
Management analyst	52%
Marketing/P.R.	47%
Doctor	34%
Lawyer	34%

Source: Bureau of Labor Statistics, 1993

"It traced the development of two childhood friends as they grew up and grew apart."

or because:

"It combined the physical comedy of the Three Stooges with the action adventure of *Raiders of the Lost Ark.* "

You want to make each example as precise and compelling as possible. After you have brainstormed a few supporting ideas, spend a couple of moments on each one, making it as specific as possible. For example, let's say we are working on an essay supporting the idea that the United States should stay out of other countries' affairs.

Too vague: When the United States sent troops to Vietnam, things didn't work out too well. (*How* didn't they work out? What were the results?)

More specific: Look at the result of the United States sending troops to Vietnam. After more than a decade of fighting in support of a dubious political regime, American casualties numbered in the tens of thousands, and we may never know how many Vietnamese lost their lives as well.

ANALYSIS OF AN ISSUE: FINAL THOUGHTS

You've picked a position, you've brainstormed, you've brought with you a template and some structure words; brainstorming should have taken about five minutes. Now it's time to write your essay. Start typing, indenting each of the four or five paragraphs. (By the way, the *tab* key on the GMAT computer does not work—to indent, just hit the spacebar a few times.) Use all the tools you've learned in this chapter. Remember to keep an eye on the time. You have only 30 minutes to complete the first essay.

If you have a minute at the end, read over your essay and do any editing that's necessary.

Then, during the next thirty minutes, you'll turn to the second essay topic.

THE SECOND TOPIC: ANALYSIS OF AN ARGUMENT

You'll be able to use all the skills we've just been discussing on the second type of essay as well—with one major change. The Analysis of an Argument essay must initially be approached just like a logical argument in the Critical Reasoning section.

An Analysis of an Argument topic requires a series of steps.

Step 1: Read the topic and separate out the conclusion from the premises.

Step 2: Since they're asking you to critique (i.e., weaken) the argument, concentrate on identifying its assumptions.

The ETS booklet describes an "outstanding" Analysis of an Argument essay as one that: "clearly identifies and insightfully analyzes important features of the argument, develops ideas cogently, organizes them logically, and connects them smoothly with clear transitions, effectively supports the main points of the critique, demonstrates superior control of language, including diction, syntactic variety, and the conventions of standard written English . . . "

Brainstorm as many different assumptions as you can think of. It helps to write these out on a piece of scratch paper or on the computer screen.

Step 3: Look at the premises. Do they actually help to prove the conclusion?

Step 4: Choose a template that allows you to attack the assumptions and premises in an organized way.

Step 5: At the end of the essay, remember to take a moment to illustrate how these same assumptions could be used to make the argument more compelling.

Step 6: Read over the essay and do some editing.

WHAT THE READERS ARE LOOKING FOR

An Analysis of an Argument topic presents you with an argument. Your job is to critique the argument's line of reasoning and the evidence supporting it and suggest ways in which the argument could be strengthened. Again, you aren't required to know any more about the subject than would any normal person—but you must be able to spot logical weaknesses. This should start to remind you of Critical Reasoning.

The essay readers will be looking for four things as they skim through your Analysis of an Argument essay at the speed of light. According to a booklet prepared by ETS, "an outstanding argument essay . . .

- ◆ clearly identifies and insightfully analyzes important features of the argument;

- ◆ develops ideas cogently, organizes them logically, and connects them smoothly with clear transitions;

- ◆ effectively supports the main points of the critique; and

- ◆ demonstrates superior control of language, including diction, syntactic variety, and the conventions of standard written English. There may be minor flaws."

To put it more simply, the readers will be looking for all the same things they were looking for in the Analysis of an Issue essay, plus one extra ingredient: a cursory knowledge of the rules of logic.

CRITICAL REASONING IN ESSAY FORM

In any GMAT argument, the first thing to do is to separate the conclusion from the premises.

Let's see how this works with an actual essay topic. Here's the Analysis of an Argument topic you saw before:

Topic:

A new medical test that allows the early detection of a particular disease will prevent the deaths of people all over the world who would otherwise die from that disease. The

Q: What are the most important aspects of writing a good Analysis of an Issue essay?

test has been extremely effective in allowing doctors to diagnose the disease 6 months to a year before it would have been spotted by conventional means.

Discuss how logically convincing you find this argument. In explaining your point of view, be sure to analyze the line of reasoning and the use of evidence in the argument. Also discuss what, if anything, would make the argument more sound and persuasive, or would help you to better evaluate its conclusion.

The conclusion in this argument comes in the first line:

A new medical test that allows the early detection of a particular disease will prevent the deaths of people all over the world who would otherwise die from that disease.

The premises are the evidence in support of this conclusion.

The test has been extremely effective in allowing doctors to diagnose the disease 6 months to a year before it would have been spotted by conventional means.

The assumptions are the *unspoken* premises of the argument—without which the argument would fall apart. Remember that assumptions are often causal, analogical, or statistical. What are some assumptions of *this* argument? Let's brainstorm.

BRAINSTORMING FOR ASSUMPTIONS

You can often find assumptions by looking for a gap in the reasoning:

Medical test → early detection: According to the conclusion, the medical test leads to the early detection of the disease. There doesn't seem to be a gap here.

Early detection → nonfatal: In turn, the early detection of the disease allows patients to survive the disease. Well, hold on a minute. Is this necessarily true? Let's brainstorm:

1. First of all, do we know that early detection will necessarily lead to survival? We don't even know if this disease is *curable*. Early detection of an incurable disease is not going to help someone survive it.

2. Second, will the test be widely available and cheap enough for general use? If the test is expensive or only available in certain parts of the world, people will continue to die from the disease.

A: Write at least four or five paragraphs, and have them clearly organized (an introduction that explains the side you are taking, a middle with your points and examples, and a conclusion to sum up your position).

3. Will doctors and patients interpret the tests correctly? The test may be fine, but if doctors misinterpret the results or if patients ignore the need for treatment, then the test will not save lives.

THE USE OF THE EVIDENCE

Okay, we've uncovered some assumptions. Now, ETS also wants to know what we thought of the argument's "use of evidence." In other words, did the premises help to prove the conclusion? Well, in fact, no, they didn't. The premise here (the fact that the test can *spot* the disease 6 months to a year earlier than conventional tests) does not really help to prove the conclusion that the test will save *lives*.

ORGANIZING THE ANALYSIS OF AN ARGUMENT ESSAY

We're ready to put this into a ready-made template. In any Analysis of an Argument essay, the template structure will be pretty straightforward: You're simply going to reiterate the argument, attack the argument in three different ways (one to a paragraph), summarize what you've said, and mention how the argument could be strengthened. From an organizational standpoint, this is pretty easy. Try to minimize your use of the word "I." *Your* opinion is not really the point in an analysis of an Argument essay.

A SAMPLE TEMPLATE

Of course, you will want to develop your *own* template for the Analysis of an Argument essay, but to get you started, here's one possible structure:

The argument that __(restatement of the conclusion)__ is not entirely logically

convincing, since it ignores certain crucial assumptions.

First, the argument assumes that _____

_____ .

Second, the argument never addresses, _____

_____ .

Finally, the argument omits _____

_____ .

Thus, the argument is not completely sound. The evidence in support of the

conclusion _____ .

Ultimately, the argument might have been strengthened by _____

_____ .

> The key to an Analysis of an Argument essay is how clearly you critique the argument.

How Would Our Brainstorming Fit Into the Template?

Here's how the assumptions we came up with for this argument would have fit into the template:

The argument that the new medical test will prevent deaths that would have occurred in the past is not entirely logically convincing, since it ignores certain crucial assumptions.

First, the argument assumes that early detection of the disease will lead to a reduced mortality rate. There are a number of reasons why this might not be true. For example, the disease might be incurable (etc. etc.).

Second, the argument never addresses the point that the existence of this new test, even if totally effective, is not the same as the widespread use of the test (etc. etc.).

Finally, even supposing the ability of early detection to save lives and the widespread use of the test, the argument still depends on the doctors' correct interpretation of the test and the patients' willingness to undergo treatment. (etc. etc.)

Thus, the argument is not completely sound. The evidence in support of the conclusion (further information about the test itself) does little to prove the conclusion—that the test will save lives—since it does not address the assumptions already raised. Ultimately, the argument might have been strengthened by making it plain that the disease responds to early treatment, that the test will be widely available around the world, and that doctors and patients will make proper use of the test.

Customizing Your Analysis of an Argument Template

Your organizational structure may vary in some ways, but it will always include the following elements: *The first paragraph* should sum up the argument's conclusion. In the *second, third, and fourth paragraphs,* you'll attack the argument and the supporting evidence. In the last paragraph, you should summarize what you've said and state how the argument could be strengthened. Here are some alternate ways of organizing your essay.

The Analysis of an Argument Essay in Six Steps

Step 1: Read the topic. Isolate the conclusion and premises.

Step 2: Identify its assumptions. Brainstorm for five minutes.

Step 3: Look at the assumptions. Do they help to prove the conclusion?

Step 4: Choose a template that allows you to attack the assumptions in an organized way.

Step 5: Illustrate how these same assumptions could be used to make the argument more compelling.

Step 6: Do some editing to correct spelling or grammar mistakes.

Variation 1:

1st paragraph: Restate the argument.

2nd paragraph: Discuss the link (or lack of same) between the conclusion and the evidence presented in support of it.

3rd paragraph: Show three holes in the reasoning of the argument.

4th paragraph: Show how each of the three holes could be plugged up by explicitly stating the missing assumptions.

Variation 2:

1st paragraph: Restate the argument and say it has three flaws.

2nd paragraph: Point out a flaw and show how it could be plugged up by explicitly stating the missing assumption.

3rd paragraph: Point out a second flaw and show how it could be plugged up by explicitly stating the missing assumption.

4th paragraph: Point out a third flaw and show how it could be plugged up by explicitly stating the missing assumption.

5th paragraph: Summarize and conclude that because of these three flaws, the argument is weak.

Analysis of an Argument: Final Thoughts

You've separated the conclusion from the premises. You've brainstormed for the gaps that weaken the argument. You've noted how the premises support (or don't support) the conclusion. Now it's time to write your essay. Start typing, indenting each of the four or five paragraphs. Use all the tools you've learned in this chapter. Remember to keep an eye on the time.

Again, if you have a minute at the end, read over your essay and do any editing that's necessary.

Q: What are the most important aspects of writing a good Analysis of an Argument essay?

PRECONSTRUCTION

In both essays, the ETS readers will be looking for evidence of your facility with standard written English. This is where preconstruction comes in. It's amazing how a little elementary preparation can enhance an essay. We'll be looking at four tricks that almost instantly improve the appearance of a person's writing:

- Structure words
- Contrast words
- Short sentence/long sentence
- The impressive book reference

STRUCTURE WORDS

In chapter 14, we brought up a problem that most students encounter when they get to the Reading Comprehension section: There isn't enough time to read the passages carefully and answer all the questions. To get around this problem, we showed you some ways to spot the overall organization of a dense reading passage in order to understand the main idea and to find specific points quickly.

When you think about it, the ETS essay readers are facing almost the identical problem: They have less than two minutes to read your essay and figure out if it's any good. There's no time to appreciate the finer points of your argument. All they want to know is whether it's well organized and reasonably lucid—and to find out, they will be looking for the *same* structural clues you have learned to look for in the reading comprehension passages. Let's mention them again:

- When entire paragraphs contradict each other, there are some useful *pairs* of words that help to make this clear:

  on the one hand/on the other hand
  the traditional view/the new view

- If you have three points to make in a paragraph, it helps to point this out ahead of time:

  There are three reasons why I believe that the Grand Canyon should be strip-mined. First . . . Second . . . Third . . .

- If you want to clue the reader in to the fact that you are about to support the main idea with examples or illustrations, the following words are useful:

  for example
  to illustrate
  for instance
  because

- To add yet another example or argument in support of your main idea, you can use one of the following words to indicate your intention:

  furthermore
  in addition
  similarly
  just as
  also
  moreover

- To indicate that the idea you're about to bring up is important, special, or surprising in some way, you can use one of these words:

  surely
  truly
  undoubtedly
  clearly

A: Write at least four or five paragraphs, and have them clearly organized (an introduction in which you state that you will analyze the reasoning of the topic, a middle to pick apart the argument by exposing assumptions, and a conclusion in which you state how the argument could be strengthened and sum up your position). Remember, this essay uses the same skills and approach you developed for the critical reasoning section of the test.

certainly
indeed
as a matter of fact
in fact
most important

◆ To signal that you're about to reach a conclusion, you might use one of these words:

therefore
in summary
consequently
hence
in conclusion
in short

How It Works

Here's a paragraph that consists of a main point and two supporting arguments:

> *I believe he is wrong. He doesn't know the facts. He isn't thinking clearly.*

Watch how a few structure words can make this paragraph classier and clearer at the same time:

> *I believe he is wrong.* **For one thing***, he doesn't know the facts.* **For another***, he isn't thinking clearly.*

> *I believe he is wrong.* **Obviously***, he doesn't know the facts.* **Moreover***, he isn't thinking clearly.*

> *I believe he is wrong* **because, first***, he doesn't know the facts, and* **second***, he isn't thinking clearly.*

> **Certainly***, he doesn't know the facts, and he isn't thinking clearly* **either.** **Consequently***, I believe he is wrong.*

The Appearance of Depth

You may have noticed that much of the structure we have been discussing thus far has involved contrasting viewpoints. Nothing will give your writing the *appearance* of depth faster than learning to use this technique. The idea is to set up your main idea by first introducing its opposite.

> *It is a favorite ploy of incoming presidents to blame the federal bureaucracy for the high cost of government, but I believe that bureaucratic waste is only a small part of the problem.*

A significant part of receiving a high score on an essay is writing clearly and providing a basic structure for your essay. The structure should consist of an introduction, a body, and a conclusion.

You may have noticed that this sentence contained a "trigger word." In this case, the trigger word "but" tells us that what was expressed in the first half of the sentence is going to be contradicted in the second half. We discussed trigger words in the Reading Comprehension chapter of this book. Here they are again:

but	however
on the contrary	although
yet	while
despite	in spite of
rather	nevertheless
instead	

By using these words, you can instantly give your writing the appearance of depth.

Example:

> *Main thought: I believe that television programs should be censored.*
>
> *While many people believe in the sanctity of free speech, I believe that television programs should be censored.*
>
> *Most people believe in the sanctity of free speech, but I believe that television programs should be censored.*

In addition to trigger words, here are a few other words or phrases you can use to introduce the view you are eventually going to decide *against*:

admittedly	true
certainly	granted
obviously	of course
undoubtedly	to be sure
one cannot deny that	it could be argued that

CONTRASTING VIEWPOINTS WITHIN A PASSAGE

Trigger words can be used to signal the opposing viewpoints of entire paragraphs. Suppose you saw an essay that began

> *Many people believe that youth is wasted on the young. They point out that young people never seem to enjoy, or even think about, the great gifts they have been given but will not always have: Physical dexterity, good hearing, good vision. However . . .*

Before beginning any essay, always brainstorm! Write your ideas out on scratch paper.

What do you think is going to happen in the second paragraph? That's right, the author is now going to disagree with the "many people" of the first paragraph.

Setting up one paragraph in opposition to another lets the reader know what's going on right away. The organization of the essay is immediately evident.

Rhythm

Many people think good writing is a mysterious talent that you either have or don't have, like good rhythm. In fact, good writing has a kind of rhythm to it, but there is nothing mysterious about it. Good writing is a matter of mixing up the different kinds of raw materials that you have available to you—phrases, dependent and independent clauses—to build sentences that don't all sound the same.

Short Sentences, Long Sentences

The ETS graders won't have time to savor your essay, but they know that effective writing mixes up short and long sentences for variety, and consequently they will be looking to see how you put sentences together. Here's an example of a passage in which all the sentences sound alike:

> Movies cost too much. Everyone agrees about that. Studios need to cut costs. No one is sure exactly how to do it. I have two simple solutions. They can cut costs by paying stars less. They can also cut costs by reducing overhead.

Why did all the sentences sound alike? Well, for one thing, they were all about the same length. For another thing, the sentences were all made up of independent clauses with the same exact setup: Subject, verb, and sometimes object. There were no dependent clauses, almost no phrases, no structure words, and, frankly, no variety at all. Here's the same passage, but this time we varied the sentence length by combining some clauses and using conjunctions. We also threw in some structure words.

> Everyone agrees that movies cost too much. Clearly, studios need to cut costs, but no one is sure exactly how to do it. I have two simple solutions: They can cut costs by paying stars less and by reducing overhead.

The Impressive Book Reference

In any kind of writing, it pays to remember who your audience will be. In this case, the essays are first going to be graded by college teaching assistants. They wouldn't be human if they didn't have a soft spot in their heart for someone who can refer to a well-known nonfiction book or a famous work of literature.

What book should you pick? Obviously it should be a book that you have actually read and liked. We do not advise picking a book if you've only seen the movie. Hollywood has a habit of changing the endings.

You might think that it would be impossible to pick a book to use as an example for an essay before you even know the topic of the essay, but it's actually pretty easy. Just to give you an idea of how it's done, let's pick a famous work of literature that most people have read at some point in their lives: Shakespeare's *Hamlet*.

Now let's take each of the topics we've been using in this chapter, and see how we could work in a reference to *Hamlet*.

Essay topic 1:

Should television and song lyrics be censored in order to curb increasing crime and violence?

. . . Where would such censorship stop? In an attempt to prevent teen suicide, would an after-school version of Shakespeare's Hamlet *be changed so that the soliloquy read, "To be, or . . . whatever"?*

Essay topic 2:

Is government bureaucracy to blame for the increased cost of government?

If you were to compare the United States government to Shakespeare's Hamlet, *the poor bureaucrats would represent the forgotten and insignificant Rosencrantz and Guildenstern, not the scheming pretenders to the throne.*

Essay topic 3:

Should the maximum amount of a medical malpractice lawsuit be capped in the interest of lowering the cost of health care?

Malpractice awards are getting out of hand. If Shakespeare's era was reportedly the most litigious age in history, surely ours must come a close second. If he were writing today, you have the feeling Hamlet might have said, "Alas poor Yorick, he should have gotten a better malpractice lawyer."

You get the idea. Since your essays may be read by the admissions officers at the schools to which you are applying, you might think it would be better to cite a book by a well-regarded economist or business guru rather than that of a playwright or novelist. As long as your example feels like an organic addition to your essay, it won't matter too much who you cite. But you may find that these economic references are harder to work into your essay—and they will almost certainly go over the head of the essay *graders*.

THE AWA

It seems unlikely that anyone is going to be rejected by a business school based on these essays, so don't bother feeling intimidated. Think of it this way: The essays represent an *opportunity* if your verbal scores are low, or if English is your second language. For the rest of us, the essays are as good a way as any to warm up (and wake up) before the sections that count.

SUMMARY

1. The GMAT writing assessment will consist of two essays to be written in thirty minutes, each using a rudimentary word processing program and the computer keyboard. The essays will be given scores that range from 1 to 6 in half-point increments.

2. The essays may be read by the schools to which you apply, but the essays will be *graded* by underpaid, overworked college instructors who have only two minutes to read each essay.

3. To score high on the writing assessment:

   A. Write as many words as possible.

   B. Use a pre-built template to organize your thoughts.

   C. Use structure words, contrast words, and a combination of short and long sentences to give the appearance of depth to your writing

   D. Refer to a well-known work of literature or nonfiction.

4. For the Analysis of an Issue topic:

   Step 1: Read the topic.

   Step 2: Decide the general position you are going to take on the issue.

   Step 3: Brainstorm. Come up with a bunch of supporting ideas or examples. It helps to write these down on a piece of scratch paper, or on your screen as long as you remember to erase them. These supporting statements are supposed to help convince the reader that your main thesis is correct.

   Step 4: Look over your supporting ideas and throw out the weakest ones. There should be three to five left over.

Step 5: Write the essay, using all the preconstruction and template tools you learned in this chapter.

Step 6: Read over the essay and edit your work.

5. For the Analysis of an Argument topic:

Step 1: Read the topic and separate out the conclusion from the premises.

Step 2: Since they're asking you to critique (i.e., weaken) the argument, concentrate on identifying its assumptions. Brainstorm as many different assumptions as you can think of. It helps to write these on a piece of scratch paper, or on your screen as long as you remember to erase them.

Step 3: Look at the premises. Do they actually help to prove the conclusion?

Step 4: Choose a template that allows you to attack the assumptions and premises in an organized way.

Step 5: At the end of the essay, remember to take a moment to illustrate how these same assumptions could be used to make the argument more compelling.

Step 6: Read over the essay and edit your work.

PART V

Answer Key to Drills

DRILL 1
(page 61)

1. 77
2. 79
3. 10
4. 16
5. choice (B)

DRILL 2
(pages 61–62)

1. $80 + 40 = 120$
2. $55 \times 100 = 5500$
3. $ab + ac - ad$
4. $c(ab + xy)$
5. $\dfrac{12y - 6y}{y} = \dfrac{y(6)}{y} = 6$, choice (B)

DRILL 3
(page 66)

1. $\dfrac{145}{24}$ or $6\dfrac{1}{24}$
2. $\dfrac{1}{5}$
3. $\dfrac{29}{3}$
4. 18
5. choice (C)

DRILL 4
(page 70)

1. 33.30
2. 266.175
3. 6.09
4. 8
5. choice (C)

DRILL 5 (Angles and Lengths)
(page 116)

1. $x = 110°$
2. $x = 50°$ $y = 130°$ $z = 130°$
3. $x = 60°$ $y = 120°$ $z = 120°$
4. $\dfrac{3}{4}$
5. choice (D)

DRILL 6 (Triangles)
(pages 121–22)

1. $x = 8$
2. $x = 60$
3. $x = 5$
4. x must be less than 11 and greater than 3
5. $3\sqrt{2}$
6. $2\sqrt{3}$
7. choice (B)

DRILL 7 (Circles)
(pages 123–24)

1. area $= 25\pi$, circumference $= 10\pi$
2. circumference $= 12\pi$
3. $60°$
4. choice (B)

Drill 8 (Data Sufficiency Basics)
(pages 143–44)

1. Choice (C). Statement (1) might *seem* to be sufficient, but remember, if $x^2 = 4$, then x could be either 2 or –2. The question is asking for the one and only value of x. Statement (1) is not sufficient. Statement (2) by itself is not sufficient either, because the question is asking for the one and only value of x. But together, the two statements are sufficient because statement (1) gets us down to two possibilities, 2 and –2, and statement (2) eliminates the positive number.

2. Choice (B). If $x^2 = 4$, then x could be either 2 or –2. The question is asking for the one and only value of x, so Statement (1) is not sufficient. You might not think statement (2) is sufficient by itself, because it only gives us a value for y, not for x. However, the question is asking for the value of x times y. If $y = 0$, then we know the value of xy. Zero times anything equals zero.

3. Choice (E). If $x^2 = 4$, then x could be either 2 or –2. The question is asking for the one and only value of x, so Statement (1) is not sufficient. If $y^2 = 9$, then y could be either 3 or –3. The question is asking for the one and only value of x, so statement (2) is not sufficient by itself either. You might think that putting the two statements together would help us arrive at an answer, but in fact, we don't know. If $x = 2$ and $y = 3$, then $xy = 6$, but what if either x or y was negative? Then xy could also equal –6.

Drill 9 (Data Sufficiency Parts and Wholes)
(pages 149–50)

1. Choice (C). Statement (1) tells us only how many people paid a deposit. This is not sufficient to answer the question, and we are down to BCE. Statement (2) tells us only what percent of the people who paid deposits actually showed up. Again, by itself, this does not give us the number of people who attended, so we can eliminate choice (B). But if we put the two statements together, we now know how many people paid deposits (70), and what percentage of those people actually attended (60%) which means we can figure out how many actual people attended.

2. Choice (D). You might have thought you needed both statements together, but in fact, either was sufficient by itself. Statement (1) tells us there are 7 ounces of pigment in a 12-ounce can. Since there are only two ingredients, this means the other ingredient must make up the rest, or 5 ounces. This is sufficient to figure out the ratio (7:5) and we are down to a fifty-fifty choice: A or D. Similarly, statement (2) tells us there are 5 ounces of alcohol in a 12-ounce can. Since there are only two ingredients, this means the other ingredient must make up the rest, or 7 ounces. Again, this is sufficient to figure out the ratio, so the answer must be (D).

3. Choice (C). To answer this question, we needed the total number of miles. Statement (1) did not give us any concrete figures— just a fraction, so it was not sufficient, and we were down to BCE. Statement (2) gave us a concrete number, but it was only for part of the distance, so we can eliminate choice (B). However, if we combine the two statements, we learn that those 12 miles must make up the remaining $\frac{2}{5}$ of the entire trip. From this we could learn the entire distance of the trip by setting up the equation $\frac{2}{5} = \frac{12}{x}$. The correct answer is choice (C).

PART ◆ VI

The Princeton Review GMAT Pre-Diagnostic Test

The Princeton Review

go online

The following pages contain practice GMAT tests so you can test just how well you've mastered the techniques in this book. No other book can give you a more accurate preview of what you can expect from the questions on the official test. We also recommend you go online at the web address below and take a free full-length, simulated GMAT exam. You'll be timed, just like on test day, and you'll receive a complete analysis of your score telling you exactly where your strengths and weaknesses are.

http://tester.review.com

GMAT

The GMAT Pre-Diagnostic

GMAT DIAGNOSTIC TEST

The purpose of this 30-minute test is to get a rough idea of your current scoring range on the GMAT and give you rough percentiles on your math and verbal skills. Using these scores as a guide, you can then select which problems to practice on from the bins of questions that follow.

To get an even more accurate assessment of where you are right now, we recommend that you take one of the computer-adaptive tests offered in our software package (included in some editions of this book, or available in computer stores everywhere) or ETS's PowerPrep.

[According to ETS, the computer-adaptive GMAT estimates your approximate scoring level after the first few questions. You then spend the rest of the test time answering questions from around that level of difficulty, chosen by the computer from bins of potential questions.]

Math Test
Time—15 minutes
10 Questions

This test is composed of both Problem Solving questions and Data Sufficiency questions.

Problem Solving Directions: Solve each problem, using any available space on the page for scratchwork. Then indicate the best of the answer choices given.

Data Sufficiency Directions: Data Sufficiency problems consist of a question and two statements, labeled (1) and (2), in which certain data are given. You have to decide whether the data given in the statements are <u>sufficient</u> for answering the question. Using the data given in the statements <u>plus</u> your knowledge of mathematics and everyday facts (such as the number of days in July or the meaning of counterclockwise), you are to fill in oval

(A)   if statement (1) ALONE is sufficient, but statement (2) alone is not sufficient to answer the question asked;

(B)   if statement (2) ALONE is sufficient, but statement (1) alone is not sufficient to answer the question asked;

(C)   if BOTH statements (1) and (2) TOGETHER are sufficient to answer the question asked, but NEITHER statement ALONE is sufficient;

(D)   if EACH statement ALONE is sufficient to answer the question asked;

(E)   if statements (1) and (2) TOGETHER are NOT sufficient to answer the question asked, and additional data specific to the problem are needed.

---

1.   If $(16)(3)^2 = x(2^3)$, then $x =$

   (A)   81
   (B)   72
   (C)   18
   (D)   16
   (E)   8

2.   At a Wall Street company, 70 percent of this year's new employees are graduates of business schools and the remainder are graduates of liberal arts colleges. If 550 new employees were hired this year, what is the difference between the number of new business school employees and the number of new liberal arts employees?

   (A)   55
   (B)   220
   (C)   240
   (D)   385
   (E)   440

GO ON TO THE NEXT PAGE.

3. Bob purchased 18 cans of soda, some of which contained diet soda. How many of the cans did not contain diet soda?

(1) Of the cans Bob purchased, the number containing diet soda is equal to the number not containing diet soda.

(2) Of the cans Bob purchased, the number containing diet soda is odd.

(A) if statement (1) ALONE is sufficient, but statement (2) alone is not sufficient to answer the question asked;

(B) if statement (2) ALONE is sufficient, but statement (1) alone is not sufficient to answer the question asked;

(C) if BOTH statements (1) and (2) TO-GETHER are sufficient to answer the question asked, but NEITHER statement ALONE is sufficient;

(D) if EACH statement ALONE is sufficient to answer the question asked;

(E) if statements (1) and (2) TOGETHER are NOT sufficient to answer the question asked, and additional data specific to the problem are needed.

4. If y is an odd integer, which of the following must be an even integer?

(A) $y + 2$
(B) $y + 6$
(C) $2y - 1$
(D) $3y$
(E) $3y + 1$

5. There are 240 doctors and nurses at a hospital. If the ratio of doctors to nurses is 5 to 7, how many nurses are at the hospital?

(A) 20
(B) 60
(C) 100
(D) 140
(E) 180

6. Laura borrowed $240, interest free, from her parents to pay for her college education. If she pays back $2\frac{1}{2}$ percent of this amount quarterly, and has already paid $42.00, for how many months has she been paying back her loan?

(A) 6
(B) 7
(C) 19
(D) 21
(E) 24

7. Marc must visit either the library or the University Center. Which of these two buildings is a greater distance from his home?

(1) It takes Marc an average of 20 minutes to ride his bike from his home to the library.

(2) It takes Marc an average of 20 minutes to ride his bike from the library to the University Center.

(A) if statement (1) ALONE is sufficient, but statement (2) alone is not sufficient to answer the question asked;

(B) if statement (2) ALONE is sufficient, but statement (1) alone is not sufficient to answer the question asked;

(C) if BOTH statements (1) and (2) TO-GETHER are sufficient to answer the question asked, but NEITHER statement ALONE is sufficient;

(D) if EACH statement ALONE is sufficient to answer the question asked;

(E) if statements (1) and (2) TOGETHER are NOT sufficient to answer the question asked, and additional data specific to the problem are needed.

GO ON TO THE NEXT PAGE.

Math

8. If when a certain integer x is divided by 5 the remainder is 2, then each of the following could also be an integer EXCEPT

(A) $\dfrac{x}{17}$

(B) $\dfrac{x}{11}$

(C) $\dfrac{x}{10}$

(D) $\dfrac{x}{6}$

(E) $\dfrac{x}{3}$

9. Is $0 < y < 1$?

(1) $0 < \sqrt{y} < 1$

(2) $y^2 = \dfrac{1}{4}$

(A) if statement (1) ALONE is sufficient, but statement (2) alone is not sufficient to answer the question asked;

(B) if statement (2) ALONE is sufficient, but statement (1) alone is not sufficient to answer the question asked;

(C) if BOTH statements (1) and (2) TO-GETHER are sufficient to answer the question asked, but NEITHER statement ALONE is sufficient;

(D) if EACH statement ALONE is sufficient to answer the question asked;

(E) if statements (1) and (2) TOGETHER are NOT sufficient to answer the question asked, and additional data specific to the problem are needed.

GO ON TO THE NEXT PAGE.

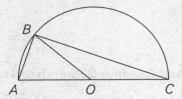

Note: Figure not drawn to scale

10. If triangle *AOB* is equilateral, *O* is the center of the semicircle *ABC,* and the radius of semicircle *ABC* is 6, what is the length of *BC*?

(A)   12

(B) $6\sqrt{3}$

(C)   10

(D) $6\sqrt{2}$

(E) $\sqrt{42}$

Verbal Test
Time—15 minutes
10 Questions

This test is made up of Sentence Corrections, Critical Reasoning, and Reading Comprehension.

Sentence Correction Directions: In Sentence Corrections, some part of the sentence or the entire sentence is underlined. Beneath each sentence you will find five ways of phrasing the underlined part. The first of these repeats the original; the other four are different. If you think the original is the best of these answer choices, choose answer A; otherwise, choose one of the others. Select the best version and fill in the corresponding oval on your answer sheet.

Reading Comprehension Directions: After reading the passage, choose the best answer to each question and fill in the corresponding oval on the answer sheet. Answer all questions following a passage on the basis of what is <u>stated</u> or <u>implied</u> in that passage.

Critical Reasoning Directions: Select the best of the answer choices given.

---

11. Violence in the stands at soccer matches has gotten so pronounced in several European countries that some stadiums have adopted new rules that aim <u>to identify fans of visiting teams and that seat them</u> in a separate area.

   (A) to identify fans of visiting teams and that seat them
   (B) to identify fans of visiting teams and seat them
   (C) to identify fans of visiting teams for seating
   (D) at identifying fans of visiting teams so as to seat them
   (E) at identifying fans of visiting teams and that seat them

12. Civic Leaders: The high cancer rate among our citizens is the result of hazardous materials produced at your plant.

   Board of Directors: Our statistics show that rates of cancer are high throughout the valley in which the plant is situated because local wells that supply drinking water are polluted, not because of the plant.

   Which of the following, if true, most seriously weakens the board's claims?

   (A) The statistics do not differentiate between types of cancer.
   (B) Nearby communities have not changed the sources of their drinking water.
   (C) Cancer-causing chemicals used at the plant are discharged into a nearby river and find their way into local wells.
   (D) The plant both uses and produces chemicals that have been shown to cause cancer.
   (E) Some of the pollutants cited by the board as contaminating the local wells have been present in the wells for decades.

GO ON TO THE NEXT PAGE.

13. Upset by the recent downturn in production numbers during the first half of the year, <u>the possibility of adding worker incentives was raised by the board of directors at its quarterly meeting</u>.

(A)   the possibility of adding worker incentives was raised by the board of directors at its quarterly meeting

(B)   the addition of worker incentives was raised as a possibility by the board of directors at its quarterly meeting

(C)   added worker incentives was raised by the board of directors at its quarterly meeting as a possibility

(D)   the board of directors raised at its quarterly meeting the possibility of worker incentives being added

(E)   the board of directors, at its quarterly meeting, raised the possibility of adding worker incentives

14. Whenever a major airplane accident occurs, there is a dramatic increase in the number of airplane mishaps reported in the media, a phenomenon that may last for as long as a few months after the accident. Airline officials assert that the publicity given the gruesomeness of major airplane accidents focuses media attention on the airline industry, and the increase in the number of reported accidents is caused by an increase in the number of news sources covering airline accidents, not by an increase in the number of accidents.

Which of the following, if true, would seriously weaken the assertions of the airline officials?

(A)   The publicity surrounding airline accidents is largely limited to the country in which the crash occurred.

(B)   Airline accidents tend to occur far more often during certain peak travel months.

(C)   News organizations do not have any guidelines to help them decide how severe an accident must be for it to receive coverage.

(D)   Airplane accidents receive coverage by news sources only when the news sources find it advantageous to do so.

(E)   Studies by government regulators show that the number of airplane flight miles remains relatively constant from month to month.

GO ON TO THE NEXT PAGE.

15. In 1978 a national study found that not only had many contractors licensed by a self-policing private guild failed to pass qualifying exams, <u>they in addition falsified their references</u>.

(A) they in addition falsified their references
(B) they had their references falsified in addition
(C) but they had also falsified their references
(D) they had also falsified their references
(E) but their references were falsified as well

16. Informed people generally assimilate information from several divergent sources before coming to an opinion. However, most popular news organizations view foreign affairs solely through the eyes of our State Department. In reporting the political crisis in foreign country B, news organizations must endeavor to find alternative sources of information.

Which of the following inferences can be drawn from the argument above?

(A) To the degree that a news source gives an account of another country that mirrors that of our State Department, that reporting is suspect.
(B) To protect their integrity, news media should avoid the influence of State Department releases in their coverage of foreign affairs.
(C) Reporting that is not influenced by the State Department is usually more accurate than are other accounts.
(D) The alternative sources of information mentioned in the passage might not share the same views as the State Department.
(E) A report cannot be seen as influenced by the State Department if it accurately depicts the events in a foreign country.

<u>Questions 17–20</u> are based on the following passage:

In Roman times, defeated enemies were generally put to death as criminals for having offended the emperor of Rome. In the Middle Ages, however, the practice of ransoming, or
5 returning prisoners in exchange for money, became common. Though some saw this custom as a step towards a more humane society, the primary reasons behind it were economic rather than humanitarian.
10 In those times, rulers had only a limited ability to raise taxes. They could neither force their subjects to fight nor pay them to do so. The promise of material compensation in the form of goods and ransom was therefore the
15 only way of inducing combatants to participate in a war. In the Middle Ages, the predominant incentive for the individual soldier was the expectation of spoils. Although collecting ransom clearly brought financial gain, keeping a
20 prisoner and arranging for his exchange had its costs. Consequently, procedures were devised to reduce transaction costs.
One such device was a rule asserting that the prisoner had to assess his own value. This
25 compelled the prisoner to establish a value without too much distortion; indicating too low a value would increase the captive's chances of being killed, while indicating too high a value would either ruin him financially or create a
30 prohibitively expensive ransom that would also result in death.

GO ON TO THE NEXT PAGE.

17. The primary purpose of the passage is to

(A) discuss the economic basis of the medieval practice of exchanging prisoners for ransom

(B) examine the history of the treatment of prisoners of war

(C) emphasize the importance of a warrior's code of honor during the middle ages

(D) explore a way of reducing the costs of ransom

(E) demonstrate why warriors of the Middle Ages looked forward to battles

18. It can be inferred from the passage that a medieval soldier

(A) was less likely to kill captured members of opposing armies than was a soldier of the Roman Empire

(B) was similar to a 20th-century terrorist in that he operated on a basically independent level and was motivated solely by economic incentives

(C) had few economic options and chose to fight because it was the only way to earn an adequate living

(D) was motivated to spare prisoners' lives by humanitarian rather than economic ideals

(E) had no respect for his captured enemies since captives were typically regarded as weak.

19. Which of the following best describes the change in policy from executing prisoners in Roman times to ransoming prisoners in the Middle Ages?

(A) The emperors of Rome demanded more respect than did medieval rulers, and thus Roman subjects went to greater lengths to defend their nation.

(B) It was a reflection of the lesser degree of direct control medieval rulers had over their subjects.

(C) It became a show of strength and honor for warriors of the Middle Ages to be able to capture and return their enemies.

(D) Medieval soldiers were not as humanitarian as their ransoming practices might have indicated.

(E) Medieval soldiers demonstrated more concern about economic policy than did their Roman counterparts.

20. The author uses the phrase "without too much distortion" (line 26) in order to

(A) indicate that prisoners would fairly assess their worth

(B) emphasize the important role medieval prisoners played in determining whether they should be ransomed

(C) explain how prisoners often paid more than an appropriate ransom in order to increase their chances for survival

(D) suggest that captors and captives often had understanding relationships

(E) show that when in prison a soldier's view could become distorted

18

GMAT Pre-Diagnostic Scoring Guide

GMAT PRE-DIAGNOSTIC SCORING GUIDE

ANSWERS TO THE PRE-DIAGNOSTIC TEST

Math:

1. C	6. D		
2. B	7. E		
3. A	8. C		
4. E	9. A		
5. D	10. B		

Verbal:

11. B	16. D
12. C	17. A
13. E	18. A
14. B	19. B
15. C	20. A

THE MATH SCORE

If you got 3 or fewer math questions correct: Your percentile rank is in the lower one-third of the testing group and you should begin by practicing the problems in Math Bin I. Once you've mastered the material in Math Bin I, you should move on to the questions in Math Bin II.

If you got between 3 and 6 math questions correct: Your percentile rank is in the middle one-third of the testing group and you should begin by practicing the problems in Math Bin II. Once you've mastered the material in Math Bin II, you should move on to the questions in Math Bin III.

If you got 7 or more math questions correct: Your percentile rank is in the top one-third of the testing group and you should begin by practicing the problems in Math Bin III.

THE VERBAL SCORE

If you got 3 or fewer verbal questions correct: Your percentile rank is in the lower one-third of the testing group and you should begin by practicing the problems in Verbal Bin I. Once you've mastered the material in Verbal Bin I, you should move on to the questions in Verbal Bin II.

If you got between 3 and 6 verbal questions correct: Your percentile rank is in the middle one-third of the testing group and you should begin by practicing the problems in Verbal Bin II. Once you've mastered the material in Verbal Bin II, you should move on to the questions in Verbal Bin III.

If you got 7 or more verbal questions correct: Your percentile rank is in the top one-third of the testing group and you should begin by practicing the problems in Verbal Bin III.

(If you want additional practice for either the math or the verbal section, it may also be helpful to do the problems in a Bin with a lower number than the one suggested. So if your math diagnostic score indicates that you should do the questions in Math Bin II, you might want to do the questions in Math Bin I as well.)

THE COMBINED SCORE

If you got 6 or fewer of the 20 total questions correct: Your combined score at the moment is less than 450.

If you got between 6 and 15 of the 20 total questions correct: Your combined score at the moment is between 450 and 550.

If you got 16 or more of the 20 total questions correct: Your combined score at the moment is above 550.

19

GMAT Pre-Diagnostic
Explanations

Math Explanations

1. If $(16)(3)^2 = x(2^3)$, then $x =$

   (A) 81
   (B) 72
   (C) 18
   (D) 16
   (E) 8

2. At a Wall Street company, 70 percent of this year's new employees are graduates of business schools and the remainder are graduates of liberal arts colleges. If 550 new employees were hired this year, what is the difference between the number of new business school employees and the number of new liberal arts employees?

   (A) 55
   (B) 220
   (C) 240
   (D) 385
   (E) 440

3. Bob purchased 18 cans of soda, some of which contained diet soda. How many of the cans did not contain diet soda?

   (1) Of the cans Bob purchased, the number containing diet soda is equal to the number not containing diet soda.

   (2) Of the cans Bob purchased, the number containing diet soda is odd.

   (A) if statement (1) ALONE is sufficient, but statement (2) alone is not sufficient to answer the question asked;

   (B) if statement (2) ALONE is sufficient, but statement (1) alone is not sufficient to answer the question asked;

   (C) if BOTH statements (1) and (2) TOGETHER are sufficient to answer the question asked, but NEITHER statement ALONE is sufficient;

   (D) if EACH statement ALONE is sufficient to answer the question asked;

   (E) if statements (1) and (2) TOGETHER are NOT sufficient to answer the question asked, and additional data specific to the problem are needed.

1. **(C)** Rather than multiply out each side of the equation, let's simplify. We can rewrite 16 as 2^4. If we cancel 2^3 from each side of the equation, we are left with $2(3)^2 = x$. The correct answer is (C) 18.

2. **(B)** What kind of problem was this? A percent problem. 70% of the 550 new employees were B-school graduates. 70% of 550 = 385. (If you were rushing you might have chosen choice (D) 385.) But you aren't done yet. The other 30% had liberal arts degrees. 30% of 550 = 165. The problem wants to know the difference between 385 and 165. To find the difference, simply subtract. The correct answer is (B) 220.

   Could we have ballparked? Sure. The difference between 70% and 30% is 40%, or slightly less than half of the 550 new employees. Choices (D) and (E) were both greater than half. Choice (A) was much too small.

3. **(A)** The original question tells us the total number of cans. Statement (1) tells us there is an equal number of diet and non-diet cans. This answers the question (there are 9 of each, not that we really needed to know to get this data sufficiency question correct.) We are down to (A) or (D).

   Statement (2) may seem to *agree* with statement (1) because we may have noticed that the number of diet cans supplied by the information in statement (1) happens to be odd. However there are lots of odd numbers. The correct answer is choice (A).

4. If y is an odd integer, which of the following must be an even integer?

   (A) $y + 2$
   (B) $y + 6$
   (C) $2y - 1$
   (D) $3y$
   (E) $3y + 1$

5. There are 240 doctors and nurses at a hospital. If the ratio of doctors to nurses is 5 to 7, how many nurses are at the hospital?

   (A) 20
   (B) 60
   (C) 100
   (D) 140
   (E) 180

4. **(E)** Variables in the answer choices means this is a plug-in problem—a total gift as long as you use our techniques—but the word "must" means you may have to plug in *twice* to be sure you have the right answer. Whenever you plug in, be sure to write the number you are using above the variable so you won't forget it as you work. Since y must be an odd integer, let's use 3. Now, all we have to do is plug 3 into each of the answer choices. Any choice that does *not* yield an even integer can be crossed off immediately. If more than one of the choices yields an even integer, we will have to plug in a second number for y to see which choice *always* yields an even number. Using 3 as our value for y, we find that choices (A), (B), (C), and (D) all yield odd numbers. Therefore the correct answer is choice (E).

5. **(D)** The key word in this problem is "ratio." To find the number of nurses, we must convert the ratio to a fraction. If the ratio of doctors to nurses is 5 to 7, then the "whole" is $5 + 7$, or 12. The fraction of nurses at the hospital is $\frac{7}{12}$. Let's set up an equation: $\frac{7}{12} = \frac{x}{240}$. The correct answer is choice (D) 140.

If you picked choice (C), you found the number of *doctors* at the hospital.

Could we have ballparked? Sure. Once we knew that the fraction of nurses at the hospital was $\frac{7}{12}$, we could see that the actual number of nurses had to be slightly more than half of the total $\left(\frac{6}{12} \text{ would be exactly half} \right)$. This allows us to eliminate choices (A), (B), and (C) because they are all less than half, and choice (E) because it is much greater than half.

Math Explanations

6. Laura borrowed $240, interest free, from her parents to pay for her college education. If she pays back $2\frac{1}{2}$ percent of this amount quarterly, and has already paid $42.00, for how many months has she been paying back her loan?

   (A) 6
   (B) 7
   (C) 19
   (D) 21
   (E) 24

7. Marc must visit either the library or the University Center. Which of these two buildings is a greater distance from his home?

   (1) It takes Marc an average of 20 minutes to ride his bike from his home to the library.

   (2) It takes Marc an average of 20 minutes to ride his bike from the library to the University Center.

   (A) if statement (1) ALONE is sufficient, but statement (2) alone is not sufficient to answer the question asked;

   (B) if statement (2) ALONE is sufficient, but statement (1) alone is not sufficient to answer the question asked;

   (C) if BOTH statements (1) and (2) TOGETHER are sufficient to answer the question asked, but NEITHER statement ALONE is sufficient;

   (D) if EACH statement ALONE is sufficient to answer the question asked;

   (E) if statements (1) and (2) TOGETHER are NOT sufficient to answer the question asked, and additional data specific to the problem are needed.

6. **(D)** Laura is paying back 2.5 percent of the loan each quarter of the year. 2.5% of $240 is $6.00. If she has already paid $42.00, that means she has paid that $6.00 for seven quarters. How many months is that? Each quarter of the year is 3 months. The correct answer is choice (D).

7. **(E)** Statement (1) only tells us the time it takes to bicycle to the library. Since it says nothing about the University Center, this is insufficient, and we are down to (B), (C), or (E).

Statement (2) only tells us the time it takes to ride from the library to the center. By itself, this is also insufficient. We're down to (C) and (E).

When we put the two statements together, we might be tempted to assume that the three sites (home, the library, and the University Center) are all in a straight line, but of course, we can't assume anything of the kind. What if Marc travels 20 minutes due north of his house to get to the library, then travels 20 minutes due south to get to the University Center, which just happens to be across the street from his home? The correct answer to this question is choice (E).

8. If when a certain integer x is divided by 5 the remainder is 2, then each of the following could also be an integer EXCEPT

(A) $\dfrac{x}{17}$

(B) $\dfrac{x}{11}$

(C) $\dfrac{x}{10}$

(D) $\dfrac{x}{6}$

(E) $\dfrac{x}{3}$

8. **(C)** As always, when there are variables in the answer choices, the easiest thing to do is plug in. If you always get a remainder of 2 when you divide x by 5, then x has to be some multiple of 5 plus 2 more. In other words, x could be 7 or 12 or 17 or 22, etc. Now, we have to go through the answer choices plugging in numbers for x that allow them to be integers as well. For example, in choice (A), if we plugged in 17 for x, that would give us $\dfrac{17}{17}$ which is an integer. Cross off choice (A). In choice (B) if we plugged in 22, we would get $\dfrac{22}{11}$ which is an integer. Cross off choice (B). In choices (D) and (E) plugging in the number 12 would make both choices integers. Only choice (C) can never be an integer as long as x can be divided by 5 with a remainder of 2. The correct answer is choice (C).

9. Is $0 < y < 1$?

   (1) $0 < \sqrt{y} < 1$

   (2) $y^2 = \dfrac{1}{4}$

   (A) if statement (1) ALONE is sufficient, but statement (2) alone is not sufficient to answer the question asked;

   (B) if statement (2) ALONE is sufficient, but statement (1) alone is not sufficient to answer the question asked;

   (C) if BOTH statements (1) and (2) TOGETHER are sufficient to answer the question asked, but NEITHER statement ALONE is sufficient;

   (D) if EACH statement ALONE is sufficient to answer the question asked;

   (E) if statements (1) and (2) TOGETHER are NOT sufficient to answer the question asked, and additional data specific to the problem are needed.

9. **(A)** To solve this "yes or no" question, plug values into the two statements. Joe Bloggs liked statement (2) because he forgot that y could equal $-\dfrac{1}{2}$. However only statement (1) answered the question: On the GMAT, square roots are always positive. The correct answer is choice (A).

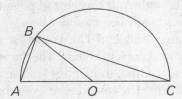

Note: Figure not drawn to scale

10. If triangle *AOB* is equilateral, *O* is the center of the semicircle *ABC,* and the radius of semicircle *ABC* is 6, what is the length of *BC*?

(A) 12

(B) $6\sqrt{3}$

(C) 10

(D) $6\sqrt{2}$

(E) $\sqrt{42}$

10. **(B)** First redraw the diagram to scale, so you can see what's going on. If you redraw carefully, making sure that *AB* = *AO* = *BO*, you will be able to guesstimate, and eliminate several answer choices even if you don't know much geometry. Use the side of your answer sheet to measure your redrawn *BC*. Is it equal to 12? Of course not. 12 is the diameter of the circle. *BC* must be smaller. Cross off choice (A). Choice (E) does not come out to a whole number, but it is close to the square root of 49, or 7. Could *BC* be this small? No way. If you drew your diagram accurately, *BC* should be a little bigger than 10. The correct answer is choice (B).

Geometrically speaking, any triangle inscribed inside a semicircle forms a 90-degree angle if one side is a diameter. If triangle *ABO* is equilateral, that means that angle *OAB* is 60 degrees. Thus triangle *ABC* is a 30-60-90 triangle, with sides 6, $6\sqrt{3}$, and 12.

Verbal Explanations

11. Violence in the stands at soccer matches has gotten so pronounced in several European countries that some stadiums have adopted new rules that aim <u>to identify fans of visiting teams and that seat them</u> in a separate area.

   (A) to identify fans of visiting teams and that seat them
   (B) to identify fans of visiting teams and seat them
   (C) to identify fans of visiting teams for seating
   (D) at identifying fans of visiting teams so as to seat them
   (E) at identifying fans of visiting teams and that seat them

11. **(B)** Go through your checklist of potential errors. Is there a misplaced modifier here? No. Is there a pronoun problem? No. Is there a parallel construction problem? Bingo! The "new rules" have two aims: first, to identify fans, and second, to seat them. The correct answer is choice (B).

12. Civic Leaders: The high cancer rate among our citizens is the result of hazardous materials produced at your plant.

   Board of Directors: Our statistics show that rates of cancer are high throughout the valley in which the plant is situated because local wells that supply drinking water are polluted, not because of the plant.

   Which of the following, if true, most seriously weakens the board's claims?

   (A) The statistics do not differentiate between types of cancer.
   (B) Nearby communities have not changed the sources of their drinking water.
   (C) Cancer-causing chemicals used at the plant are discharged into a nearby river and find their way into local wells.
   (D) The plant both uses and produces chemicals that have been shown to cause cancer.
   (E) Some of the pollutants cited by the board as contaminating the local wells have been present in the wells for decades.

12. **(C)** This is a causal argument. The civic leaders are saying that the plant's hazardous waste is the cause of high cancer rates in the area. The company directors propose an alternate cause: polluted drinking water. How do we weaken the directors' argument? The correct answer is choice (C), which says that it is the hazardous wastes from the company that are contaminating the drinking water. In other words, there is no alternate cause; the primary cause is creating the secondary cause that the company is trying to blame. (A), (B), and (E) are outside the scope of the argument. Choice (D) is attractive, but does not directly attack the board's claims, nor does it say that the cancerous materials are contaminating the environment.

13. Upset by the recent downturn in production numbers during the first half of the year, <u>the possibility of adding worker incentives was raised by the board of directors at its quarterly meeting</u>.

  (A) the possibility of adding worker incentives was raised by the board of directors at its quarterly meeting
  (B) the addition of worker incentives was raised as a possibility by the board of directors at its quarterly meeting
  (C) added worker incentives was raised by the board of directors at its quarterly meeting as a possibility
  (D) the board of directors raised at its quarterly meeting the possibility of worker incentives being added
  (E) the board of directors, at its quarterly meeting, raised the possibility of adding worker incentives

14. Whenever a major airplane accident occurs, there is a dramatic increase in the number of airplane mishaps reported in the media, a phenomenon that may last for as long as a few months after the accident. Airline officials assert that the publicity given the gruesomeness of major airplane accidents focuses media attention on the airline industry, and the increase in the number of reported accidents is caused by an increase in the number of news sources covering airline accidents, not by an increase in the number of accidents.

Which of the following, if true, would seriously weaken the assertions of the airline officials?

  (A) The publicity surrounding airline accidents is largely limited to the country in which the crash occurred.
  (B) Airline accidents tend to occur far more often during certain peak travel months.
  (C) News organizations do not have any guidelines to help them decide how severe an accident must be for it to receive coverage.
  (D) Airplane accidents receive coverage by news sources only when the news sources find it advantageous to do so.
  (E) Studies by government regulators show that the number of airplane flight miles remains relatively constant from month to month.

13. **(E)** This is a misplaced modifier question. Who was "upset by the recent downturn?" It was the board of directors. This eliminates choices (A), (B), and (C). Choice (E) correctly positions the prepositional phrase "at its quarterly meeting" and avoids the passive "being added in choice (D)."

14. **(B)** This is a statistical argument. The officials are asserting that there is in fact no increase in actual mishaps during the months after an accident, but an increase in the number of news sources *reporting* the mishaps—in other words, they are arguing that the statistics are not representative. To weaken this assertion, we would have to show that the statistics are in fact representative. Choice (B) does this by implying that certain months are more likely to have more frequent accidents due to high volume of flights. Choice (A) is outside the scope of the argument. Choices (C), (D), and (E) would all *strengthen* the assertions of the officials.

Verbal Explanations

15. In 1978 a national study found that not only had many contractors licensed by a self-policing private guild failed to pass qualifying exams, <u>they in addition falsified their references</u>.

   (A) they in addition falsified their references
   (B) they had their references falsified in addition
   (C) but they had also falsified their references
   (D) they had also falsified their references
   (E) but their references were falsified as well

15. **(C)** One of ETS's favorite idiomatic expressions is "not only . . . but also." Only choice (C) uses the idiom correctly with a parallel active verb.

16. Informed people generally assimilate information from several divergent sources before coming to an opinion. However, most popular news organizations view foreign affairs solely through the eyes of our State Department. In reporting the political crisis in foreign country B, news organizations must endeavor to find alternative sources of information.

   Which of the following inferences can be drawn from the argument above?

   (A) To the degree that a news source gives an account of another country that mirrors that of our State Department, that reporting is suspect.
   (B) To protect their integrity, news media should avoid the influence of State Department releases in their coverage of foreign affairs.
   (C) Reporting that is not influenced by the State Department is usually more accurate than are other accounts.
   (D) The alternative sources of information mentioned in the passage might not share the same views as the State Department.
   (E) A report cannot be seen as influenced by the State Department if it accurately depicts the events in a foreign country.

16. **(D)** To get an inference question correct, you almost never actually want to infer. Look for an answer that seems ludicrously obvious. Choice (A) implies that the State Department's views are always likely to diverge from other news sources, which is not only silly, but something ETS would be unlikely to say. (B) implies that the State Department should never be used as a news source, which goes way too far. (C) also goes much further than the passage itself. (E) is a bit bizarre, since sometimes the State Department is bound to be right. (D) is the correct answer because the argument makes it clear that the "alternative" sources of information would provide the "divergent" opinions mentioned in the first sentence.

Questions 17–20 are based on the following passage.

In Roman times, defeated enemies were generally put to death as criminals for having offended the emperor of Rome. In the Middle Ages, however, the practice of ransoming, or
5 returning prisoners in exchange for money, became common. Though some saw this custom as a step towards a more humane society, the primary reasons behind it were economic rather than humanitarian.
10 In those times, rulers had only a limited ability to raise taxes. They could neither force their subjects to fight nor pay them to do so. The promise of material compensation in the form of goods and ransom was therefore the
15 only way of inducing combatants to participate in a war. In the Middle Ages, the predominant incentive for the individual soldier was the expectation of spoils. Although collecting ransom clearly brought financial gain, keeping a
20 prisoner and arranging for his exchange had its costs. Consequently, procedures were devised to reduce transaction costs.
One such device was a rule asserting that the prisoner had to assess his own value. This
25 compelled the prisoner to establish a value without too much distortion; indicating too low a value would increase the captive's chances of being killed, while indicating too high a value would either ruin him financially or create a
30 prohibitively expensive ransom that would also result in death.

17. The primary purpose of the passage is to

(A) discuss the economic basis of the medieval practice of exchanging prisoners for ransom

(B) examine the history of the treatment of prisoners of war

(C) emphasize the importance of a warrior's code of honor during the middle ages

(D) explore a way of reducing the costs of ransom

(E) demonstrate why warriors of the Middle Ages looked forward to battles

17. **(A)** Choice (A) correctly summarizes the main idea of the first paragraph. While choice (D) reflects a part of the passage, it does not encompass the main idea of the passage.

18. It can be inferred from the passage that a medieval soldier

    (A) was less likely to kill captured members of opposing armies than was a soldier of the Roman Empire.
    (B) was similar to a 20th-century terrorist in that he operated on a basically independent level and was motivated solely by economic incentives
    (C) had few economic options and chose to fight because it was the only way to earn an adequate living
    (D) was motivated to spare prisoners' lives by humanitarian rather than economic ideals
    (E) had no respect for his captured enemies since captives were typically regarded as weak.

18. **(A)** The first paragraph gives us the information to answer this question. Note the trigger word ("however") that underscores the difference between the Roman era and the Middle Ages.

19. Which of the following best describes the change in policy from executing prisoners in Roman times to ransoming prisoners in the Middle Ages?

    (A) The emperors of Rome demanded more respect than did medieval rulers, and thus Roman subjects went to greater lengths to defend their nation.
    (B) It was a reflection of the lesser degree of direct control medieval rulers had over their subjects.
    (C) It became a show of strength and honor for warriors of the Middle Ages to be able to capture and return their enemies.
    (D) Medieval soldiers were not as humanitarian as their ransoming practices might have indicated.
    (E) Medieval soldiers demonstrated more concern about economic policy than did their Roman counterparts.

19. **(B)** The correct answer can be found in the second paragraph.

20. The author uses the phrase "without too much distortion" (line 26) in order to

(A) indicate that prisoners would fairly assess their worth

(B) emphasize the important role medieval prisoners played in determining whether they should be ransomed

(C) explain how prisoners often paid more than an appropriate ransom in order to increase their chances for survival

(D) suggest that captors and captives often had understanding relationships

(E) show that when in prison a soldier's view could become distorted

20. **(A)** To get the correct answer, we had to understand the meaning of the quoted words, but it also helped to read the rest of the paragraph which talked about a value that was neither too low nor too high.

PART VII

The Princeton Review GMAT Diagnostic Test

Math Test
Bin One
14 Questions

This test is composed of both Problem Solving questions and Data Sufficiency questions.

Problem Solving Directions: Solve each problem, using any available space on the page for scratchwork. Then indicate the best of the answer choices given.

Data Sufficiency Directions: Data Sufficiency problems consist of a question and two statements, labeled (1) and (2), in which certain data are given. You have to decide whether the data given in the statements are <u>sufficient</u> for answering the question. Using the data given in the statements <u>plus</u> your knowledge of mathematics and everyday facts (such as the number of days in July or the meaning of *counterclockwise*), you are to fill in oval

(A) if statement (1) ALONE is sufficient, but statement (2) alone is not sufficient to answer the question asked;

(B) if statement (2) ALONE is sufficient, but statement (1) alone is not sufficient to answer the question asked;

(C) if BOTH statements (1) and (2) TOGETHER are sufficient to answer the question asked, but NEITHER statement ALONE is sufficient;

(D) if EACH statement ALONE is sufficient to answer the question asked;

(E) if statements (1) and (2) TOGETHER are NOT sufficient to answer the question asked, and additional data specific to the problem are needed.

94.08 —
 A —

94.07 —

1. A portion of a thermometer above is calibrated to show degrees in equal increments. If the temperature indicates a reading at level *A*, what is the temperature?

   (A) 94.069
   (B) 94.070
   (C) 94.079
   (D) 94.080
   (E) 94.790

2. Starting at 9 a.m. on a certain day, snow began to fall at a rate of $1\frac{1}{4}$ inches every two hours until 3 p.m. If there were already $2\frac{1}{4}$ inches of snow on the ground at 9 a.m., how many inches of snow were on the ground at 3 p.m. that day?

   (A) $3\frac{3}{4}$

   (B) 6

   (C) 7

   (D) $7\frac{1}{2}$

   (E) $9\frac{3}{4}$ GO ON TO THE NEXT PAGE.

3. What is the area of triangular region *T*?

   (1)   The base of triangle *T* is 12.

   (2)   The ratio of the height of *T* to the base of *T* is 3:1.

   (A)   if statement (1) ALONE is sufficient, but statement (2) alone is not sufficient to answer the question asked;

   (B)   if statement (2) ALONE is sufficient, but statement (1) alone is not sufficient to answer the question asked;

   (C)   if BOTH statements (1) and (2) TO-GETHER are sufficient to answer the question asked, but NEITHER statement ALONE is sufficient;

   (D)   if EACH statement ALONE is sufficient to answer the question asked;

   (E)   if statements (1) and (2) TOGETHER are NOT sufficient to answer the question asked, and additional data specific to the problem are needed.

4. The owner of a boutique decides to calculate the percentage of customers who purchase hats. If 40 percent of the store's customers decide to purchase items, and of those customers 15 percent purchase hats, what percent of the store's customers purchase hats?

   (A)   4%
   (B)   6%
   (C)   15%
   (D)   24%
   (E)   55%

5. The result obtained when *x* is multiplied by *y* is equal to ten times the result obtained when *y* is subtracted from *x*. If *y* equals 5, what does *x* equal?

   (A)   50
   (B)   25
   (C)   15
   (D)   10
   (E)   5

6. In 1988, was the number of people in City *X* greater than three times the number of people in City *Y*?

   (1)   In 1988, there were approximately 1.1 million more people in City *X* than in City *Y*.

   (2)   In 1988, the 300,000 Mormons in City *X* made up 20 percent of its population, and the 141,000 Buddhists in City *Y* made up 30 percent of its population.

   (A)   if statement (1) ALONE is sufficient, but statement (2) alone is not sufficient to answer the question asked;

   (B)   if statement (2) ALONE is sufficient, but statement (1) alone is not sufficient to answer the question asked;

   (C)   if BOTH statements (1) and (2) TO-GETHER are sufficient to answer the question asked, but NEITHER statement ALONE is sufficient;

   (D)   if EACH statement ALONE is sufficient to answer the question asked;

   (E)   if statements (1) and (2) TOGETHER are NOT sufficient to answer the question asked, and additional data specific to the problem are needed.

GO ON TO THE NEXT PAGE.

7. $(165)^2 - (164)^2 =$

(A)   1
(B)   2
(C)   4
(D) 325
(E) 329

8. If point X is directly north of point Y and directly west of point Z, what is the distance from point X to point Z?

(1)   The distance from Y to Z is 20.

(2)   The distance from X to Y is equal to half the distance from Y to Z.

(A)   if statement (1) ALONE is sufficient, but statement (2) alone is not sufficient to answer the question asked;

(B)   if statement (2) ALONE is sufficient, but statement (1) alone is not sufficient to answer the question asked;

(C)   if BOTH statements (1) and (2) TO-GETHER are sufficient to answer the question asked, but NEITHER statement ALONE is sufficient;

(D)   if EACH statement ALONE is sufficient to answer the question asked;

(E)   if statements (1) and (2) TOGETHER are NOT sufficient to answer the question asked, and additional data specific to the problem are needed.

9. The formula $E = \sqrt{\dfrac{a}{6}}$ describes the relationship between the length of the edge E of a cube and the surface area a of the cube. How much longer is the edge of a cube with a surface area of 1350 than the edge of one with a surface area of 600?

(A)   5
(B)   15
(C) 150
(D) 250
(E) 750

10. Is v equal to the average (arithmetic mean) of $s, t,$ and u?

(1) $s + t + u = 3v$

(2) $\dfrac{s+t+u}{6} = \dfrac{v}{2}$

(A)   if statement (1) ALONE is sufficient, but statement (2) alone is not sufficient to answer the question asked;

(B)   if statement (2) ALONE is sufficient, but statement (1) alone is not sufficient to answer the question asked;

(C)   if BOTH statements (1) and (2) TO-GETHER are sufficient to answer the question asked, but NEITHER statement ALONE is sufficient;

(D)   if EACH statement ALONE is sufficient to answer the question asked;

(E)   if statements (1) and (2) TOGETHER are NOT sufficient to answer the question asked, and additional data specific to the problem are needed.

GO ON TO THE NEXT PAGE.

11. $\left[1 - \left(\dfrac{2}{3} \right)^2 \right]^2 =$

(A) $-\dfrac{1}{3}$

(B) $\dfrac{1}{27}$

(C) $\dfrac{125}{729}$

(D) $\dfrac{25}{81}$

(E) $\dfrac{5}{9}$

12. What is the maximum capacity in cups of a pail that contains only sand and is filled to three-fourths of its capacity?

(1) If one cup of sand were added to the pail, it would be filled to seven-eighths of its capacity.

(2) If two cups were removed from the pail, it would be filled to one-half of its capacity.

(A) if statement (1) ALONE is sufficient, but statement (2) alone is not sufficient to answer the question asked;

(B) if statement (2) ALONE is sufficient, but statement (1) alone is not sufficient to answer the question asked;

(C) if BOTH statements (1) and (2) TO-GETHER are sufficient to answer the question asked, but NEITHER statement ALONE is sufficient;

(D) if EACH statement ALONE is sufficient to answer the question asked;

(E) if statements (1) and (2) TOGETHER are NOT sufficient to answer the question asked, and additional data specific to the problem are needed.

GO ON TO THE NEXT PAGE.

13. After reading $\frac{3}{5}$ of his biology homework on Monday night, Bernie read $\frac{1}{3}$ of his remaining homework on Tuesday night. What fraction of his original homework would Bernie have to read on Wednesday night to complete his biology assignment?

(A) $\frac{1}{15}$

(B) $\frac{2}{15}$

(C) $\frac{4}{15}$

(D) $\frac{2}{5}$

(E) $\frac{4}{5}$

14. What is the value of x?

(1) $x^2 = 4x$

(2) x is an even integer.

(A) if statement (1) ALONE is sufficient, but statement (2) alone is not sufficient to answer the question asked;

(B) if statement (2) ALONE is sufficient, but statement (1) alone is not sufficient to answer the question asked;

(C) if BOTH statements (1) and (2) TOGETHER are sufficient to answer the question asked, but NEITHER statement ALONE is sufficient;

(D) if EACH statement ALONE is sufficient to answer the question asked;

(E) if statements (1) and (2) TOGETHER are NOT sufficient to answer the question asked, and additional data specific to the problem are needed.

NO TEST MATERIAL ON THIS PAGE

Math Test
Bin Two
14 Questions

This test is composed of both Problem Solving questions and Data Sufficiency questions.

Problem Solving Directions: Solve each problem, using any available space on the page for scratchwork. Then indicate the best of the answer choices given.

Data Sufficiency Directions: Data Sufficiency problems consist of a question and two statements, labeled (1) and (2), in which certain data are given. You have to decide whether the data given in the statements are <u>sufficient</u> for answering the question. Using the data given in the statements <u>plus</u> your knowledge of mathematics and everyday facts (such as the number of days in July or the meaning of *counterclockwise*), you are to fill in oval

(A) if statement (1) ALONE is sufficient, but statement (2) alone is not sufficient to answer the question asked;

(B) if statement (2) ALONE is sufficient, but statement (1) alone is not sufficient to answer the question asked;

(C) if BOTH statements (1) and (2) TOGETHER are sufficient to answer the question asked, but NEITHER statement ALONE is sufficient;

(D) if EACH statement ALONE is sufficient to answer the question asked;

(E) if statements (1) and (2) TOGETHER are NOT sufficient to answer the question asked, and additional data specific to the problem are needed.

---

1. If $x = \dfrac{5}{6} + \dfrac{15}{18} - \dfrac{10}{12}$, then $(x-1)^3 =$

    (A) $-\dfrac{1}{216}$

    (B) $-\dfrac{1}{6}$

    (C) $\dfrac{1}{6}$

    (D) $\dfrac{27}{216}$

    (E) $\dfrac{125}{216}$

2. If the temperature rises 25 percent from d degrees to 60 degrees, then $60 - d =$

    (A) 12
    (B) 30
    (C) 35
    (D) 48
    (E) 85

GO ON TO THE NEXT PAGE.

3. Is x^3 equal to 125?

    (1) $x > 4$

    (2) $x < 6$

    (A) if statement (1) ALONE is sufficient, but statement (2) alone is not sufficient to answer the question asked;

    (B) if statement (2) ALONE is sufficient, but statement (1) alone is not sufficient to answer the question asked;

    (C) if BOTH statements (1) and (2) TO-GETHER are sufficient to answer the question asked, but NEITHER statement ALONE is sufficient;

    (D) if EACH statement ALONE is sufficient to answer the question asked;

    (E) if statements (1) and (2) TOGETHER are NOT sufficient to answer the question asked, and additional data specific to the problem are needed.

4. If $x \neq 1$, then $\dfrac{3x^2 + 6x - 9}{3x - 3} =$

    (A) $x + 1$
    (B) $x - 1$
    (C) $3x + 1$
    (D) $x + 3$
    (E) $3x + 3$

5. Over a seven-week period a company monitored the output of two of its branches, C and D. Each week the company calculated how many units were produced in each branch. The branch that produced the greatest number of units for four or more of the seven weeks was considered the more efficient branch. Which office was deemed the more efficient?

    (1) Over the seven-week period Branch C produced twice as many units as Branch D.

    (2) The branch that was more efficient was known by the fifth week.

    (A) if statement (1) ALONE is sufficient, but statement (2) alone is not sufficient to answer the question asked;

    (B) if statement (2) ALONE is sufficient, but statement (1) alone is not sufficient to answer the question asked;

    (C) if BOTH statements (1) and (2) TO-GETHER are sufficient to answer the question asked, but NEITHER statement ALONE is sufficient;

    (D) if EACH statement ALONE is sufficient to answer the question asked;

    (E) if statements (1) and (2) TOGETHER are NOT sufficient to answer the question asked, and additional data specific to the problem are needed.

GO ON TO THE NEXT PAGE.

$$a = \left(\frac{1}{10}\right)^2$$

$$b = \frac{1}{5}$$

$$c = \sqrt{\frac{1}{100}}$$

6. The values of *a, b,* and *c* are shown above. Which of the following is correct?

    (A) $a < b < c$
    (B) $a < c < b$
    (C) $b < c < a$
    (D) $c < a < b$
    (E) $c < b < a$

7. All of the tickets for two real estate seminars, *F* and *G*, were either purchased or given away, and the ratio of *F* tickets to *G* tickets was 2 to 1. Of the total number of *F* tickets and *G* tickets, what percentage was purchased?

    (1) The total number of *F* tickets and *G* tickets is 240.

    (2) Of the *F* tickets, exactly 60 percent were purchased, and of the *G* tickets, exactly 80 percent were purchased.

    (A) if statement (1) ALONE is sufficient, but statement (2) alone is not sufficient to answer the question asked;

    (B) if statement (2) ALONE is sufficient, but statement (1) alone is not sufficient to answer the question asked;

    (C) if BOTH statements (1) and (2) TO-GETHER are sufficient to answer the question asked, but NEITHER statement ALONE is sufficient;

    (D) if EACH statement ALONE is sufficient to answer the question asked;

    (E) if statements (1) and (2) TOGETHER are NOT sufficient to answer the question asked, and additional data specific to the problem are needed.

8. If $\frac{1}{y} = 3\frac{1}{2}$, then $\frac{1}{y+2} =$

    (A) $\frac{7}{16}$

    (B) $\frac{4}{7}$

    (C) $\frac{7}{9}$

    (D) $\frac{7}{8}$

    (E) $\frac{16}{7}$

9. The function * is defined by the equation $a * b = \frac{ab}{b-a}$, where $a \neq b$. Which of the following has a value of 3?

    (A) 1 * 3
    (B) 3 * 0
    (C) 2 * 6
    (D) 6 * 2
    (E) 4 * –1

GO ON TO THE NEXT PAGE.

10. What is the greatest common factor of positive integers x and y?

 (1) The greatest common factor of $\dfrac{x}{2}$ and $\dfrac{y}{2}$ is 5.

 (2) x and y are even.

 (A) if statement (1) ALONE is sufficient, but statement (2) alone is not sufficient to answer the question asked;

 (B) if statement (2) ALONE is sufficient, but statement (1) alone is not sufficient to answer the question asked;

 (C) if BOTH statements (1) and (2) TO-GETHER are sufficient to answer the question asked, but NEITHER statement ALONE is sufficient;

 (D) if EACH statement ALONE is sufficient to answer the question asked;

 (E) if statements (1) and (2) TOGETHER are NOT sufficient to answer the question asked, and additional data specific to the problem are needed.

11. A computer is programmed to generate a list of multiples of prime numbers 2, 3, and 5, as shown below:

Program 1—*List multiples of 2*
Program 2—*List multiples of 3*
Program 3—*List multiples of 5*

How many integers between 1 and 100 will appear on all three of the lists of the programs produced above?

 (A) None
 (B) 1
 (C) 3
 (D) 5
 (E) An infinite number of integers

12. If x and y are positive integers, is $x + 4y$ odd?

 (1) y is odd.

 (2) x is odd.

 (A) if statement (1) ALONE is sufficient, but statement (2) alone is not sufficient to answer the question asked;

 (B) if statement (2) ALONE is sufficient, but statement (1) alone is not sufficient to answer the question asked;

 (C) if BOTH statements (1) and (2) TO-GETHER are sufficient to answer the question asked, but NEITHER statement ALONE is sufficient;

 (D) if EACH statement ALONE is sufficient to answer the question asked;

 (E) if statements (1) and (2) TOGETHER are NOT sufficient to answer the question asked, and additional data specific to the problem are needed.

GO ON TO THE NEXT PAGE.

13. A grocer is storing small cereal boxes in large cartons that measure 25 inches by 42 inches by 60 inches. If the measurement of each small cereal box is 7 inches by 6 inches by 5 inches, then what is the maximum number of small cereal boxes that can be placed in each large carton?

   (A)   25
   (B)   210
   (C)   252
   (D)   300
   (E)   420

14. Sue is now 10 years younger than Jane. If in 5 years Jane will be twice as old as Sue, how old will Sue be in 3 years?

   (A)   6
   (B)   8
   (C)   11
   (D)   14
   (E)   18

NO TEST MATERIAL ON THIS PAGE

Math Test
Bin Three
14 Questions

This test is composed of both **Problem Solving questions and Data Sufficiency questions.**

Problem Solving Directions: Solve each problem, using any available space on the page for scratchwork. Then indicate the best of the answer choices given.

Data Sufficiency Directions: Data Sufficiency problems consist of a question and two statements, labeled (1) and (2), in which certain data are given. You have to decide whether the data given in the statements are <u>sufficient</u> for answering the question. Using the data given in the statements <u>plus</u> your knowledge of mathematics and everyday facts (such as the number of days in July or the meaning of *counterclockwise*), you are to fill in oval

(A) if statement (1) ALONE is sufficient, but statement (2) alone is not sufficient to answer the question asked;

(B) if statement (2) ALONE is sufficient, but statement (1) alone is not sufficient to answer the question asked;

(C) if BOTH statements (1) and (2) TOGETHER are sufficient to answer the question asked, but NEITHER statement ALONE is sufficient;

(D) if EACH statement ALONE is sufficient to answer the question asked;

(E) if statements (1) and (2) TOGETHER are NOT sufficient to answer the question asked, and additional data specific to the problem are needed.

---

1. A store raised the price of an item by exactly 10 percent. Which of the following could NOT be the resulting price of the item?

    (A) $5.50
    (B) $7.60
    (C) $11.00
    (D) $12.10
    (E) $75.90

2. The price for a pair of cuff links is $1.00. The price for a 5-pair package of cuff links is $3.40. The 5-pair package is what percent cheaper per pair than 5 pairs purchased separately?

    (A)   63%
    (B)   62%
    (C)   47%
    (D)   32%
    (E)   20%

GO ON TO THE NEXT PAGE.

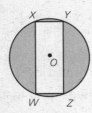

3. Rectangle *WXYZ* is inscribed in a circle with center *O* as shown above. If the diameter of the circle is equal to 16, then what is the area of the shaded region?

(1) *WZ = OW*
(2) *XW < XY*

(A) if statement (1) ALONE is sufficient, but statement (2) alone is not sufficient to answer the question asked;
(B) if statement (2) ALONE is sufficient, but statement (1) alone is not sufficient to answer the question asked;
(C) if BOTH statements (1) and (2) TO-GETHER are sufficient to answer the question asked, but NEITHER statement ALONE is sufficient;
(D) if EACH statement ALONE is sufficient to answer the question asked;
(E) if statements (1) and (2) TOGETHER are NOT sufficient to answer the question asked, and additional data specific to the problem are needed.

4. Is rectangular block *B* a cube?

(1) At least two faces of rectangular block *B* are square.
(2) The volume of rectangular block *B* is 64.

(A) if statement (1) ALONE is sufficient, but statement (2) alone is not sufficient to answer the question asked;
(B) if statement (2) ALONE is sufficient, but statement (1) alone is not sufficient to answer the question asked;
(C) if BOTH statements (1) and (2) TO-GETHER are sufficient to answer the question asked, but NEITHER statement ALONE is sufficient;
(D) if EACH statement ALONE is sufficient to answer the question asked;
(E) if statements (1) and (2) TOGETHER are NOT sufficient to answer the question asked, and additional data specific to the problem are needed.

5. In a certain flower shop, which stocks four types of flowers, there are $\frac{1}{3}$ as many violets as carnations, and $\frac{1}{2}$ as many tulips as violets. If there are equal numbers of roses and tulips, what percent of the flowers in the shop are carnations?

(A) 10%
(B) 33%
(C) 40%
(D) 50%
(E) 60%

6. If *x*, *y*, and *z* are non-zero numbers such that $1 \geq y > x$ and *xy = z*, which of the following CANNOT be true?

(A) *y > z*
(B) *y = z*
(C) *z = x*
(D) *x > z*
(E) *z > 0*

GO ON TO THE NEXT PAGE.

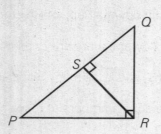

7. In the figure above, what is the length of *PQ* times the length of *RS*?

   (1)   The length of *PQ* is 5.

   (2)   The length of *QR* times the length of *PR* is equal to 12.

   (A)   if statement (1) ALONE is sufficient, but statement (2) alone is not sufficient to answer the question asked;

   (B)   if statement (2) ALONE is sufficient, but statement (1) alone is not sufficient to answer the question asked;

   (C)   if BOTH statements (1) and (2) TO-GETHER are sufficient to answer the question asked, but NEITHER statement ALONE is sufficient;

   (D)   if EACH statement ALONE is sufficient to answer the question asked;

   (E)   if statements (1) and (2) TOGETHER are NOT sufficient to answer the question asked, and additional data specific to the problem are needed.

8. A company bought a total of 60 computers and 20 printers to modernize billing operations. If the price of each computer was three times the price of each printer, what percent of the total cost of the purchase was the total cost of the printers?

   (A)   10%
   (B)   11%
   (C)   15%
   (D)   20%
   (E)   25%

9. If *P* is a set of integers and 3 is in *P*, is every positive multiple of 3 in *P*?

   (1)   For any integer in *P*, the sum of 3 and that integer is also in *P*.

   (2)   For any integer in *P*, that integer minus 3 is also in *P*.

   (A)   if statement (1) ALONE is sufficient, but statement (2) alone is not sufficient to answer the question asked;

   (B)   if statement (2) ALONE is sufficient, but statement (1) alone is not sufficient to answer the question asked;

   (C)   if BOTH statements (1) and (2) TO-GETHER are sufficient to answer the question asked, but NEITHER statement ALONE is sufficient;

   (D)   if EACH statement ALONE is sufficient to answer the question asked;

   (E)   if statements (1) and (2) TOGETHER are NOT sufficient to answer the question asked, and additional data specific to the problem are needed.

10. A machine costs *m* dollars per day to maintain and *n* cents for each unit it produces. If the machine is operated 7 days a week and produces *r* units in a week, which of the following is the total cost, in dollars, of operating the machine for a week?

   (A) $7m + 100nr$

   (B) $\dfrac{700m + nr}{100}$

   (C) $m + nr$

   (D) $\dfrac{7m + 100nr}{100}$

   (E) $700mnr$

GO ON TO THE NEXT PAGE.

11. A car averages 40 miles per hour for the first 6 hours of a trip and averages 60 miles per hour for each additional hour of travel time. If the average speed for the entire trip is 55 miles per hour, how many hours long is the trip?

(A) 8
(B) 12
(C) 16
(D) 18
(E) 24

12. If t is a multiple of prime number s, is t a multiple of s^2?

(1) $s < 4$

(2) $t = 18$

(A) if statement (1) ALONE is sufficient, but statement (2) alone is not sufficient to answer the question asked;

(B) if statement (2) ALONE is sufficient, but statement (1) alone is not sufficient to answer the question asked;

(C) if BOTH statements (1) and (2) TOGETHER are sufficient to answer the question asked, but NEITHER statement ALONE is sufficient;

(D) if EACH statement ALONE is sufficient to answer the question asked;

(E) if statements (1) and (2) TOGETHER are NOT sufficient to answer the question asked, and additional data specific to the problem are needed.

13. How many integers between 100 and 150, inclusive, can be evenly divided by neither 3 nor 5?

(A) 33
(B) 28
(C) 27
(D) 26
(E) 24

	s	
u	t	8
	4	

14. A computer generates non-zero numbers for the figure above so that the product of the numbers along any vertical column is equal to the product of the numbers in any horizontal row. What number does s represent?

(1) u equals 6.

(2) t equals 2.

(A) if statement (1) ALONE is sufficient, but statement (2) alone is not sufficient to answer the question asked;

(B) if statement (2) ALONE is sufficient, but statement (1) alone is not sufficient to answer the question asked;

(C) if BOTH statements (1) and (2) TOGETHER are sufficient to answer the question asked, but NEITHER statement ALONE is sufficient;

(D) if EACH statement ALONE is sufficient to answer the question asked;

(E) if statements (1) and (2) TOGETHER are NOT sufficient to answer the question asked, and additional data specific to the problem are needed.

Verbal Test
Bin One
17 Questions

This test is made up of Sentence Corrections, Critical Reasoning, and Reading Comprehension.

Sentence Correction Directions: In Sentence Corrections, some part of the sentence or the entire sentence is underlined. Beneath each sentence you will find five ways of phrasing the underlined part. The first of these repeats the original; the other four are different. If you think the original is the best of these answer choices, choose answer A; otherwise, choose one of the others. Select the best version and fill in the corresponding oval on your answer sheet.

Reading Comprehension Directions: After reading the passage, choose the best answer to each question and fill in the corresponding oval on the answer sheet. Answer all questions following a passage on the basis of what is stated or implied in that passage.

Critical Reasoning Directions: Select the best of the answer choices given.

1. Despite the recent election of a woman to the office of prime minister, the status of women in Pakistan is little changed from how it was in the last century.

   (A) is little changed from how it was
   (B) is a little changed from how it was
   (C) has changed little
   (D) has changed little from how it has been
   (E) is little changed from the way it was

2. In the last twenty years, despite the chauvinism of European connoisseurs, Californian wines are respected throughout the world.

   (A) are respected
   (B) are becoming better respected
   (C) which have gained respect
   (D) have gained respect
   (E) have since become respected

3. A mail-order company recently had a big jump in clothing sales after hiring a copywriter and a graphic artist to give its clothing catalog a magazine-like format designed to appeal to a more upscale clientele. The company is now planning to launch a housewares catalog using the same concept.

   The company's plan assumes that

   (A) other housewares catalogs with maga-zine-like formats do not already exist
   (B) an upscale clientele would be interested in a housewares catalog
   (C) the same copywriter and graphic artist could be employed for both the clothing and housewares catalogs
   (D) a magazine-like format requires a copy-writer and a graphic artist
   (E) customers to whom the old clothing catalog appealed would continue to make purchases from catalogs with the new format

GO ON TO THE NEXT PAGE.

4. Recently there has been increased debate <u>over if a budget surplus should go toward lower taxes or increased spending</u> on social programs.

   (A) over if a budget surplus should go toward lower taxes or increased spending
   (B) over whether a budget surplus should go toward lowering taxes or increasing spending
   (C) about a budget surplus going toward lower taxes or increasing spending
   (D) about if lower taxes should come from a budget surplus or spending increases
   (E) concerning a budget surplus and its going toward lower taxes or increased spending

5. Chicago, <u>where industrial growth in the nineteenth century was more rapid than any other American city</u>, was plagued by labor troubles like the Pullman Strikes of 1894.

   (A) where industrial growth in the nineteenth century was more rapid than any other American city
   (B) which had industrial growth in the nineteenth century more rapid than that of other American cities
   (C) which had growth industrially more rapid than any other American city in the nineteenth century
   (D) whose industrial growth in the nineteenth century was more rapid than any other American city
   (E) whose industrial growth in the nineteenth century was more rapid than that of any other American city

6. Television programming experts maintain that with each 1% increase in the prime-time ratings of a television station there is a 3.5% increase in the number of people who watch its evening news program. However, in the last ten years at Channel NTR, there was only one year of extremely high prime-time ratings and, during that year, fewer people than ever watched Channel NTR's evening news program.

   Which of the following conclusions can properly be drawn from the statements above?

   (A) When a news program has good ratings, the channel as a whole will have good ratings.
   (B) The programming experts neglected to consider daytime news programs.
   (C) The year of high ratings at NTR was a result of two hit shows that were subsequently canceled because of contractual problems.
   (D) The ten-year period in question is not representative of normal viewing patterns.
   (E) Prime-time ratings are not the only factor affecting how many people watch an evening news program.

7. With total sales <u>of less than three hundred thousand dollars and fewer</u> new subscribers than last year, the New England Theatre Company is in danger of losing its building.

   (A) of less than three hundred thousand dollars and fewer
   (B) lower than three hundred thousand dollars and less
   (C) lesser than three hundred thousand dollars and fewer
   (D) fewer than three hundred thousand dollars and less
   (E) of fewer than three hundred thousand dollars and of fewer

GO ON TO THE NEXT PAGE.

8. The people least likely to be audited by the Internal Revenue Service this year are those who have been audited at least once since 1985 and who were found to have made no mistakes in filing their returns during that audit.

   Of the following people, who is MOST likely to be audited by the IRS?

   (A) A person who was audited in 1986 but was not found to have made any mistakes in filing his return.
   (B) A person who was audited in 1986 and whose lawyer corrected several mistakes in the tax return prior to the filing deadline.
   (C) A person whose spouse was convicted of tax fraud in 1987, who was then audited and found to have made no mistakes.
   (D) A person who was last audited in 1984, and had no mistakes uncovered by the IRS during that audit.
   (E) A person who was audited in each of the past five years, but was found to have made no mistakes in any of the filings.

9. A recent *New York Times* editorial criticized the city's election board for, first of all, failing to replace outmoded voting machines prone to breakdowns, and <u>secondarily, for their failure to</u> investigate allegations of corruption involving board members.

   (A) secondarily, for their failure to
   (B) secondly, for their failure to
   (C) secondly, that they failed and did not
   (D) second, that they failed to
   (E) second, for failing to

10. James's grade point average puts him in the top third of the graduating class of college A. Nestor is in the top tenth of the same class. Elizabeth has the same grade point average as Nestor. Nancy has a lower grade point average than Elizabeth.

    If the information above is true, which of the following must also be true?

    (A) James has a higher grade point average than Elizabeth.
    (B) James has a higher grade point average than Nancy.
    (C) Nestor has a higher grade point average than Nancy.
    (D) Elizabeth and Nancy both have a higher grade point average than James.
    (E) Nestor and James both have a higher grade point average than Nancy.

11. <u>Two week notice being given to employers before leaving</u> a job is the generally accepted protocol.

    (A) Two week notice being given to employers before leaving
    (B) Giving notice to employers of two weeks before having to leave
    (C) Two weeks' notice to give to employers before leaving
    (D) Giving notice to employers two weeks before leaving
    (E) To give two weeks' worth of notice before having to leave

GO ON TO THE NEXT PAGE.

Questions 12–17 are based on the following passage:

The Romans—for centuries the masters of war and politics across Europe, Northern Africa, and Asia Minor—have often been criticized for producing few original thinkers outside the

5   realm of politics. This criticism, while in many ways true, is not without its problems. It was, after all, the conquest of Greece that provided Rome with its greatest influx of educated subjects. Two of the great disasters in intellec-

10   tual history—the murder of Archimedes and the burning of Alexandria's library—both occurred under Rome's watch. Nevertheless, a city that was able to conquer so much of the known world could not have been devoid of the

15   creativity that characterizes so many other ancient empires.

Engineering is one endeavor in which the Romans showed themselves capable. Their aqueducts carried water hundreds of miles

20   along the tops of vast arcades. Roman roads, built for the rapid deployment of troops, criss-cross Europe and still form the basis of numer-ous modern highways that provide quick access between many major European and

25   African cities. Indeed, a large number of these cities owe their prominence to Rome's eco-nomic and political influence.

Many of those major cities lie far beyond Rome's original province, and Latin-derived

30   languages are spoken in most Southern Euro-pean nations. Again a result of military influ-ence, the popularity of Latin and its offspring is difficult to overestimate. During the centuries of ignorance and violence that followed Rome's

35   decline, the Latin language was the glue that held together the identity of an entire continent. While seldom spoken today, it is still studied widely, if only so that such masters of rhetoric as Cicero can be read in the original.

40   It is Cicero and his like who are perhaps the most overlooked legacy of Rome. While far from being a democracy, Rome did leave behind useful political tools that serve the American republic today. "Republic" itself is

45   Latin for "the people's business," a notion cherished in democracies worldwide. Senators owe their name to Rome's class of elders; Representatives owe theirs to the Tribunes who seized popular prerogatives from the Senatorial

50   class. The veto was a Roman notion adopted by the historically aware framers of the Constitu-tion, who often assumed pen names from the lexicon of Latin life. These accomplishments, as monumental as any highway or coliseum,

55   remain prominent features of the Western landscape.

12.   The author describes "two of the great disasters in intellectual history" (lines 9–12) in order to

(A)   establish a point directly related to the main argument

(B)   show that certain historical claims are inaccurate

(C)   demonstrate the importance of certain historical data

(D)   disprove the claims made by others with a different view

(E)   concede the partial accuracy of an opposing view

13.   According to the passage, ancient Roman roads

(A)   connected many major cities in ancient Europe

(B)   are engineering marvels unequaled in modern times

(C)   are similar in some respects to modern highways

(D)   were products of democratic political institutions

(E)   caused the development of modern European cities

GO ON TO THE NEXT PAGE.

14. According to the passage, which of the following accurately describes the Latin language?

   I. It spread in part due to Rome's military power.
   II. It is reflected in modern political concepts.
   III. It is spoken today in some parts of Europe.

   (A) I only
   (B) II only
   (C) I and II only
   (D) I and III only
   (E) II and III only

15. It can be inferred from the passage that the framers of the Constitution

   (A) were familiar with certain aspects of Roman government
   (B) were similar to the Roman elders
   (C) embraced the veto as the hallmark of Roman democracy
   (D) overlooked Cicero's contributions to the theory of democracy
   (E) formed a government based on world-wide democracy

16. The primary purpose of the passage is to

   (A) reveal the indifferent attitude taken by the ancient Romans toward the fine arts
   (B) discuss the lasting accomplishments achieved by ancient Romans
   (C) analyze the use of the Latin language by the framers of the Constitution
   (D) show that the construction of roads and aqueducts could not have been accomplished in ancient Greece
   (E) compare the destruction of the library at Alexandria to the murder of Archimedes

17. Which of the following is NOT described in the passage as a part of ancient Roman life that left a lasting legacy?

   (A) The Latin language
   (B) Military accomplishments
   (C) An extensive system of roads
   (D) A democratic system of government
   (E) Wide-ranging economic influence

NO TEST MATERIAL ON THIS PAGE

Verbal Test
Bin Two
18 Questions

This test is made up of Sentence Corrections, Critical Reasoning, and Reading Comprehension.

Sentence Correction Directions: In Sentence Corrections, some part of the sentence or the entire sentence is underlined. Beneath each sentence you will find five ways of phrasing the underlined part. The first of these repeats the original; the other four are different. If you think the original is the best of these answer choices, choose answer A; otherwise, choose one of the others. Select the best version and fill in the corresponding oval on your answer sheet.

Reading Comprehension Directions: After reading the passage, choose the best answer to each question and fill in the corresponding oval on the answer sheet. Answer all questions following a passage on the basis of what is <u>stated</u> or <u>implied</u> in that passage.

Critical Reasoning Directions: Select the best of the answer choices given.

---

1. IRS provision 354-B requires <u>that an S corpora-
    tion with assets of greater than $200,000 send
    W-2 forms to their full- and part-time employees
    on or before Jan. 31</u>.

    (A) that an S corporation with assets of
         greater than $200,000 send W-2 forms
         to their full- and part-time employees
         on or before Jan. 31
    (B) an S corporation with assets of greater
         than $200,000 send W-2 forms to their
         full- and part-time employees on or
         before Jan. 31
    (C) that an S corporation with assets of
         greater than $200,000 send W-2 forms
         to its full- and part-time employees on
         or before Jan. 31
    (D) an S corporation with assets of greater
         than $200,000 to send W-2 forms to
         their full- and part-time employees on
         Jan. 31 or before
    (E) an S corporation with assets of greater
         than $200,000 send W-2 forms to its
         full- and part-time employees on or
         before Jan. 31

Questions 2–3 are based on the following:

Investing in real estate would be a profitable venture at this time. A survey in *House* magazine revealed that 85% of the magazine's readers are planning to buy a second home over the next few years. A study of the real estate industry, however, revealed that the current supply of homes could only provide for 65% of that demand each year.

2. Which of the following, if true, reveals a weak-
    ness in the evidence cited above?

    (A) Real estate is a highly labor-intensive
         business.
    (B) Home builders are not evenly distributed
         across the country.
    (C) The number of people who want second
         homes has been increasing each year
         for the past ten years.
    (D) Readers of *House* magazine are more
         likely than most people to want
         second homes.
    (E) *House* magazine includes articles about
         owning a second home as well as
         articles about building a second home.

GO ON TO THE NEXT PAGE.

3. Which of the following, if true, would undermine the validity of the investment advice in the paragraph above?

    (A) Some home owners are satisfied with only one home.
    (B) About half of the people who buy homes are investing in their first home.
    (C) About half of the people who buy homes have to take out a mortgage to do so.
    (D) Only a quarter of the homes that are built are sold within the first two weeks.
    (E) Only a quarter of those who claim that they want a second home actually end up purchasing one.

4. <u>Just as the European countries of the early eighteenth century sought to exploit the resources of our continent, so too</u> are we now attempting to extract energy and minerals from the ocean bed.

    (A) Just as the European countries of the early eighteenth century sought to exploit the resources of our continent, so too
    (B) The European countries of the early eighteenth century sought to exploit the resources of our continent, and in a similar way
    (C) Like the case of the European countries of the early eighteenth century who sought to exploit the resources of our continent, so too
    (D) As in the exploitation of the resources of our continent by European countries of the early eighteenth century,
    (E) Similar to the European countries which sought in the early eighteenth century to exploit the resources of our continent

5. Traffic safety experts predict that the installation of newly designed air bags in all cars in the United States would reduce the average number of fatalities per traffic accident by 30 percent. In order to save lives, the Department of Transportation (DOT) is considering requiring automobile manufacturers to install air bags of this design in all cars produced after 1998.

    Which of the following, if true, represents the strongest challenge to the DOT's proposal?

    (A) Air bags of the new design are more given to being inadvertently triggered, an occurrence that can sometimes result in fatal traffic accidents.
    (B) The DOT is planning to require automobile manufacturers to produce these air bags according to very strict specifications.
    (C) After installing air bags in new cars, automobile manufacturers will experience an increase in sales.
    (D) The proposed air bag installation program will adversely affect the resale of cars manufactured prior to 1998.
    (E) As production costs increase, the profits of many domestic automobile dealers show a marked decrease.

GO ON TO THE NEXT PAGE.

6. An attempt <u>to ratify the Equal Rights Amendment, begun almost two decades ago,</u> has been unsuccessful despite efforts by many important groups, including the National Organization for Women.

   (A) to ratify the Equal Rights Amendment, begun almost two decades ago,
   (B) begun almost two decades ago, for ratifying the Equal Rights Amendment
   (C) begun for ratifying the Equal Rights Amendment almost two decades ago
   (D) at ratifying the Equal Rights Amendment, begun almost two decades ago,
   (E) that has begun almost two decades ago to ratify the Equal Rights Amendment

7. A newly discovered disease is thought to be caused by a certain bacterium. However, recently released data notes that the bacterium thrives in the presence of a certain virus, implying that it is actually the virus that causes the new disease.

   Which of the following pieces of evidence would most support the data's implication?

   (A) In the absence of the virus, the disease has been observed to follow infection by the bacterium.
   (B) The virus has been shown to aid the growth of bacterium, a process which often leads to the onset of the disease.
   (C) The virus alone has been observed in many cases of the disease.
   (D) In cases where the disease does not develop, infection by the bacterium is usually preceded by infection by the virus.
   (E) Onset of the disease usually follows infection by both the virus and the bacterium.

8. When evidence of financial wrongdoing by an elected official surfaces, it is the electorate who must decide <u>whether the evidence warrants censuring him or ousting him</u> from office.

   (A) whether the evidence warrants censuring him or ousting him
   (B) if there is evidence that warrants a censure or an ousting of him
   (C) whether or not the evidence warrants the censuring or ousting of him
   (D) if there is evidence that warrants censuring him or his ousting
   (E) if the evidence would warrant that he be censured or that he be ousted

GO ON TO THE NEXT PAGE.

9. Because of a recent drought in Florida during the orange-growing season, the price of oranges this season will be three times the usual price. This will drive up the cost of producing orange juice and thus push up the price of orange juice for the consumer.

Which of the following, if true, most seriously weakens the argument above?

(A) The recent drought was not as severe as scientists predicted.

(B) States other than Florida also supply oranges to orange juice manufacturers.

(C) Other ingredients are used in the production of orange juice.

(D) Last year the price of oranges was actually lower than the average price over the past ten years.

(E) The price of oranges will eventually be $0.48 per crate.

10. Because the enemy's new ship is the quietest and it is therefore the most elusive submarine, it is being increasingly viewed by the military as a threat to security.

(A) and it is therefore the most elusive submarine, it is being increasingly viewed

(B) it is therefore the most elusive of submarines, and it has increased the view

(C) and therefore the most elusive submarine, it is being increasingly viewed

(D) and therefore it is the most elusive of submarines, there is an increasing view

(E) therefore being the most elusive of submarines, it is increasingly viewed

11. The economic forces that may affect the new public offering of stock include sudden downturns in the market, hedging and other investor strategies for preventing losses, loosening the interest rates in Washington, and fearing that the company may still be undercapitalized.

(A) loosening the interest rates in Washington, and fearing that the company may still be undercapitalized

(B) loosening the interest rates in Washington, and a fear of the company still being undercapitalized

(C) a loosening of the interest rates in Washington, and fearing that the company may still be undercapitalized

(D) a loosening of the interest rates in Washington, and a fear of the still undercapitalized company

(E) a loosening of the interest rates in Washington, and a fear that the company may still be undercapitalized

GO ON TO THE NEXT PAGE.

Questions 12–18 are based on the following passage:

Anthropologists who study orangutans, distant cousins of the human race, find in the animals' behavior hints of how our earliest ancestors may have lived. It has long been
5　accepted that primates originally dwelt in the treetops and only migrated to the ground as forests began to dwindle. While to a certain extent all primates except humans spend at least some time dwelling in trees, the orangu-
10　tan hardly ever ventures to the forest floor. Adult orangutans can grow as heavy as 330 pounds and live for decades, requiring copious amounts of fruit simply to stay alive. Thus, they become very jealous of the territory where they
15　find their food. Compounding this territoriality are the breeding habits of orangutans, since females can only breed every few years and, like humans, give birth not to litters but single offspring.
20　Consequently, orangutans are solitary, territorial animals who have difficulty foraging in any part of the forest where they were not raised. Orangutans taken from poachers by customs agents undergo incredible hardship on
25　their return to the wild. Incorrectly relocating a male orangutan is especially problematic, often ending in the animal's death at the hands of a rival who sees not only his territory but also the females of his loosely knit community under
30　threat from an outsider. While humans, like chimpanzees, are more gregarious and re-sourceful than orangutans, the latter provide anthropologists with useful information about the behavior of prehominid primates and how
35　apelike behavior influenced our ancestors' search for food and family beneath the forest's canopy.

12. The primary purpose of this passage is to

 (A) describe some behavioral and evolution-ary characteristics of orangutans
 (B) analyze the reasons why early primates left their forest dwellings
 (C) illustrate the dangers posed to orangu-tans by poachers
 (D) show how orangutan behavior differs from that of other primates
 (E) criticize anthropologists who misinterpret orangutan behavior

13. The author of the passage discusses "orangu-tans taken from poachers" (line 23) in order to

 (A) stress the importance of preserving orangutans as a species
 (B) indicate the widespread practice of animal poaching
 (C) refute the theory that orangutans can live in a variety of environments
 (D) contrast the behavior of orangutans with that of other apes
 (E) emphasize the consequences of orangu-tan territoriality

14. The passage indicates that it is difficult to return orangutans to the wild for which of the follow-ing reasons?

 I. The threat posed by newcomers to other orangutans' territory
 II. The conflict between males over available females
 III. The scarcity of available food in the orangutan's environment

 (A) I only
 (B) I and II only
 (C) I and III only
 (D) II and III only
 (E) I, II, and III

GO ON TO THE NEXT PAGE.

15. Which of the following can be inferred about differences between the behavior of orangutans and that of other ape species?

   (A) While orangutans spend much of their time in the treetops, other apes live exclusively on the ground.
   (B) Orangutans and other types of apes are all sociable species, but orangutans are more likely to bond for life.
   (C) Apes such as chimpanzees rely less upon their size than the average orangutan does.
   (D) Orangutans spend less time in the company of other members of their species than do some other apes.
   (E) Because of their stringent territoriality, orangutans are less likely to elude capture by poachers than are other apes.

16. According to the author, anthropologists study the behavior of orangutans in order to

   (A) prevent orangutans from becoming the target of poaching
   (B) assist customs agents in the relocation of orangutans
   (C) analyze the causes and consequences of contemporary human behavior
   (D) prevent larger orangutans from eliminating their weaker rivals
   (E) better understand the factors that influenced human evolution

17. Which of the following are factors that the author indicates contribute to the orangutan's territoriality?

   (A) The lack of available food and the antisocial nature of orangutans
   (B) The orangutan's need for large quantities of food and the infrequency with which they mate
   (C) The threat posed by poachers and the orangutan's inability to protect itself from them
   (D) The difficulties that orangutans face when compelled to socialize with other ape species such as chimpanzees
   (E) The constant dangers that present themselves whenever one orangutan encounters another

18. It can be inferred from the passage that one development responsible for the evolution of distinct ape species was

   (A) early primates' inability to survive in the forest
   (B) the shrinking of the available primitive forest
   (C) the growth of human and chimpanzee communities
   (D) the orangutan's eventual dominance of the treetops
   (E) the encroachment of other species into the primitive forest

**Verbal Test
Bin Three
17 Questions**

This test is made up of Sentence Corrections, Critical Reasoning, and Reading Comprehension.

Sentence Correction Directions: In Sentence Corrections, some part of the sentence or the entire sentence is underlined. Beneath each sentence you will find five ways of phrasing the underlined part. The first of these repeats the original; the other four are different. If you think the original is the best of these answer choices, choose answer A; otherwise, choose one of the others. Select the best version and fill in the corresponding oval on your answer sheet.

Reading Comprehension Directions: After reading the passage, choose the best answer to each question and fill in the corresponding oval on the answer sheet. Answer all questions following a passage on the basis of what is <u>stated</u> or <u>implied</u> in that passage.

Critical Reasoning Directions: Select the best of the answer choices given.

---

1. Like the government that came before it, which set new records for growth, <u>laissez-faire capitalism is the cornerstone of the new government</u>.

   (A) laissez-faire capitalism is the cornerstone of the new government
   (B) the cornerstone of the new government is laissez-faire capitalism
   (C) laissez-faire capitalism is the new government's cornerstone
   (D) the new government has made laissez-faire capitalism its cornerstone
   (E) the new government has a laissez-faire cornerstone of capitalism

2. During the 1980s it became clear <u>that soliciting private funds was far more efficient for environmentalists who sought financial aid</u> than to go to state or federal agencies.

   (A) that soliciting private funds was far more efficient for environmentalists who sought financial aid
   (B) that for environmentalists who sought financial aid, it was far more efficient to solicit private funds
   (C) that for environmentalists seeking financial aid, private organizations were far more efficient to go to
   (D) for environmentalists seeking financial aid, going to private organizations was far more efficient
   (E) for environmentalists who sought financial aid, private organizations were far more efficient

GO ON TO THE NEXT PAGE.

Questions 3–4 are based on the following:

Local phone companies have monopolies on phone service within their areas. Cable television can be transmitted via the wires that are already in place and owned by the phone companies. Cable television companies argue that if the telephone companies were to offer cable service, these telephone companies would have an unfair advantage, because their cable transmissions could be subsidized by the profits of their monopolies on phone service.

3. Which of the following, if true, would ease the cable companies' fear of unfair competition?

   (A) In order to use existing telephone wire, telephone companies would need to modernize their operations, a process so expensive it would virtually wipe out all profit from their monopoly for the foreseeable future.

   (B) If a phone company were to offer cable service within a particular area, it would have a monopoly within that area.

   (C) The cost of television service, whether provided by cable or telephone companies, scales; that is, the total cost of transmission rises only marginally as more homes are added to the network.

   (D) Cable programming that offers more channels is already available through satellite dish, but the initial cost of the dish is extremely high.

   (E) Cable television will never be able to compete with the burgeoning video rental industry, especially as more homes now have videocassette recorders than ever did before.

4. On the basis of the information provided in the passage above, which of the following questions can be answered?

   (A) Are phone companies as efficient as cable companies in providing reliable and inexpensive service?

   (B) If phone companies were allowed to provide cable service, would they want to do so?

   (C) Do the cable companies believe that the local phone companies make a profit on phone service?

   (D) Are local phone companies forbidden to offer cable service?

   (E) Is it expected that phone companies will have a monopoly on cable service?

5. The major areas of medicine in which lasers are effective <u>is in the cutting and closing of blood vessels, and in the destruction</u> of tumors.

   (A) is in the cutting and closing of blood vessels, and in the destruction

   (B) are the cutting and closing of blood vessels, and also the case of destroying

   (C) are the cutting, closing of blood vessels, and in the destroying

   (D) are the cutting and closing of blood vessels, and the destruction

   (E) is in the cutting and closing of blood vessels, and the destroying

GO ON TO THE NEXT PAGE.

6. Since the movie was released seventeen UFOs have been sighted in the state, <u>which is more than had been sighted</u> in the past ten years , together.

   (A) which is more than had been sighted
   (B) more than had been sighted
   (C) more than they had sighted
   (D) more than had reported sightings
   (E) which is more than had reported sightings

7. In the past year, there has been a large drop in the number of new cars sold, due to harsh economic conditions in the marketplace and high taxes. At the same time, the average price paid for a new car has risen dramatically.

Which of the following, if true, best explains the increase in the average price of a new car?

   (A) The price of used cars has climbed steadily over the past ten years.
   (B) There will be a tax reduction later in the year which is expected to aid moderate and low income families.
   (C) The market for expensive cars has been unaffected by the current economic conditions.
   (D) Economic conditions are expected to get significantly worse before the end of the year.
   (E) Low demand for trucks and vans has led to lower production in the factories.

8. Ignoring the admonitions of his staff, the chief financial officer accepted the advice of the consulting company because <u>he believed that the standardized accounting procedures would prove not only inexpensive but</u> reliable indicators of economic performance.

   (A) he believed that the standardized accounting procedures would prove not only inexpensive but
   (B) the standardized accounting procedures will prove both inexpensive and also
   (C) he believed the standardized accounting procedures would prove themselves to be both inexpensive and
   (D) he believed that the standardized accounting procedures would prove to be both inexpensive and
   (E) standardized accounting procedures will prove his belief that they are both inexpensive and

GO ON TO THE NEXT PAGE.

9. A light bulb company produces 2,000 light bulbs per week. The manager wants to ensure that standards of quality remain constant from week to week. The manager, therefore, claims that out of 2,000 light bulbs produced per week, 500 light bulbs are rejected.

Of the following, the best criticism of the manager's plan is that the plan assumes that

(A) light bulb manufacturers cannot accept all light bulbs that are produced

(B) the overall quality of the light bulbs would not be improved if the total number of light bulbs produced were reduced

(C) each light bulb that is reviewed is worthy of being reviewed

(D) it is difficult to judge the quality of a light bulb

(E) the 1,500 light bulbs that are accepted will be of the same quality from week to week

10. A large rise in the number of housing starts in the coming year should boost new construction dollars by several billion dollars, _making the construction industry's economic health much more robust than five years ago_.

(A) making the construction industry's economic health much more robust than five years ago

(B) and make the construction industry's economic health much more robust than five years ago

(C) making the construction industry's economic health much more robust than it was five years ago

(D) to make the construction industry's economic health much more robust than five years ago

(E) in making the construction industry's economic health much more robust than it was five years ago

GO ON TO THE NEXT PAGE.

Questions 11–17 are based on the following passage:

The two main theories of arbitration may be described as judicial and political. One might even go so far as to characterize them by saying that the first is based on how arbitration
5   is supposed to work, while the second is based on how it does in fact work.

The judicial theory implies that a "just" solution of the dispute does in fact exist, and that it is the duty of the arbitrator to decide on
10   the principles and the facts involved. The arbitrator sits as a private judge, called upon to determine the legal rights and the economic interests of the parties involved as these rights and interests are demonstrated by the informa-
15   tion provided by the parties themselves. The political theory, on the other hand, regards arbitration as an extension of both collective bargaining and, of course, collective coercion. The arbitrator functions as a sensitive instru-
20   ment of sorts, accurately recording the relative strengths of the parties and making sure that the lion gets his share.

To some extent, however, these opposing theories represent a confusion between arbitra-
25   tion and conciliation, the act of appeasing both parties to a dispute without necessarily rendering a just or pragmatic decision. The notion of compromise that dominates conciliation may also guide arbitration, although, in the process
30   of arbitration, the result necessarily requires the decision of an outsider rather than an accommodation between the parties themselves. Nevertheless, since to some the idea of arbitration necessarily involves absolute "rights,"
35   compromise is likely to be regarded as the solution of the timid or the unprincipled. Arbitration grounded in political theory, while more likely to permit conciliation, is therefore less preferable to both parties in a dispute,
40   despite the obvious practicality of compromise.

11. The primary purpose of the passage is to

(A) provide examples of the social failures that make arbitration necessary
(B) describe the origin of two theories of arbitration
(C) compare two conflicting theories of dispute arbitration
(D) discuss the relative merits of arbitration and conciliation
(E) outline the successive stages of collective bargaining

12. It can be inferred from the passage that all of the following are elements of the political theory of arbitration EXCEPT

(A) an evaluation of the balance of power between disputing parties
(B) a willingness on the part of both parties to accept compromise
(C) a relative disregard of the importance of moral right in the dispute
(D) an understanding that any compromise must appear to be just
(E) an extension of collective bargaining

13. Which of the following, if true, would most effectively weaken the author's assessment of the drawbacks of the political theory of arbitration?

(A) Litigation is becoming a more popular alternative to arbitration.
(B) A system of checks and balances was put in place to reduce the likelihood of finding biased arbitrators.
(C) Contending parties in most disputes establish compromise as one of their most important goals.
(D) The process of arbitration uncovered new strategies for avoiding conflicts between contending parties.
(E) Resolution of the problem of the opposing rights of the parties involved in labor settlements can be achieved.

GO ON TO THE NEXT PAGE.

14. It can be inferred from the passage that the political theory of arbitration

    (A) will eventually be replaced by a more efficient system of judicial compromise
    (B) is not solely concerned with principles of justice
    (C) suffers from most disputants' unwillingness to accept compromise
    (D) may replace conciliation as the most practical means of resolving disputes
    (E) is unlikely to be chosen by disputants unless they are coerced

15. According to the judicial theory of arbitration, an arbitrator would base his or her decision on

    (A) information supplied by the parties involved in arbitration
    (B) the notion of compromise that dominates conciliation
    (C) decisions rendered by judges in similar cases
    (D) the relative strengths of the parties involved
    (E) whatever appears to both parties to be a fair settlement of the dispute

16. It can be inferred from the passage that efforts at conciliation are

    (A) unlikely to be highly regarded by proponents of the judicial theory of arbitration
    (B) absent from most well-regarded theories of arbitration
    (C) most effective when neither party is responsible for a final decision
    (D) inextricably linked with the concept of "rights"
    (E) necessary to any dispute resolution under current theories of arbitration

17. According to the passage, the political theory of arbitration

    (A) leaves no room for dissension
    (B) implies that there is a just solution to all disputes
    (C) directly contradicts the notion of compromise
    (D) is grounded in political theory
    (E) is based on how arbitration actually works

ANSWER KEY

MATH DIAG			VERBAL DIAG		
Bin 1	**Bin 2**	**Bin 3**	**Bin 1**	**Bin 2**	**Bin 3**
1. C	1. A	1. B	1. C	1. C	1. D
2. B	2. A	2. D	2. D	2. D	2. B
3. C	3. E	3. A	3. B	3. E	3. A
4. B	4. D	4. E	4. B	4. A	4. C
5. D	5. E	5. E	5. E	5. A	5. D
6. B	6. B	6. B	6. E	6. A	6. B
7. E	7. B	7. B	7. A	7. C	7. C
8. C	8. A	8. A	8. D	8. A	8. D
9. A	9. C	9. A	9. E	9. B	9. E
10. D	10. A	10. B	10. C	10. C	10. C
11. D	11. C	11. E	11. D	11. E	11. C
12. D	12. B	12. E	12. E	12. A	12. D
13. C	13. D	13. C	13. A	13. E	13. C
14. E	14. B	14. A	14. C	14. B	14. B
			15. A	15. D	15. A
			16. B	16. E	16. A
			17. D	17. B	17. E
			18. B		

VIII

GMAT Diagnostic Test Answers and Explanations

MATH BIN 1

QUESTIONS	EXPLANATIONS

1. A portion of a thermometer above is calibrated to show degrees in equal increments. If the temperature indicates a reading at level *A*, what is the temperature?

   (A) 94.069
   (B) 94.070
   (C) 94.079
   (D) 94.080
   (E) 94.790

2. Starting at 9 a.m. on a certain day, snow began to fall at a rate of $1\frac{1}{4}$ inches every two hours until 3 p.m. If there were already $2\frac{1}{4}$ inches of snow on the ground at 9 a.m., how many inches of snow were on the ground at 3 p.m. that day?

   (A) $3\frac{3}{4}$

   (B) 6

   (C) 7

   (D) $7\frac{1}{2}$

   (E) $9\frac{3}{4}$

---

1. **(C)** In this decimal question, choices (A) and (E) are off the scale. Choices (B) and (D) are the smallest and greatest numbers on the scale, but the mercury in the thermometer is a little less than 94.08. The correct answer is choice (C).

2. **(B)** It snowed from 9 a.m. until 3 p.m., for a total of six hours. The rate of snowfall was $1\frac{1}{4}$ inches every <u>two</u> hours. So to find the snowfall during those three 2-hour periods, multiply $1\frac{1}{4}$ times 3, for a total of $3\frac{3}{4}$ inches. You'll notice that this is the number in answer choice (A), but we aren't quite done yet. There were already $2\frac{1}{4}$ inches on the ground. To get the total number of inches, we need to add $3\frac{3}{4}$ to $2\frac{1}{4}$. The answer is (B) 6.

   By the way, if you picked choice (E), you probably thought the rate of snowfall was $1\frac{1}{4}$ inches per hour. As usual, ETS made sure your answer was there waiting for you. Could we have ballparked this problem a bit? Sure. There were already $2\frac{1}{4}$ inches on the ground, and the snow was falling at a rate of $1\frac{1}{4}$ every two hours. Clearly choice (A) was going to be too small.

MATH BIN 1

QUESTIONS	EXPLANATIONS

3. What is the area of triangular region T?

  (1) The base of triangle T is 12.

  (2) The ratio of the height of T to the base of T is 3:1.

  (A) if statement (1) ALONE is sufficient, but statement (2) alone is not sufficient to answer the question asked;

  (B) if statement (2) ALONE is sufficient, but statement (1) alone is not sufficient to answer the question asked;

  (C) if BOTH statements (1) and (2) TOGETHER are sufficient to answer the question asked, but NEITHER statement ALONE is sufficient;

  (D) if EACH statement ALONE is sufficient to answer the question asked;

  (E) if statements (1) and (2) TOGETHER are NOT sufficient to answer the question asked, and additional data specific to the problem are needed.

3. (C) The area of a triangle is

$$\frac{\text{base} \times \text{height}}{2}$$

Statement (1) alone gives us the base, but not the height, so we are down to (B), (C), or (E). Statement (2) alone gives us the ratio of the height to the base, but doesn't give us a specific number for either, so eliminate (B). Let's see if the *combination* of the two statements will help. If the base is 12 and the ratio of the height to the base is 3:1, then we can figure out exactly what the height is as well:

$$\frac{3}{1} = \frac{x}{12}$$

The correct answer is choice (C). Remember, in Data Sufficiency you don't have to solve a problem; you merely have to know that you *can* solve a problem based on either or both of the statements.

4. The owner of a boutique decides to calculate the percentage of customers who purchase hats. If 40 percent of the store's customers decide to purchase items, and of those customers 15 percent purchase hats, what percent of the store's customers purchase hats?

  (A) 4%
  (B) 6%
  (C) 15%
  (D) 24%
  (E) 55%

4. (B) This is a cosmic plug-in problem. Let's say there were 100 customers. 40 of them purchase something. The problem says that 15% of the 40 purchase hats. 15% of 40 is 6. The correct answer is choice (B). We could have used ballparking to eliminate choice (E), which was greater than the percentage of customers who bought *anything*, let alone hats.

MATH BIN 1

QUESTIONS	EXPLANATIONS

5. The result obtained when x is multiplied by y is equal to ten times the result obtained when y is subtracted from x. If y equals 5, what does x equal?

    (A) 50
    (B) 25
    (C) 15
    (D) 10
    (E) 5

5. **(D)** Let's translate the first sentence: $xy = 10(x - y)$. If $y = 5$, then x must equal 10. The correct answer is choice (D).

6. In 1988, was the number of people in City X greater than three times the number of people in City Y?

    (1) In 1988, there were approximately 1.1 million more people in City X than in City Y.

    (2) In 1988, the 300,000 Mormons in City X made up 20 percent of its population, and the 141,000 Buddhists in City Y made up 30 percent of its population.

    (A) if statement (1) ALONE is sufficient, but statement (2) alone is not sufficient to answer the question asked;

    (B) if statement (2) ALONE is sufficient, but statement (1) alone is not sufficient to answer the question asked;

    (C) if BOTH statements (1) and (2) TOGETHER are sufficient to answer the question asked, but NEITHER statement ALONE is sufficient;

    (D) if EACH statement ALONE is sufficient to answer the question asked;

    (E) if statements (1) and (2) TOGETHER are NOT sufficient to answer the question asked, and additional data specific to the problem are needed.

6. **(B)** Statement (1) tells us how many *more* people were in City X than in City Y, but since we don't know the total population of either, we can't definitively answer this "yes or no" question. We're down to (B), (C), or (E).

At first glance, statement (2) may not seem helpful since it talks about Mormons and Buddhists, but in fact, this statement is sufficient. The 300,000 Mormons make up 20% of the population of City X, meaning that we can compute the entire population (five times 300,000, not that we needed to know the exact figure.) The 141,000 Buddhists make up 30% of City Y, meaning that we can compute the entire population of City Y as well. Is this information enough to answer this question with a definitive yes or no? Of course. The correct answer is choice (B).

MATH BIN 1

QUESTIONS	EXPLANATIONS

7. $(165)^2 - (164)^2 =$

    (A)   1
    (B)   2
    (C)   4
    (D) 325
    (E) 329

7. **(E)** Rather than multiply out completely, let's focus on the units digit of both numbers. We may not need to know exactly what 165^2 equals, if we know what its units digit equals. 5^2 gives us a units digit of 5, so whatever the entire number will be, its units digit will be 5. We may not need to know exactly what 164^2 equals, if we know what its units digit equals. 4^2 gives us a units digit of 6, so whatever the entire number is going to be, its units digit will be 6. The problem asks you to subtract the second number from the first. Again, we don't know what either number is exactly, but we do know that the first number ends in a 5 and the second ends in a 6. When you subtract one from the other, what will the units digit be?

$$\begin{array}{r} \underline{,\underline{}\,5} \\ -\,\underline{,\underline{}\,6} \\ \hline 9 \end{array}$$

The correct answer is (E), 329.

MATH BIN 1

QUESTIONS	EXPLANATIONS

8. If point X is directly north of point Y and directly west of point Z, what is the distance from point X to point Z?

  (1)   The distance from Y to Z is 20.

  (2)· The distance from X to Y is equal to half the distance from Y to Z.

  (A) if statement (1) ALONE is sufficient, but statement (2) alone is not sufficient to answer the question asked;

  (B) if statement (2) ALONE is sufficient, but statement (1) alone is not sufficient to answer the question asked;

  (C) if BOTH statements (1) and (2) TO-GETHER are sufficient to answer the question asked, but NEITHER statement ALONE is sufficient;

  (D) if EACH statement ALONE is sufficient to answer the question asked;

  (E) if statements (1) and (2) TOGETHER are NOT sufficient to answer the question asked, and additional data specific to the problem are needed.

8. **(C)** Remember, in geometry problems where there is no diagram, your first step should be to draw your own. In this case, your diagram should look like this:

Statement (1) tells us the distance from Y to Z. This is one side (the hypotenuse, as it happens) of the right triangle, but since we don't know any of the angles except for angle YXZ (which must be 90 degrees), we will need one other side in order to figure out the third. We're down to (B), (C), or (E).

Statement (2) tells us that the distance from X to Y is half the distance from Y to Z. By itself, this gives us no actual numbers. We're down to (C) or (E).

Putting the two statements together, we know that YZ is 20 and that XY is half of that, or 10. Using the Pythagorean theorem ($a^2 + b^2 = c^2$) we could figure out the distance from X to Z. Thus the correct answer is choice (C).

9. The formula $E = \sqrt{\dfrac{a}{6}}$ describes the relationship between the length of the edge E of a cube and the surface area a of the cube. How much longer is the edge of a cube with a surface area of 1350 than the edge of one with a surface area of 600?

  (A)   5
  (B)   15
  (C) 150
  (D) 250
  (E) 750

9. **(A)** While this looks like a geometry problem, it is actually simply a matter of plugging the numbers provided into the formula. Let's start with the surface area of 600. To find $\sqrt{\dfrac{600}{6}}$, first divide 600 by 6 to get 100. The square root of $100 = 10$. To find $\sqrt{\dfrac{1350}{6}}$, first divide 1350 by 6 to get 225. The square root of $225 = 15$. The problem asks how much longer 15 is than 10. The correct answer is choice (A) 5.

MATH BIN 1

QUESTIONS	EXPLANATIONS

10. Is y equal to the average (arithmetic mean) of s, t, and u?

    (1) $s + t + u = 3v$

    (2) $\dfrac{s+t+u}{6} = \dfrac{v}{2}$

    (A)   if statement (1) ALONE is sufficient, but statement (2) alone is not sufficient to answer the question asked;

    (B)   if statement (2) ALONE is sufficient, but statement (1) alone is not sufficient to answer the question asked;

    (C)   if BOTH statements (1) and (2) TO-GETHER are sufficient to answer the question asked, but NEITHER statement ALONE is sufficient;

    (D)   if EACH statement ALONE is sufficient to answer the question asked;

    (E)   if statements (1) and (2) TOGETHER are NOT sufficient to answer the question asked, and additional data specific to the problem are needed.

10. **(D)** The average of any three numbers is the sum of those numbers divided by 3. In this "yes or no" question, you are being asked if the average of three numbers equals v. By dividing both sides by 3, statement (1) can be rewritten as

$$\frac{s+t+u}{3}=v$$

Obviously, this answers the question. We're down to (A) or (D).

By dividing both sides by 2, statement (2) can be rewritten as

$$\frac{s+t+u}{3}=\frac{2v}{2}$$

As soon as we cancel the 2's on the right, we see that statement (2) also answers the question. The correct answer is choice (D).

11. $\left[1-\left(\dfrac{2}{3}\right)^{2}\right]^{2} =$

    (A) $-\dfrac{1}{3}$

    (B) $\dfrac{1}{27}$

    (C) $\dfrac{125}{729}$

    (D) $\dfrac{25}{81}$

    (E) $\dfrac{5}{9}$

11. **(D)** Use PEMDAS to perform the operations in the correct order. Start with the innermost set of parentheses: First, square $\dfrac{2}{3}$; then subtract that from 1; finally, square the result. The correct answer is choice (D). You could have used ballparking to eliminate choice (A), because the square of any number is always positive.

MATH BIN 1

QUESTIONS	EXPLANATIONS

12. What is the maximum capacity in cups of a pail that contains only sand and is filled to three-fourths of its capacity?

   (1) If one cup of sand were added to the pail, it would be filled to seven-eighths of its capacity.

   (2) If two cups were removed from the pail, it would be filled to one-half of its capacity.

   (A) if statement (1) ALONE is sufficient, but statement (2) alone is not sufficient to answer the question asked;

   (B) if statement (2) ALONE is sufficient, but statement (1) alone is not sufficient to answer the question asked;

   (C) if BOTH statements (1) and (2) TOGETHER are sufficient to answer the question asked, but NEITHER statement ALONE is sufficient;

   (D) if EACH statement ALONE is sufficient to answer the question asked;

   (E) if statements (1) and (2) TOGETHER are NOT sufficient to answer the question asked, and additional data specific to the problem are needed.

12. **(D)** In this fraction problem, we must convert fractions to actual numbers. Statement (1) says that 1 cup of sand would fill the pail from $\frac{3}{4}$ to $\frac{7}{8}$. This translates to a change of $\frac{1}{8}$. Thus, one cup $= \frac{1}{8}$ of the pail. The pail holds a total of 8 cups. This answers the question, so we are down to (A) or (D).

Statement (2) says that removing two cups would reduce the pail from $\frac{3}{4}$ to $\frac{1}{2}$. In other words, the difference $\left(\frac{1}{4}\right)$ is equal to 2 cups, and the entire pail holds 8 cups. This, too, answers the question, so the correct answer is choice (D).

MATH BIN 1

QUESTIONS	EXPLANATIONS

13. After reading $\frac{3}{5}$ of his biology homework on Monday night, Bernie read $\frac{1}{3}$ of his remaining homework on Tuesday night. What fraction of his original homework would Bernie have to read on Wednesday night to complete his biology assignment?

   (A) $\frac{1}{15}$

   (B) $\frac{2}{15}$

   (C) $\frac{4}{15}$

   (D) $\frac{2}{5}$

   (E) $\frac{4}{5}$

13. **(C)** To get this fraction problem correct, you needed to remember the concept of "the rest." If Bernie reads $\frac{3}{5}$ of his homework on Monday, that means $\frac{2}{5}$ remains to be read. He reads $\frac{1}{3}$ of the $\frac{2}{5}$ (remember, in math the word "of" always means multiply) or $\frac{2}{15}$ on Tuesday. How much of his assignment has he done so far? $\frac{3}{5} + \frac{2}{15}$. Using the bowtie, this works out to $\frac{11}{15}$. How much remains? The correct answer is choice (C), $\frac{4}{15}$.

14. What is the value of x?

   (1) $x^2 = 4x$

   (2) x is an even integer.

   (A) if statement (1) ALONE is sufficient, but statement (2) alone is not sufficient to answer the question asked;

   (B) if statement (2) ALONE is sufficient, but statement (1) alone is not sufficient to answer the question asked;

   (C) if BOTH statements (1) and (2) TOGETHER are sufficient to answer the question asked, but NEITHER statement ALONE is sufficient;

   (D) if EACH statement ALONE is sufficient to answer the question asked;

   (E) if statements (1) and (2) TOGETHER are NOT sufficient to answer the question asked, and additional data specific to the problem are needed

14. **(E)** You might think that if $x^2 = 4x$, then x must equal 4, but this is not necessarily so. What if x were 0? In data sufficiency, when ETS asks for the value of x, they mean the one and only value of x. Statement (1) gives us two possible values. It is not sufficient, and we are down to (B), (C), or (E).

Statement (2) by itself narrows down the answer to every single even integer in the world, which is not very helpful.

Combining the two statements might at first appear to help. If statement (1) gives us two alternatives (4 and 0), wouldn't statement (2) (which limits the answer to only even integers) eliminate one of them? Well, no. 4 and 0 are *both* even integers. The correct answer is choice (E).

MATH BIN 2

QUESTIONS	EXPLANATIONS

1. If $x = \dfrac{5}{6} + \dfrac{15}{18} - \dfrac{10}{12}$, then $(x-1)^3 =$

   (A) $-\dfrac{1}{216}$

   (B) $-\dfrac{1}{6}$

   (C) $\dfrac{1}{6}$

   (D) $\dfrac{27}{216}$

   (E) $\dfrac{125}{216}$

1. **(A)** In this fraction problem, many students would be tempted to use a common denominator of 36. However, if you take a second to look at the fractions involved, you will notice that the second two fractions can be reduced to $\dfrac{5}{6}$ and $\dfrac{5}{6}$. This saves a lot of time. x turns out to equal $\dfrac{5}{6} + \dfrac{5}{6} - \dfrac{5}{6}$ —in other words, $\dfrac{5}{6}$. Now let's plug in $\dfrac{5}{6}$ for x in the second part of the equation. $\left(\dfrac{5}{6} - 1\right)^3 = \left(-\dfrac{1}{6}\right)^3$. The correct answer is choice (A), $-\dfrac{1}{216}$.

Could we have ballparked? Sure. As soon as you know that the number in the parentheses is going to be negative, you could have eliminated choices (C), (D), and (E). A negative number to an odd power always stays negative.

2. If the temperature rises 25 percent from d degrees to 60 degrees, then $60 - d =$

   (A)   12
   (B)   30
   (C)   35
   (D)   48
   (E)   85

2. **(A)** ETS wants you to write an equation here. The correct equation would be $d + .25d = 60$. Then you would have to subtract your result from 60 to get the final answer. However, there is a much faster way. Let's work backward. Ordinarily, when you work backward you want to start with choice (C), but in this case choice (B) is much easier: If $60 - d = 30$, then $d = 30$, which is a nice round number to work with. Let's see if plugging in 30 for d makes the problem work. According to the problem, the temperature rises 25% from d degrees to 60 degrees. If $d = 30$, could this be true? No way! 25% of 30 is only a bit more than 7. D must be much larger. And if d is much larger, then $60 - d$, which is what we are looking for, must be much smaller than choice (B). There is only one choice smaller than (B). The correct answer is choice (A) 12.

MATH BIN 2

QUESTIONS	EXPLANATIONS

3. Is x^3 equal to 125?

   (1) $x > 4$

   (2) $x < 6$

   (A) if statement (1) ALONE is sufficient, but statement (2) alone is not sufficient to answer the question asked;

   (B) if statement (2) ALONE is sufficient, but statement (1) alone is not sufficient to answer the question asked;

   (C) if BOTH statements (1) and (2) TOGETHER are sufficient to answer the question asked, but NEITHER statement ALONE is sufficient;

   (D) if EACH statement ALONE is sufficient to answer the question asked;

   (E) if statements (1) and (2) TOGETHER are NOT sufficient to answer the question asked, and additional data specific to the problem are needed.

3. **(E)** The question "Is $x^3 = 125$?" can be rewritten as "Is $x = 5$?" This is a "yes or no" question, and the best way to tackle it is to plug in twice. In statement (1), we can plug in 5, in which case the answer to the question "is $x^3 = $ to 125" is "yes," or 6, in which case the answer is "no." Thus, since we are getting two different answers depending on the numbers we plug in, statement (1) is not sufficient. We're down to (B), (C), or (E).

In statement (2), we can plug in 5, in which case the answer is "yes," or 4, in which case the answer is "no." Eliminate choice (B).

To see if the answer is (C), we must choose a number that satisfies the conditions of both statements (1) and (2) at the same time. We can plug in 5, in which case the answer is "yes." You may have been tempted to choose (C) at this point since no other integer will satisfy the two equations at the same time, but does this problem limit us to picking integers? Nope. What about 4.5? Or 5.2? In either of these cases, the answer would be "no." Thus, since we are getting two different answers depending on the numbers we plug in, the combination of statements (1) and (2) is not sufficient either, and the correct answer is choice (E).

4. If $x \neq 1$, then $\dfrac{3x^2 + 6x - 9}{3x - 3} =$

   (A) $x + 1$
   (B) $x - 1$
   (C) $3x + 1$
   (D) $x + 3$
   (E) $3x + 3$

4. **(D)** You could use the quadratic formula, but it would be just as easy to plug in since there are variables in the answer choices. Pick a value for x, solve the equation and then find out which answer choice yields the same number. If we let $x = 2$, we get $\dfrac{15}{3}$, or 5. Which answer choice equals 5? That's right, choice (D) $x + 3$. Or you could just factor out the $(3x - 3)$ from the numerator, cancel it out of the both the numerator and denominator, and you end up with $(x + 3)$.

MATH BIN 2

QUESTIONS	EXPLANATIONS

QUESTIONS

5. Over a seven-week period a company monitored the output of two of its branches, C and D. Each week the company calculated how many units were produced in each branch. The branch that produced the greatest number of units for four or more of the seven weeks was considered the more efficient branch. Which office was deemed the more efficient?

(1) Over the seven-week period Branch C produced twice as many units as Branch D.

(2) The branch that was more efficient was known by the fifth week.

(A) if statement (1) ALONE is sufficient, but statement (2) alone is not sufficient to answer the question asked;

(B) if statement (2) ALONE is sufficient, but statement (1) alone is not sufficient to answer the question asked;

(C) if BOTH statements (1) and (2) TOGETHER are sufficient to answer the question asked, but NEITHER statement ALONE is sufficient;

(D) if EACH statement ALONE is sufficient to answer the question asked;

(E) if statements (1) and (2) TOGETHER are NOT sufficient to answer the question asked, and additional data specific to the problem are needed.

EXPLANATIONS

5. **(E)** While statement (1) makes Branch C seem pretty darn capable, we must answer the question based on the criteria given in the question: The branch that's considered more efficient is considered the branch that produced the greatest number of units for four or more of the seven weeks. Statement (1) doesn't tell us *when* Branch C produced its units. Perhaps all Branch C's units were produced in the last week. In spite of the fact that, according to the statement, Branch C produced many more units than Branch D, it doesn't necessarily fit the criteria. We're down to (B), (C), or (E).

Statement (2) by itself isn't sufficient either. We're down to answer choices (C) or (E). The combination of the two statements might seem to be sufficient, but we still don't know if it was Branch C that was the more efficient. The correct answer is choice (E).

QUESTIONS	EXPLANATIONS

6.
$$a = \left(\frac{1}{10}\right)^2$$

$$b = \frac{1}{5}$$

$$c = \sqrt{\frac{1}{100}}$$

The values of *a, b,* and *c* are shown above. Which of the following is correct?

(A) $a < b < c$
(B) $a < c < b$
(C) $b < c < a$
(D) $c < a < b$
(E) $c < b < a$

6. **(B)** The first step in this medium problem is to simplify the values of $a, b,$ and c. $a = \frac{1}{100}$, $b = \frac{1}{5}$, and $c = \frac{1}{10}$. The correct answer is choice (B).

7. All of the tickets for two real estate seminars, *F* and *G*, were either purchased or given away, and the ratio of *F* tickets to *G* tickets was 2 to 1. Of the total number of *F* tickets and *G* tickets, what percentage was purchased?

(1) The total number of *F* tickets and *G* tickets is 240.

(2) Of the *F* tickets, exactly 60 percent were purchased, and of the *G* tickets, exactly 80 percent were purchased.

(A) if statement (1) ALONE is sufficient, but statement (2) alone is not sufficient to answer the question asked;

(B) if statement (2) ALONE is sufficient, but statement (1) alone is not sufficient to answer the question asked;

(C) if BOTH statements (1) and (2) TOGETHER are sufficient to answer the question asked, but NEITHER statement ALONE is sufficient;

(D) if EACH statement ALONE is sufficient to answer the question asked;

(E) if statements (1) and (2) TOGETHER are NOT sufficient to answer the question asked, and additional data specific to the problem are needed.

7. **(B)** Using information from statement (1), which gives us the total number of tickets, and from the question itself, which gives us the ratio of one type of ticket to another, we can figure out exactly how many *F* tickets and *G* tickets there were. But this doesn't help us to figure out what percentage of these tickets were purchased as opposed to given away. We're down to (B), (C), or (E).

Statement (2) does not give us the total number of actual tickets, but in this case, that doesn't matter. All we need to know to answer the question is the percentage of each type that were purchased, and the ratio of one type to the other. The correct answer is choice (B).

Still confused about why statement (2) is sufficient? Let's plug in. The ratio of *F* to *G* was 2 to 1, so let's say there were 20 *F* tickets and 10 *G* tickets, for a total of 30 tickets. Statement (2) says 60% of the *F* tickets (60% of 20 = 12) and 80% of the *G* tickets (80% of 10 = 8) were purchased. That's a total of 20 tickets purchased out of a total of 30. Can we figure out what percentage that is? Of course.

MATH BIN 2

QUESTIONS	EXPLANATIONS

8. If $\dfrac{1}{y} = 3\dfrac{1}{2}$, then $\dfrac{1}{y+2} =$

   (A) $\dfrac{7}{16}$

   (B) $\dfrac{4}{7}$

   (C) $\dfrac{7}{9}$

   (D) $\dfrac{7}{8}$

   (E) $\dfrac{16}{7}$

8. **(A)** $3\dfrac{1}{2}$ is equal to $\dfrac{7}{2}$. If $\dfrac{1}{y} = \dfrac{7}{2}$, then $y = \dfrac{2}{7}$. We can now plug this value into the equation:

$$\frac{1}{y+2} = \frac{1}{\dfrac{2}{7} + \dfrac{14}{7}} = \frac{7}{16}$$

The correct answer is choice (A).

9. The function * is defined by the equation $a * b = \dfrac{ab}{b-a}$, where $a \neq b$. Which of the following has a value of 3?

   (A) 1 * 3
   (B) 3 * 0
   (C) 2 * 6
   (D) 6 * 2
   (E) 4 * –1

9. **(C)** Answering a function problem is simply a matter of following directions. In this case, the directions say that whenever you see two numbers a and b with a * between them, you should multiply them and then divide by $b - a$. Now you have to try out each of the answer choices until you find the one that equals 3. The correct answer is choice (C).

MATH BIN 2

QUESTIONS	EXPLANATIONS

10. What is the greatest common factor of positive integers x and y?

(1) The greatest common factor of $\dfrac{x}{2}$ and $\dfrac{y}{2}$ is 5.

(2) x and y are even.

(A) if statement (1) ALONE is sufficient, but statement (2) alone is not sufficient to answer the question asked;

(B) if statement (2) ALONE is sufficient, but statement (1) alone is not sufficient to answer the question asked;

(C) if BOTH statements (1) and (2) TO-GETHER are sufficient to answer the question asked, but NEITHER statement ALONE is sufficient;

(D) if EACH statement ALONE is sufficient to answer the question asked;

(E) if statements (1) and (2) TOGETHER are NOT sufficient to answer the question asked, and additional data specific to the problem are needed.

---

10. (A) As usual, whenever you see variables, you should try to plug in. Statement (1) tells us that the greatest common factor of $\dfrac{x}{2}$ and $\dfrac{y}{2}$ is 5. Let's plug in some numbers for x and y that make this true. How about 10 for x and 20 for y. How did we pick these numbers? Well, first of all, $\dfrac{x}{2}$ and $\dfrac{y}{2}$ have to be non-fraction numbers in order to be divisible by *any* integer, which means that x and y must both be divisible by 2. Second of all, to have 5 as a factor, both x and y have to be divisible by 5. If x and y have to be divisible by both 2 and by 5, they both have to be divisible by 2 times 5, or 10. You could also just mess around until you find two numbers that work. If $x = 10$ and $y = 20$, then what is the greatest common factor of x and y? You got it: 10. Because this is a Data Sufficiency question, the exact answer doesn't matter, but it is important to be sure that you will always get the same answer. You could try plugging in a few more values for x and y, but in this case, you won't find a greater common factor than 10. We're down to (A) or (D).

While it appears to agree with statement (1), statement (2) gives us much less specific information. By plugging in, you'll see that there could be many different answers to the question using statement (2). The correct answer is choice (A).

---

11. A computer is programmed to generate a list of multiples of prime numbers 2, 3, and 5, as shown below:

Program 1—*List multiples of 2*
Program 2—*List multiples of 3*
Program 3—*List multiples of 5*

How many integers between 1 and 100 will appear on all three of the lists of the programs produced above?

(A) None
(B) 1
(C) 3
(D) 5
(E) An infinite number of integers

---

11. (C) To appear on all three lists, a number would have to be a multiple of 2, 3, and 5, all at the same time. What kind of number is a multiple of all three of these numbers? A number that has 2, 3, and 5 as factors. If we multiply $2 \times 3 \times 5$, we get 30. 30 is therefore a multiple of 2, 3, and 5. How many numbers like this are there between 1 and 100? 30 is the first one, 60 is the second, and 90 is the third. The correct answer is choice (C) 3.

12. If x and y are positive integers, is $x + 4y$ odd?

   (1) y is odd.

   (2) x is odd.

   (A) if statement (1) ALONE is sufficient, but statement (2) alone is not sufficient to answer the question asked;

   (B) if statement (2) ALONE is sufficient, but statement (1) alone is not sufficient to answer the question asked;

   (C) if BOTH statements (1) and (2) TOGETHER are sufficient to answer the question asked, but NEITHER statement ALONE is sufficient;

   (D) if EACH statement ALONE is sufficient to answer the question asked;

   (E) if statements (1) and (2) TOGETHER are NOT sufficient to answer the question asked, and additional data specific to the problem are needed.

12. **(B)** "Is $x + 4y$ odd?" is a "yes or no" question. Before we look at the statements, notice that 4 times *any* integer is always going to be even. Thus, in this case, it doesn't matter whether y is even or odd. We don't need to know anything about y. Since $4y$ will always be even, what number plus an even number makes an odd number? That's right: An odd number. To answer this question affirmatively, x would have to be odd. To answer this question in the negative, x would have to be even. Since this is a "yes or no" question, in which either a yes *or* a no is sufficient to answer the question, all we need to know is *something* about x. Statement (1) tells us nothing about x. So is $x + 4y$ odd? It might be and it might not. This statement is not sufficient to answer the question definitively. We're down to (B), (C), or (E).

Statement (2) tells us that x is odd. If this is the case, then $x + 4y$ will *always* be odd. The correct answer is choice (B). Note that on this question, the too-obvious answer is choice (C). If you were in a hurry, you might think you needed to know about both x and y to answer the question.

MATH BIN 2

QUESTIONS	EXPLANATIONS

13. A grocer is storing small cereal boxes in large cartons that measure 25 inches by 42 inches by 60 inches. If the measurement of each small cereal box is 7 inches by 6 inches by 5 inches, then what is the maximum number of small cereal boxes that can be placed in each large carton?

    (A) 25
    (B) 210
    (C) 252
    (D) 300
    (E) 420

13. **(D)** This volume problem is potentially difficult because there may be more than one way to stack the boxes inside the carton. We need to find the *maximum* number that will fit. Let's start by worrying about one layer of cereal boxes inside the carton—in other words, let's start in two dimensions instead of three. Later we'll worry about the height of the box, but for now consider a rectangle that is 25 by 42.

As with any geometry problem without a diagram, it is essential that you make your own drawing. How many smaller rectangles measuring 5 by 7 will fit in this larger 25 by 42 rectangle? You can actually draw in the smaller boxes if you want. You will notice that you can fit 5 sides of 5 inches along the 25 inch side. You can fit 6 sides of 7 inches along the 42 inch side. This means that you can fit 5 × 6, or 30 boxes in one layer of the carton. Now, how many layers of boxes fit in the carton? The carton is 60 inches tall. Each of the boxes is 6 inches tall. How many layers of 6 inches fit into 60? That's right, 10. The correct answer to this problem is 10 times 30, which is choice (D) 300. We know this is the maximum number because we used up all the space in the carton.

MATH BIN 2

QUESTIONS	EXPLANATIONS

14. Sue is now 10 years younger than Jane. If in 5 years Jane will be twice as old as Sue, how old will Sue be in 3 years?

   (A) 6
   (B) 8
   (C) 11
   (D) 14
   (E) 18

14. **(B)** This is a great problem for working backward. Instead of writing an equation, just try plugging the answer choices back into the problem until you find the correct answer. As usual, you want to start with choice (C).

Let's suppose for a moment that Sue will be (C) 11 years old in 3 years. That means that right now she is 8. The problem says Sue is now 10 years younger than Jane. If Sue is now 8, then Jane is now 18.

According to the problem, in five years Jane will be twice as old as Sue. Let's see if these numbers make that true: In five years, Sue will be 13 and Jane will be 23. Obviously, choice (C) is wrong, so we eliminate it. At this point in most backsolving problems you can tell whether you need a larger or a smaller number, which enables you to eliminate several other answer choices as well. However, sometimes you may not be able to see in which direction you should go. Can you tell in this case if we want a larger or a smaller number? You may have noticed that in choice (C), Sue's age ended up being slightly *more* than half Jane's age. Sue's age will have to start out a bit smaller to make the problem work. However, if you didn't notice that, don't get worried. Rather than wasting time trying to figure out which direction to go in, just pick a direction and see what happens. At worst, you'll just try each of the answers until you get the right one.

Let's try choice (B). If Sue will be 8 in three years, then she is 5 right now. Sue is now 10 years younger than Jane, so Jane is 15 right now. In five years, Sue will be 10 and Jane will be 20. Bingo! Jane's age in five years will be twice Sue's. The correct answer is choice (B). Note that choice (E), the Joe Bloggs answer in this question, was simply the sum of all the numbers in the problem.

MATH BIN 3

1. A store raised the price of an item by exactly 10 percent. Which of the following could NOT be the resulting price of the item?

   (A) $5.50
   (B) $7.60
   (C) $11.00
   (D) $12.10
   (E) $75.90

1. **(B)** In this question, four of the five choices could be the result of raising a price by 10%. One of them could not. You might have noticed that it was relatively easy to figure out two of the choices. Choice (A) $5.50 was clearly the result of adding 10% of $5.00 (50 cents) to $5.00. Choice (C) was clearly the result of adding 10% of $10.00 (or $1) to $10.00. Thus, we could eliminate (A) and (C). If this was as far as you could get, it made sense to guess among the remaining answer choices. Remember, if you can eliminate even one choice, you should guess. To eliminate the other two answer choices was tougher, and it helped to try to extrapolate from one of the choices that was easier to see. For example, we knew that choice (C) was the result of adding 10% of $10 (or $1) to $10. Mathematically, what did we do? We took an amount x, added 10% of x to that and set it equal to $11.00:

$$x + .1(x) = \$11.$$

and x turned out to equal $10, a round number.

Let's try this with choice (D) $12.10:

$$x + .1(x) = \$12.10$$

If you do the math, x turns out to equal $11.00, a round number. We can eliminate choice (D).

Let's try it with choice (B) $7.60. This time, x is *not* a round number at all; it works out to about $6.9090..., a repeating decimal. The correct answer is choice (B).

2. The price for a pair of cuff links is $1.00. The price for a 5-pair package of cuff links is $3.40. The 5-pair package is what percent cheaper per pair than 5 pairs purchased separately?

   (A) 63%
   (B) 62%
   (C) 47%
   (D) 32%
   (E) 20%

2. **(D)** The five-pair package costs $3.40, which works out to 68 cents per pair, as opposed to the $1.00 per pair if purchased individually. Thus, the savings per pair if you buy the package is 32 cents. What percent cheaper is this? $\frac{32}{100}$, or choice (D).

MATH BIN 3

QUESTIONS	EXPLANATIONS

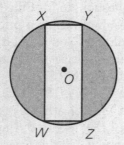

3. Rectangle *WXYZ* is inscribed in a circle with center *O* as shown above. If the diameter of the circle is equal to 16, then what is the area of the shaded region?

(1) *WZ* = *OW*

(2) *XW* < *XY*

(A) if statement (1) ALONE is sufficient, but statement (2) alone is not sufficient to answer the question asked;

(B) if statement (2) ALONE is sufficient, but statement (1) alone is not sufficient to answer the question asked;

(C) if BOTH statements (1) and (2) TO-GETHER are sufficient to answer the question asked, but NEITHER statement ALONE is sufficient;

(D) if EACH statement ALONE is sufficient to answer the question asked;

(E) if statements (1) and (2) TOGETHER are NOT sufficient to answer the question asked, and additional data specific to the problem are needed.

3. **(A)** Remember, in Data Sufficiency, the diagrams are *never* drawn to scale. Always make it a point to redraw the diagram as the two statements give you information. To get the area of the shaded region, we need to subtract the area of the rectangle from the area of the circle. The question itself gives us the diameter of the circle (16), which enables us to find its area. Now all we need is the area of the rectangle. Statement (1) tells us that the base of the rectangle is equal to the radius of the circle (1/2 of the diameter), which we know to be 8. We don't have the height of the rectangle, but we can figure it out. *WZ* = 8. *WY* is equal to the diameter of the circle, or 16. These two segments form two sides of a right triangle *WZY*. We can use the Pythagorean theorem to find the third side *ZY*. We're down to (A) or (D).

Statement (2) merely tells us that one side of the rectangle is less than another. This does not help to answer the question. The correct answer is choice (A).

MATH BIN 3

4. Is rectangular block B a cube?

   (1) At least two faces of rectangular block B are square.

   (2) The volume of rectangular block B is 64.

   (A) if statement (1) ALONE is sufficient, but statement (2) alone is not sufficient to answer the question asked;

   (B) if statement (2) ALONE is sufficient, but statement (1) alone is not sufficient to answer the question asked;

   (C) if BOTH statements (1) and (2) TO-GETHER are sufficient to answer the question asked, but NEITHER statement ALONE is sufficient;

   (D) if EACH statement ALONE is sufficient to answer the question asked;

   (E) if statements (1) and (2) TOGETHER are NOT sufficient to answer the question asked, and additional data specific to the problem are needed.

4. **(E)** This is a "yes or no" question. Statement (1) tells us that 2 faces of the block are square. A rectangular block has 6 faces. If all 6 are square, then the block is a cube. But if only some of them are square, then the block is not a cube. If you try drawing this yourself, you will see that it is possible to sometimes get a cube and sometimes get a rectangular solid, so we are down to (B), (C), or (E).

Statement (2) tells us that the volume of the block is 64. You may have realized that 64 is the cube root of 4, and decided that this means the solid must be a cube with dimensions $4 \times 4 \times 4$. Unfortunately, there are other dimensions that would also yield a block with a volume of 64. We're down to (C) or (E).

Combining the two statements does not help either. It is still possible to draw this as a cube $(4 \times 4 \times 4)$ or as a rectangular solid $(2 \times 2 \times 16)$. The correct answer is choice (E). Joe Bloggs might have picked (A) under the mistaken impression that if any side of the solid was a square, then the entire solid must be a cube. Joe might also have picked choice (C), feeling that the best way to answer this question was to throw the kitchen sink at it.

MATH BIN 3

QUESTIONS	EXPLANATIONS

5. In a certain flower shop, which stocks four types of flowers, there are $\frac{1}{3}$ as many violets as carnations, and $\frac{1}{2}$ as many tulips as violets. If there are equal numbers of roses and tulips, what percent of the flowers in the shop are carnations?

(A) 10%
(B) 33%
(C) 40%
(D) 50%
(E) 60%

5. (E) As an algebra question, this is pretty tough. However, if you plug in, it is pretty easy. There are $\frac{1}{3}$ as many violets as carnations. Let's say there are 30 carnations. That would mean there are 10 violets. There are $\frac{1}{2}$ as many tulips as violets, which means there are 5 tulips. And there are equal numbers of roses and tulips, which means there are 5 roses. Let's add this up

> *30 carnations*
> 10 violets
> 5 tulips
> 5 roses
> _____
> *50 flowers*

What percent are carnations? $\frac{30}{50} = \frac{x}{100}$. The correct answer is choice (E), 60%. Choice (B) was the Joe Bloggs answer.

6. If x, y, and z are non-zero numbers such that $1 \geq y > x$ and $xy = z$, which of the following CANNOT be true?

(A) $y > z$
(B) $y = z$
(C) $z = x$
(D) $x > z$
(E) $z > 0$

6. (B) As soon as you see variables in the answer, you should be thinking "plugging in." In order for (B) to be true, x would have to equal 1. This is impossible, since x must be smaller than y and only y can equal 1. The correct answer is choice (B).

MATH BIN 3

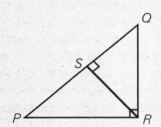

7. In the figure above, what is the length of *PQ* times the length of *RS*?

    (1)   The length of *PQ* is 5.

    (2)   The length of *QR* times the length of *PR* is equal to 12.

    (A)   if statement (1) ALONE is sufficient, but statement (2) alone is not sufficient to answer the question asked;

    (B)   if statement (2) ALONE is sufficient, but statement (1) alone is not sufficient to answer the question asked;

    (C)   if BOTH statements (1) and (2) TO-GETHER are sufficient to answer the question asked, but NEITHER statement ALONE is sufficient;

    (D)   if EACH statement ALONE is sufficient to answer the question asked;

    (E)   if statements (1) and (2) TOGETHER are NOT sufficient to answer the question asked, and additional data specific to the problem are needed.

7. **(B)** Statement (1) only gives the length of *PQ*, so we're down to (B), (C), or (E). At first glance, statement (2) doesn't seem to help, but in fact it is sufficient to answer the question. The key to this problem is area. The area of any triangle is $\frac{base \times height}{2}$, but you can consider any side of the triangle to be the base. For example, the area of this figure could be written as $\frac{PQ \times RS}{2}$, or as $\frac{QR \times PR}{2}$. In other words, these are equivalent equations, and the correct answer is choice (B). Joe Bloggs might have taken the kitchen sink approach to this one and chosen (C).

MATH BIN 3

8. A company bought a total of 60 computers and 20 printers to modernize billing operations. If the price of each computer was three times the price of each printer, what percent of the total cost of the purchase was the total cost of the printers?

   (A) 10%
   (B) 11%
   (C) 15%
   (D) 20%
   (E) 25%

8. **(A)** This is a cosmic plugging in problem. Notice that no specific price is ever mentioned. You could use an equation to solve this problem, but it would be infinitely easier to plug in prices. The problem says that the price of each computer was three times the price of a printer. Let's make the price of a printer $100, which would make the price of a computer $300. 20 printers at $100 each works out to $2,000, and 60 computers at $300 each works out to $18,000. The question wants to know what percent of the total cost was the cost of all the printers. The total cost (using the numbers we plugged in) was $20,000. The cost of the printers was $2,000.

$$\frac{\$2,000}{\$20,000} = \frac{x}{100}$$

The correct answer is choice (A), 10%. Notice that choice (D) was a Joe Bloggs answer, merely repeating a number from the problem itself.

9. If P is a set of integers and 3 is in P, is every positive multiple of 3 in P?

   (1) For any integer in P, the sum of 3 and that integer is also in P.

   (2) For any integer in P, that integer minus 3 is also in P.

   (A) if statement (1) ALONE is sufficient, but statement (2) alone is not sufficient to answer the question asked;

   (B) if statement (2) ALONE is sufficient, but statement (1) alone is not sufficient to answer the question asked;

   (C) if BOTH statements (1) and (2) TO-GETHER are sufficient to answer the question asked, but NEITHER statement ALONE is sufficient;

   (D) if EACH statement ALONE is sufficient to answer the question asked;

   (E) if statements (1) and (2) TOGETHER are NOT sufficient to answer the question asked, and additional data specific to the problem are needed.

9. **(A)** To find the answer to this "yes or no" question, try plugging into the two statements, starting with the one number that you know is in the set: 3. Statement (1) gives us all the positive multiples of 3. Statement (2) gives us all the negative multiples of 3, plus 0. The correct answer is choice (A). Joe might have picked (D).

MATH BIN 3

QUESTIONS	EXPLANATIONS

10. A machine costs *m* dollars per day to maintain and *n* cents for each unit it produces. If the machine is operated 7 days a week and produces *r* units in a week, which of the following is the total cost, in dollars, of operating the machine for a week?

   (A) $7m + 100nr$

   (B) $\dfrac{700m + nr}{100}$

   (C) $m + nr$

   (D) $\dfrac{7m + 100nr}{100}$

   (E) $700mnr$

10. **(B)** Given the variables in the answer choices, this is yet another plug-in problem. Let's pick 5 for *m*, 200 for *n*, and 8 for *r*. Of course, any numbers will work, but the problem was much easier to figure out if we picked a number for *n* that easily converted into dollars, since the answer to the question is supposed to be in dollars. Based on these numbers, one week would cost $35 in maintenance and $16 for production, for a total cost of $51. Now all we have to do is figure out which answer choice equals 51 when we plug in our numbers for *m*, *n*, and *r*. The correct answer is choice (B).

MATH BIN 3

QUESTIONS	EXPLANATIONS

11. A car averages 40 miles per hour for the first 6 hours of a trip and averages 60 miles per hour for each additional hour of travel time. If the average speed for the entire trip is 55 miles per hour, how many hours long is the trip?

    (A)   8
    (B) 12
    (C) 16
    (D) 18
    (E) 24

11. **(E)** As soon as you see the words "car" and "trip," you should be thinking $R \times T = D$. Did you also notice that this problem could be solved by working backward? Let's start with choice (C), 16 hours.

The first 6 hours were driven at 40 mph for a total of 240 miles. That leaves 10 hours at 60 mph for a total of 600 miles. To find the average speed, divide the total distance (840) by the total number of hours (16). If the result is 55 mph, we have our answer. Unfortunately, $\frac{840}{16} = 52.5$, so we can cross off choice (C), but we can do even better than that: We can also cross off choices (A) and (B). To get from 52.5 up to 55, we need a *greater* number of hours. The answer is either (D) or (E). Let's try (E) 24.

The first 6 hours were driven at 40 mph for a total of 240 miles. That leaves 18 hours at 60 mph for a total of 1080 miles. To find the average speed, divide the total distance (1320) by the total number of hours (24). The result is 55 mph, and the correct answer is choice (E). You could probably have used ballparking to eliminate choice (B). If the first six hours were driven at 40 mph and the second six hours were driven at 60 mph, what would the average speed have been? That's right: 50 mph. We needed a larger number. This would have allowed you to eliminate choice (A) as well as choice (B).

MATH BIN 3

QUESTIONS	EXPLANATIONS

12. If t is a multiple of prime number s, is t a multiple of s^2?

(1) $s < 4$

(2) $t = 18$

(A) if statement (1) ALONE is sufficient, but statement (2) alone is not sufficient to answer the question asked;

(B) if statement (2) ALONE is sufficient, but statement (1) alone is not sufficient to answer the question asked;

(C) if BOTH statements (1) and (2) TOGETHER are sufficient to answer the question asked, but NEITHER statement ALONE is sufficient;

(D) if EACH statement ALONE is sufficient to answer the question asked;

(E) if statements (1) and (2) TOGETHER are NOT sufficient to answer the question asked, and additional data specific to the problem are needed.

12. **(E)** To solve this "yes or no" question, you have to plug in. Let's begin with statement (1). s must be less than 4 and prime; let's make $s = 3$. The information in the question says that t is a multiple of s. Let's make $t = 9$. Now, let's ask the question: Is t a multiple of s^2? In this case, the answer is "yes." 9 is a multiple of 9. If the answer to this question is *always* "yes" then statement (1) is sufficient, but if we can find even one case where the answer is "no," then statement (1) is no good. Let's try again by keeping $s = 3$, but this time let's plug in 12 for t. Again, let's ask the question: Is t a multiple of s^2? In this case, the answer is "no." 12 is not a multiple of 9. Since the answer is sometimes yes and sometimes no, statement (1) is not sufficient and we're down to (B), (C), or (E).

Statement (2) says that $t = 18$, but gives us no information about s. Let's plug in 3 for s again. 18 is a multiple of 3. Now, let's ask the question: Is 18 a multiple of s^2? Yes. 18 is a multiple of 9. If the answer is always yes, then statement (2) is sufficient, but to make sure, let's try plugging in another number. We still have $t = 18$, but make $s = 2$. 18 is a multiple of 2, so now let's ask the question: Is 18 a multiple of s^2? In this case, the answer is "no." 18 is not a multiple of 4. Thus statement (2) is not sufficient either, and we are down to (C) or (E).

Combining both statements in this case is not going to help either. The numbers we plugged in above will satisfy both statements, and still sometimes yield a "yes," and other times yield a "no." The correct answer to this question is choice (E). Joe Bloggs is probably pretty tempted by (C), because it appears to give information about both s and t.

MATH BIN 3

QUESTIONS	EXPLANATIONS

13. How many integers between 100 and 150, inclusive, can be evenly divided by neither 3 nor 5?

    (A) 33
    (B) 28
    (C) 27
    (D) 26
    (E) 24

13. **(C)** Let's first figure out how many integers between 100 and 150 can be divided by 5. You could count it out on your fingers ("100, 105, 110, 115..." etc.), which gives you 11, or you could subtract 100 from 150 and then divide by 5, which gives you 10, and then you have to remember that the problem says "inclusive" meaning you have to add one more, which gives you 11.

Now, let's figure out how many integers between 100 and 150 can be divided by 3. Again, you could count on your fingers or you could subtract 100 from 150 and then divide by 3, which gives you 16, plus one, since 150 itself is divisible by 3. 11 + 17 = 28, which is answer choice (B), but we aren't done yet. There were four numbers in the 3 pile that were also in the 5 pile, and we can't count count them twice— 105, 120, 135, and 150. 28 − 4 = 24 numbers divisible by 3 or 5. But, the question asks how many of the integers between 100 and 150 inclusive are NOT divisible by 3 or 5. There are 51 integers between 100 and 150 inclusive. Of these, 24 are divisible by either 3 or 5. So 51 − 24 gives us the correct answer of 27.

MATH BIN 3

	s	
u	t	8
	4	

14. A computer generates non-zero numbers for the figure above so that the product of the numbers along any vertical column is equal to the product of the numbers in any horizontal row. What number does s represent?

(1) u equals 6.

(2) t equals 2.

(A) if statement (1) ALONE is sufficient, but statement (2) alone is not sufficient to answer the question asked;

(B) if statement (2) ALONE is sufficient, but statement (1) alone is not sufficient to answer the question asked;

(C) if BOTH statements (1) and (2) TO-GETHER are sufficient to answer the question asked, but NEITHER statement ALONE is sufficient;

(D) if EACH statement ALONE is sufficient to answer the question asked;

(E) if statements (1) and (2) TOGETHER are NOT sufficient to answer the question asked, and additional data specific to the problem are needed.

14. **(A)** Joe thinks you need both u and t to get s, so he picks choice (C). However, all you need is u. Here's why: We know that $u \times t \times 8 = s \times t \times 4$ so $8u = 4s$. If $u = 6$, here's what the equation would look like:

$$6 \times 8 \times t = s \times 4 \times t$$

Since t is a common term in both, it will cancel out if we divide both sides by t. We're left with $48 = s \times 4$. The correct answer is choice (A).

VERBAL BIN 1

QUESTIONS	EXPLANATIONS

1. Despite the recent election of a woman to the office of prime minister, the status of women in Pakistan <u>is little changed from how it was</u> in the last century.

   (A) is little changed from how it was
   (B) is a little changed from how it was
   (C) has changed little
   (D) has changed little from how it has been
   (E) is little changed from the way it was

2. In the last twenty years, despite the chauvinism of European connoisseurs, Californian wines <u>are respected</u> throughout the world.

   (A) are respected
   (B) are becoming better respected
   (C) which have gained respect
   (D) have gained respect
   (E) have since become respected

3. A mail order company recently had a big jump in clothing sales after hiring a copywriter and a graphic artist to give its clothing catalog a magazine-like format designed to appeal to a more upscale clientele. The company is now planning to launch a housewares catalog using the same concept.

   The company's plan assumes that

   (A) other housewares catalogs with magazine-like formats do not already exist
   (B) an upscale clientele would be interested in a housewares catalog
   (C) the same copywriter and graphic artist could be employed for both the clothing and housewares catalogs
   (D) a magazine-like format requires a copywriter and a graphic artist
   (E) customers to whom the old clothing catalog appealed would continue to make purchases from catalogs with the new format

1. **(C)** The pronoun "it" in this stem sentence is ambiguous. To what noun does it refer? If you said "the status of women" you were right, that was the sentence's *intention*, but the anal ETS test writers want the antecedent of a pronoun to be crystal-clear. Choices (A), (B), (D), and (E) all contain the ambiguous "it." Choice (C), by avoiding the pronoun completely, is the clearest version of the sentence.

2. **(D)** This is a tense question. "In the last twenty years" implies a continued action over time—which needs the perfect tense. This eliminates choices (A) and (B). Choice (C) creates a sentence fragment. Choice (E) isn't bad, but the word "since" is a bit redundant because the sentence began with "in the last twenty years." Choice (D) is best.

3. **(B)** This is an analogy argument. The magazine-like houseware catalog is being launched because the company expects it to appeal to the same upscale clientele that its clothing catalog appealed to. The key word in the passage that might have alerted you to the analogy was the word "same." The assumption on which this argument depends is that the two catalogues are analogous—that it actually will attract the same clientele. (A), (C), (D), and (E) are all outside the scope of the argument. The correct answer is choice (B).

VERBAL BIN 1

QUESTIONS	EXPLANATIONS

4. Recently there has been increased debate <u>over if a budget surplus should go toward lower taxes or increased spending</u> on social programs.

    (A) over if a budget surplus should go toward lower taxes or increased spending

    (B) over whether a budget surplus should go toward lowering taxes or increasing spending

    (C) about a budget surplus going toward lower taxes or increasing spending

    (D) about if lower taxes should come from a , budget surplus or spending increases

    (E) concerning a budget surplus and its going toward lower taxes or increased spending

4. **(B)** This is an idiom question. Do you have debate (A) over if, (B) over whether, (C) about, (D) about if, or (E) concerning? The correct answer is choice (B).

5. Chicago, <u>where industrial growth in the nineteenth century was more rapid than any other American city</u>, was plagued by labor troubles like the Pullman Strikes of 1894.

    (A) where industrial growth in the nineteenth century was more rapid than any other American city

    (B) which had industrial growth in the nineteenth century more rapid than that of other American cities

    (C) which had growth industrially more rapid than any other American city in the nineteenth century

    (D) whose industrial growth in the nineteenth century was more rapid than any other American city

    (E) whose industrial growth in the nineteenth century was more rapid than that of any other American city

5. **(E)** The clue that let you know that this was an apples-and-oranges question was the word "than." In choice (A) the sentence is comparing actions. To make the sentence correct, choice (A) would have had to read, " . . . was more rapid than *it was in* any other American city." Choices (B), (C), (D), and (E) all attempt to get around this by comparing nouns instead (which means, of course, that they will need some version of the replacement noun, "that of.") Choice (B) is wrong because, among other things, it suggests that "the nineteenth century" was rapid. To be correct, it would need to say "those of" other cities. Choices (C) and (D) forget to put in any replacement noun at all. The correct answer is choice (E).

QUESTIONS	EXPLANATIONS

6. Television programming experts maintain that with each 1% increase in the prime-time ratings of a television station there is a 3.5% increase in the number of people who watch its evening news program. However, in the last ten years at Channel NTR, there was only one year of extremely high prime-time ratings and, during that year, fewer people than ever watched Channel NTR's evening news program.

Which of the following conclusions can properly be drawn from the statements above?

(A) When a news program has good ratings, the channel as a whole will have good ratings.

(B) The programming experts neglected to consider daytime news programs.

(C) The year of high ratings at NTR was a result of two hit shows that were subsequently canceled because of contractual problems.

(D) The ten-year period in question is not representative of normal viewing patterns.

(E) Prime-time ratings are not the only factor affecting how many people watch an evening news program.

6. **(E)** This is a causal argument. According to the experts, high prime-time ratings cause the ratings of the evening news show to increase as well. However, at Channel NTR, this was not found to be true. What conclusion can we draw from this? The correct answer is choice (E), which asks us to consider that there might be alternate causes. (A), (B), and (C) are outside the scope of the argument, while choice (D) would have been more likely to be correct had this been a statistical argument.

7. With total sales <u>of less than three hundred thousand dollars and fewer</u> new subscribers than last year, the New England Theatre Company is in danger of losing its building.

(A) of less than three hundred thousand dollars and fewer

(B) lower than three hundred thousand dollars and less

(C) lesser than three hundred thousand dollars and fewer

(D) fewer than three hundred thousand dollars and less

(E) of fewer than three hundred thousand dollars and of fewer

7. **(A)** This question is about quantity words. Do you use "fewer" or "less" when you are talking about money? It depends. If you had six one-dollar bills, we would say that you had *fewer* than seven, because dollar bills can be counted with assurance. If you had six thousand dollars, we would say that you had *less* than seven thousand, because we have no idea how many actual bills you had. Thus, the correct answer is choice (A).

8. The people least likely to be audited by the Internal Revenue Service this year are those who have been audited at least once since 1985 and who were found to have made no mistakes in filing their returns during that audit.

   Of the following people, who is MOST likely to be audited by the IRS?

   (A) A person who was audited in 1986 but was not found to have made any mistakes in filing his return.
   (B) A person who was audited in 1986 and whose lawyer corrected several mistakes in the tax return prior to the filing deadline.
   (C) A person whose spouse was convicted of tax fraud in 1987, who was then audited and found to have made no mistakes.
   (D) A person who was last audited in 1984, and had no mistakes uncovered by the IRS during that audit.
   (E) A person who was audited in each of the past five years, but was found to have made no mistakes in any of the filings.

8. **(D)** According to the passage, you are least likely to be audited if you have recently been audited and found not to have made mistakes. Thus it would seem evident that you would be most likely to be audited if you had not been audited for a while, but when you were last audited you were found to have made lots of mistakes. Unfortunately, there is no answer choice like that. We need the best choice we can find. Choice (B) seems attractive at first, but as long as the lawyer corrected the mistakes before the IRS caught them, choice (B) is effectively identical to choice (A). Choice (C) seems attractive because the spouse was convicted of tax fraud, but if you picked it, you were thinking beyond the scope of the argument. This taxpayer was audited recently and no mistakes were found. Choice (E) describes a person who is extremely unlikely to be audited given the criteria outlined in the argument. Thus, choice (D) is the best answer: The taxpayer has not been audited since 1984, and although he or she was not then found to have made any mistakes, this is the furthest away we can get from the criteria.

9. A recent *New York Times* editorial criticized the city's election board for, first of all, failing to replace outmoded voting machines prone to breakdowns, and <u>secondarily, for their failure to</u> investigate allegations of corruption involving board members.

   (A) secondarily, for their failure to
   (B) secondly, for their failure to
   (C) secondly, that they failed and did not
   (D) second, that they failed to
   (E) second, for failing to

9. **(E)** This is a parallel construction question, containing a list of two parts; each must be expressed the same way. There's no point trying to fix the part of the sentence that isn't underlined, so we know that the first part must be correct as is: ". . . for, first of all, failing to . . ."

   The second part must mimic the first. The correct answer is choice (E).

QUESTIONS	EXPLANATIONS

10. James's grade point average puts him in the top third of the graduating class of college A. Nestor is in the top tenth of the same class. Elizabeth has the same grade point average as Nestor. Nancy has a lower grade point average than Elizabeth.

If the information above is true, which of the following must also be true?

(A) James has a higher grade point average than Elizabeth.
(B) James has a higher grade point average than Nancy.
(C) Nestor has a higher grade point average than Nancy.
(D) Elizabeth and Nancy both have a higher grade point average than James.
(E) Nestor and James both have a higher grade point average than Nancy.

10. **(C)** This is an all-some-most question. The clue that gives this away is the word "must" in the question. It is often helpful to sketch out all-some-most questions for yourself. A sketch might look like this:

Nestor = Elizabeth

↓   ↓

James - ? - Nancy

Nestor and Elizabeth are equivalent. Nancy has a lower average than Elizabeth, but we don't know where she ranks in terms of James. Now, just read through the choices for something that MUST be true. The correct answer is choice (C).

11. <u>Two week notice being given to employers before leaving</u> a job is the generally accepted protocol.

(A) Two week notice being given to employers before leaving
(B) Giving notice to employers of two weeks before having to leave
(C) Two weeks' notice to give to employers before leaving
(D) Giving notice to employers two weeks before leaving
(E) To give two weeks' worth of notice before having to leave

11. **(D)** ETS has an aversion to the word "being," which usually creates a passive voice. This eliminates choice (A). In choice (B), the prepositional phrase "of two weeks" is too far away from "notice" (the noun that it is supposed to modify), giving the mistaken impression that the phrase instead modifies "employers." "Two weeks' notice" is a correct idiomatic expression, but we eliminate choices (C) and (E) due to awkwardness. The correct answer is choice (D).

QUESTIONS	EXPLANATIONS

Questions 12–17 are based on the following passage:

The Romans—for centuries the masters of war and politics across Europe, Northern Africa, and Asia Minor—have often been criticized for producing few original thinkers outside the
5 realm of politics. This criticism, while in many ways true, is not without its problems. It was, after all, the conquest of Greece that provided Rome with its greatest influx of educated subjects. Two of the great disasters in intellec-
10 tual history—the murder of Archimedes and the burning of Alexandria's library—both occurred under Rome's watch. Nevertheless, a city that was able to conquer so much of the known world could not have been devoid of the
15 creativity that characterizes so many other ancient empires.

Engineering is one endeavor in which the Romans showed themselves capable. Their aqueducts carried water hundreds of miles
20 along the tops of vast arcades. Roman roads, built for the rapid deployment of troops, criss-cross Europe and still form the basis of numer-ous modern highways that provide quick access between many major European and
25 African cities. Indeed, a large number of these cities owe their prominence to Rome's eco-nomic and political influence.

Many of those major cities lie far beyond Rome's original province, and Latin-derived
30 languages are spoken in most Southern Euro-pean nations. Again a result of military influ-ence, the popularity of Latin and its offspring is difficult to overestimate. During the centuries of ignorance and violence that followed Rome's
35 decline, the Latin language was the glue that held together the identity of an entire continent. While seldom spoken today, it is still studied widely, if only so that such masters of rhetoric as Cicero can be read in the original.
40 It is Cicero and his like who are perhaps the most overlooked legacy of Rome. While far from being a democracy, Rome did leave behind useful political tools that serve the American republic today. "Republic" itself is

45 Latin for "the people's business," a notion cherished in democracies worldwide. Senators owe their name to Rome's class of elders; Representatives owe theirs to the Tribunes who seized popular prerogatives from the Senatorial
50 class. The veto was a Roman notion adopted by the historically aware framers of the Constitu-tion, who often assumed pen names from the lexicon of Latin life. These accomplishments, as monumental as any highway or coliseum,
55 remain prominent features of the Western landscape.

Reading Comprehension Passage Overview

Paragraph one says that ancient Rome has been criticized for lack of originality, but the criticism is wrong.

Paragraph two gives the example of Rome's engineering innovations.

Paragraph three gives the example of the influence of their language (Latin) on other languages.

Paragraph four gives the example of Rome's political innovations.

QUESTIONS	EXPLANATIONS

12. The author describes "two of the great disasters in intellectual history" (lines 9–12) in order to

   (A) establish a point directly related to the main argument

   (B) show that certain historical claims are inaccurate

   (C) demonstrate the importance of certain historical data

   (D) disprove the claims made by others with a different view

   (E) concede the partial accuracy of an opposing view

12. **(E)** This specific question has a line number. Remember to read a bit above and below the cited lines. The two disasters cited are mentioned to give an example of Rome's failings, before countering with a number of Rome's successes. The best answer was choice (E).

13. According to the passage, ancient Roman roads

   (A) connected many major cities in ancient Europe

   (B) are engineering marvels unequaled in modern times

   (C) are similar in some respects to modern highways

   (D) were products of democratic political institutions

   (E) caused the development of modern European cities

13. **(A)** This specific question also has a good lead phrase: "Roman roads." You'll find it in the second paragraph. Choice (C) is wrong because these roads are not just similar to modern highways—they form the *basis* of these highways. Choice (E) is a bit too extreme. The cities may owe their prominence to these roads, but they were not "caused" by the roads. The correct answer (choice (A)) is a paraphrase of lines 20–25.

14. According to the passage, which of the following accurately describes the Latin language?

   I. It spread in part due to Rome's military power.

   II. It is reflected in modern political concepts.

   III. It is spoken today in some parts of Europe.

   (A) I only

   (B) II only

   (C) I and II only

   (D) I and III only

   (E) II and III only

14. **(C)** This is a specific question with a good lead phrase: "Latin language." You'll find it in the third paragraph. The correct answer is choice (C). If you were tempted by statement III, remember that while Latin derivatives are widely spoken today, the passage says Latin itself is "seldom spoken today." If you said, "Well, what about the Vatican?" you forgot that as far as ETS is concerned, only what's said in the passage is relevant.

VERBAL BIN 1

QUESTIONS	EXPLANATIONS

15. It can be inferred from the passage that the framers of the Constitution

    (A) were familiar with certain aspects of Roman government
    (B) were similar to the Roman elders
    (C) embraced the veto as the hallmark of Roman democracy
    (D) overlooked Cicero's contributions to the theory of democracy
    (E) formed a government based on world-wide democracy

15. **(A)** This specific question also has a good lead phrase: "framers of the Constitution." You'll find it in the last paragraph. You may have been down to choices (A) and (C). Choice (C) used extreme language and went a bit too far. Great as the veto is, did the founding fathers consider it the "hallmark" of democracy? The passage doesn't say so. The correct answer was choice (A).

16. The primary purpose of the passage is to

    (A) reveal the indifferent attitude taken by the ancient Romans toward the fine arts
    (B) discuss the lasting accomplishments achieved by ancient Romans
    (C) analyze the use of the Latin language by the framers of the Constitution
    (D) show that the construction of roads and aqueducts could not have been accomplished in ancient Greece
    (E) compare the destruction of the library at Alexandria to the murder of Archimedes

16. **(B)** The first paragraph puts forth the idea that, despite criticism leveled against it, ancient Rome had many lasting accomplishments. The following three paragraphs give examples of these accomplishments.

17. Which of the following is NOT described in the passage as a part of ancient Roman life that left a lasting legacy?

    (A) The Latin language
    (B) Military accomplishments
    (C) An extensive system of roads
    (D) A democratic system of government
    (E) Wide-ranging economic influence

17. **(D)** In the fourth paragraph, it is explicitly stated that despite its political innovations, Rome was "far from being a democracy." All of the other choices are touched upon somewhere in the passage.

VERBAL BIN 2

1. IRS provision 354-B requires <u>that an S corporation with assets of greater than $200,000 send W-2 forms to their full- and part-time employees on or before Jan. 31</u>.

   (A) that an S corporation with assets of greater than $200,000 send W-2 forms to their full- and part-time employees on or before Jan. 31

   (B) an S corporation with assets of greater than $200,000 send W-2 forms to their full- and part-time employees on or before Jan. 31

   (C) that an S corporation with assets of greater than $200,000 send W-2 forms to its full- and part-time employees on or before Jan. 31

   (D) an S corporation with assets of greater than $200,000 to send W-2 forms to their full- and part-time employees on Jan. 31 or before

   (E) an S corporation with assets of greater than $200,000 send W-2 forms to its full- and part-time employees on or before Jan. 31

1. **(C)** This is a pronoun question. The pronoun in question is the plural "their," which is referring to the singular "S corporation." We can thus eliminate (A), (B), and (D). Choice (E) requires the infinitive "to send." The correct answer is choice (C).

VERBAL BIN 2

QUESTIONS	EXPLANATIONS

Questions 2–3 are based on the following:

Investing in real estate would be a profitable venture at this time. A survey in *House* magazine revealed that 85% of the magazine's readers are planning to buy a second home over the next few years. A study of the real estate industry, however, revealed that the current supply of homes could only provide for 65% of that demand each year.

2. Which of the following, if true, reveals a weakness in the evidence cited above?

   (A) Real estate is a highly labor-intensive business.
   (B) Home builders are not evenly distributed across the country.
   (C) The number of people who want second homes has been increasing each year for the past ten years.
   (D) Readers of *House* magazine are more likely than most people to want second homes.
   (E) *House* magazine includes articles about owning a second home as well as articles about building a second home.

2. **(D)** This is a statistical argument. The conclusion, that it would be a good idea to invest in real estate, is based on a survey that implies that there will be more demand than supply. To weaken a statistical argument, we need to show that the survey was not representative. Which choice does this? Answer choice (D) shows that the readers of *House* magazine are more likely to want to buy a house than the general public—making the survey less than representative. The rest of the answer choices were out of the scope of the argument.

3. Which of the following, if true, would undermine the validity of the investment advice in the paragraph above?

   (A) Some home owners are satisfied with only one home.
   (B) About half of the people who buy homes are investing in their first home.
   (C) About half of the people who buy homes have to take out a mortgage to do so.
   (D) Only a quarter of the homes that are built are sold within the first two weeks.
   (E) Only a quarter of those who claim that they want a second home actually end up purchasing one.

3. **(E)** Question 2 was asking us to weaken the evidence. Question 3 is asking us to weaken the conclusion that was based on the evidence. In both cases, the correct answer will show that the statistics are not representative. In question 3 the correct answer is choice (E), which does exactly this. If only a quarter of the people who claimed in the survey to want a second home actually buy one, this undermines the validity of the survey, and thus the validity of the investment advice as well.

4. <u>Just as the European countries of the early eighteenth century sought to exploit the resources of our continent, so too</u> are we now attempting to extract energy and minerals from the ocean bed.

(A) Just as the European countries of the early eighteenth century sought to exploit the resources of our continent, so too

(B) The European countries of the early eighteenth century sought to exploit the resources of our continent, and in a similar way

(C) Like the case of the European countries of the early eighteenth century who sought to exploit the resources of our continent, so too

(D) As in the exploitation of the resources of our continent by European countries of the early eighteenth century,

(E) Similar to the European countries which sought in the early eighteenth century to exploit the resources of our continent

4. **(A)** The idiom, "Just as . . . so too" is correct as written. Each of the other choices uses variations on unidiomatic expression instead. The correct answer is choice (A).

5. Traffic safety experts predict that the installation of newly designed air bags in all cars in the United States will reduce the average number of fatalities per traffic accident by 30 percent. In order to save lives, the Department of Transportation (DOT) is considering requiring automobile manufacturers to install air bags of this design in all cars produced after 1998.

Which of the following, if true, represents the strongest challenge to the DOT's proposal?

(A) Air bags of the new design are more given to being inadvertently triggered, an occurrence that can sometimes result in fatal traffic accidents.

(B) The DOT is planning to require automobile manufacturers to produce these air bags according to very strict specifications.

(C) After installing air bags in new cars, automobile manufacturers will experience an increase in sales.

(D) The proposed air bag installation program will adversely affect the resale of cars manufactured prior to 1998.

(E) As production costs increase, the profits of many domestic automobile dealers show a marked decrease.

5. **(A)** Choices (D) and (E) are negative aspects of the DOT's proposal, but negative only in an economic sense. Choice (A) represents a stronger challenge to the proposal, since it raises the possibility that the new design that is supposed to save lives may inadvertently cost additional lives.

VERBAL BIN 2

QUESTIONS	EXPLANATIONS

6. An attempt <u>to ratify the Equal Rights Amendment, begun almost two decades ago,</u> has been unsuccessful despite efforts by many important groups, including the National Organization for Women.

   (A) to ratify the Equal Rights Amendment, begun almost two decades ago,

   (B) begun almost two decades ago, for ratifying the Equal Rights Amendment

   (C) begun for ratifying the Equal Rights Amendment almost two decades ago

   (D) at ratifying the Equal Rights Amendment, begun almost two decades ago,

   (E) that has begun almost two decades ago to ratify the Equal Rights Amendment

6. **(A)** This is an idiom question. Do you attempt *to* do something, do you attempt *at* something, or do you attempt *for* something? The correct answer is choice (A).

7. A newly discovered disease is thought to be caused by a certain bacterium. However, recently released data notes that the bacterium thrives in the presence of a certain virus, implying that it is actually the virus that causes the new disease.

Which of the following pieces of evidence would most support the data's implication?

   (A) In the absence of the virus, the disease has been observed to follow infection by the bacterium.

   (B) The virus has been shown to aid the growth of bacterium, a process which often leads to the onset of the disease.

   (C) The virus alone has been observed in many cases of the disease.

   (D) In cases where the disease does not develop, infection by the bacterium is usually preceded by infection by the virus.

   (E) Onset of the disease usually follows infection by both the virus and the bacterium.

7. **(C)** The last line of this argument gives away its type: "... the virus that *causes* ..." The cause of a certain disease was thought to be one thing, but now is believed to be something else. Recent evidence suggests that the cause is a virus (which also nourishes the bacterium once thought to be the cause of the disease). To support a causal argument, you take away possible alternate causes. Choice (C) does this by showing that while both virus and bacterium are often present at the same time, the virus has been found *without* the bacterium in many cases of the disease. Choice (A) directly contradicts this, suggesting that the bacterium is the sole cause. Choices (B) and (E) suggest that the virus plays a supporting role to the bacterium. Choice (D) is outside the scope of the argument. The correct answer is choice (C).

VERBAL BIN 2

8. When evidence of financial wrongdoing by an elected official surfaces, it is the electorate who must decide <u>whether the evidence warrants censuring him or ousting him</u> from office.

 (A) whether the evidence warrants censuring him or ousting him
 (B) if there is evidence that warrants a censure or an ousting of him
 (C) whether or not the evidence warrants the censuring or ousting of him
 (D) if there is evidence that warrants censuring him or his ousting
 (E) if the evidence would warrant that he be censured or that he be ousted

8. **(A)** This question involves parallel construction. The evidence warrants one of two choices, and both must be expressed in the same way. The correct answer is choice (A), which expresses both choices as verbs. Choice (E) might have been correct, but the correct idiomatic expression (as far as ETS is concerned) is to decide *whether*, not to decide *if*.

9. Because of a recent drought in Florida during the orange-growing season, the price of oranges this season will be three times the usual price. This will drive up the cost of producing orange juice and thus push up the price of orange juice for the consumer.

 Which of the following, if true, most seriously weakens the argument above?

 (A) The recent drought was not as severe as scientists predicted.
 (B) States other than Florida also supply oranges to orange juice manufacturers.
 (C) Other ingredients are used in the production of orange juice.
 (D) Last year the price of oranges was actually lower than the average price over the past ten years.
 (E) The price of oranges will eventually be $0.48 per crate.

9. **(B)** According to the passage, a drought in Florida will drive up the overall price of orange juice. Let's use this question as a scope workshop.

 Choice (A): According to the argument, there was a drought in Florida. This is not changed by saying the drought was less severe than scientists had predicted before the drought.

 Choice (B): This seriously weakens the argument. If the drought in Florida only affects part of this year's orange crop—the part produced in Florida—then the price of orange juice might not be so severely affected.

 Choice (C): While other materials may be used in the making of orange juice, we have to feel that oranges are at least an important ingredient. If the drought decreases the Florida orange crop, this is likely to affect prices unless there is another supply.

 Choice (D): Who cares that the price was lower than usual last year? The argument says only that it will go up *this* year.

 Choice (E): Since we have nothing to compare it to, the price per crate is meaningless.

VERBAL BIN 2

QUESTIONS	EXPLANATIONS
10. Because the enemy's new ship is the quietest <u>and it is therefore the most elusive submarine, it is being increasingly viewed</u> by the military as a threat to security.	10. **(C)** This is also a parallel construction problem. The introductory clause expresses two desirable characteristics of a submarine, but the two characteristics are expressed in different ways. There is no need for a repetition of the verb or a pronoun, which eliminates all the answers but choice (C).

    (A) and it is therefore the most elusive submarine, it is being increasingly viewed

    (B) it is therefore the most elusive of submarines, and it has increased the view

    (C) and therefore the most elusive submarine, it is being increasingly viewed

    (D) and therefore it is the most elusive of submarines, there is an increasing view

    (E) therefore being the most elusive of submarines, it is increasingly viewed

11. The economic forces that may affect the new public offering of stock include sudden downturns in the market, hedging and other investor strategies for preventing losses, <u>loosening the interest rates in Washington, and fearing that the company may still be undercapitalized</u>.

    (A) loosening the interest rates in Washington, and fearing that the company may still be undercapitalized

    (B) loosening the interest rates in Washington, and a fear of the company still being undercapitalized

    (C) a loosening of the interest rates in Washington, and fearing that the company may still be undercapitalized

    (D) a loosening of the interest rates in Washington, and a fear of the still undercapitalized company

    (E) a loosening of the interest rates in Washington, and a fear that the company may still be undercapitalized

11. **(E)** This sentence contains a list of several nouns: "Sudden downturns," "hedging, other strategies," etc. The correct answer must contain all nouns. Choices (A), (B), and (C) all contain a verb-like thing. Since "loosening" is an action, you must put the article "a" in front of it to make it a noun. "Fearing" is also an action, but the noun form of "fearing" is simply "fear." This eliminates choices (A), (B), and (C). Choice (D) suggests that it is the "company" that is feared. Choice (E) is best.

VERBAL BIN 2

QUESTIONS	EXPLANATIONS

Questions 12–18 are based on the following passage:

Anthropologists who study orangutans, distant cousins of the human race, find in the animals' behavior hints of how our earliest ancestors may have lived. It has long been
5 accepted that primates originally dwelt in the treetops and only migrated to the ground as forests began to dwindle. While to a certain extent all primates except humans spend at least some time dwelling in trees, the orangu-
10 tan hardly ever ventures to the forest floor. Adult orangutans can grow as heavy as 330 pounds and live for decades, requiring copious amounts of fruit simply to stay alive. Thus, they become very jealous of the territory where they
15 find their food. Compounding this territoriality are the breeding habits of orangutans, since females can only breed every few years and, like humans, give birth not to litters but single offspring.
20 Consequently, orangutans are solitary, territorial animals who have difficulty foraging in any part of the forest where they were not raised. Orangutans taken from poachers by customs agents undergo incredible hardship on
25 their return to the wild. Incorrectly relocating a male orangutan is especially problematic, often ending in the animal's death at the hands of a rival who sees not only his territory but also the females of his loosely knit community under
30 threat from an outsider. While humans, like chimpanzees, are more gregarious and re-sourceful than orangutans, the latter provide anthropologists with useful information about the behavior of prehominid primates and how
35 apelike behavior influenced our ancestors' search for food and family beneath the forest's canopy.

Reading Comprehension Passage Overview

This is a science passage and, like many real ETS passages, not particularly well written. Paragraph one says the orangutan, studied by scientists for its resemblance to early humans, lives in trees and is very territorial. Paragraph two describes the orangutan's solitary territorial behavior, which resembled that of early humans.

VERBAL BIN 2

QUESTIONS	EXPLANATIONS

12. The primary purpose of this passage is to

    (A) describe some behavioral and evolutionary characteristics of orangutans

    (B) analyze the reasons why early primates left their forest dwellings

    (C) illustrate the dangers posed to orangutans by poachers

    (D) show how orangutan behavior differs from that of other primates

    (E) criticize anthropologists who misinterpret orangutan behavior

12. **(A)** The answer to this general question came from understanding the main idea. The passage did not analyze the *reasons* primates left trees (B), or devote itself to a discussion of poachers (C), or do a point-by-point comparison of orangutans with other primates (D), or criticize anthropologists (E). The correct answer is choice (A).

13. The author of the passage discusses "orangutans taken from poachers" (line 23) in order to

    (A) stress the importance of preserving orangutans as a species

    (B) indicate the widespread practice of animal poaching

    (C) refute the theory that orangutans can live in a variety of environments

    (D) contrast the behavior of orangutans with that of other apes

    (E) emphasize the consequences of orangutan territoriality

13. **(E)** This specific question has a line number. Remember to read a bit above and below the cited lines. The answer to this question actually came just *below* the quote. The poacher example is simply a further illustration of orangutans' territorial nature. The correct answer is choice (E).

14. The passage indicates that it is difficult to return orangutans to the wild for which of the following reasons?

    I. The threat posed by newcomers to other orangutans' territory

    II. The conflict between males over available females

    III. The scarcity of available food in the orangutan's environment

    (A) I only

    (B) I and II only

    (C) I and III only

    (D) II and III only

    (E) I, II, and III

14. **(B)** In this case, the question is discussing the same topic you were just reading about for question number 13. Both statements I and II were mentioned in lines 28–30. Statement III was not. The correct answer is choice (B).

QUESTIONS	EXPLANATIONS

15. Which of the following can be inferred about differences between the behavior of orangutans and that of other ape species?

    (A) While orangutans spend much of their time in the treetops, other apes live exclusively on the ground.

    (B) Orangutans and other types of apes are all sociable species, but orangutans are more likely to bond for life.

    (C) Apes such as chimpanzees rely less upon their size than the average orangutan does.

    (D) Orangutans spend less time in the company of other members of their species than do some other apes.

    (E) Because of their stringent territoriality, orangutans are less likely to elude capture by poachers than are other apes.

15. **(D)** This is a specific question with no line number, and, really, no lead word. We're looking for differences between orangutans and other types of apes. The only other type of monkey mentioned is the chimpanzee who is said to be more gregarious in lines 30–32. The correct answer is choice (D).

16. According to the author, anthropologists study the behavior of orangutans in order to

    (A) prevent orangutans from becoming the target of poaching

    (B) assist customs agents in the relocation of orangutans

    (C) analyze the causes and consequences of contemporary human behavior

    (D) prevent larger orangutans from eliminating their weaker rivals

    (E) better understand the factors that influenced human evolution

16. **(E)** This specific question also has a good lead word: "anthropologists." We found it in two places, at the very beginning and the very end of the passage. You were probably down to choices (C) and (E). Why was (C) wrong? Because anthropologists only see parallels with *early* man.

VERBAL BIN 2

QUESTIONS	EXPLANATIONS

17. Which of the following are factors that the author indicates contribute to the orangutan's territoriality?

   (A) The lack of available food and the antisocial nature of orangutans

   (B) The orangutan's need for large quantities of food and the infrequency with which it mates

   (C) The threat posed by poachers and the orangutan's inability to protect itself from them

   (D) The difficulties that orangutans face when compelled to socialize with other ape species such as chimpanzees

   (E) The constant dangers that present themselves whenever one orangutan encounters another

17. **(B)** This specific question also has a good lead word: "Territoriality." You'll find it in the second half of the first paragraph, which discusses two causes: the need for large amounts of food, and breeding habits. You were probably down to (A) or (B). Why was (A) wrong? It didn't discuss both food and breeding habits. Choice (B) was correct.

18. It can be inferred from the passage that one development responsible for the evolution of distinct ape species was

   (A) early primates' inability to survive in the forest

   (B) the shrinking of the available primitive forest

   (C) the growth of human and chimpanzee communities

   (D) the orangutan's eventual dominance of the treetops

   (E) the encroachment of other species into the primitive forest

18. **(B)** The second sentence of the first paragraph ends, "...and only migrated to the ground as forests began to dwindle." That gives us choice (B).

VERBAL BIN 3

QUESTIONS	EXPLANATIONS

QUESTIONS

1. Like the government that came before it, which set new records for growth, <u>laissez-faire capitalism is the cornerstone of the new government</u>.

   (A) laissez-faire capitalism is the cornerstone of the new government
   (B) the cornerstone of the new government is laissez-faire capitalism
   (C) laissez-faire capitalism is the new government's cornerstone
   (D) the new government has made laissez-faire capitalism its cornerstone
   (E) the new government has a laissez-faire cornerstone of capitalism

2. During the 1980s it became clear <u>that soliciting private funds was far more efficient for environmentalists who sought financial aid</u> than to go to state or federal agencies.

   (A) that soliciting private funds was far more efficient for environmentalists who sought financial aid
   (B) that for environmentalists who sought financial aid, it was far more efficient to solicit private funds
   (C) that for environmentalists seeking financial aid, private organizations were far more efficient to go to
   (D) for environmentalists seeking financial aid, going to private organizations was far more efficient
   (E) for environmentalists who sought financial aid, private organizations were far more efficient

EXPLANATIONS

1. **(D)** This is a misplaced modifier. What follows "Like the government that came before it" must be an actual government. This eliminates choices (A), (B), and (C). Choice (E) doesn't make much sense, because "laissez-faire" should modify "capitalism," not "cornerstone." So the correct answer is choice (D).

2. **(B)** The stem sentence here has a parallel construction problem: "that soliciting . . . was more efficient than . . . to go . . ." *Going* would have been correct, but this part of the sentence was not underlined. We needed to fix the first part of the sentence to agree with the infinitive construction of the second part of the sentence. The correct answer is choice (B).

VERBAL BIN 3

QUESTIONS	EXPLANATIONS

Questions 3–4 are based on the following:

Local phone companies have monopolies on phone service within their areas. Cable television can be transmitted via the wires that are already in place and owned by the phone companies. Cable television companies argue that if the telephone companies were to offer cable service, these telephone companies would have an unfair advantage, because their cable transmissions could be subsidized by the profits of their monopolies on phone service.

3. Which of the following, if true, would ease the cable companies' fear of unfair competition?

   (A) In order to use existing telephone wire, telephone companies would need to modernize their operations, a process so expensive it would virtually wipe out all profit from their monopoly for the foreseeable future.

   (B) If a phone company were to offer cable service within a particular area, it would have a monopoly within that area.

   (C) The cost of television service, whether provided by cable or telephone companies, scales; that is, the total cost of transmission rises only marginally as more homes are added to the network.

   (D) Cable programming that offers more channels is already available through satellite dish, but the initial cost of the dish is extremely high.

   (E) Cable television will never be able to compete with the burgeoning video rental industry, especially as more homes now have videocassette recorders than ever did before.

3. **(A)** Choices (C), (D), and (E) are outside the scope of the argument. Choice (B) would not ease the fears of the cable companies—rather the reverse. The correct answer is choice (A).

4. On the basis of the information provided in the passage above, which of the following questions can be answered?

   (A) Are phone companies as efficient as cable companies in providing reliable and inexpensive service?
   (B) If phone companies were allowed to provide cable service, would they want to do so?
   (C) Do the cable companies believe that the local phone companies make a profit on phone service?
   (D) Are local phone companies forbidden to offer cable service?
   (E) Is it expected that phone companies will have a monopoly on cable service?

4. **(C)** To conclusively answer a question, neither the question nor the answer can be hypothetical. Choices (A), (B), and (E) discuss events that might or might not happen in the future. Choice (D) is not discussed in the passage. The correct answer is choice (C), because the cable companies' position is based on their assumption or knowledge that the telephone companies are turning a profit.

5. The major areas of medicine in which lasers are effective is in the cutting and closing of blood vessels, and in the destruction of tumors.

   (A) is in the cutting and closing of blood vessels, and in the destruction
   (B) are the cutting and closing of blood vessels, and also the case of destroying
   (C) are the cutting, closing of blood vessels, and in the destroying
   (D) are the cutting and closing of blood vessels, and the destruction
   (E) is in the cutting and closing of blood vessels, and the destroying

5. **(D)** The subject of this sentence is "areas," which is plural, but the verb is singular. This eliminates choices (A) and (E). Choices (B) and (C) are not parallel. As you know, some nouns require an "–ing" ending. "Cutting" is one. But, the noun form of "destroy" is not "the destroying," it's "the destruction." The correct answer is choice (D).

QUESTIONS	EXPLANATIONS

6. Since the movie was released, seventeen UFOs have been sighted in the state, <u>which is more than had been sighted</u> in the past ten years together.

    (A) which is more than had been sighted
    (B) more than had been sighted
    (C) more than they had sighted
    (D) more than had reported sightings
    (E) which is more than had reported sightings

6. **(B)** The pronoun "which" is supposed to refer to a particular noun, but in this sentence, that noun does not really exist. (The noun would be "sightings.") This gets rid of (A) and (E). (C) throws in another pronoun, which doesn't help, and (D) gives the impression that it was the UFOs that had reported the sightings. The correct answer is choice (B).

7. In the past year, there has been a large drop in the number of new cars sold, due to harsh economic conditions in the marketplace and high taxes. At the same time, the average price paid for a new car has risen dramatically.

Which of the following, if true, best explains the increase in the average price of a new car?

    (A) The price of used cars has climbed steadily over the past ten years.
    (B) There will be a tax reduction later in the year which is expected to aid moderate and low income families.
    (C) The market for expensive cars has been unaffected by the current economic conditions.
    (D) Economic conditions are expected to get significantly worse before the end of the year.
    (E) Low demand for trucks and vans has led to lower production in the factories.

7. **(C)** *Used* cars, a tax reduction sometime in the *future*, a change of economic conditions in the *future*, and the demand for *trucks* are all irrelevant in explaining the recent increase in the price of new cars. Thus, choice (C) seems to be the best answer, even if we aren't immediately sure why. This is a tough question, and you may not have seen during the minute and some-odd seconds that you had to spend on it during the test why (C) would explain the increase in the "average price paid for a new car." However, if harsh economic situations are preventing ordinary people from buying cars, but not preventing rich people from buying expensive cars, then the "average price paid for a car" would rise.

8. Ignoring the admonitions of his staff, the chief financial officer accepted the advice of the consulting company because <u>he believed that the standardized accounting procedures would prove not only inexpensive but</u> reliable indicators of economic performance.

    (A) he believed that the standardized accounting procedures would prove not only inexpensive but

    (B) the standardized accounting procedures will prove both inexpensive and also

    (C) he believed the standardized accounting procedures would prove themselves to be both inexpensive and

    (D) he believed that the standardized accounting procedures would prove to be both inexpensive and

    (E) standardized accounting procedures will prove his belief that they are both inexpensive and

8. **(D)** The sentence as written needs a "but also" to complement its "not only." Choice (A) is gone. In choice (B) the "also" is redundant, since it is next to the word "and." In choice (C), it is implied that "procedures" can "prove themselves." Be careful of this construction. Don't attribute active abilities to things that, in and of themselves, can't act. In choice (E), the pronoun "they" is ambiguous. Choice (D) is best.

9. A light bulb company produces 2,000 light bulbs per week. The manager wants to ensure that standards of quality remain constant from week to week. The manager, therefore, claims that out of 2,000 light bulbs produced per week, 500 light bulbs must be rejected.

Of the following, the best criticism of the manager's plan is that the plan assumes that

    (A) light bulb manufacturers cannot accept all light bulbs that are produced

    (B) the overall quality of the light bulbs would not be improved if the total number of light bulbs produced were reduced

    (C) each light bulb that is reviewed is worthy of being reviewed

    (D) it is difficult to judge the quality of a light bulb

    (E) the 1,500 light bulbs that are accepted will be of the same quality from week to week

9. **(E)** The manager's aim is constant quality, yet his solution—to reject 500 bulbs every week—presupposes that there will be exactly 500 defective bulbs every week. Choice (E) points this out. If you chose choice (C), you were in too much of a hurry. If (C) had said, "each light bulb that is *rejected* is worthy of being *rejected*," that would have been a better answer.

VERBAL BIN 3

QUESTIONS	EXPLANATIONS

10. A large rise in the number of housing starts in the coming year should boost new construction dollars by several billion dollars, <u>making the construction industry's economic health much more robust than five years ago</u>.

   (A)   making the construction industry's economic health much more robust than five years ago

   (B)   and make the construction industry's economic health much more robust than five years ago

   (C)   making the construction industry's economic health much more robust than it was five years ago

   (D)   to make the construction industry's economic health much more robust than five years ago

   (E)   in making the construction industry's economic health much more robust than it was five years ago

10. **(C)** This is an apples-and-oranges question. The key word here is "than." What is being compared are two actions, which means we need "it was" after the "than." We are down to choices (C) and (E). Choice (E) confuses the participial phrase "making..." by the inclusion of the word "in." The correct answer is choice (C).

VERBAL BIN 3

QUESTIONS	EXPLANATIONS

Questions 11–17 are based on the following passage:

The two main theories of arbitration may be described as judicial and political. One might even go so far as to characterize them by saying that the first is based on how arbitration
5 is supposed to work, while the second is based on how it does in fact work.

The judicial theory implies that a "just" solution of the dispute does in fact exist, and that it is the duty of the arbitrator to decide on
10 the principles and the facts involved. The arbitrator sits as a private judge, called upon to determine the legal rights and the economic interests of the parties involved as these rights and interests are demonstrated by the informa-
15 tion provided by the parties themselves. The political theory, on the other hand, regards arbitration as an extension of both collective bargaining and, of course, collective coercion. The arbitrator functions as a sensitive instru-
20 ment of sorts, accurately recording the relative strengths of the parties and making sure that the lion gets his share.

To some extent, however, these opposing theories represent a confusion between arbitra-
25 tion and conciliation, the act of appeasing both parties to a dispute without necessarily render-ing a just or pragmatic decision. The notion of compromise that dominates conciliation may also guide arbitration, although, in the process
30 of arbitration, the result necessarily requires the decision of an outsider rather than an accom-modation between the parties themselves. Nevertheless, since to some the idea of arbitra-tion necessarily involves absolute "rights,"
35 compromise is likely to be regarded as the solution of the timid or the unprincipled. Arbitration grounded in political theory, while more likely to permit conciliation, is therefore less preferable to both parties in a dispute,
40 despite the obvious practicality of compromise.

Reading Comprehension Passage Overview

Paragraph one compares two theories of arbitration—judicial and political.
Paragraph two briefly describes each theory.
Paragraph three relates arbitration to the idea of conciliation, and ultimately decides that the judicial theory of arbitration is preferable.

VERBAL BIN 3

QUESTIONS	EXPLANATIONS

11. The primary purpose of the passage is to

    (A)   provide examples of the social failures that make arbitration necessary

    (B)   describe the origin of two theories of arbitration

    (C)   compare two conflicting theories of dispute arbitration

    (D)   discuss the relative merits of arbitration and conciliation

    (E)   outline the successive stages of collective bargaining

11. (C) The passage did not mention the larger social failures that might make arbitration necessary (A), nor the origin of the theories (B) or the stages of bargaining (E). The confusion between arbitration and conciliation *was* discussed, but was this the main idea of the passage? Nope. The correct answer was choice (C), a good paraphrase of the main idea of the passage.

12. It can be inferred from the passage that all of the following are elements of the political theory of arbitration EXCEPT

    (A)   an evaluation of the balance of power between disputing parties

    (B)   a willingness on the part of both parties to accept compromise

    (C)   a relative disregard of the importance of moral right in the dispute

    (D)   an understanding that any compromise must appear to be just

    (E)   an extension of collective bargaining

12. (D) This specific question has a good lead phrase: "political theory." Running your finger down the passage, you would find it on line 16. Remember, this is an EXCEPT question—the choice that was *not* discussed in relation to political theory is correct: choice (D). This was said about judicial theory a bit earlier in the passage.

13. Which of the following, if true, would most effectively weaken the author's assessment of the drawbacks of the political theory of arbitration?

    (A)   Litigation is becoming a more popular alternative to arbitration.

    (B)   A system of checks and balances was put in place to reduce the likelihood of finding biased arbitrators.

    (C)   Contending parties in most disputes establish compromise as one of their most important goals.

    (D)   The process of arbitration uncovered new strategies for avoiding conflicts between contending parties.

    (E)   Resolution of the problem of the opposing rights of the parties involed in labor settlements can be achieved.

13. (C) Litigation, biased arbitrators, new strategies for avoiding conflicts, and resolution of the rights of different parties—all of these are outside the scope of this passage.

Choice (C) is correct because if the two parties' goal is compromise, then compromise would actually *be* the "just or pragmatic" decision.

VERBAL BIN 3

QUESTIONS	EXPLANATIONS

14. It can be inferred from the passage that the political theory of arbitration

    (A) will eventually be replaced by a more efficient system of judicial compromise

    (B) is not solely concerned with principles of justice

    (C) suffers from most disputants' unwillingness to accept compromise

    (D) may replace conciliation as the most practical means of resolving disputes

    (E) is unlikely to be chosen by disputants unless they are coerced

14. **(B)** This specific question has the same lead phrase we found in question 2: "political theory." The answer to the question can be found in lines 15–22. We know from the beginning of the paragraph that the judicial theory is "just." But the sentence that describes the political theory begins with the trigger word "on the other hand." We also see it described as "collective coercion." The correct answer is choice (B).

15. According to the judicial theory of arbitration, an arbitrator would base his or her decision on

    (A) information supplied by the parties involved in arbitration

    (B) the notion of compromise that dominates conciliation

    (C) decisions rendered by judges in similar cases

    (D) the relative strengths of the parties involved

    (E) whatever appears to both parties to be a fair settlement of the dispute

15. **(A)** This specific question has a good lead phrase: "judicial theory." We'll find it at the beginning of the second paragraph. Choices (B), (D), and (E) would all be true of the political theory, not the judicial theory. Choice (C) is not mentioned in the passage. The correct answer is choice (A).

VERBAL BIN 3

QUESTIONS	EXPLANATIONS

16. It can be inferred from the passage that efforts at conciliation are

    (A) unlikely to be highly regarded by proponents of the judicial theory of arbitration

    (B) absent from most well-regarded theories of arbitration

    (C) most effective when neither party is responsible for a final decision

    (D) inextricably linked with the concept of "rights"

    (E) necessary to any dispute resolution under current theories of arbitration

16. **(A)** This specific question also has a good lead phrase: "conciliation." We'll find it in the third paragraph. (B) and (C) are not discussed in the passage. Choice (D) gets it wrong: Compromise is not compatible with absolute "rights." Choice (E) is too extreme. Which of the two theories is conciliation linked to? If you said political, you are doing just fine—so the answer is choice (A).

17. According to the passage, the political theory of arbitration

    (A) leaves no room for dissension

    (B) implies that there is a just solution to all disputes

    (C) directly contradicts the notion of compromise

    (D) is grounded in political theory

    (E) is based on how arbitration actually works

17. **(E)** The answer to this question is in lines 5–6. Choices (A), (B), and (C) are all based on the judicial theory. Choice (D) might have seemed tempting, but it was pretty broad for a specific question. The correct answer was choice (E).

Afterword

About The Princeton Review Course

The Princeton Review GMAT Course is a six-week course to prepare students for the GMAT.

Students are assigned to small classes (no more than fifteen students) grouped by ability. Everyone in your math class is scoring at your math level; everyone in your verbal class is scoring at your verbal level. This enables your teacher to focus each lesson on your problems because everybody else in your class has precisely the same problems.

Each week you will cover one math area and one verbal area. If you don't understand a particular topic thoroughly, some courses expect you to listen to audiocassettes.

Not so with The Princeton Review.

If you want more work on a topic, you can come to an extra-help session later in the week. If after coming to an extra-help class you want still more practice, you can request free private tutoring with your instructor.

Four times during the course you will take a diagnostic test that is evaluated by computer. Each diagnostic test is constructed according to the statistical design of actual GMATs. The computer evaluation of your diagnostic tests is used to assign you to your class, as well as to measure your progress. The computer evaluation tells you what specific areas you need to concentrate on. We know how busy you are. We don't ask you to spend time on topics you already understand.

Princeton Review instructors undergo a strict selection process and a rigorous training period. All of them have done exceedingly well on standardized tests like the GMAT, and most of them have gone to highly competitive colleges. All Princeton Review instructors are chosen because we believe they can make the course enjoyable as well as instructive.

Our materials are updated each year to reflect changes in the test design and improved techniques.

ARE YOUR BOOKS JUST LIKE YOUR COURSES?

Since our SAT book first came out in 1986, many students and teachers have asked us, "Are your books just like your courses?"

No.

We like to think that this book is fun, informative, and well written, but no book can capture the rigor and advantages of our course structure, or the magic of our instructors. It isn't easy to raise GMAT scores. Our course is spread over six weeks and requires class participation, diagnostic exams, and some homework.

Moreover, this book cannot contain all of the techniques we teach in our course for a number of reasons. Some of our techniques are too difficult to explain, without a trained Princeton Review teacher to describe and demonstrate them. Also, this book is written for the average student. Classes in our course are grouped by ability so that we can gear our techniques to each student's level. A 500-level Princeton Review student learns different techniques from those learned by a 400- or 600-level Princeton Review student.

IF YOU'D LIKE MORE INFORMATION

The Princeton Review offers courses in hundreds of cities around the country and around the world. For the office nearest you, call 1-800-2-REVIEW.

GMAT Diagnostic Software

ABOUT THE SOFTWARE

The diagnostic tests on the CD-ROM were designed to help you practice your test-taking skills, pacing, and techniques in an environment that is very much like the real GMAT. We want to make sure your testing experience is as realistic as possible. Each test has a dedicated pool of questions, and each question drawn from that pool depends on how you answered the previous question—just like an actual GMAT.

In addition to the four full-length GMATs on the disc, you can practice specific question types with drills. The drill questions also come out of a dedicated pool of questions that will not show up on the tests. However, when you have completed all four full GMATs, the entire question pool (over 2,000 questions) is opened into the drills. So, although you may see some repeat questions at that point, you can drill as much as you need to. We've even included some suggestions for using the drills (see below).

Although the software allows you to take a single section of the test on its own, we recommend trying to take an entire test in one sitting. Remember—you want to simulate real testing conditions. And don't forget to use scratch paper—that screen-to-scratch paper conversion is very important. We also advise making good use of the review features—look at the explanations for questions you missed, and determine which sections are giving you the most trouble.

SYSTEM REQUIREMENTS

WINDOWS™
486/66 MHz or higher
Windows 95, 98
16 MB RAM
15 MB Hard Disk space
SVGA Monitor (256 Colors)
Double-speed CD-ROM or faster
Mouse

MACINTOSH®
Power PC
System 7.1 or higher
16 MB RAM
15 MB Hard Disk space
256 Color Monitor (640 x 480 pixels)
Double-speed CD-ROM or faster
Mouse

INSTALLATION AND START-UP

Windows:

Close all other applications.
Check that your monitor is set to 256 colors.

1. Insert the CD in your CD-ROM drive.

2. From your Start Menu, select **Run**.

3. Type D: setup and press **Enter**. (If your CD-ROM drive is not drive D:, type the appropriate letter)

4. Follow the onscreen instructions until installation is complete.

5. Once setup is complete, if you want to begin immediately, you can check "Yes, I want to run GMAT Diagnostic now" and select **Finish.** Otherwise, just select Finish.

To run the software later, make sure the CD is in your CD-ROM drive, and simply select **GMAT Diagnostic** from the *Princeton Review* folder in Programs from the Start Menu.

Macintosh:

1. Insert the CD in your CD-ROM drive

2. Double click the GMAT Diagnostic Installer icon

3. Follow the onscreen instructions until installation is complete.

To run the software, make sure the CD is in your CD-ROM drive, and simply double click the *Tester* icon located in the *GMAT Diagnostic* folder on your hard drive.

USING GMAT DIAGNOSTIC TESTS

THE MAIN MENU

Each time you launch your GMAT Diagnostic, you will begin with the main menu screen. From this screen, you can **Take a Test**—one of four GMAT Diagnostics (which can be taken section by section or as a whole test), **Review a Test** you've already taken, or **Practice a Section** with drills. You can also exit the software, by clicking **Quit** on the upper-right corner.

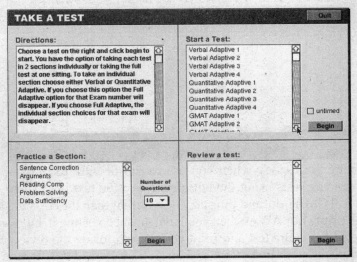

TAKING A TEST

Each full-length GMAT consists of 4 sections: Two Analytical Writing Assessments (Analysis of an Issue, Analysis of an Argument), Verbal and Quantitative. Our software will obviously not score the Writing sections, but they are useful as practice. Our software includes some non-scored experimental questions in the multiple-choice sections just like the real GMAT.

If you choose to take an individual section, you can only take the corresponding section separately as well. Likewise, if you take a full test, the corresponding sections become unavailable.

You also have the option of taking an untimed test by clicking the "untimed" box above the Begin button. For a true testing experience this option is only recommended if you have a documented learning disability and will be taking the real GMAT untimed.

To start a test, select one from the list and click **Begin**. If you have chosen one of the full GMATs, you will start with the first AWA essay.

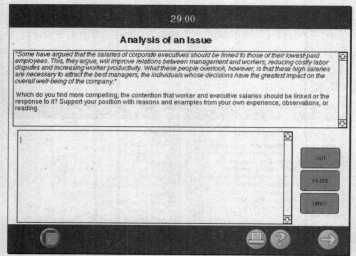

You may begin typing your essay when you are ready. Be sure to practice cutting, pasting, and undoing during your practice tests using the buttons next to the text box. These are designed to work exactly as those on the real GMAT do, and thus may be different than the cut-and-paste functions you are accustomed to. You can print your AWA when you have finished writing it, but we recommend you wait until you have completed the entire test and print your AWA during the review mode.

When you have completed your first essay, click the **NEXT QUESTION** button at the bottom right of the screen to proceed to the next essay. To skip the AWA portion of the test entirely, click the **STOP TEST** button—doing so will send you to the multiple-choice portion of the test and you will not be able to return to the AWA. In an actual GMAT, you will have a 1:00 minute break between essays, but this diagnostic has no break between essays.

After completing the second essay, click **NEXT QUESTION** again and you will have a 5 minute break before beginning the multiple-choice section of the test.

The multiple-choice portion of the GMAT begins with the Directions Screen.

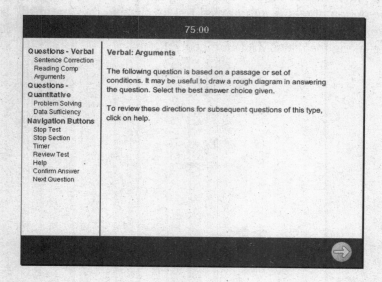

This is also the **Help** screen. If you need to review the directions for any type of question or the functions of any of the buttons on your screen, simply click the **Help** button at the bottom of any active testing screen and this screen will reappear. You can then click on the topic on which you need help.

Since the timer starts as soon as you click **Begin**, you should not spend unnecessary time on the Directions Screen. Please review all of the section directions (provided in the book) before taking the diagnostic tests. The buttons on the actual GMAT are also explained in the book (*see page 38*), but please read the TOOLBAR section below because the buttons on these diagnostic tests are slightly different.

Unlike the actual GMAT, there is no warning that you are nearing the end of a section, so pay attention to the timer.

Here is a sample test question screen:

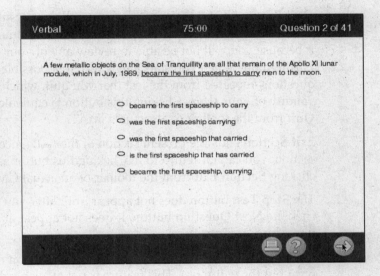

To select an answer, click on the oval next to the answer or the answer itself, and then click the **NEXT QUESTION** button which will turn into a **CONFIRM ANSWER** button. Click that button again to move to the next question. Remember, once you click **CONFIRM ANSWER,** you cannot return to that question.

THE TOOLBAR

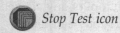 *Stop Test icon*

Clicking **STOP TEST** during the multiple-choice sections will give you the following warning:

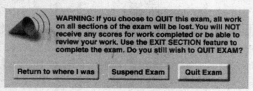

Return to Where I Was does exactly what you think it does.

Quit Exam will end the exam and erase all your results. We have included this button for emergency purposes, but we recommend that you never use it because you will not be able to review any of your work on that test. Furthermore, when you start a new test, it is possible that there will be questions repeated from the test that you quit, which will compromise the validity of your score. Clicking this button is equivalent to clicking **Test Quit** from the toolbar of an actual GMAT.

Exit Section ends the present section of the test. Once you have exited a section, you cannot return to it. Clicking this button is equivalent to clicking **Section Exit** from the toolbar of an actual GMAT.

The **Stop Test** button does not appear until after you select an answer and click the **Next Question** button. It does not appear at all on the first question of any section.

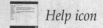 *Print icon*

Clicking **PRINT** will print the question presently on the screen. You cannot print out the entire test. This feature is not available during a real GMAT.

 Help icon

Clicking **HELP** will bring you to the Directions Screen (see above) just as it does on an actual GMAT.

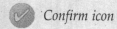 *Next icon*

Clicking **NEXT** will change the button into **CONFIRM.** In the actual GMAT, these are two separate buttons.

Confirm icon

Clicking **CONFIRM ANSWER** will record your answer and bring you the next question. Before confirming, you have one last chance to change your answer.

Ending a Section and Finishing the Test

When you reach the end of a section, you will see this message:

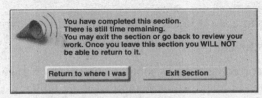

Return to where I was allows you to continue working on the last question in the section only. You cannot review the test at this time.

Exit Section will end your time on the section. Choose this option if you are finished with the section. If you have another section remaining, you will now have a 5 minute break and then the computer will start the next section. If you would like a longer break, you can also wait until time runs out on this section.

When you reach the end of the last section of the test and choose **Exit Section**, you will receive a message that reads, "You have reached the end of the exam." Select **Exit** to proceed.

The Score Report

When you have completed a test, you will see a screen that asks you to wait while your exam is scored. Then you will see your **SCORE REPORT**. This report gives you detailed information about your test. You can view the results of each section by selected a section from the pull-down menu in the upper-right corner, or you can print the full report by clicking the **Print** button.

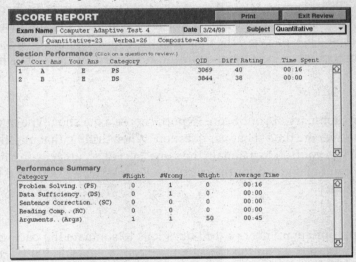

You can view this **SCORE REPORT** at another time by selecting this test from the Review a Test section of the Main Menu.

Reviewing Your Test

You may review any question from your test by clicking on the question number in the **SCORE REPORT**. This will display the correct and incorrect answers. The review mode will show you a green checkmark to indicate the credited response, and show your answer as the darkened oval. To view an explanation for an answer choice, click on the answer (the words in the answer, not on the oval). These explanations do not print. To return to the **SCORE REPORT**, click on the **STOP SECTION** button.

PRACTICE A SECTION—TAKING DRILLS

To take a drill, select a question type from the **Practice a Section** menu, select whether you want 5 or 10 questions, and click **Begin.**

The drill screens look the same as the testing screens, with the following functional differences:

- The questions are untimed.

- You are shown the correct answer as soon as you select an answer. So, while there is no need to confirm answers, you cannot change answers while using the drills.

- You can view explanations immediately once you've answered by clicking on the answer choice—not the oval. But unlike **Reviewing a Test**, you cannot go back to a question once you have moved on to the next.

We've designed our drills so that you will not jeopardize the accuracy of any of your practice tests by seeing questions early. We have secured a group of about 400 questions for you to drill before you complete the tests. Once you have completed all four tests, you may see questions you saw previously in a test or drill (we want you to be able to drill to your heart's content), but at this point seeing questions again will not affect the utility of these drills. Remember that questions tend to fall into predictable patterns – that's part of what makes the GMAT a standardized test.

You can use the drills to increase your familiarity with a particular question type, to target specific weaknesses, or to increase your speed or accuracy. Here are some suggestions:

Building accuracy

After you've taken a test, view the **Performance Summary** on your **Score Report** and find a question type whose accuracy you wish to improve. Note the average time per question. To increase your accuracy on that type of question, double the average amount of time spent per question and try to get each drill question right in that time. Then decrease the time slightly, while staying at 100% accuracy. This drilling method helps you improve your performance in the first third of the test, where accuracy is more important than speed.

Building speed

From the **Performance Summary** of your **Score Report**, choose a question type in which you are already very accurate. Note the average time spent per question. When drilling that question type, decrease that time slightly and challenge yourself to maintain the same level of accuracy with this decreased time. This drilling method helps you build speed for the middle of the test, where you need to move more quickly without sacrificing accuracy.

Practicing pacing

You can choose the appropriate number of drill questions to simulate the pacing of an actual test. For example, if your target score is 25 on the Quantitative section, aim for 100% accuracy on the first 10 questions in the first 25 minutes of the test. You can simulate this in a drill by working five Problem Solving and then five Data Sufficiency questions in 25 minutes.

ABOUT THE AUTHOR

Geoff Martz attended Dartmouth College and Columbia University before joining The Princeton Review in 1985 as a teacher and writer. Martz headed the development team that designed the Review's GMAT course. He is the author or coauthor of *Cracking the ACT, Paying for College, Cracking the GED,* and *How to Survive Without Your Parents' Money.*

NOTES

NOTES

NOTES

NOTES

NOTES

NOTES

FIND US...

International

Hong Kong
4/F Sun Hung Kai Centre
30 Harbour Road, Wan Chai,
Hong Kong
Tel: (011)85-2-517-3016

Japan
Fuji Building 40, 15-14
Sakuragaokacho, Shibuya Ku,
Tokyo 150, Japan
Tel: (011)81-3-3463-1343

Korea
Tae Young Bldg, 944-24,
Daechi- Dong, Kangnam-Ku
The Princeton Review—ANC
Seoul, Korea 135-280,
South Korea
Tel: (011)82-2-554-7763

Mexico City
PR Mex S De RL De Cv
Guanajuato 228 Col. Roma
06700 Mexico D.F., Mexico
Tel: 525-564-9468

Montreal
666 Sherbrooke St.
West, Suite 202
Montreal, QC H3A 1E7 Canada
Tel: 514-499-0870

Pakistan
1 Bawa Park - 90 Upper Mall
Lahore, Pakistan
Tel: (011)92-42-571-2315

Spain
Pza. Castilla, 3 - 5° A, 28046
Madrid, Spain
Tel: (011)341-323-4212

Taiwan
155 Chung Hsiao East Road
Section 4 - 4th Floor,
Taipei R.O.C., Taiwan
Tel: (011)886-2-751-1243

Thailand
Building One, 99 Wireless Road
Bangkok, Thailand 10330
Tel: 662-256-7080

Toronto
1240 Bay Street, Suite 300
Toronto M5R 2A7 Canada
Tel: 800-495-7737
Tel: 716-839-4391

Vancouver
4212 University Way NE,
Suite 204
Seattle, WA 98105
Tel: 206-548-1100

National (U.S.)

We have more than 60 offices around the U.S. and run courses at over 400 sites. For courses and locations within the U.S. call 1-800- 2- Review and you will be routed to the nearest office.

www.review.com

Expert Advice

Talk About It

www.review.com

Pop Surveys

Paying for it

www.review.com

THE PRINCETON REVIEW

Getting in

Word du Jour

www.review.com

Find-O-Rama School & Career Search

www.review.com

Best Schools

Finding it

www.review.com